Rural Communism in France, 1920–1939

RURAL COMMUNISM IN FRANCE, 1920–1939

Laird Boswell

Cornell University Press

ITHACA AND LONDON

First published 1998 by Cornell University Press.

Printed in the United States of America.

Library of Congress Cataloging-in-Publication Data

Boswell, Laird.
    Rural communism in France, 1920–1939 / Laird Boswell.
        p.   cm.
    Includes index.
    ISBN 0-8014-3421-1 (cloth : alk. paper)
        1. Communism—France.   2. Communism and agriculture—France.   3. France—Rural conditions.   4. France—Politics and government—1914–1940.   I. Title.
    HX263.B59   1998
    335.43'0944'0902—dc21   97-44193

Cornell University Press strives to utilize environmentally responsible suppliers and materials to the fullest extent possible in the publishing of its books. Such materials include vegetable-based, low-VOC inks and acid-free papers that are also either recycled, totally chlorine-free, or partly composed of nonwood fibers.

Cloth printing   10 9 8 7 6 5 4 3 2 1

Within each individualistic small property owner there is a potential Communist.

                    —Paul-Vaillant Couturier, *A ceux des champs* (1920)

Contents

Maps

Figures

Acknowledgments

This book has been long in the making, and it is a pleasure to thank institutions and individuals who have helped make it possible. The research was undertaken with funding from the Social Science Research Council, the George Lurcy Foundation, and a Bourse Chateaubriand from the French Ministère des Affaires Etrangères. The University of California at Berkeley, the Allan Sharlin Memorial Foundation, and the National Endowment for the Humanities (summer stipend) all provided support for various stages of writing and revision. I am grateful to all these institutions for their financial assistance.

The Cartographic Laboratory at the University of Wisconsin at Madison transformed my amateurish sketches into maps and provided generous funding for this undertaking. Parts of chapters 2 and 3 have appeared in the *Journal of Interdisciplinary History* 23 (1993): 719–49, and are used here with the permission of its editors and MIT Press, Cambridge, Massachusetts, copyright © 1993 by the Massachusetts Institute of Technology.

I am indebted to many individuals as well. Lynn Hunt ranks at the top of this list. This book owes much to her unfailing support, her critical advice, and her keen vision of the historian's craft. Martin Malia, the most francophile of Russian historians, pushed me to think more rigorously and to question my assumptions. At the California Institution of Technology, Philip Hoffman and J. Morgan Kousser taught me much of what I know about quantitative methods, and I have learned much from their respective works. In France, Alain Corbin, Annie Kriegel, Pierre Vallin, Georges Dauger, and especially Louis Pérouas offered advice throughout the research process. I am particularly grateful to the two anonymous readers for Cornell University Press whose close reading of the manuscript helped to make this a better book. Suzanne Desan has been an inspiring friend and colleague. Thought-provoking conversations with Carolyn Dean and Leonard Moore helped me keep things in perspective. I owe thanks to all the old rural Communist militants in Corrèze who gave of their time and insight. Without them, and without the extensive documentation that the enlightened archivist of Corrèze, Guy Quincy, kindly let me consult without resorting to multiple *dérogations*, this book would not have been possible. Florence Bernault and Suzanne know why the final thanks can be addressed only to them.

L. B.

Abbreviations

AC	Archives Communales
ADC	Archives Départementales de la Corrèze
ADCR	Archives Départementales de la Creuse, Guéret
ADD	Archives Départementales de la Dordogne, Périgueux
ADHV	Archives Départementales de la Haute-Vienne, Limoges
AN	Archives Nationales, Paris
ARAC	Association Républicaine des Anciens Combattants
BSLSAC	*Bulletin de la Société des Lettres, Sciences, et Arts de la Corrèze*
CGPT	Confédération Générale des Paysans Travailleurs
CGT	Confédération Générale du Travail
CGTU	Confédération Générale du Travail Unitaire
CPF	Conseil Paysan Français
CS	Commissaire Spécial
DCM	Délibérations du Conseil Municipal
FAAC	Fédération des Associations Agricoles Corréziennes
FDSEA	Fédération Départementale des Syndicats d'Exploitants Agricoles
FNSEA	Fédération Nationale des Syndicats d'Exploitants Agricoles
FTT	Fédération des Travailleurs de la Terre
GPU	Russian Secret Police (tr.)
JIH	*Journal of Interdisciplinary History*
MI	Ministre de l'Intérieur
MODEF	Mouvement de Coordination et de Défense des Exploitations Agricoles Familiales
MSSNAC	*Mémoires de la Société des Sciences Naturelles et Archéologiques de la Creuse*
PC	Préfet Corrèze
PCF	Parti Communiste Français
PCI	Partito Comunista Italiano
PCTC	*Le Prolétaire du Centre et le Travailleur de la Corrèze*
PD	Préfet Dordogne
PHV	Préfet Haute-Vienne

Pop C	*Le Populaire du Centre*
Prol C	*Le Prolétaire du Centre*
Prol D	*Le Prolétaire de la Dordogne*
RFSP	*Revue Française de Science Politique*
sfio	Section Française de l'Internationale Ouvrière
SG	Sûreté Générale
SP	Sous-Préfet
SPT	Syndicats des Paysans Travailleurs
TC	*Le Travailleur de la Corrèze*
TCCHV	*Le Travailleur, Corrèze, Creuse, Haute-Vienne*
TCHV	*Le Travailleur, Creuse, Haute-Vienne*
TCO	*Le Travailleur du Centre Ouest*
TT	*Le Travailleur de la Terre*
VP	*La Voix Paysanne*

Rural Communism in France, 1920–1939

Introduction

The rolling hills northwest of Tulle, the administrative capital of Corrèze, have been a bastion of rural communism ever since the Communist Party was established there in late December 1920. It was among the small villages in this area—two of which have been Communist ever since the Communist Party's birth—that I conducted some of my most rewarding interviews with smallholding peasants who had been active in the Communist Party during the interwar years. One of those I spoke to, François Monédière, a small farmer in the village of Beaumont (the locations of interviews are shown in map 1), had been active in both the Party and the agricultural trade union movement during the 1920s and 1930s. Monédière had been—and still was, despite his age—an exemplary rural Communist militant.

The first thing I noticed when I entered the Monédière farmhouse in Beaumont was the full-length statue of Lenin that occupied the central position on the mantel. Seeing that it had caught my attention, Monédière proudly explained that he had brought it back from his only trip to the Soviet Union; his voice filled with conviction, he added that Lenin would always remain "the greatest man," for he was the father of the most successful revolution ever made.[1] Monédière's statue of the Russian revolutionary was no isolated display: as early as the 1920s peasants in Limousin and Dordogne publicly exhibited their sympathy for the Communist movement in a variety of ways.

François Chastagnol was one of many inhabitants of the remote, impoverished Corrèze village of Tarnac who, unable to make ends meet on the rugged Millevaches plateau, migrated to Paris in the first decades of the century in search of stable employment. A clubfoot disqualified Chastagnol for

---

[1] Interview with François Monédière, Beaumont, 31 July 1984. Unless otherwise noted, interviews were conducted in Corrèze.

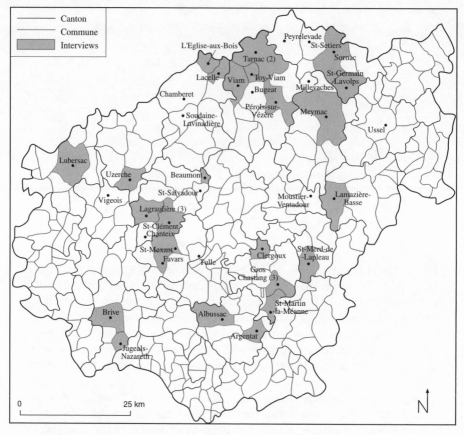

Map 1. Corrèze: sites of interviews (number of interviews in parentheses)

work as a mason or taxi driver, the jobs taken by most Tarnacois migrants. He worked instead as a tailor in the Belle Jardinière department store. With his savings he purchased an old house in the Tarnac hamlet of La Bessette for his elderly parents, who had worked all their lives as agricultural wage laborers. In the mid-1920s, Chastagnol attached two marble plaques engraved with the hammer and sickle to the outside of this modest dwelling. On the first, he inscribed "Villa Lenin" in honor of the Bolshevik leader, who had died shortly before, and on the second, "Villa Clémentine Rose" in memory of his wife. Chastagnol's gesture clearly was in keeping with Tarnac's reputation as the reddest village in Limousin, if not in all of France: 73 percent of Tarnac's votes were cast in favor of the Communist list in 1924; twelve years later the Party was gathering an even 80 percent of the vote. According to the story told in Tarnac today, it was not until the end of the Vichy regime that the *milice* managed to remove Chastagnol's unusual plaque from the public eye. And since then, as a sign of the rural exodus that has hit these areas, the abandoned house has crumbled to the ground.[2]

This sort of display of revolutionary sympathies was not unusual in interwar Limousin and Périgord, nor was it confined to those who had migrated. The Communist mayor of Favars, a small village west of Tulle (Corrèze), flew the red flag on the roof of his brand-new pigpen in the late 1930s. Eventually it caught the attention of local authorities. In the small *bourg* of Le Buisson (Dordogne), a peasant celebrated the end of the harvest by planting a red flag atop his haystack and inviting the railroad workers who had assisted him to a banquet, which ended with the singing of the "International."[3] Antoine Bouniol, a peasant in St-Hilaire-Foissac (Corrèze), went even further by having the hammer and sickle sculpted on the gable of his stone barn. To make the Communist symbol more visible to passers-by, he painted it red against a blue background. After the Nazi-Soviet pact in August 1939 and the banning of the Communist Party that September, the Tulle gendarmerie ordered Bouniol to destroy this seditious and all-too-visible emblem.[4] People who chose to have their political *engagement* remembered by having the hammer and sickle sculpted on their gravestones, as Panteix Pardoux of St-Gilles-les-Forêts (Haute-Vienne) did, were luckier; Vichy administrators did not go so far as to have those emblems removed (figure 1).[5]

It is a bit surprising at first to find individuals exhibiting leftist symbols on their homes in one of the more rural, isolated, and backward regions of interwar France. It was one thing for the Communists of the village of Albussac (Corrèze) to post the hammer and sickle above their meeting place, with a sign reading, "The Peasant Center of Albussac";[6] it was quite another for an individual to do so, especially in a commune that was not nearly so one-sidedly leftist as Tarnac. Today such public displays of attachment to communism have disappeared, but the symbols are still to be seen indoors. In the homes of old peasant Communists it is not rare to find some record of their political affiliation—a flag, medal, certificate, or photograph—posted prominently on the wall.

Communist municipalities in the countryside also used emblems and flags to defy the local authorities. In the village of Beauregard (Dordogne), the newly reelected Communist Party municipality, led by their peasant mayor, Baptiste Dujaric, celebrated its 1929 victory by offering a banquet on the symbolic date of August 4 to commemorate the abolition of privileges. The

[2] Interview with René Monzac, Tarnac, 8 August 1984.

[3] ADC 1M73; *Prol C*, 29 July 1923.

[4] ADC 1M71, Gendarmerie Nationale, Brigade de Lapleau, 4 November 1939. See also *La Croix de la Corrèze*, 12 November 1939, cited in the Archives de la Fédération du Parti Communiste Français de la Corrèze (Tulle).

[5] Panteix Pardoux (1859–1937) was an active Communist militant in St-Gilles-les-Forêts. Thanks to Georges Guingouin for bringing this gravestone to my attention.

[6] ADC 1M77, Gendarmerie Nationale, 10 April 1936; *TCCHV*, 2 and 30 May 1936; interview with Henri Peuch, Brive, 23 August 1983.

Figure 1. The grave of Panteix Pardoux (1859–1937) in St-Gilles-les-Forêts, Haute-Vienne. (Photo by Laird Boswell.)

participants met at the town hall to fetch the red flag, which was then borne aloft by a group of young women who sang the "International" as they led the group to the banquet. After the meal, an even larger crowd took the red flag back to the town hall and struck up the "International" once again.[7] On May 1, 1930, Gabriel Texier, the combative mayor of Ambazac (Haute-Vienne), raised the Soviet flag over the town hall in place of the French Tricolor. When he refused an order to take it down, the prefect suspended him from duty for three months. A little over one year later, on July 14, 1931, Texier had the town hall balcony draped in red with an inscription that read, "July 14, 1789: fall of the Bastille; July 14, 1931: the Republic imprisons working-class militants. Workers, judge!" The police ordered him to remove the banner, and once more he refused. In more isolated villages such as Sornac (Corrèze), the Communist municipality was not disturbed when it celebrated Bastille Day in 1935 by raising both the Tricolor and the red flag over the town hall.[8]

Rural Communists in Limousin and Dordogne did not limit themselves to displaying the Communist Party's emblem in its various forms in both public and private places. In Communist-run La Coquille (Dordogne), the Party cell set up an Esperanto group to translate letters that their "Russian comrades" had written in the international language. A common tongue, the cell argued, would unite the world's workers and become a potent weapon in the hands of *les travailleurs*.[9] The rural inhabitants of La Coquille and of the few other communes where militants established Esperanto groups were not convinced that the effort was worthwhile, and the experiment ended in failure. The Parti Communiste Français (PCF) was more successful in its attempts to introduce Russian vocabulary. The correspondents of the regional Communist newspaper often called themselves *rabcors* (meaning "worker correspondents of the proletarian press"—something of an irony in a rural area), and a few of them, presumably inspired by the inquisitive tactics of the Russian secret police (GPU), signed their articles Guépéou. Rural militants also felt compelled to describe their enemies as kulaks, despite the fact that well-to-do peasants were virtually nonexistent in Limousin. Dismayed by the slow sales of his book on small-scale forestry and the creation of pastureland, the Corrèze Communist leader Marius Vazeilles warned small peasants that they soon would be at a disadvantage, because the local kulaks had bought their copies long ago.[10]

There was, of course, much more to rural communism than flag-waving, awkward mimicking of Russian vocabulary, and other exhibitions of one's

---

[7] *TCO*, 24 August 1929.

[8] ADHV 1M173; AN F[7] 13127, CS Limoges to SG, 14 July 1931; *TCO*, 27 July 1935.

[9] *Prol C*, 10 July 1921; *TCO*, 15 February 1930.

[10] *TCO*, 26 August 1933. The term was also used by rural militants to describe large property holders; *TCO*, 1 August 1931. For brief comments on Russian vocabulary, Annie Kriegel, *Le pain et les roses: Jalons pour une histoire des socialismes* (Paris, 1968), 207–8n.

convictions. But symbols do have their importance, particularly Communist symbols in an agricultural region such as Corrèze. During the interwar years a shared imagery proved critical to forging the identity of the new party in the making, in both urban and rural areas. At the very least, the widespread display of symbols vividly attests to the remarkable influence the Communist movement enjoyed in one of the most rural, isolated areas of France.

French communism has been characterized by enduring strength in some rural areas, particularly in departments along the northern and western edge of the Massif Central and along the Mediterranean littoral. Why has the PCF generally done best (and continued to do so even in the 1980s, a period of vertiginous electoral decline) in rural departments that, from a sociological perspective, hardly correspond to the image one has of the Party of the working class? The massive literature on the Communist Party and on French elections sheds little light on this problem. The Party's strength in rural areas has been ignored by historians and political scientists alike.[11]

Over the years, the Party's success at the polls in rural departments has been attributed to the existence of what is alternatively termed a leftist tradition (*tradition de gauche*) and a highly advanced democratic tradition (*tradition démocratique très avancée*).[12] According to this interpretation, successive generations of voters in the countryside, determined to vote as far left as possible, cast their ballots in logical succession always further to the left (*toujours plus à gauche*), beginning with the Démocrates Socialistes in 1849, then moving on to the Radicals, the Socialists in the first decades of the twentieth century, and to the Communists after 1920. While this argument certainly contains a germ of truth, it raises more problems than it solves. Few things are as difficult to explain as traditions, particularly voting traditions. Tradition well may be the principal component of the electorate's choice in some regions, but this is difficult to prove. Moreover, the *tradition de gauche* argument does not satisfactorily explain why rural inhabitants in some leftist departments never moved beyond radicalism, whereas others gave a bet-

[11] For overviews see Henry W. Ehrmann, "The French Peasant and Communism," *American Political Science Review* 46 (1952): 19–43; Gordon Wright, "Communists and Peasantry in France," in *Modern France: Problems of the Third and Fourth Republics*, ed. E. M. Earle (Princeton, 1951), 219–31, and "French Farmers in Politics" *South Atlantic Quarterly* 51 (1952): 356–65; Claude Ezratty, "Les communistes," in *Les paysans et la politique dans la France contemporaine*, ed. Jacques Fauvet and Henri Mendras (Paris, 1958); Pierre Gaborit, "Le Parti communiste et les paysans," in Yves Tavernier et al., *L'univers politique des paysans dans la France contemporaine* (Paris, 1972), 197–222; Jean Irigaray, "Le Parti communiste et ses électeurs paysans," *Esprit*, October 1966, 404–12; Gérard Belloin, *Renaud Jean, le tribun des paysans* (Paris, 1993); Stéphane Baumont, "De Renaud Jean à André Lajoinie: Les agriculteurs et le communisme," paper presented to the Association des Ruralistes Français, Bordeaux, 15–16 November 1990; Jean-Paul Molinari, *Les ouvriers communistes* (Thonon-les-Bains, 1991), 180–92; Sally Sokoloff, "Communism and the French Peasantry, with special reference to the Allier, 1919–39" (Ph.D. thesis, London University, 1975).

[12] François Goguel, *Géographie des élections françaises sous la Troisième et la Quatrième République* (Paris, 1970), 78.

ter reception to Socialist or Communist candidates. It is telling that electoral sociologists such as François Goguel have advanced tradition to explain Communist voting only in those areas where the presence of a large working class cannot be invoked as the basis of Communist Party support.[13] Industrialized regions presumably also have political traditions, but they are not seen as key to communism's strength.

I question standard interpretations of rural support for communism—those based on long-standing voting traditions, "red republicanism," "red cultures," or family structures—and propose a renewed analysis of both how and why the French Communist Party, after its creation in December 1920, established itself with such success in certain rural regions of France. Whereas most analyses of French communism focus on institutional and political aspects of the Party's history or on its "anthropologically diverse" implantation in urban, working-class areas, I argue that the Communist Party's enduring presence on the French political scene cannot be explained apart from its strong performance in parts of the countryside.[14]

From a national perspective, rural communism was but a succession of paradoxes:[15] an ostensibly Marxist party well established in the countryside among a peasantry better known for its conservatism; a workers' party with strong roots among the smallholding peasantry, tenant farmers, sharecroppers, rural artisans, and shopkeepers; a party closely linked to the Soviet Union, which never denounced the appalling toll of forced collectivization yet did well among small peasants and French "kulaks"; an oppositional political party, devoid of connections within the state apparatus, which was in no position to deliver the political goods and favors that were the bread and butter of politics in the countryside. But these kinds of paradoxes are more complex than they appear at first sight. After all, this was not the first time that Marxism, in however vulgarized and watered down a form, found an audience in rural areas.[16] From the point of view of the peasantry, rural communism was a coherent response to unfulfilled desires for political and social reform, the fears born of the Great War, the crisis of a quickly declining rural sector in search of salvation and identity.

The PCF's enduring rural implantation was at the heart of its identity (even if the Party itself considered it to be peripheral). Historians seeking to account for the PCF's domestic roots—its ability to establish itself within a

[13] Ibid., 78; François Goguel, *Chroniques électorales: Les scrutins politiques en France de 1945 à nos jours* (Paris, 1981–83), 1: 80–84, and *Initiation aux recherches de géographie électorale* (Paris, 1949), 51–52.

[14] On urban regions see Annie Fourcaut, *Bobigny, banlieue rouge* (Paris, 1986); Tyler Stovall, *The Rise of the Paris Red Belt* (Berkeley, 1990). See also Michel Hastings, *Halluin la rouge, 1919–1939: Aspects d'un communisme identitaire* (Lille, 1991); Jean-Pierre A. Bernard, *Paris Rouge, 1944–1964: Les communistes français dans la capitale* (Seyssel, 1991).

[15] "Purest paradox," in the words of Gordon Wright, "Four Red Villages in France," *Yale Review*, Spring 1952, 361.

[16] Tony Judt, *Socialism in Provence, 1871–1914* (Cambridge, 1979).

range of social groups and regions—no longer can write off the countryside as a mere appendage, easily explained away by "tradition." Nor was rural communism an urban import spread by working-class militants. On the contrary, the PCF fared best in the countryside when rural militants took charge, resisted the intrusion of their comrades from the city, and pressed the flesh in village cafés, fairs, markets, and shops.

The French Communist Party was born in the aftermath of the Great War at the December 1920 Tours Congress, which cemented the split within the French Socialist Party. Under strong pressure from Lenin, who wanted to establish parties of the Bolshevik type throughout the West to prepare for worldwide revolution, the majority of French Socialists voted to adhere to the famous twenty-one conditions of the Communist International (Comintern) and create a new Communist party. The young party met with considerable difficulty in its early years. Purged and "bolshevized" in the early 1920s, it followed the zigzags of Soviet policy, culminating in the disastrous "class against class" sectarian experiment (1927–34). In mid-1934, partly under prodding from the Comintern, the PCF reversed its stand, came out of its isolation, and began to forge alliances with other parties on the left. Not until the 1936 elections, which saw the victory of a Popular Front coalition (Communists, Socialists, and Radicals), did the PCF enter the mainstream of French politics and become a national party. It would remain a linchpin of French social, political, and cultural life for the next half century.[17] After Hitler's takeover of power in 1933 and the subsequent banning of the German Communist Party, the PCF remained the largest Communist party in the West.

While this book contributes to the reconceptualization of communism's history, it also looks at contemporary rural political behavior. Few questions have been as hotly debated as how and when (in the nineteenth-century) French peasants became integrated within the nation, and when their forms of political behavior lost their distinctive character.[18] Interest in twentieth-century rural history has been more modest, and focused on the post–World War II years, when mechanization and the Common Market gave the decisive blow to the remnants of the old rural society. The disappearance of the peasantry has been one of the major events in the social history of twentieth-century France, and the transformations of the French countryside have been

[17] The best history of the PCF is Stéphane Courtois and Marc Lazar, *Histoire du Parti communiste français* (Paris, 1995).

[18] The classic analysis, which exaggerates the backwardness of rural society, is Eugen Weber, *Peasants into Frenchmen: The Modernization of Rural France, 1870–1914* (Stanford, 1976). A few examples from a vast literature: Maurice Agulhon, *La république au village* (Paris, 1979); Ted Margadant, *French Peasants in Revolt: The Insurrection of 1851* (Princeton, 1979); P. M. Jones, *Politics and Rural Society: The Southern Massif Central, c. 1750–1880* (Cambridge, 1985); Laura Levine Frader, *Peasants and Protest: Agricultural Workers, Politics, and Unions in the Aude, 1850–1914* (Berkeley, 1991).

considerable in every respect.[19] This rural revolution did not come without pain, or without social and political costs. At the Great War's end, close to 54 percent of France's population still lived in the countryside, and though by 1930 the balance had shifted in favor of urban areas, the depopulation of rural areas was a slow process. In 1931, 36 percent of the active population were still engaged in agriculture, versus 34 percent in industry.[20] The weight of the countryside was even stronger in the world of politics: during the interwar years rural constituents still elected the majority of deputies (not to mention senators). And yet successive governments showed meager foresight in their management of agricultural issues, their support for the modernization of farming equipment and techniques, and the consolidation of land-holdings. France's agricultural productivity and mechanization remained below the levels attained by Belgium, Holland, and Great Britain.

The "triple crisis" of French agriculture in the 1930s put the state and urban society to the test.[21] The political class appealed to key rural constituencies through favorable tax laws, programs designed to reduce market supply (and thus support prices), subsidies to promote exports, and, more frequently, import barriers to keep out foreign wheat, fruits and vegetables, or meat. Over the long term, however, the state's efforts lacked coherence and imagination, and the results were not convincing. It was no accident that communism founded one of its rural bastions in the home district of Henri Queuille, an influential Corrèze Radical politician and frequent minister of agriculture during the interwar years.

Rural communism was a response to the profound dissatisfaction with the state's standoffish attitude in the face of the transformations of rural economy, society, and culture. Low-grade hostility toward and suspicion of the state (but not, in general, the Republic) was endemic in many French rural regions between the wars. Granted, the state did intervene, at times massively, to support agriculture. But the perception in the countryside, especially in less fortunate areas, was that rural society was ever more on the fringe of the nation's interest. France was becoming an increasingly urban society, and the city dwellers were making the decisions. Urban merchants and intermediaries were responsible for the peasantry's plight. The small-

---

[19] Henri Mendras, *La fin des paysans* (Arles, 1984); Gordon Wright, *Rural Revolution in France: The Peasantry in the Twentieth Century* (Stanford, 1964); Peter Amann, *The Corncribs of Buzet: Modernizing Agriculture in the French Southwest* (Princeton, 1990); Susan Carol Rogers, *Shaping Modern Times in Rural France: The Transformation and Reproduction of an Aveyronnais Community* (Princeton, 1991); Suzanne Berger, *Peasants against Politics: Rural Organization in Brittany, 1911–1967* (Cambridge, Mass., 1972).

[20] Serge Berstein and Pierre Milza, *Histoire de la France au XXe siècle* (Brussels, 1995), 277; Direction de la Statistique Générale, *Résultats statistiques du recensement général de la population effectué le 8 mars 1936* (Paris, 1943), 1, pt. 3: 8.

[21] The expression is Robert Paxton's and refers to the combined effect of the Depression, the loss of interest in rural society, and the political crisis of representation in the countryside. See his excellent discussion in *Le temps des chemises vertes: Révoltes paysannes et fascisme rural, 1929–1939*, trans. Jean-Pierre Bardos (Paris, 1996), 23–85.

holding peasants, who had paid more than their share of the "blood tax" during the Great War, reacted bitterly to the decline of their influence in society. And the omnipresence of the French state was felt all the way to the grass-roots. The state's departmental representative, the prefect, kept a watchful eye on politics and budgets in the smallest of rural communes and intervened to limit municipal initiatives. In periods of tight fiscal policies, rural inhabitants resented the state's lack of investment in local infrastructure. But to peasants in Limousin and Dordogne—unlike those in the west and the north, where suspicion of the state encompassed a hatred of civil servants—a career in the *fonctionnariat* was seen as potential salvation in an agricultural world on the decline.[22] Opposition to the state in this region was a demand for a more interventionist, social state that would defend small property owners while granting them increased autonomy at the local level.

Communism's presence in the countryside was not solely a French phenomenon. Communism's rural character in the years after World War II was even more pronounced in Finland. Finnish Communists built strongholds in the industrialized south and especially among small farmers in the rural northern and eastern parts of the country. The strength of the Italian Communist Party (PCI) in the countryside was the most impressive, although the Fascists' seizure of power postponed the development of peasant communism in Italy to the second half of the twentieth century. The PCI was better established in agricultural areas of central Italy (Emilia-Romagna, Tuscany, Umbria, Marches), where it received the support of sharecroppers and agricultural workers, than in northern, industrialized regions (Piedmont, Lombardy) and the northeast (Venezia). Communism gained strength in the southern countryside (the Mezzogiorno) in the 1950s and 1960s.[23] Unlike their French counterparts, Italian Communists implanted themselves within a rural society that had been the site of bitter social movements in the years after both the Great War (Emilia-Romagna, the Po Valley) and World War II (Sicily and the southern boot). Peasants who had no land (sharecroppers, agricultural workers) had far greater weight in Italy than in France, where the great majority were smallholders—a circumstance of no small consequence for rural communism's social basis in both countries. In European nations where rural society was still influential—especially in France, Italy, and Finland, where industrialization walked hand in hand with the preservation of a large agricultural sector—rural support was critical to communism's success.

Today both peasants and Communists have largely disappeared. Peasants have been replaced by farmers (in 1993, 5.3 percent of the active population

---

[22] On the west and the north, ibid., 69.

[23] Sidney Tarrow, *Peasant Communism in Southern Italy* (New Haven, 1967); Paul Ginsborg, "The Communist Party and the Agrarian Question in Southern Italy, 1943–48," *History Workshop Journal* 17 (1984): 81–101, and *A History of Contemporary Italy: Society and Politics, 1943–1988* (London, 1990), 121–29, 200–204; Marc Lazar, *Maisons rouges: Les Partis communistes français et italien de la Libération à nos jours* (Paris, 1992).

worked in agriculture), and the smallholding peasantry is a concept of the past. Rural society and culture have undergone profound transformations, and the countryside increasingly is inhabited by urbanites in search of pastoral peace. The Creuse, saddled with the lowest population density in the nation, is commonly referred to as a "desert." Communism also is a movement of the past. The collapse of communism in the Soviet Union, along with its increasing marginalization in the West, has brought a historical epoch to a close. Communism was one of the central social and political (not to mention intellectual) movements of twentieth-century Europe, both East and West, and its decline has provoked a still ongoing realignment in society and political life. Now that communism is no longer a subject of polemical debate, we can look back and analyze its social and cultural roots.

The scope of this book is limited in both time and place. I have focused my attention on the interwar years in order to trace the genesis of the Communist Party's strength among the peasantry. If rural communism reached its apogee in the late 1940s and early 1950s, it was thanks to the foundations that had been laid over the previous two decades, and not, as some observers have argued, just to the PCF's role in the Resistance and its ensuing aura at the time of the Liberation. The Limousin, one of the areas where the French Communist Resistance was strongest, had been a bastion of rural communism since the 1920s. The choice of geographical area was more difficult. Instead of conducting a national study that would run the risk of superficiality, I focus on the three departments of Limousin (Corrèze, Creuse, Haute-Vienne) and Dordogne (map 2). By a comparative perspective I hope to avoid problems that often plague departmental monographs.[24]

The Corrèze, Dordogne, and Haute-Vienne were at one time or another among the half-dozen departments where the Communist Party enjoyed considerable influence in the countryside during the 1920s and 1930s. The Corrèze was one of the Party's most faithful electoral bastions (around 20 percent of the vote except in 1932) and it has remained so to the present day. PCF successes in Haute-Vienne—the Socialist Party's interwar stronghold—did not achieve the same consistency, but on two occasions (1928 and 1936) the Party scored well at the polls. Communism's influence in this department was essentially concentrated within a limited number of rural communes. In Dordogne, the Communists stagnated slightly over the 10 percent mark until 1936, when they more than doubled their strength (to 22 percent). The Creuse, which was the only one of the four departments where the Communist movement never managed to get off the ground during the interwar period, is a good example of a rural area where the Party met with

[24] For an initial overview of Corrèze communism, see Philippe Gratton, "Le communisme rural en Corrèze," in his *Les paysans français contre l'agrarisme* (Paris, 1972), 13–42; and Gérard Monédiaire, "Intersection politique d'espaces: Le communisme rural en Limousin," *Ethnologia* (Limoges) 33–36 (1985): 77–102.

Map 2. France: departments

success only *after* World War II. All four departments, however, have been solid Communist strongholds ever since 1945. They illustrate the different chronological paths followed in the PCF's gradual implantation in the French countryside.

The Limousin departments constitute a coherent geographical unit in the northwestern corner of the Massif Central, to which one can add the northern part of Dordogne, better known as the Nontronnais.[25] Limousin's often hilly landscape is composed of plateaus formed of crystalline rocks; the soil is poor, shallow, and impermeable.[26] At the juncture of the three depart-

---

[25] Geographers consider that the Nontronnais (Périgord Vert) is part of Limousin. The Nontronnais belonged to the diocese of Limoges as far back as the fifth century.

[26] The rock structure is composed of acidiferous rocks (granite and schist) that degrade into poor soils. Heathlands (*landes*) still subsist in parts of Limousin. Guy Bouet and André Fel, *Le Massif central* (Paris, 1983).

ments, the Montagne Limousine, which culminates at close to 1,000 meters, forms the most desolate part of the region (see map 3). Winters are long and rigorous. Similarly difficult conditions prevail in the Combrailles (Creuse) and the southeastern plateaus (Corrèze). The Montagne is bordered to the north, west, and southwest by a series of rolling highlands, ranging between 200 and 500 meters in altitude, where the climate is less harsh and the land better suited to agriculture (Basse-Marche, Haute-Marche, Vienne-Moyenne, and southwestern plateaus). In Dordogne, where economic and agricultural life is concentrated in the more fertile valleys, the sedimentary rock plateaus (chalk and sand) are considerably lower (150 to 200 meters). The climate in Périgord, as well as in Corrèze's Brive Basin, is more temperate and meridional.

Bocage—pastureland surrounded by hedges and trees—predominates in the countryside of Limousin (and to a lesser extent of Dordogne). The impermeable soil and above-average rainfall give birth to large numbers of rivers and streams, particularly on the high Millevaches Plateau, located in the heart of the Montagne.[27] The Limousin has a long agricultural and pastoral tradition, and the raising of livestock of all kinds has increased considerably since the end of the nineteenth century. These were anything but fertile agricultural regions: in 1933 both Corrèze and Dordogne ranked seventy-second out of ninety departments in wheat yields per hectare.[28]

The Limousin's unity is historical and administrative as well as geographical. The diocese of Limoges, founded in the fifth century, covered present-day Limousin, and the region's administrative entity was consolidated under the monarchy.[29] In recent times the region has centered on its capital, Limoges. The Dordogne, like all departments on the periphery of the Massif Central, was oriented toward neighboring regions—the Bassin Aquitain and in particular the port of Bordeaux. Both Limousin and Dordogne have suffered from their isolation (the main north–south and east–west routes of communication bypass the region) and their lack of urbanization. They have watched industrial growth from the sidelines, and the few industries (porcelain in Limoges, textiles, leather work, paper products) are dispersed and little developed. Agriculture remained the predominant activity during the interwar years.

Limousin and Dordogne ranked among the poorest, most isolated and underprivileged regions in France. Rural housing, particularly outside migrant areas, was more often than not substandard; indoor toilets and running water were a luxury, and electrification proceeded at a slow pace. Few

[27] The name Millevaches, derived from *mille vaches*, is said to signify *mille sources* (a thousand springs).

[28] Statistique Générale de la France, *Annuaire statistique, 1934* (Paris, 1935), 104.

[29] On the differences between the Limousin departments, Jean Boutier and Louis Pérouas, "La Corrèze, limousine ou méridionale? Une approche historique," in Louis Pérouas et al., *Les Limousins en quête de leur passé* (Limoges, 1986), 156–58. A diocese was founded in Tulle (Corrèze) in the fourteenth century but it covered only fifty or so parishes. Most of Corrèze remained attached to the Limoges diocese.

Map 3. Limousin and Dordogne: regions

rural inhabitants owned automobiles, and even fewer purchased tractors. When tens of thousands of refugees from Alsace-Lorraine arrived in Haute-Vienne and Dordogne in the early days of the Phoney War, in the fall of 1939, they were profoundly shocked by the miserable living conditions. Put up in farmhouses with neither toilets, running water, nor electricity, the refugees from the well-to-do east, many of them from the city of Strasbourg, complained that the local people were "three hundred years behind the times," "savages," lived in "filthy" villages, and had little more than bread, turnips, and wine on their tables.[30] The contrast between one of the nation's

[30] Archives Départementales du Bas-Rhin (Strasbourg) 98AL292, Contrôle Postal, April 1940.

most prosperous regions and one of its most backward could not have been more marked. Limousin and Périgord lagged behind in other areas as well. Except in Creuse, where an age-old tradition of temporary migration to the cities had promoted reading skills among the men, literacy rates fell below the national average. In 1921 Haute-Vienne had the second highest percentage of male illiterates (17.3 percent) in the nation (after Corsica); Corrèze and Dordogne (both at 15.2 percent) tied for fourth place, with illiteracy rates more than double France's average.[31]

To this day, the inhabitants of Limousin share a strong regional identity along with a sentiment of underprivilege.[32] The Limousin also shares with Dordogne a common leftist political tradition. While differences do exist among the four departments, their similar geographical, social, and economic characteristics render comparisons fruitful and relevant. Only the southern half of Périgord (the Dordogne River valley and wine-growing areas around Bergerac) constitutes a case apart, more akin to the bordering Lot-et-Garonne, where Renaud Jean headed a powerful rural Communist movement. Contrasting this area with Limousin should help determine whether the PCF's fortunes were anchored to a specific regional situation.

This book is based in part on interviews with thirty-four surviving Communist Party militants in Corrèze who had been active between the wars. It has become commonplace to note that oral history is an exercise fraught with perils, but so are other methodologies. Oral history can be of inestimable value to the contemporary historian.[33] The list of people I interviewed, initially put together with the help of membership rosters from the Fédération du Parti Communiste Français de la Corrèze, is not meant to be "representative" in any statistical sense of the word. Surviving rural militants, their ranks thinned by death and emigration, who could be tracked down were too few and far between to make this goal a possibility. Most were at least seventy years of age at the time of the interviews.

My principal objective was to encourage those I interviewed to speak about themselves, their life, their work, their political involvement, and their fellow Party militants. I never used a fixed questionnaire because I felt it would inhibit discussion; my aim, on the contrary, was to foster spontaneity. As I spoke to old Communist peasants in Corrèze, I learned countless details concerning other Party members, the local political scene, village life, and the *mentalité* of the people I was interviewing. Through no other source

---

[31] Statistique Générale de la France, *Résultats statistiques du recensement général de la population effectué le 6 mars 1921* (Paris, 1927), 1, pt. 2: 40.

[32] *Le Monde*, 9–10 February 1986. See also *Limousin et Limousins: Image régionale et identité culturelle*, ed. Maurice Robert (Limoges, 1988), 284–88.

[33] Two of the interviews were conducted with former Haute-Vienne militants. On oral history, Paul Thompson, *The Voice of the Past: Oral History* (Oxford, 1988) and Philippe Joutard, *Ces voix qui nous viennent du passé* (Paris, 1983).

have I obtained such a rich, clear picture of what it was like to be a politically involved peasant in interwar Corrèze. The people I have spoken with have taught me much, and some of their testimony has allowed me to develop my argument with far more confidence than I could have done had I relied solely on archival and printed sources. I have changed the names of the interviewees in order to protect the confidentiality of those who are still alive.

The majority of the people I interviewed worked the land. Half had been (and some still were) smallholding peasants; three were tenant farmers and four were temporary migrants who spent much of their lives tilling the soil. The migrant workers (five in all) included a peasant who drove a taxi in Paris for twenty years before returning to farm his land, and others who had worked as masons in Paris or in neighboring Cantal. The remaining militants I spoke to consisted of three village schoolteachers, two local employees, a doctor, a worker in Brive, and a village carpenter. Only a few of those interviewed held positions within the interwar Communist Party; the highest ranking had been treasurer of the Corrèze PCF. Five had held electoral offices (usually as municipal councillors) during the 1930s, and almost twice that number had been elected to positions of higher rank (mayor, *conseiller général*) in the decades after World War II.

Those interviewed thus provide a mix between grass-roots militants, whose degree of political involvement did not go much beyond their village cell, to some who had been active on the municipal or cantonal level, and finally to a small group who assumed leadership positions in the 1960s, 1970s, and 1980s (a former editor of the PCF rural paper *La Terre*, a deputy to the European Parliament, a president of the Corrèze Conseil Général). They also represented a mixture of political views within the Communist Party. All agreed that rural militants were more open and less sectarian than their urban counterparts. Some older members who had "retired" from Party activities looked upon the past with nostalgia, and had a vision of communism that seemed frozen in time. The most hard-line among them regretted the growing internal debate within the Party, and regretted (without saying so) destalinization and its consequences. In the Montagne, said one, "we don't fall over during the first windstorm"; unlike the intellectuals who had quit the Party at the time of the Soviet invasion of Hungary, "a peasant or a worker [who had thought] a bit more" before joining stayed on.[34] Others—a minority—welcomed the winds of reform blowing through the PCF and the growing contestation of Georges Marchais's leadership. And one prefigured the increasing anti-immigrant feelings in French society by railing against the Turks (a small minority) in a nearby town who lived off the dole and benefited from public housing. Finally, the old militants I spoke to found

[34] Interview with Maurice Bans, Viam, 7 October 1983.

themselves in a diversity of financial situations. Some still worked, others lived adequately if not comfortably off their pensions, while others lived in poverty, scratching a living from unproductive mountain land and occupying substandard farmhouses with few modern amenities; the lucky ones owned an old automobile. All militants—even those who openly displayed doubts about the PCF—were proud they had remained "faithful."

The emphasis on voting behavior in chapters 2 and 3 may require a few words of explanation. Electoral analysis has fallen out of fashion among historians, in part because of the widespread (though erroneous) belief that understanding voting requires little more than commonsensical analysis, and in part because interpretations of politics have shifted increasingly toward the realm of culture and language. But elections remain critical to a comprehension of political and social movements in democratic societies. In the French case, they provide the historian with an outstanding and reliable measure of public opinion (outside Corsica there was little systematic voter fraud). Interwar Limousin and Dordogne society was highly civic-minded and politicized. In isolated rural areas, voting remained the key political act in men's lives.

The electoral process was at the heart of the PCF's activity in Limousin and Dordogne. Of all political parties, only the Communists regularly presented candidates for legislative office in all districts of the region regardless of their chances of success. Campaigns offered unique opportunities for the Party to galvanize militants, reactivate dormant cells or create new ones, and spread its propaganda among the electorate. And much available evidence underlines just how much importance the Party attached to election results, as this was one of the few means at its disposal, especially in rural areas, to measure its influence among the electorate. As militants in the village of St-Pierre-Chérignat (Creuse) put it: "You have a magnificent weapon, your ballot. Know how to use it." [35]

Finally, a note on vocabulary. In interwar France the term "peasant" (*paysan*) referred in its broad sense to anyone who worked the land. The Communists followed this usage, although at times they distinguished between agricultural workers (*les travailleurs des champs*) and peasants (*paysans travailleurs, petits paysans*, or *cultivateurs*), a category that included property-owning peasants, sharecroppers, and tenant farmers. The Limousin and Dordogne countryside was predominantly populated by peasants who farmed their own land, and in the eyes of the Communists their similar income levels qualified them all, regardless of the size of their holdings, as small or "toiling" peasants. Only those who employed more than one agricultural worker were considered to be *gros paysans*. I follow the contemporary definition and use the word "peasant" to designate a person who tills

[35] Uncatalogued electoral leaflet, Bibliothèque Nationale.

the soil; whenever the evidence has allowed me to do so, however, I have distinguished between the peasantry's various components.

The book's organization is thematic rather than chronological. The year-to-year *histoire événementielle* of communism in Limousin and Dordogne is of only moderate interest and mirrors the history of the movement in other regions. Chapters 1 through 3 outline the PCF's fortunes in the countryside on the national level and examine the historical roots and the sociocultural structure of the Communist electorate in Limousin and Dordogne. The remaining chapters contextualize rural Communist successes during the interwar years and analyze how rural voters influenced, appropriated, and refashioned the Party's discourse. Together, voters, militants, and local leaders forged an original political movement that offers rich lessons about the nature of communism and rural society in twentieth-century France.

I   A Critical Constituency

During the first fifteen years of its existence, the French Communist Party occupied a semimarginal position on the French political scene. The 1936 Popular Front, and later the Liberation years, marked the PCF's full emergence as a national political party and a major force in French politics. It was a national party because it gathered support from an ever-larger geographical base, from the industrial north to the Paris region and through large portions of central and southwestern France to the Mediterranean coast. It was a major force in both a social and a political sense: socially through its growing influence among the working class and its control of the Confédération Générale du Travail (CGT) trade union; politically because its newly found strength enabled it to influence, make, and unmake coalitions. Even when the Cold War encouraged sectarianism and isolation, the PCF's control of one-fifth of the French electorate ensured its continued impact on the nation's affairs.

The PCF's growing strength in the countryside contributed to these achievements. The Party's rural character—even if it often was downplayed by its bureaucratic apparatus and later much ignored by historians—had a profound, long lasting impact on its development. Voters elected Communist deputies, departmental representatives, and municipal councilors in rural districts. The Party organized cells and recruited members in agricultural regions. But the PCF did not implant itself simultaneously in all its future rural bastions, nor did it do so for the same historical and sociological reasons. In certain agricultural regions, the Communists had a significant base of support from the very beginning, whereas in other rural areas they would have to wait until the mid 1930s, 1940s, or 1950s to anchor themselves firmly. In parts of France they captured the support of smallholding peasants and rural artisans and shopkeepers, while in other regions they found greater sympathy among agricultural workers or sharecroppers. We can gauge the PCF's presence in the countryside by examining its accomplishments in three realms: its ability to recruit members and leaders, its successes and failures at the polls, and its attempts to organize the agricultural world. The rural Communist presence in Limousin and Dordogne was not an isolated, exceptional phenomenon dependent on local circumstances and historical contingencies; it was part of a nationwide trend.

Peasants and the Origins of French Communism

The relationship between peasants and the PCF dates back to the Party's founding moments at the Congrès de Tours, which resulted in the definitive scission of French socialism in December 1920. Numerous delegates to the congress claimed that rural members of their departmental federations were far more radicalized than their urban counterparts. The Cantal delegate explained that village sections of the Section Française de l'Internationale Ouvrière (SFIO) had voted unanimously in favor of joining the Third International. In Ain, Allier, Ariège, Aube, Charente, Corrèze, Creuse, Drôme, and elsewhere, peasant support for Lenin's party seems to have been equally important.[1] Only in a minority of departments did rural militants choose to remain within the Socialist Party.

The social background of those militants who backed the PCF's creation has long been the object of considerable controversy. Political parties often are marked strongly by the circumstances surrounding their origin, and the French Communists worked hard to counter the perception that they were a foreign body imposed on the French socialist tradition. From an ideological point of view, it was critical for the PCF to have its roots within the French working class. Historians close to the Communist Party (along with the Party itself) have, for obvious reasons, underlined the central role played by workers in the events leading up to the birth of the PCF, but this claim is not always easy to sustain.[2] In the early 1960s Annie Kriegel challenged this interpretation when she argued that enthusiasm for joining the Third International in late 1920 tended to be greatest among new, young, and peasant members of the Socialist Party. The PCF, then, was not the logical outgrowth of the French working-class movement; rather, its founding was linked to the complex nitty-gritty social and political circumstances of the postwar period. That large numbers of rural militants favored the Third International did not necessarily mean that they were further to the left than other SFIO

---

[1] *Le Congrès de Tours* (Paris, 1980). For Cantal see 245.

[2] Roger Pierre, *Les origines du syndicalisme et du socialisme dans la Drôme, 1850–1920* (Paris, 1970), 245. Other historians have stressed the small number of peasant delegates at Tours: *Congrès de Tours*, 78–81; and Jean-Louis Robert, "Les origines du PCF," in Roger Bourderon et al., *Le PCF étapes et problèmes, 1920–1972* (Paris, 1981), 17–39.

members: the dividing line at the Tours Congress did not correspond to the divisions between reformists and revolutionaries.[3]

In fact, the peasant impetus in favor of the Third International was not as strong, unanimous, or straightforward as Kriegel suspected; nor was the role of the working-class leadership in the countryside as important as PCF-aligned historians argued in response. The Cher's delegate at Tours thought that backing for the new International was strongest among peasants, small-holders, and winegrowers, while Socialist militants in the towns of Bourges and Vierzon gave a cool reception to Moscow's twenty-one conditions.[4] Claude Pennetier has shown, however, that support in Cher for the Third International was not significantly stronger within the agricultural world than among the working class, and no social group appears to have played a leading role.[5] In Hérault, where Socialist militants voted against the Third International, there equally was no clear-cut occupational division, although after the Tours Congress agricultural and industrial workers tended to join the new Communist party, while small property holders remained loyal to the sfio. Var rural militants—often from newly founded socialist groups—tended to vote in favor of the new International, while in Allier, which cast over 60 percent of its votes at Tours in favor of the PCF, rural sections approved of the twenty-one conditions, while urban sections around Montluçon and Commentry opposed them.[6] Rural backing for the new International on the eve of the Tours Congress thus was far from homogeneous on a national level. Peasants and other rural militants did not display *less* enthusiasm—quite the contrary—about Moscow's twenty-one conditions than did other social groups.

Rural Communist Leaders

The young Communist party benefited from the hard work and charisma of a generation of rural leaders who did much to cement the Party's credibility in the countryside. Few of these leaders—was this surprising in a party obsessed with the working class?—achieved national prominence. Working

[3] Annie Kriegel, *Aux origines du communisme français, 1914–1920* (Paris, 1964), 2:834–43, 868–69.

[4] Ibid., 246.

[5] Claude Pennetier, *Le socialisme dans le Cher, 1851–1921* (La Charité-sur-Loire and Paris, 1982), 252, 262. See also P. and M. Pigenet, *Terres de luttes* (Paris, 1977), 110–12.

[6] Jean Sagnes, *Le mouvement ouvrier en Languedoc: Syndicalistes et socialistes de l'Hérault de la fondation des bourses du travail à la naissance du Parti communiste* (Toulouse, 1980), 279–86; Sally Sokoloff, "Communism and the French Peasantry, with special reference to the Allier, 1919–1939" (Ph.D. thesis, London University, 1975), 173–78; Jacques Girault, *Le Var rouge: Les Varois et le socialisme de la fin de la Première Guerre mondiale au milieu des années 1930* (Paris, 1995), 208.

outside the limelight, rural leaders played an essential role running the Party at the grass roots, training a new generation of militants, and tailoring the PCF's policies to local circumstances. Many of them had experienced the horrors of the Great War and had been politically active in its turbulent aftermath. Often engaged in professions closely linked to the agricultural world—if they did not work the land themselves—they knew how to reach out to the peasantry and address its concerns. More by lack of interest than by design, the PCF gave rural militants considerable leeway during the first years of its existence. When the Party apparatus cracked down during the periods of bolshevization (1924–27) and class against class (1927–34), rural leaders usually held their own. Throughout the interwar years they would successfully defend the interests of their constituents in the face of militants "parachuted" from Paris to gain control of distant rural PCF federations. Over the long term it was this rural leadership, often laboring anonymously and far from the hubbub and factionalism of the capital city, that put the PCF on the map in the French countryside, and helped transform it from a semimarginal political party to a national one.

Three rural Communist leaders—Marius Vazeilles, Renaud Jean and Waldeck Rochet—achieved national prominence during the interwar years. Marius Vazeilles, the bearded nursery tree gardener who campaigned tirelessly in favor of poor peasants on the Corrèze's harsh Millevaches plateau, became one of the Party's leading peasant experts, and is one of the key figures in this book (see chapter 6). Renaud Jean (a pseudonym for Jean Jean) had greater national stature than Vazeilles within the Party, and was one of the first true peasants to make his mark in it. Born in 1887 to a family of radical-socialist sharecroppers turned smallholding peasants in the southwest (Samazan, Lot-et-Garonne), Renaud Jean started working at an early age on the family farm. At twenty he joined the SFIO and began organizing sharecroppers. Called to the front in 1914, Renaud Jean was severely wounded in September of that year; his war experience left him with a lame leg and contributed to his pacifism. In 1919, while secretary general of the Lot-et-Garonne Socialists, Renaud Jean ran for deputy as a wounded veteran (in an appeal to peasant antimilitarism), taking advantage of the bitter strikes that had begun in neighboring Landes in support of a new sharecroppers' union. Profiting from divisions among his opponents and dissatisfaction with the Bloc National government, Renaud Jean was elected to the Chamber of Deputies in a Lot-et-Garonne by-election two weeks before the December 1920 Congrès de Tours, and attended that congress as a partisan of the Third International.

Passionate and disinterested, Renaud Jean was a powerful public speaker who could move an audience. His rural roots, down-to-earth style, and Gascon accent ensured that even those lukewarm to his views would give him a hearing. When much of rural political life still took place at small town fairs and in village squares, and when public meetings were open to sympathizers and political opponents alike, the oratory skills at which Renaud Jean excelled were the sine qua non of mobilizing rural inhabitants. He could harangue a crowd, capture its attention, denounce the horrendous cost of the Great War, support the claims both of the landless and of property owners, and criticize the "machinations" of the capitalist class. Second only to the right-wing propagandist Henry Dorgères, Renaud Jean was one of the last great peasant orators and organizers of twentieth-century France.

Along with Vazeilles, Renaud Jean was a principal author of the PCF's agrarian program drafted in 1921, and, like many other peasant Communist leaders, he believed in the peasantry's revolutionary character. Unlike Vazeilles, who remained a peasant expert with a solid regional base, Renaud Jean became a high-ranking member of the PCF, and one of the few mavericks within the Party and the International (clashing with Trotsky in 1922) who, despite his opposition to certain policies, such as the class-against-class tactic, managed to survive through agility and luck. Known in 1920 as the "peasant deputy," he was one of the few PCF leaders to have consistent success (in 1924, 1932, and 1936) in the countryside. After the Popular Front elections Renaud Jean became head of the PCF parliamentary group and president of the powerful agricultural commission in the Chamber of Deputies. In the late 1930s, however, the Party gradually eased him out of his leadership role in peasant affairs to make way for the up-and-coming Waldeck Rochet.[7]

Rochet was of a different mold. Born in 1905, the son of a small village artisan in Saône-et-Loire, Rochet began tending cows at age eight and only attended school during the winter months. At age seventeen he hired himself out as a truck gardener. He joined the Communist youth organization one year later and the PCF in 1924. Rochet soon became an active, dedicated, and popular militant in Saône-et-Loire. Though not a talented public speaker, he knew how to address rural audiences. In 1931 Rochet was selected to attend the International Leninist School in Moscow, and on his return to France fifteen months later, he became a full-time Party cadre. In 1934 Rochet, who had been increasingly involved in rural issues, was placed at the head of the PCF's peasant section. By 1937 he was in charge of the PCF's peasant weekly (of which more below) and gradually eclipsed Renaud Jean as Party peasant spokesperson. In 1964, Rochet became the first militant of rural origin named secretary general of the PCF.[8]

Waldeck Rochet differed substantially from Communist peasant leaders of an earlier generation. Too young to have experienced the war or to have been involved in the Socialist movement, Rochet was a first-generation Com-

[7] Gérard Belloin, Renaud Jean: Le tribun des paysans (Paris, 1993); Dictionnaire biographique du mouvement ouvrier français, 1919–1939 (Paris, 1991), 40:43–50; Philippe Robrieux, Histoire intérieure du Parti communiste (Paris, 1980–84), 4:470–72; Gordon Wright, Rural Revolution in France: The Peasantry in the Twentieth Century (Stanford, 1964), 192–97.

[8] Dictionnaire biographique, 40:233–39; Robrieux, Histoire intérieure, 4:475–87.

munist militant who quickly became a professional Party worker. Vazeilles and Renaud Jean, for their part, had political experience before they joined the PCF, were largely self-taught, and owed their social promotion and grass-roots political achievements less to the PCF than to their own hard work. Their enduring accomplishments in the countryside allowed them to preserve a certain independence.

The Rural Membership

Especially in Corrèze and Lot-et-Garonne, the rural leadership existed in symbiosis with a membership sociologically quite different from that of the traditional urban, militant working-class PCF. Peasants played an active role in the formation of the Communist Party, and they have continued to support the Party to varying degrees. In mid-1924 the Party reported to the Comintern that one-fourth (12,500) of its members lived in the countryside; how many of those people belonged to the agricultural occupations remains unknown.[9] The following year, Pierre Sémard, then secretary general of the Communist Party, estimated that peasants constituted 15 percent of the PCF's membership—far fewer than workers (75 percent) but more than revolutionaries of middle-class origin (see table 1.1). A 1929 survey published by *L'Humanité* confirmed these figures and provided a more detailed membership breakdown, which showed that peasants outnumbered agricultural workers.[10] These national figures masked important regional disparities: close to 44 percent of Languedoc's militants in 1928 came from the agricultural world, and two-thirds of them were agricultural workers. In Cher, peasants and agricultural workers joined the PCF in similar numbers (16 versus 18 percent) during the interwar years. More significantly, 64 percent of Cher militants lived either in villages or in small towns without industry. Finally, in Pyrénées-Orientales, on the Spanish border, peasants (18.9 percent) and agricultural workers (6.1 percent) accounted for one-quarter of the known PCF militants in 1937; the actual percentages probably were higher, for this number failed to include militants in the department's most heavily agricultural cantons.[11] In rural areas the Party rarely possessed a clear sense of who its militants were.

[9] Figure cited in Robert Wohl, *French Communism in the Making, 1914–1924* (Stanford, 1966), 394–95. By people who "belonged to the agricultural occupations" I mean all those who worked the land: agricultural workers, sharecroppers, tenant-farmers, and property-owning peasants.

[10] The Party had 38,447 members in that year. Philippe Buton, "Les effectifs du Parti communiste français, 1920–1984," *Communisme* 7 (1985): 8.

[11] AN F⁷ 13091, "Rapport sur la situation économique de la région du Languedoc et l'organisation du Parti." Anne-Marie and Claude Pennetier, "Les militants communistes du Cher," in *Sur l'implantation du Parti communiste français dans l'entre-deux-guerres*, ed. Jacques Girault (Paris, 1977), 264; Michel Cadé, *Le parti des campagnes rouges: Histoire du Parti communiste dans les Pyrénées-Orientales, 1920–1939* (Vinça, 1988), 275–81.

Table 1.1. Peasants and agricultural workers in PCF membership, 1925–1979 (percent)

	1925	1929	1954	1959	1966	1979
Peasants	15%	9.9%	9.4%	8.2%	6.6%	2.4%
Agricultural workers		4.5	4.8	5.0	3.2	1.1
All peasants and agricultural workers	15%	14.4%	14.2%	13.2%	9.8%	3.5%

Sources: Philippe Robrieux, *Histoire intérieure du Parti communiste*, vol. 1 (Paris, 1980), 250; Danielle Tartakowsky, *Les premiers communistes français* (Paris, 1980), 124; Philippe Buton, "Les effectifs du Parti communiste français, 1920–1984," *Communisme* 7 (1985), 20; Stéphane Courtois, "Les délégués aux congrès du PCF et l'évolution de l'appareil communiste, 1956–1985," *Communisme* 10 (1986), 100; François Platone, "Les adhérents de l'apogée: La composition du PCF en 1979," *Communisme* 7 (1985).

The proportion of peasants and agricultural workers in the Party remained roughly the same in the mid-1950s after a decade of seesawing membership levels. While PCF membership was ten times larger during the 1950s than in 1929, the Communists continued to recruit peasant members at the same rate as they had done in the past. The percentage of agricultural militants declined rapidly in the 1960s and 1970s, reflecting the dramatic rural exodus. This precipitous downturn was apparent even in bastions such as Corrèze, where peasant militants traditionally had been the heart and soul of the PCF. In 1970, peasants still made up 27.5 percent of Corrèze's militants; nine years later this figure had dropped to 15.9 percent. Only Dordogne, Allier, Lot-et-Garonne, and Gers had a higher percentage of peasant militants.[12]

Compared to the Italian Communist Party, the PCF's rural militant strength was more modest and geographically concentrated. In 1954, one-third of PCI members worked in the agricultural professions. Membership composition on both sides of the Alps largely reflected the different makeup of rural society: the French recruited best among peasant smallholders (66 percent of all agricultural militants in France versus 22 percent in Italy), and, to some extent, agricultural workers, but did poorly among sharecroppers. The Italians, for their part, found their strongest rural supporters among agricultural workers and among *mezzadri* (sharecroppers) in their stronghold of Emilia-Romagna; by the mid-1950s 16 percent of their members in this region were *mezzadri* and 24 percent were agricultural workers.[13] The dissimilar social profiles of the French and Italian rural Com-

[12] Guy Lord, "Le PCF: Structures et organisation d'une fédération départementale," paper delivered at the European Consortium for Political Research, Paris, 1973, 11; 1979 data from Jean-Paul Molinari, *Les ouvriers communistes* (Thonon-les-Bains, 1991), 189.

[13] Marc Lazar, *Maisons rouges: Les Partis communistes français et italien de la Libération à nos jours* (Paris, 1992), 218–19, 400. In 1954, 17.8% of the PCI's members were agricultural workers; they were followed by sharecroppers (12.2%) and smallholders (3.9%).

munist Party memberships meant that these parties faced different tasks: the French appealed to a constituency of peasant proprietors, while the Italians secured support among the landless. Tensions among sharecroppers', agricultural workers', and peasant smallholders' interests made the agricultural policies of the PCF and PCI into tightrope exercises.

In the years after the Liberation, the Communist Party capitalized on its popularity in the countryside by establishing over 12,000 rural cells. After this initial surge of enthusiasm, however, the Communists proved unable to keep many of these cells afloat, and by 1954 only half of them remained in existence.[14] This precipitous decline in rural cells, which occurred during a time when the Party lost over half its members, clearly was attributable to the exodus of rural militants. Rural cells declined in number until the early 1960s (4,810 in 1962), but regained their mid-1950s level by 1967. After the mid-1950s, losses in peasant membership led to a reduction in the size of rural cells, but over the long term did not lead to a substantial downturn in the number of cells. As a consequence, some cells in the countryside tended to be skeletal and their activity nonexistent.

The Rural Electorate

Peasants also supported the Communist Party by voting for it in both local and national elections. In the absence of opinion polls it is difficult to estimate the Communist electorate's social composition during the interwar years. The percentage of people working the land who backed the Communist Party reached a peak in the years after the Liberation (22 percent) and remained at significant levels in the early 1950s before declining rapidly (table 1.2). If anything, these figures underestimate rural support for the PCF, because some voters may have hesitated to admit their sympathy for Communist candidates when pollsters knocked at their doors. Moreover, the PCF's strength in the countryside did not derive solely from the agricultural world. The Communists also received the backing of rural artisans, shopkeepers, workers, and employees who lived in close contact with the peasants. François Goguel ventures that peasants accounted for 25 to 30 percent of voters who cast their ballots for the PCF in 1951, and of these, 8 to 10 percent were agricultural workers.[15] In Italy, agricultural voters formed a much larger share of the PCI's electorate (36 percent in 1958); if we follow Dogan's conjectures, the Italian left (Communists and Socialists) cornered two-thirds of the votes of sharecroppers and agricultural workers

---

[14] Roger Martelli, "Le PCF et la 'guerre froide' 1947–1953," in Bourderon et al., *Le PCF étapes et problèmes*, 351; Annie Kriegel, *Les communistes français, 1920–1970* (Paris, 1985), 105; Jacques Fauvet, *Histoire du Parti communiste français* (Paris, 1965), 2:328.

[15] François Goguel, "Esquisse d'une description sociologique du Parti communiste français," *Lumière et vie* 28 (1956): 16–17.

Table 1.2. Peasants and agricultural workers in PCF electorate, 1948–1988 (percent)

	1948	1952	1956	1967	1978	1986	1988
Peasants		5%					
Agricultural workers		8	5%				
All peasants and agricultural workers	22%	13%	5%	9%	4%	3%	1%

Sources: Jean Ranger, "L'évolution du vote communiste en France depuis 1945," in Frédéric Bon et al., *Le communisme en France* (Paris, 1969), 243; "Le Parti communiste et ses électeurs," *Sondages* 3 (1952), 50; Roger Martelli, "L'année 1956," in Roger Bourderon et al., *Le PCF étapes et problèmes, 1920–1972* (Paris, 1981); François Platone, *Les électorats sous la Cinquième République* (Paris, 1991).
Note: Polls rarely distinguished between peasants and agricultural workers. Data for 1948 are from an opinion poll; other figures are all from pre- and postlegislative elections surveys.

Table 1.3. Support for the PCF among peasants and agricultural workers, 1948–1993 (percent)

	1948	1947–51	1956[a]	1967	1978	1986	1993
Small peasants	22%		14.9%				
Agricultural workers			28.5				
All peasants[b] and agricultural workers		17%	14.3%	13%	6%	6%	3%

Sources: In 1948 respondents were asked: "Quel parti, depuis la Libération, a mené la politique la plus favorable au pays?" See *Sondages*, October 15, 1948, 198–99. The figure for 1947–51 is the average of three IFOP surveys and for 1956 is a "conjectural estimate": Mattei Dogan, "Political Cleavage and Social Stratification in France and Italy," in *Party Systems and Voter Alignments*, ed. Seymour M. Lipset and Stein Rokkan (New York, 1967), 129–95; François Platone, *Les électorats sous la Cinquième République* (Paris, 1991); Philippe Habert et al., *Le vote sanction: Les élections législatives des 21 et 28 mars 1993* (Paris, 1993).
[a]The figures do not yield the total given because these are the results of separate surveys.
[b]Small, middling, and large farmers.

(particularly in the central regions), while garnering only 12 percent of the smallholding peasants' votes.[16] The purely smallholding peasants' share of the French Communist vote is harder to pinpoint—the polls are not always accurate and do not always distinguish clearly between peasants and agricultural workers—though one can estimate that, through the 1960s, between 5 and 15 percent of the Party's supporters were peasants. By 1986 the Party's agricultural electorate had dwindled to a mere 3 percent.

In the 1940s and 1950s the Party also gathered the support of a notable proportion of the total agricultural electorate (table 1.3). Close to 15 per-

[16] Mattei Dogan, "La stratificazione sociale dei suffragi," in *Elezioni e comportamento politico in Italia*, ed. Alberto Spreafico and Joseph La Palombara (Milan, 1963), 437, 439.

cent of all small peasants are estimated to have voted for the Communist Party in 1956 (for a total of some 500,000 votes), joined by over 28 percent of all agricultural workers. In contrast, 49 percent of the French working-class electorate voted Communist that year.[17] In the decades to follow, the Party's share of the peasant vote declined markedly. By 1986, the PCF was receiving only 7 percent of the agricultural vote; its support was far stronger among male *agriculteurs* (11 percent) than among females (2 percent)—no doubt a reflection of the higher degree of Catholic practice among rural women.[18]

While the drop in the Communist Party's share of the vote since the 1950s (from 25.6 percent in 1951 to 20 percent in 1968, 16.1 percent in 1981, and 9.2 percent in 1993) coincided with an even more precipitous decline in peasant support for communism, it cannot be attributed primarily to "the proletarianization and urbanization of the poorest peasantry." In fact, the rural exodus may well have been a key source of urban militants (and voters), just as it was in northern Italy, where the PCI gathered the votes of southern immigrants.[19] The downturn in peasant support is but one factor in the erosion of communism's electoral support. Deindustrialization, the declining strength of the working class, the changing social and economic character of the Paris suburbs, the inflexibility of PCF policies, and the declining prestige (and later collapse) of the Soviet Union and the international Communist movement all helped to sap the Communist Party's foundations.

Ever since its birth, the Communist Party has found the peasantry to be an important, faithful, and dedicated electoral base. A poll of the Communist electorate published in 1952 revealed that peasants attached greater importance to doctrine (50 percent) than did workers (44 percent) or employees (42 percent). And for 83 percent of the peasants, voting Communist was a sign of confidence in the Party itself; this figure was lower among the rural Communist electorate as a whole (71 percent) and dropped to 53 percent in urban areas.[20]

The Political Geography of Rural Communism

At the heart of the Communist Party's strengths and weaknesses was its concentration in a few rural regions. The PCF's interwar rural zones of sup-

---

[17] Mattei Dogan, "Political Cleavage and Social Stratification in France and Italy," in *Party Systems and Voter Alignments*, ed. Seymour M. Lipset and Stein Rokkan (New York, 1967), 141.

[18] Figures differ slightly from those in table 3.1; see Nona Mayer, "Pas de chrysanthèmes pour les variables sociologiques," in *Mars 1986: La drôle de défaite de la gauche*, ed. Elisabeth Dupoirier and Gérard Grundberg (Paris, 1986), 162.

[19] Sally Sokoloff, "Peasant Leadership and the French Communist Party, 1921–1940," *Historical Reflections/Réflexions historiques* 4 (1977): 155n. For the rural exodus argument, Kriegel, *Les communistes*, 104–5; on Italy, Lazar, *Maisons rouges*, 189.

[20] "Le Parti communiste et ses électeurs," *Sondages* 3 (1952): 54–55.

port were all in central and southern France, south of the Loire River (whereas the "peasant fascist" Dorgères movement was strongest north of that line). Communist bastions in the countryside were concentrated along the Mediterranean coast from Gard to the Italian border, in parts of Aquitaine, in Limousin, and in the broad triangle formed by the Bourbonnais, Berry, and Nivernais on the northern edge of the Massif Central. Poverty, isolation, and distance from the Party's northern industrial strongholds characterized some of these departments. The PCF's appeal, however, was not based on social and economic factors alone or limited to areas with similar socioeconomic traits. The Communists also appealed to networks of sociability and culture (or recreated them where they had disappeared) in village communities.[21]

The Party's geographical implantation was sketched out as early as 1924, when the Communists presented themselves before the electorate for the very first time and received 9.8 percent of the valid votes cast nationwide (map 4). Four distinct regions of Communist strength emerged in that year: among industrial areas along the northern border, from Nord, to Ardennes, Moselle, and Bas-Rhin; in the Paris basin; in a number of rural departments on the northern and western edges of the Massif Central; and finally just off the Mediterranean coast in Gard and Vaucluse (for the location of departments see map 2). The PCF had its highest level of support in the overwhelmingly rural department of Lot-et-Garonne (southeast of Bordeaux), where the Communist ticket, led by Renaud Jean, gathered over 30 percent of the votes cast. The Communists received impressive support in Cher (over 26 percent) and Corrèze (20.6 percent), and did relatively well in Allier, Nièvre, and Dordogne.[22] Seven of the seventeen departments in which support was strongest were predominantly rural.

In the remaining interwar legislative elections (1928, 1932, 1936) the Communist Party's zones of support in the countryside remained similar. In 1928, once again, a rural department, Cher, gave the Communists their highest nationwide score (31.2 percent). In two subsequent elections, Cher and Lot-et-Garonne trailed the Party's industrial bastion, Seine, by only a few percentage points. Most of communism's strength in the countryside was located between these two agricultural departments: the Party's implantation ran from Agenais (Lot-et-Garonne) to the northeast in a wide band that encompassed Périgord, Limousin, Bourbonnais, Berry, and Nièvre. As early as 1928, the Communists made important advances in both Allier and Haute-Vienne.

Thanks to its important electoral gains in 1936, the Party established itself—somewhat gingerly, to be sure—in many rural departments from

[21] Roger Martelli, *Le rouge et le bleu: Essai sur le communisme dans l'histoire française* (Paris, 1995), 143; Cadé, *Le parti des campagnes rouges.*

[22] Note that the figures cited in the text are percentages of valid votes (used to determine the winning candidate) while the maps are drawn as a percentage of the registered voters (and thus take abstentions into account).

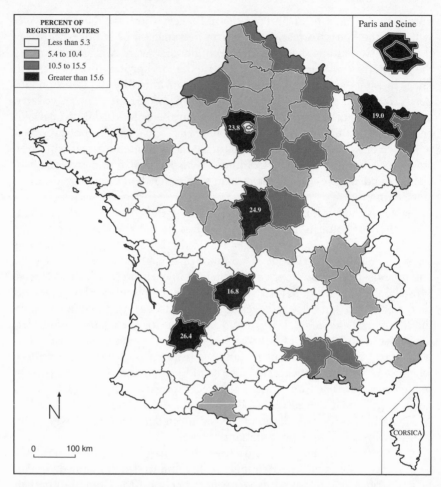

Map 4. France: Communist vote, 1924. (Adapted from Georges Lachapelle, *Elections législatives du 11 mai 1924* [Paris, 1924].)

which it had been virtually absent in the past (map 5). Communism's major gains in the countryside came in Dordogne (22 percent) and Saône-et-Loire (12.3 percent), and along the Mediterranean coast and the lower Rhône valley (Gard [27.7 percent], Var [28.4 percent], Alpes-Maritimes [17.7 percent], Pyrénées-Orientales [20.6 percent], Vaucluse [24 percent], and Drôme [18.4 percent]). Of the twenty-five departments where the Communist Party received more than 15 percent of the vote, ten were rural in character, and three—Lot-et-Garonne, Corrèze, and Dordogne—had over 60 percent of their active male population engaged in agriculture.[23] Fifteen departments

[23] The nationwide average was 33.1%. Direction de la Statistique Générale, *Résultats statistiques du recensement de la population effectué le 8 mars 1936* (Paris, 1943), 1, pt. 3: 8, 12–13.

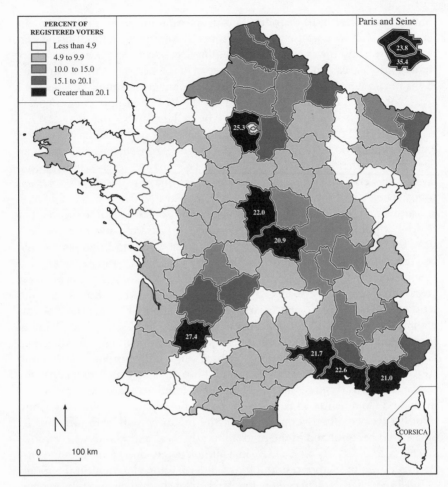

PERCENT OF
REGISTERED VOTERS

☐ Less than 4.9
▨ 4.9 to 9.9
▨ 10.0 to 15.0
▨ 15.1 to 20.1
■ Greater than 20.1

Paris and Seine

23.8
35.4

25.3

22.0

20.9

27.4

21.7

22.6

21.0

N

0   100 km

CORSICA

Map 5. France: Communist vote, *1936*. (Adapted from Claude Leleu, *Géographie des élections françaises depuis 1936* [Paris, 1971], 211.)

gave the PCF over 20 percent of the vote: in eight of them a greater proportion of the active population worked in agriculture than in industry (Lot-et-Garonne, Dordogne, Corrèze, Cher, Allier, Gard, Vaucluse, and Pyrénées Orientales). Voters elected Communist deputies in rural districts of Dordogne (two), Lot-et-Garonne (two), Gard (two), Corrèze, Cher, and Var. Maurice Thorez, the Party's secretary general, noted with satisfaction that the Communists had succeeded both in industrial areas and in the countryside, and he singled out these departments for praise.[24]

The PCF's growing strength in the countryside brought added benefits. Of the seventy-two Communist deputies elected in 1936, ten came from rural

[24] *Cahiers du Bolchévisme*, 16 May 1936, 488.

(in two cases semirural) districts. This proportion increased in the years after World War II. Because of rural France's overrepresentation in the National Assembly, fewer votes were required to elect representatives there than in urban areas; the opposite was true in Party bastions around Paris and in the north, which over time had been gerrymandered to minimize the left's representation. This fact was not lost on the PCF, and only encouraged it to pursue its work in the countryside. The PCF became a national party in the true sense of the word when it acquired a strong parliamentary presence, and recruited voters (and thus elected mayors, *conseillers généraux*, and deputies) in urban and agricultural areas. The Party's presence in the countryside was crucial to the consolidation of its image as *un grand parti national*. The PCF's growing rural success demonstrated that it was not a "one-constituency party" with a geographically and socially restricted base. For sectors of public opinion that thought that the peasantry incarnated essential values of the French nation, the PCF's success in the countryside could be reassuring; it certainly added to the Party's legitimacy and acceptance.

Some of the Communist Party's strongest bastions during the interwar years thus were located outside of large industrial areas. But those who worked the land did not necessarily constitute the PCF's only pool of voters in these regions. Rural departments such as Cher, Allier, Gard, Haute-Vienne, and Var had significant pockets of industry: mining in Allier and Gard, porcelain factories in Haute-Vienne, shipbuilding in Var. In Cher and Allier, the Party's strength was found both in small and medium-sized industrial towns (Bourges and Vierzon in Cher and, to a lesser extent, Montluçon and Commentry in Allier) and in the countryside.[25] In Var, the Communist Party acquired support within the urban coastal strip (Toulon, La Seyne, and beyond) and in the predominantly rural hinterland, where voters elected a PCF deputy in 1936.[26] In Haute-Vienne, on the other hand, the Party did best in the poorest and most underdeveloped agricultural regions.

In all rural departments where the Party did well, the key question remains whether its support came from those who worked in agriculture (and if so, whether from peasants, agricultural workers, or sharecroppers), or whether the Party retained strong backing from artisans, shopkeepers, workers, or employees who lived in rural settings. Answering this question is complicated by the fact that social categories are not always clear-cut in the countryside: artisans, workers, and shopkeepers (some of them temporary

[25] Sokoloff, "Communism and the French Peasantry"; Anne-Marie and Claude Pennetier, "Influence et implantation de la Fédération communiste du Cher, 1921–1936" (mémoire de maîtrise, Université de Paris I, 1971). Georges Dupeux attributes 1936 Communist successes in Cher and Var to the votes of workers in Vierzon (Cher) and Toulon (Var). See *Le Front populaire et les élections de 1936* (Paris, 1959), 148–50.

[26] Jacques Girault et al., "Remarques sur l'étude de l'électorat communiste," *Cahiers d'histoire de l'institut Maurice Thorez*, January 1973, 37; and Girault, "Parti communiste et électorat: L'exemple du Var en 1936," in *Sur l'implantation du Parti communiste*, ed. Girault, 273–99.

migrants), ranging from woodcutters to masons, miners, café owners, blacksmiths, and taxi drivers, simultaneously practiced their trades and cultivated plots of land. Living in rural areas, however, may have been more important than their occupations in shaping their political outlooks.

Those observers who have gone beyond the standard leftist tradition argument and ventured to estimate the social composition of the rural Communist electorate have argued that it varied greatly within regions, and that the Party gathered support not only from peasant smallholders but from a variety of occupational groups. Jacques Girault, writing on Var in the 1930s, found that the presence of workers helped the Party; in certain cantons Communists captured substantial support among cultivators, and in other areas their supporters tended to be winegrowers. Claude Mesliand estimates that one-fifth of the peasants in the most heavily agricultural villages of nearby Vaucluse, spurred by "republican dynamism," cast their ballots for the PCF. Michel Cadé's work on Pyrénées-Orientales suggested that the Party's rural electorate was composed of rural workers (miners and textile workers) and "peasant workers," as well as small property owners and agricultural workers in winegrowing areas. The PCF's limited strength in rural districts of Puy-de-Dôme is thought to have come from workers who lived in rural settings and temporary migrants. Sally Sokoloff has proposed that, contrary to common assumptions, the bulk of the Party's backers just to the north, in Allier, was composed not of sharecroppers but of small property owners and tenant farmers from the Montluçon area. Gordon Wright, in a national overview of the years after World War II, thought that the Party's staunchest rural supporters were farm laborers, marginal tenant farmers, and sharecroppers, while it also made inroads among smallholders and "moderately prosperous small tenants"; a "considerable share" of the Party's support also came from small towns in rural areas.[27]

These estimates of the Communist vote should be considered hypotheses, based as they are on little verifiable evidence, and the authors in question often violate basic statistical rules to reach their conclusions.[28] Support for the Communist Party in the French countryside was not necessarily homogeneous in its occupational composition, and depended greatly on the local social structure. It is reasonable to assume that an important percentage of

[27] *Sur l'implantation du Parti communiste*, ed. Girault, 273–300; Claude Mesliand, *Paysans du Vaucluse, 1860–1939* (Aix-en-Provence, 1989), 2:759; Cadé, *Le parti des campagnes rouges*, 17, 83, 132, 260; Jean-Pierre Vaudon, "L'implantation du Parti communiste dans les milieux ruraux des arrondissements d'Issoire et de Thiers de 1920 à 1936," *Le mouvement social* 74 (1974): 89–96; Sokoloff, "Communism and the French Peasantry," 264. Sokoloff later argued that the Party's rural support also came from forestry workers who worked a plot of land on the side, and from smallholding winegrowers. See "Land Tenure and Political Tendency in Rural France: The Case of Sharecropping," *European Studies Review* 20 (1980): 376–77; Wright, "Communists and Peasantry," 227, 229.

[28] Sokoloff, Girault, and Vaudon are prone to the ecological fallacy when they draw links between specific social groups and the PCF vote.

the Party's backing in villages and hamlets in highly agricultural areas came from people who earned their living from the land.

The Geography of Membership

The geographical implantation of the Communist Party's militants during the interwar years resembled that of its voters. The Party's rural electoral strongholds generally were bastions of militancy as well. The Corrèze, Lot-et-Garonne, Pyrénées-Orientales, Gard, Drôme, Var, and Alpes-Maritimes counted over 90 members of the Communist Party per 10,000 inhabitants in 1937; these figures were equaled or surpassed only in the Paris Basin, the north, and part of Lorraine.[29] The density of Party membership was significant in most other areas of Communist electoral strength in the countryside. In the late 1920s and early 1930s, the PCF's unpopular strategy resulted in a downturn in membership: between 1925 and 1933 the Party lost over 50 percent of its militants nationwide, but these losses were lower than average in the Paris Basin and in a large area of central and south-central France encompassing Cher, Allier, the three Limousin departments, and Dordogne.[30] Given the difficulty of recruiting, mobilizing, and preserving militants in the countryside, the Party's accomplishments are all the more remarkable, and demonstrate that rural communism was far from being a purely electoral phenomenon.

After World War II, the Communist Party's membership became increasingly ruralized. Of twelve departments where the density of Communist militants was over 300 per 10,000 inhabitants in 1946, only one—Pas-de-Calais, ranked ninth—was industrial; the others, in order of importance, were the largely rural Basses-Alpes, Corrèze, Corsica, Ariège, Allier, Dordogne, Haute-Vienne, Drôme, Gard, Hautes-Alpes, and Lot. The proportion of Communist militants declined in the more urban departments. According to Philippe Buton, the twenty-eight most urban, industrial departments had a mean density of 75 PCF militants per 10,000 inhabitants in 1937, while the thirty-three most rural ones claimed a density of 43 per 10,000. Two years after the Liberation this relationship had been reversed: the density of Party militants reached 216 in highly rural departments but dropped to 191 in industrial ones. Between 1946 and 1952 the Party lost nearly 60 percent of its members, and its center of gravity continued to shift toward central and southern rural France. By 1979, the PCF's membership bastions had been reduced to the northern and western edges of the Massif Central, as well as a few departments along the Mediterranean coast.[31]

[29] Buton, "Les effectifs," 12.

[30] Annie Kriegel, *Le pain et les roses: Jalons pour une histoire des socialismes* (Paris, 1968), 218–25; Buton, "Les effectifs."

[31] Buton, "Les effectifs," 14, and maps on pp. 15, 17, 22; by the same author, *Les lendemains qui déchantent: Le Parti communiste français à la Libération* (Paris, 1993), 271–77. The

The Ruralization of Communist Support

What was true of the Communist Party's militants was generally true of its voters. The electoral maps of the late 1940s and early 1950s confirm the Party's growing strength in large parts of rural France, including Côtes-du-Nord, Finistère, Charente, Yonne, Basses-Alpes, and Savoie, where it had not been particularly successful in the past (map 6). Communism's two major rural zones of support remained the northern and western edges of the Massif Central and the southeastern corner of the country. The Party advanced substantially along the western Mediterranean coast (Pyrénées-Orientales, Aude, Hérault) and in the Alps. By 1956, however, the Communists in the southeast had already fallen back on their old strongholds along the southern littoral.

The Communists still continued to do best among the rural bastions they had established during the interwar years: while the Party's nationwide share of the vote dropped from 28.8 percent to 25.6 percent between 1946 and 1951, it progressed in Allier, Creuse, Corrèze, Haute-Vienne, Drôme, and Gard. On the other hand, some of the heaviest Communist losses in 1951 came in rural departments where the Party had been poorly implanted during the interwar years, and where it made modest gains after the Liberation.[32] When the Communist Jacques Duclos ran for President in 1969, he did best in three areas of old rural Communist strength: Haute-Vienne, Corrèze, and Allier.

The map of rural Communist support has remained unchanged since the mid-1950s. The Party's successive setbacks have been spread evenly among electoral districts and departments, and this decline has resulted in the gradual disappearance from communism's map of those rural areas where the PCF was only moderately established.[33] By 1986, when Communist strength in the Midi nosedived, the Party had come almost full circle: its presence among rural departments increasingly resembled that of the interwar years (map 7). The Limousin was, as it had been in 1967 and 1978, the region where the PCF fared best. The Party's four highest-scoring departments all could be found in central France and were all long-standing Party centers: Cher (24.7 percent), Allier (22.2 percent), Haute-Vienne (20.8 percent), and Corrèze (19.1 percent). In all of these departments but Cher, however, the Party's candidates lost a significant share of the vote. As late as 1981 the Communists, led by Marcel Rigout, future minister under the second Mauroy government, still received 33.4 percent of the vote in Haute-Vienne

---

PCF still had militants in the Nord and the Paris region, but there were proportionately more of them in central or southern *rural* France.

[32] Cantal, Aveyron, Deux-Sèvres, Vendée, Calvados, and Orne.

[33] François Platone and Jean Ranger, "L'échec électoral du Parti communiste," in *1981: Les élections de l'alternance*, ed. Alain Lancelot (Paris, 1986), 74; Jean Ranger, "L'évolution du vote communiste en France depuis 1945," in Frédéric Bon et al., *Le communisme en France* (Paris, 1969), 213–14.

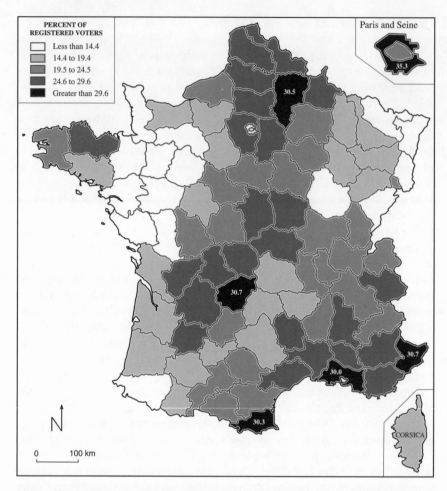

**PERCENT OF
REGISTERED VOTERS**

Less than 14.4
14.4 to 19.4
19.5 to 24.5
24.6 to 29.6
Greater than 29.6

Paris and Seine

35.3

30.5

30.7

30.7

30.0

N

30.3

CORSICA

0   100 km

Map 6. France: Communist vote, November 1946. (Adapted from Claude Leleu, *Géographie des élections françaises depuis 1936* [Paris, 1971], 246.)

(27.1 percent in Corrèze), and three years earlier they had captured the department's three seats in the Chamber of Deputies.

Peasant support for communism and the Party's presence in the countryside have both declined since the 1950s. At first it may seem paradoxical that peasant backing for the Communist Party has reached an all-time low when the Party continues to do best in some parts of the countryside. The Communists, however, score well only in a limited number of rural, depopulated departments, and the support they receive from peasants, sharecroppers, and tenant farmers is not of major significance on a national level. Furthermore, the social composition of the PCF's electorate in its rural bastions has changed as the percentage of the active population engaged in agriculture continues to decline.

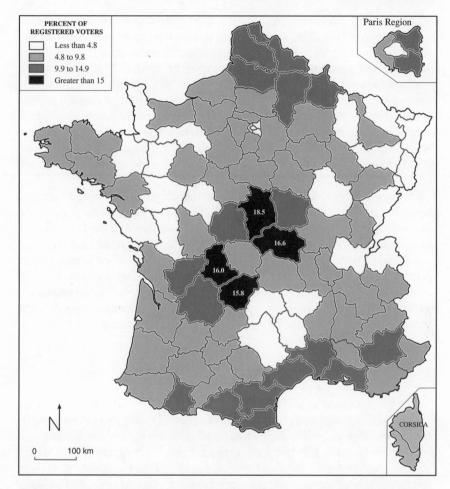

PERCENT OF
REGISTERED VOTERS

☐ Less than 4.8
▨ 4.8 to 9.8
▨ 9.9 to 14.9
■ Greater than 15

Paris Region

18.5

16.6

16.0

15.8

N

0   100 km

CORSICA

Map 7. France: Communist vote, 1986. (Adapted from "Les élections législatives du 16 mars 1986," *Le Monde: Dossiers et documents*, March 1986.)

The downturn in PCF strength among the agricultural professions can be attributed to a variety of factors. The Communists have been hurt by the continuing rural exodus of peasants and agricultural workers from poor areas where the Party traditionally has done well. French Communists have found it difficult to recruit the young, even within their rural strongholds, and many Party officials in these areas admit that their militants and voters are aging and not being replaced at the rate at which they pass away. The case of Maurice Bans, the Communist mayor of the small Corrèze village of Viam for over forty years (1935 to 1983, save for the Vichy interlude) before he finally retired at eighty-one, is not so exceptional as it may seem. Commenting on the problem, he told me, "You know, I stayed [as mayor] twenty years too long. I told them [the Party] twenty years ago, 'You've got to replace me.' It's unacceptable—it's been half a century. What does it prove? It proves that there are no young people to replace me? It proves bad things. It worked here because for the time being we're unbeatable." When I asked, "And your successor, is he young?" he replied, "He's young, yes, he's young—well, fifty years old!" He laughed. "We call fifty young here!"[34]

Faced with the difficult task of recruiting leaders, militants, and voters in regions that have suffered from economic crisis and depopulation, the PCF is satisfied when it manages to hold its own. In a few cases the Communists have actually gained votes in these areas: in the 1984 elections to the European Parliament, the Party's few advances on the national level were found in rural regions of Corrèze and Dordogne.

There can be nothing encouraging for the Communists in the fact that their present-day bastions are on the decline from both demographic and socioeconomic perspectives. In the 1930s and 1940s, when the Party was on the offensive, its spreading implantation in rural areas could be interpreted as a sign of its vitality and its growing ability to appeal to broad sectors of French society. Today the Party is unquestionably on the defensive. Its strength in a few rural departments is a reminder of how much influence it has lost in rural and industrial areas. From a geographical perspective, the Communists can no longer claim to be *un grand parti national*.

Organizing the Agricultural World

The Communists made a sustained effort to increase their influence through agricultural trade unions and the press. During the interwar years these endeavors met with limited success. Although the Communists and their peasant leader, Renaud Jean, managed to gain control of the Socialist Party weekly aimed at the rural world, *La Voix Paysanne*, after the Tours Congress, they could not increase its circulation significantly. Reliable figures are few, but the number of subscribers probably never surpassed 10,000 and averaged below 5,000.[35] Despite Renaud Jean's efforts, the Communist weekly never gained widespread acceptance in the countryside, and its financial condition was disastrous. The only widely read PCF publications in rural areas were weekly departmental papers that devoted their inside pages to local news, something that was difficult to do on a large scale for national publications. *L'Humanité*, the Communist Party's daily newspaper, had few subscribers in agricultural regions.

In January 1937, the Communist Party launched *La Terre*, a new weekly

[34] Interview with Maurice Bans, Viam, 7 October 1983.

[35] In December 1921, the *VP* had 4,700 subscribers, and according to Gratton, the paper's total circulation had reached 9,000 in March of that year. See AN F^7 13627; *VP*, 24 December 1921, 10 April 1926; and Philippe Gratton, *Les paysans français contre l'agrarisme* (Paris, 1972), 105.

for the "defense of French peasants." Headed by Waldeck Rochet, *La Terre* was far more successful than the *Voix Paysanne*, and it reached a print run of 30,000 copies by the end of the year and 33,000 in 1939.[36] The birth of *La Terre* was a clear snub to Renaud Jean, whose independence was not always appreciated by the PCF leadership and the Comintern. Renaud Jean continued publishing *La Voix Paysanne* through April 1937, when, unable to make ends meet, he closed shop and joined *La Terre*.

After the Liberation, the printing of *La Terre* exploded: it reached 199,000 copies in late 1944 and 293,000 in 1946 (of which 125,000 to 160,000 were distributed to subscribers). These figures dropped off substantially by the mid-1960s, but the paper still had a print run of some 150,000 copies in those years, and by 1982 the figure had risen to 200,000.[37] Until recently *La Terre* was the most widely read agricultural weekly in France; in 1966, it was estimated that the paper reached approximately 8 to 9 percent of all French farms.[38] The Communist weekly outdistanced its two major rivals in a large area of central and southeastern France (Auvergne, Limousin, Aquitaine, Midi-Pyrénées) as well as in Provence, while doing poorly in the northern part of the country from Normandy to Alsace-Lorraine.[39] The newspaper's popularity over the years has been the result of its excellent coverage of agricultural issues, ranging from price supports to technical matters concerning cattle raising, fertilizers, and seeds. *La Terre*'s reporting of national and world news is, more often than not, pulled straight out of *L'Humanité*, and its analysis of rural politics reflects the Party line. Though the weekly's influence extends far beyond a thinning kernel of Communist militants, it is unclear whether *La Terre*'s success has helped the PCF minimize its setbacks in the countryside.[40]

The Communists have also made a consistent effort to gain a foothold in the agricultural trade union movement. During the interwar period, under the leadership of Renaud Jean and Marius Vazeilles, they attempted to lay the foundations of a nationwide Communist agricultural trade union. The Fédération des Travailleurs de la Terre (FTT) was founded in Corrèze in 1920 by Marius Vazeilles and gained strength as the years went on, but it

---

[36] For *La Terre*'s 1937 print run see Parti Communiste Français, *Deux ans d'activité au service du peuple: Rapports du Comité Central pour le IXe Congrès National du Parti communiste français, Arles, 25–29 décembre 1937* (n.p., n.d.), 61. For 1939 Robrieux, *Histoire intérieure*, 2:216–17.

[37] Buton, *Les lendemains*, 278; Robrieux, *Histoire intérieure*, 2:216–17; Claude Ezratty, "Les communistes," in *Les paysans et la politique dans la France contemporaine*, ed. Jacques Fauvet and Henri Mendras (Paris, 1958), 77. Figures for the 1960s from Kriegel, *Les communistes français*, 105 and 41n. For 1982 see *L'Humanité*, 30 April 1983.

[38] *La Terre* was outdistanced by the conservative weekly *France Agricole*; see Jacques Longeot, "Les damnés de la terre," *Autrement* 78 (1986): 59. For 1966, Jean Irigaray, "Le Parti communiste et ses électeurs paysans," *Esprit*, October 1966, 404.

[39] René Poupry, "L'information des agriculteurs," in Yves Tavernier et al., *L'univers politique des paysans dans la France contemporaine* (Paris, 1972), 357.

[40] Corrèze, one of the Party's strongest rural federations, had 1,200 peasant members and 4,200 subscribers to *La Terre* in 1970; Lord, "Le PCF: Structures et organisation."

was never able to expand significantly outside of that department. In the hope of grouping together agricultural unions (particularly the Communist-supported Syndicat des Paysans Travailleurs) and, in regions where no organizations existed, individual peasants sympathetic to its views, the Party formed in the mid-1920s the Conseil Paysan Français (CPF), which was the French branch of the Moscow-based Peasants' International. The CPF gave way in 1929 to the Confédération Générale des Paysans Travailleurs (CGPT), which achieved greater success, particularly during the economic crisis that hit the countryside in the 1930s.[41]

The Party's strategy was to organize Syndicats des Paysans Travailleurs where no agricultural trade unions existed or where Communist militants found it impossible to work within present ones. In all other areas, Communist peasants were encouraged to work within existing organizations either to gain control altogether or at least to achieve sufficient strength to influence policy decisions. The purpose of this tactic was to avoid the marginalization of the Communists in the world of agricultural syndicalism. As a consequence, communism's influence within agricultural trade unionism is difficult to evaluate. The few figures we do have concerning those peasant unions close to the Communist Party confirm their limited influence: 200 delegates took part in the first congress of the Conseil Paysan Français in 1926; they represented over 13,000 members of 110 unions (of which 80 appear to have been Communist).[42] The strength of the CGPT and its predecessors was concentrated in a few departments where the Communist Party was well implanted.

Other Communist efforts to penetrate the rural world never had more than regional success. The Party-backed Confédération Générale du Travail Unitaire (CGTU) attempted to group agricultural workers in the Fédération Unitaire de l'Agriculture throughout the interwar period; in 1933, however, this union could claim only 4,000 members.[43] In 1937 the Communists launched the Union des Jeunesses Agricoles de France in the hope of organizing young peasants, but this organization got off the ground only in a small number of departments (Corrèze in particular) before the PCF was banned in September 1939.[44]

After World War II the outline of the PCF's policy remained substantially unchanged: the Party encouraged militants and sympathizers to join major

[41] For an interpretation that places the origins of Communist agricultural trade unions within the context of a "power struggle" between Renaud Jean and Marius Vazeilles, consult Belloin, *Renaud Jean*, 119–41.

[42] Gratton, *Les paysans français contre l'agrarisme*, 108.

[43] AN F[7] 13628, report of the Préfecture de Police, 15 June 1933; Archives de la Préfecture de Police (Paris), Ba 318.

[44] *TC*, 2 February 1938. The UJAF made the inflated claim of 9,000 members in 1938, 1,060 of whom were in Limousin and Dordogne. Parti Communiste Français, *1937–1938: Du Congrès d'Arles à la Conférence de Gennevilliers: Une année de lutte pour le pain, la paix et la liberté* (n.p., n.d.), 274.

agricultural organizations in the hope that they would gain sufficient influence to make their voices heard. Only in April 1959 did the Communists judge it necessary to support the agricultural trade unionists of Corrèze, Landes, and Charentes (among others) who had been excluded from the mainstream Fédération Nationale des Syndicats d'Exploitants Agricoles (FNSEA) in launching the Mouvement de Coordination et de Défense des Exploitations Agricoles Familiales (MODEF), which has remained close to the Party ever since that time.[45] As its name indicates, the MODEF has centered its strategy on defending small family farms (not sharecroppers or landless laborers), and while it has enjoyed some successes, it has never been in a position to challenge seriously the leading role of the FNSEA in most rural areas. The MODEF claimed a membership of 60,000 in 1968 and 200,000 in 1977, but the number of active members was probably substantially lower.[46] The relationship between the MODEF and the PCF is complex and sometimes contradictory, and the organization cannot be considered a simple Party transmission belt.

Rural communism was critical to the Party's larger fortunes. As the Communist Party became increasingly ruralized in the postwar years, it came to depend more on the countryside for support at the polls and elsewhere. In these circumstances, one might have expected the rural world to be the recipient of considerable interest and solicitude on the part of the Communist apparatus, but the opposite was the case. The leadership was indifferent to the peasants, and they clearly occupied a secondary position within PCF discourse when they were not absent altogether. The Party left rural matters in the hands of Renaud Jean and Marius Vazeilles, whose roles in the PCF hierarchy were marginalized more than respected. The Communist Party's standoffish attitude toward the countryside had the unintended consequence of giving rural militants considerable autonomy in determining policy, and this was a key source of their achievements. In urban areas and in factories, the Communists kept much closer tabs on local leaders.

The Party's relative indifference to things rural had much to do with its inflexibility on doctrinal and tactical matters. Despite the fact that their membership and electorate were sociologically varied, the Communists remained wedded to the belief that the working class was the key to their progress. PCF leaders had a frozen vision of communism, which evolved little in response to changes in society and in the social composition of their support. For the leadership, Communist successes in rural Corrèze or Allier paled in comparison with its achievements in industrial regions. The Party's

---

[45] In 1968 the meaning of MODEF was changed to Mouvement de Défense des Exploitants Familiaux. The best overview of MODEF remains Yves Tavernier, "Le mouvement de défense des exploitants familiaux," in Tavernier et al., *L'univers politique*, 467–95.

[46] François Tello, "Données sur l'origine et l'implantation du MODEF," *Cahiers d'histoire de l'Institut Maurice Thorez* 28 (1978): 80.

coolness to rural matters was also related to the peasant component of its agricultural base. To appeal on a national level to this constituency would be to address the issue of private property head-on—a can of worms best avoided, in the minds of hard-line leaders. Thus the issue was left largely to militants at the grass roots. From this perspective, the Italian Communists, whose agricultural electorate was largely landless, faced an easier task.

Rural communism was founded on ambivalence. The PCF came to depend on the countryside's contribution to its national strength, but the Party and its urban militants remained divorced from the rural base. And surely there were times when the apparatus felt threatened by the Party's rural strength and its growing deproletarianization.[47] As a result, the countryside was placed on the back burner and the Party's rural policy stagnated. Had the PCF deployed the same amount of resources and energy in the countryside as in urban areas, it might have developed in other ways. It would also have been a different kind of political party.

---

[47] On deproletarianization, Buton, *Les lendemains*, 265–96.

2   The Party of Stability

The complex political divisions of France have posed a challenge to generations of social scientists. Fascinated by the country's political map throughout the contemporary period, and convinced that electoral geography was the key to understanding French politics at the local and national levels, they have sought long and hard for explanations. Why do certain political parties do well in certain areas and not in others? Does the geography of politics change over time, and if so, why? What kinds of links can be uncovered between electoral choice and age, sex, occupation, and religion (to list but a few variables)? Why does one find countless communes that are identical in everything except their politics? Why, for example, is the political orientation of the *Corrézien* village of Meyrignac, where the Communist Party obtained no votes in 1936, so different from that of the nearby settlements of Beaumont and Grandsaigne, where the Party received 36 percent and 54 percent of the vote in the same year?[1] Scholars have met with much difficulty in their attempts to understand such regional and local political differences. Even the protagonists—militants or mid-level Communist Party politicians—are frequently puzzled and frustrated by the complex political geography within which they operate.

The Limits of Cartography

French historians, joined until recently by political scientists, generally have resorted to the cartographical approach to explain the pattern of French politics, plotting election results on maps to identify the locational

[1] AN C10045.

strengths and weaknesses of political parties. These maps have been drawn by department, by electoral district, by canton, and, much less frequently, by commune. The enduring emphasis on geography in the study of elections in France has become an original component of French political culture. The countless maps, and their accompanying commentaries, published in the press at election time, as well as the various atlases, guides, and essays on political, economic, and social geography that regularly appear in bookstores, are vivid testimony to this fact.[2] Much of this interest, both within the academy and among the general public, can be attributed to the close ties (largely absent in the English-speaking world) between the disciplines of history and geography in France. French fascination with cartography as a key to explaining political and social history is unique in the historiography of any contemporary European nation. Maps have constituted both the strong point and the central weakness of the French school of electoral geography.

The discipline of electoral geography traces its contemporary roots back to André Siegfried's *Tableau politique de la France de l'ouest sous la Troisième République*, first published in 1913. Siegfried's most famous (though least commercially successful) book, which played a central role in the development of French political science, was largely ignored for over thirty years, and Siegfried himself returned to his work on elections only in the late 1930s and 1940s.[3] Electoral geography firmly established itself only after World War II under the leadership of François Goguel, who, like Siegfried, was an avid cartographer. The late 1940s, and especially the 1950s were the heydays of the growing discipline that Goguel had renamed electoral sociology. Goguel's prolific work exerted a powerful influence on the field, and his *Géographie des élections françaises sous la Troisième et la Quatrième République*, first published in 1951, is still considered a classic.[4] Goguel's book, which is little more than a compilation of departmental maps accompanied by the briefest of commentary, has served as a model to generations of postwar historians and political scientists. Goguel himself encouraged his students to follow Siegfried's example and conduct detailed departmental electoral analyses; once a sufficient number of these monographs had been completed, Goguel hoped to propose a more in-depth interpretation of the

[2] Among the latest, Hervé Le Bras and Emmanuel Todd, *L'invention de la France: Atlas anthropologique et politique* (Paris, 1981); Hervé Le Bras, *Les trois France* (Paris, 1986); Emmanuel Todd, *La nouvelle France* (Paris, 1988); and, of far higher quality, Frédéric Bon and Jean-Paul Cheylan, *La France qui vote* (Paris, 1988); Roger Brunet, *La carte, mode d'emploi* (Paris, 1987).

[3] André Siegfried, *Tableau politique de la France de l'Ouest sous la Troisième République* (Paris, 1913) and *Géographie électorale de l'Ardèche sous la IIIᵉ République* (Paris, 1949); Pierre Favre, *Naissances de la science politique en France, 1870–1914* (Paris, 1989).

[4] Surveys of the field include Georges Dupeux and François Goguel, *Sociologie électorale* (Paris, 1951); Charles Morazé et al., *Etudes de sociologie électorale* (Paris, n.d.); *Nouvelles études de sociologie électorale*, ed. François Goguel (Paris, 1954); and Claude Leleu, *Géographie des élections françaises depuis 1936* (Paris, 1971).

nation's political geography.[5] While some of these studies have contributed to our knowledge of regional political differences, many have done little more than further the growing departmentalization of French history; the analyses of electoral results they propose are devoid of any meaningful historical *problématique*.[6]

Though Goguelian electoral geography is no longer as fashionable as it once was, fascination with the cartographical approach to political and social life remains. In *L'invention de la France* (1981) Hervé Le Bras and Emmanuel Todd attempted to renew the field by publishing an "anthropological" atlas of France that takes the department as its unit of reference. Their refreshingly provocative analysis is, unfortunately, methodologically unsound. In this and other works that have received considerable attention, the authors compare maps of everything from voting behavior to suicide rates, family and property structure, illegitimate births, and alcoholism. Maps, however, can be designed to illustrate a wide variety of situations, and Le Bras and Todd freely admit that they constructed maps that best supported their argument.[7] A similarity in the appearance of maps representing different social, economic, cultural, and political factors is no indication of a relationship between them. Le Bras's belief that readers can perform reliable eyeball correlations by comparing two maps of France is insupportable in practice, as well as statistical nonsense.[8]

The geographical obsession of French electoral studies has thus not been without drawbacks. Electoral geographers have sometimes drawn conclusions that are not justified by their maps, and they have often skated on thin ice in their attempts to estimate the origins and social composition of a given party's electorate. At its worst, the cartographical approach amounts to little more than correlation through intimidation:[9] faced with a deluge of maps in support of a particular argument, the uninformed reader can only acquiesce. One of the central and often unacknowledged problems that has plagued electoral geography is that no common standards exist for assessing the associations between maps: where an author discerns a relationship, readers may see none at all.

[5] François Goguel, *Initiation aux recherches de géographie électorale* (Paris, 1949), 9, and for examples of local studies, Jean Pataut, *Sociologie électorale de la Nièvre au XXᵉ siècle, 1902–1951* (Paris, 1956); Jean Micheu-Puyou, *Histoire électorale du département des Basses-Pyrénées sous la IIIᵉ et la IVᵉ République* (Paris, 1965).

[6] As early as 1955 Raymond Aron expressed concern about the "microscopic" nature of these inquiries: "Réflexions sur la politique et la science politique française," in *Etudes politiques* (Paris, 1972), 300–314; Jacques Rougerie, "Faut-il départementaliser l'histoire de France?" *Annales, économies, sociétés, civilisations* 21 (1966): 178–93.

[7] Le Bras and Todd, *L'invention de la France*, 89. For an excellent critique see Jean-René Tréanton, "Faut-il exhumer Le Play? ou Les héritiers abusifs," *Revue française de sociologie* 25 (1984): 458–83.

[8] Le Bras, *Les trois France*, 23–25.

[9] I owe this apt expression to J. Morgan Kousser.

Historians (as opposed to political scientists and geographers) have displayed little methodological innovation in their studies of French elections.[10] Correlational analysis and other more advanced quantitative techniques have never been used as widely in France as in Germany or the United States, and until recently only a few isolated historians worked with them. The methodological simplicity of historical studies of French electoral geography presents major advantages. Whereas other researchers' use of obscure calculations may have alienated their audiences, the French, by using a straightforward approach to focus on geography, retained their readers' interest. Research in electoral geography has raised critical questions that continue to be debated. Efforts by geographers and political scientists to represent cartographically the outcomes of sophisticated statistical calculations have produced some suggestive results.[11] But the field is at an impasse. Certain key questions cannot be answered satisfactorily by the use of cartography alone, however sophisticated. The relationship between voting and economic, social, or religious factors is best clarified by some form of statistical analysis. Do French political parties have geographical roots that reach far back in time, or has their support been fundamentally unstable? Is it possible to trace the shifting allegiances of voters? Do the electorates of major political parties differ substantially in their social composition? To answer these and other questions, a quantitative approach is both a profitable and necessary complement to a geographical study.

This chapter proposes a detailed examination of voting traditions and past electoral behavior in Limousin and Dordogne from the mid–nineteenth century through the Popular Front era. The objective is to identify the principal characteristics of the Communist vote and isolate what distinguished it— spacially, historically, structurally—from that of other political parties. This study of voting proceeds along two broad fronts. I first draw a geographical profile of the Communist Party's backing over time, using a correlational analysis of village-level electoral results. The purpose of the correlational study is to identify short- and long-term geographical variations in a political party's implantation. The results will enable us to see if locational continuity existed in the PCF's bases of support, and thus permit us to discuss in greater detail its political and geographical roots. Over the longer term it will be possible to trace whether the Communists, as has often been argued, benefited from a *toujours plus à gauche* tradition going back to the Démocrates Socialistes in 1849. Second, using a technique inelegantly termed

[10] René Rémond, "L'apport des historiens aux études électorales," in *Explication du vote: Un bilan des études électorales en France*, ed. Daniel Gaxie (Paris, 1985), 34–48. For a different view, Daniel Gaxie, "Sur l'analyse historique des phénomènes électoraux: Les attentes d'un politologue," *Vingtième siècle: Revue d'histoire* 8 (1985): 93–105.

[11] Bon and Cheylan, *La France qui vote*. The authors use principal components analysis to study the territorial structure and evolution of major political groups. By mapping the results of regression residuals they develop an original method of conveying complex information. See also Brunet, *La carte*, 108–11.

ecological regression, I estimate individual-level voter behavior between successive elections in Corrèze. How loyal were Communist voters to their party? Whom had they supported before the Communist Party was founded in December 1920? And finally, did the Communists meet with success in their attempts to capture large numbers of voters from competing political parties? [12]

The statistical analysis is based on the first-round results (by canton and by commune) of nine legislative elections between 1898 and 1936, for all political parties in Limousin and Dordogne. Other parties have been included in this study because the Communist Party's specificity is best understood when its electoral behavior is compared to that of its opponents. And the need to understand the genesis of rural communism has forced me back in time—to 1849 and 1898—in search of elements that may contribute to a historical explanation of the PCF's voting patterns.

Support for the Communist Party was unequal in Limousin and Périgord. The Communists established their strongest base in Corrèze, where their backing remained relatively stable, averaging 19.6 percent of the vote over the four interwar elections. Just to the north, in Creuse, the Party's efforts never met with consistent success, and its support usually was lower here than in the nation as a whole. In Dordogne, the Communist Party hovered around the 13 percent mark in the 1920s, lost support in 1932, then more than doubled its score to 22 percent of the vote—one of the better results in the nation—in the 1936 Popular Front elections. In Haute-Vienne, results seesawed considerably, but a strong showing in 1928 (21 percent) and to a lesser degree in 1936 demonstrated that the PCF could be successful in this area when it presented more suitable candidates and policies (table 2.1).

These results were achieved within varying political contexts. The Creuse, Corrèze, and Dordogne remained areas of important—although steadily declining—radical influence. This decline was most apparent in Creuse, where the Radicals had been replaced by the Socialists as the dominant party by the early 1930s. In Corrèze, radicalism remained the principal political force until it nose-dived in 1936 and in the process was overtaken by both socialism, which had grown consistently since 1928, and communism. The Radicals never gave up their leading position in Dordogne, and together with centrist leaders they dominated the political landscape there until the Popular Front. Support for the right, already low by national standards, fell consistently in all three departments during the interwar years, and in Corrèze and Dordogne this downturn began even before World War I.

The Haute-Vienne Socialist bastion constitutes a different case. Here the Socialists reigned supreme as early as 1914, when they obtained 55 percent

---

[12] More detailed versions of the tables reproduced below can be found in Laird Boswell, "The French Rural Communist Electorate," *JIH* 23 (1993): 719–49. See the Appendix for details on the data and methodology.

Table 2.1. Percent of valid votes cast for parties of left and right, Limousin and Dordogne, 1906–1936

	Parti Communiste	Parti Socialiste	Radical candidates[a]	Other left candidates	Right candidates
Corrèze					
1906		0.4%	55.2%	11.4%	32.9%
1910		3.4	64.5	5.4	26.5
1914		7.9	56.3	4.7	31.0
1919		23.9	36.9	–	39.2
1924	20.8%	–	50.5	–	28.6
1928	21.1	11.4	33.5	5.7	28.4
1932	15.2	19.5	41.3	4.6	19.5
1936	21.6	34.3	18.9	6.7	18.5
Creuse					
1910		5.1	56.8	36.3	1.5
1914		15.5	68.3	16.0	–
1919		19.1	32.6	27.4	10.5
1924	6.9	28.0	37.6	–	26.5
1928	14.0	30.9	32.6	9.0	13.4
1932	5.8	50.9	19.3	12.1	11.8
1936	11.4	47.8	21.9	2.2	16.7
Dordogne					
1910		6.9	34.8	21.7	36.2
1914		10.1	28.2	17.3	44.3
1919		12.5	21.7	–	55.7
1924	13.5	–	47.4	–	37.5
1928	13.7	10.0	25.5	9.4	37.1
1932	9.0	13.3	39.8	17.6	20.3
1936	22.0	16.7	23.6	17.8	18.9
Haute-Vienne					
1910		37.5	42.4	2.8	17.1
1914		55.6	27.8	2.1	11.9
1919		51.2	–	–	46.5
1924	6.0	58.0	–	–	34.5
1928	21.0	34.9	4.1	3.3	36.6
1932	11.0	44.5	–	5.2	39.2
1936	17.1	46.9	1.8	–	33.4

Sources: Electoral results are from AN C7208 (1906); C6781 (Socialist vote, district of Bellac, Haute-Vienne, reconstructed from *bulletins nuls*), C7228 (1910); C7243, C7251 (1914); C10002, C10006 (1919); C10011, C10016 (1924); C10021, C10027 (1928); C10031-32, 10039 (1932); C10045-46, C10055 (1936); ADC 3M189–202 (1906-36); ADCR 3M304 (1928); ADD 3M90 (1936); ADHV 3M162 (1910); 3M164 (1919); *Le Journal de Bergerac*, 17 and 24 May 1924; *L'Union Sarladaise*, 18 May 1924.

Note: Figures do not always add up to 100% because a few minor candidates whose political affiliation was unclear have been omitted.

[a] Including dissidents from the Radical-Socialist Party and Radical-leaning candidates.

of the vote, and by 1919 the Radicals, who had received the backing of 42 percent of the voters only nine years earlier, had been eliminated from the political scene. The strength of socialism in Haute-Vienne left little room for the center left, and so may have contributed to the more notable presence of the interwar right, although its score still remained well under the nationwide average.

The Limousin and Dordogne thus were characterized by an overwhelmingly and consistently strong left. The first four decades of the century witnessed an important reordering in the ranking of left political parties: broadly speaking, the Radicals declined, while the Socialists and Communists established themselves, although not always consistently or simultaneously. This shift was reflected as well in the political affiliations of the region's deputies: as the number of Radical and Conservative deputies fell, the number of Socialist and even Communist representatives rose. Five Communist deputies represented this area during the interwar period: the first, François Aussoleil, was elected on the Corrèze Socialist ticket in 1919, and joined the Communist Party after the December 1920 Tours Congress. He failed in his bid for reelection in 1924. Jules Fraisseix, who served one term in office, was elected Communist deputy of Haute-Vienne in 1928. In 1936 the Party reaped the fruits of the Popular Front alliance by electing two Communist deputies in Dordogne (Paul Loubradou and Gustave Saussot), and one in Corrèze (Marius Vazeilles).

The Party of Stability

Throughout Limousin and Dordogne the Communist vote in the 1920s and 1930s was characterized by remarkable geographical continuity. The correlations of the Party's interwar electoral results are, in the great majority of cases, far stronger than those of any other political party.[13] In Corrèze the correlations of the Communist Party's score in pairs of successive elections grow consistently stronger over time, never dipping below .77 (1924–28) and reaching the .84 mark for the 1932 and 1936 elections (table 2.2) (to see the change between succeeding elections, read the correlation matrix diagonally; read it vertically to observe changes over the longer term). These results suggest that the Party benefited from similar geographical patterns of support throughout the period. By and large, the same communes backed the Party from election to election, and they did so in the same relative order: communes that voted heavily for the Communists in 1924 would, in the majority of cases, tend to do so again in future elections, just as those that

[13] A high correlation coefficient indicates that support for the political party concerned is geographically stable, whereas a low coefficient indicates change in the geographical base of support for that party. Correlation coefficients measure whether a party's share of the vote changes (up or down) by widely different levels in all communes.

Table 2.2. Correlation of percent of Socialist and Communist votes, Limousin and Dordogne, by commune (percent of registered voters)

	Parti Socialiste				Parti Communiste		
	1906	1910	1914	1919	1924	1928	1932
Corrèze							
N	71	125	191	290	290	290	290
Parti Socialiste							
1910	.623						
1914	.518	.545					
1919	.452	.462	.591				
Parti Communiste							
1924	.523	.420	.530	.698			
1928	.531	.327	.615	.717	.774		
1932	.466	.231	.349	.649	.760	.802	
1936	.508	.347	.331	.633	.721	.748	.846
Haute-Vienne							
	1898						
N	63	205	205	206	206	206	206
Parti Socialiste							
1910	.327						
1914	.205	.781					
1919	.378	.627	.740				
Parti Communiste							
1924	.501	.328	.237	.361			
1928	.504	.595	.497	.601	.728		
1932	.568	.543	.430	.477	.735	.836	
1936	.449	.448	.395	.461	.716	.819	.876
Dordogne[a]							
N = 47							
Parti Socialiste							
1914		.584					
1919		.467	.815				
Parti Communiste							
1924		.385	.756	.827			
1928		.414	.647	.651	.769		
1932		.263	.679	.753	.862	.793	
1936		.274	.609	.507	.595	.686	.693
Creuse							
N = 266							
Parti Communiste							
1924			.405				
1928			.620	.480			
1932			.624	.504	.776		
1936			.489	.278	.581	.662	

Sources: For electoral results, see table 2.1.
[a]By canton.

had failed to support communism generally would behave similarly in years to come. Changes in the Communist vote were not restricted to specific communes but were across the board, and this had clearly been the case since 1924, when the Party first presented candidates to the electorate. Throughout the 1920s and 1930s the Party's communal geographical ordering of support remained broadly similar.

The principal characteristic of the Communist vote was its locational stability. The Party underwent no major electoral realignment during this period; on the contrary, its geographic base of support continuously strengthened between successive elections. The long-term correlations from 1924 are remarkably consistent as well (1924–36: .72), thus clearly demonstrating the Party's long-term geographical stability. This enduring stability throughout the interwar years distinguishes the Communists from their Socialist and Radical opponents, who may have enjoyed moderate geographical continuity between consecutive elections but rarely did so over any lengthier time period.

The Communist Party's territorial stability was unaffected by variations in the percentage of votes it received for legislative elections. In comparison with its turnout in Creuse, Dordogne and Haute-Vienne, the Party's score in Corrèze fluctuated only moderately, never dipping below 15 percent or advancing beyond 22 percent of the vote. The correlational analysis demonstrates that these gains (1932–36: +6.4 percent) and losses (1928–32: −5.9 percent) were not confined to any particular region but were, on the contrary, relatively evenly spread out among all Corrèze communes, regardless of how well or poorly the Party was established.

The PCF's geographical permanence was equally impressive in neighboring Haute-Vienne, and by the late 1930s it was even more firmly anchored there than in Corrèze (table 2.2). The Party's impressive gains and losses (1924–28: +15.05 percent of the vote; 1928–32: −10 percent) were not concentrated within specific areas of Haute-Vienne but were, by and large, evenly distributed among all communes, regardless of how well the Party was implanted. Communes thus reacted in similar fashion to changes both in the general political climate and in the Communist Party's national and local efforts. The Party remained strong in Haute-Vienne even though fluctuations in voter support were greater and more frequent there than in Corrèze.

In Dordogne the Communist party was, once again, the most geographically stable of political parties, although this territorial permanence at the cantonal level was not quite as consistent as it was in Corrèze and Haute-Vienne (table 2.2). Finally, in Creuse the PCF failed to secure a stable base of support in its early years. Only as of 1928 did the *Creusois* Communists achieve a notable degree of locational continuity, although the coefficients indicate that this stability was weaker than in the rest of Limousin (table 2.2).

The remarkable stability of the Communist vote in Limousin and Dordogne should not obscure the fact that the Party's base of support underwent a small, gradual, long-term shift. The strong correlation between the Corrèze Communist vote in 1924 and its counterpart in 1936 (.72) nonetheless indicates that some locational change occurred in the Party's implantation; had this not been the case, the correlation would be near perfect. Among what kind of communes did these shifts take place? Table 2.3, which measures the evolution of the Communist vote between 1924 and 1936, reveals that the Party progressed most in those 196 communes where it was poorly or moderately established in the mid-1920s (these were areas where it received less than its departmental average); it was among these villages that support for communism tended to be most volatile. On the other hand, the Party lost support in villages where it received between 30 to 40 percent of the vote in its early years, while holding its own in those twenty-two communes where it had obtained the backing of over 45 percent of those who had cast their ballots. Communist strongholds (and this was true in Haute-Vienne as well) proved exceptionally faithful in their support of the Party. This finding confirms what the coefficient initially suggested: behind a backdrop of stability there nonetheless was some change. Over a twelve-year period the PCF's votes had been partly redistributed (the vote total itself changed little—see table 2.1), to the benefit of a large majority of communes where the Party was poorly implanted. The Communists thus had achieved one of their objectives, which was to improve their score in areas of weakness. Their second and most important objective, however—to gain a larger share of the vote—remained unfulfilled.

The electoral stability of the Communist vote throughout Limousin and Dordogne distinguished it from its rivals. Major changes in the Communist Party's line, such as the adoption of the class-against-class tactic in November 1927, did not lead to significant alterations in the Party's implantation. No other political force acquired such a solid, unchanging base of support between the wars or evinced such striking similarity of electoral behavior from one department to another. None of the Party's opponents on the left could conserve their geographical base for any extended period of time. Only the conservative parties, to a lesser degree than the Communist Party, succeeded in preserving their communal implantation in both the short and intermediary terms. The PCF truly was the party of stability, a stability that constituted both the source of its success and a major barrier to its development. The Communists successfully preserved their zones of strength; they had great difficulty, however, finding new supporters in areas where they were poorly established.

The case of Dordogne, with its different geographical and political makeup, suggests that electoral stability was not a regional phenomenon confined solely to Limousin, but was far broader in scope. Studies of the PCF's electorate reveal that this stability existed throughout France from the

Table 2.3. Change in Communist vote, Corrèze, 1924–1936 (percent)

	Number of communes	1924	1936	Change
% of PCF vote in 1924				
Less than 5%	58	2.5%	8.7%	+6.2%
5–10	53	7.7	13.6	+5.9
10–15	51	12.7	17.4	+4.7
15–20	34	17.4	21.3	+3.9
20–25	16	22.9	21.8	−1.1
25–30	19	28.1	27.2	−0.9
30–35	15	33.4	21.9	−11.5
35–40	20	37.8	31.6	−6.2
40–45	2	43.2	51.5	+8.3
45–50	11	47.5	47.3	−0.2
50+	11	58.2	57.0	−1.2
Total	290	20.7%	21.6%	+0.9%

Sources: ADC 3M196, AN C10045.

mid-1950s through the 1980s, during periods of both expansion and vertiginous decline. This was probably the case during the interwar years as well.[14]

The Socialist Heritage

The origins of the PCF's stable patterns of support can be traced back to the Socialist Party in the years before the December 1920 Tours Congress. In Corrèze, the SFIO vote between adjacent elections in the first two decades of the century correlated strongly (although not so strongly as for the Communists later on), suggesting that in its formative years in Corrèze, socialism established a geographical base of support before the Communists inherited and strengthened it in the early 1920s. Communes that voted Socialist in 1906, 1910, and 1914 (in whatever proportion) had a marked tendency to vote Communist early on, although this relationship clearly had weakened by the early 1930s. The Socialist vote in 1914 is more highly correlated with the Communist vote in 1928 ($r = .61$) than with any vote in any other election, including the Socialist vote in 1919 (table 2.2). In short, the communes that supported the Socialists before World War I did not tend to do so after 1920. Instead, they turned to communism.

The results are even more significant for the 1919 elections, when every

[14] François Platone and Jean Ranger, "L'échec électoral du Parti communiste," in *1981: Les élections de l'alternance*, ed. Alain Lancelot (Paris, 1986), 70–133; Robert Ponceyri, *Gaullisme électoral et Cinquième République: Les élections en France depuis 1958 et la mutation du système politique* (Toulouse, 1985). Bon and Cheylan, *La France qui vote*, 53, underscore the PCF's extraordinary territorial stability under the Fifth Republic.

Corrèze town and village had SFIO candidates on the ballot: communes voting for the Socialists in that year are an excellent predictor of those that would support the PCF throughout the 1920s and 1930s. Areas of prewar Socialist strength became regions of Communist strength, just as areas of Socialist weakness predicted Communist weakness. In both Corrèze and Dordogne, the Communist Party stepped into the shoes of the pre-1920 SFIO, leaving the Socialist Party in the difficult position of having to carve out a new long-term geographical and political base for itself. The Communists appropriated the old Socialist locational base more quickly and successfully in departments such as Corrèze and Dordogne, where they faced no independent Socialist ticket in 1924. In the 1920s and 1930s the Communists became the geographic heirs of the pre-1920 Socialist Party, and thus could claim to be the sole continuators of the Socialist tradition.

A similar situation prevailed in Haute-Vienne, where communism became an electoral tradition, though the political situation in this department hardly resembled that of its southeastern neighbor. The Socialist party was by far the most powerful political force in Haute-Vienne, dominating key aspects of political life. The Communists, in the minority within the SFIO at the time of the Tours Congress, found themselves unable to make up the ground they had lost at the start, and played second fiddle to the Socialists throughout the 1920s and 1930s. In 1924 the Socialists, not the Communists, assumed the territorial heritage of the pre-Tours SFIO. This proved to be a short-lived accomplishment, however; by the late 1920s, the Communists succeeded in appropriating most of the late nineteenth- and early twentieth-century Socialist geographical base (table 2.2), despite the parties' unequal relationship. The new SFIO, on the other hand, lost its geographical base of support in the late 1920s, and by the Popular Front years the association with the Socialist vote before the Congrès de Tours had disappeared almost entirely. There was also a slight time lag in Creuse before the PCF proved able to assume the old Socialist party's locational heritage (table 2.2).

The Communist vote in Limousin and Dordogne thus was strongly associated with the Socialist vote in 1898 (Haute-Vienne), 1906 (Corrèze), 1910, 1914, and 1919 (in the region as a whole), although the strength of this relationship varied among departments. In each case, faced with widely diverging political situations, the Communists successfully managed to preserve and enlarge the territorial base of the old Socialist Party.

A Long-Standing Leftist Tradition?

The final question that the correlational analysis can resolve is whether communism was, from an electoral perspective, somewhat of a "new" phenomenon that could be traced back to socialism in the early decades of the century, or whether its geographical roots lie further back in time. In other words, was communism, as the proponents of the *toujours plus à gauche* theory have argued, the end point of a long-standing leftist voting tradition in the countryside that began with the Démocrates Socialistes (also known as the Démoc-Soc) in 1849, or even in 1848?

This argument was first proposed in the 1920s by Daniel Halévy in his classic book on rural life in central France. It later was developed and popularized by Ernest Labrousse and François Goguel.[15] For Goguel, only a founding event, the 1849 Montagnard vote, could account for communism's 1946 strength in departments such as Corrèze, where social and economic factors could not explain why peasants turned to the PCF. Communism, he argued, "purely and simply succeeded Ledru-Rollin's Montagne. It owes its strength to the fact that it is 'the furthest on the left' of French parties, the successor of socialism twenty years ago and radicalism fifty years ago."[16] This explanation was extended by Goguel, and other leading observers of French political life, to all rural regions where the Party scored well at the polls. Rural communism, in short, was the outgrowth of an old republican tradition, and was nothing but "an old bottle, with a new label"; the contents remained unchanged.[17]

The tradition argument, based on the haphazard visual correlations characteristic of much French electoral geography, poses more problems than it solves. While observers have been quick to invoke tradition as an all-encompassing explanation of political behavior, they never investigate the critical question of how voting traditions are transmitted. Moreover, the proponents of the *tradition de gauche* interpretation fail to provide convincing explanations of why large numbers of peasants, sharecroppers, tenant farmers, artisans, shopkeepers, and rural workers never moved beyond support for the Radical Socialists (and their allies), whereas others cast their ballots in favor of Socialist and Communist candidates. In other words, why did some electors vote *toujours plus à gauche* and others not? What evidence can be advanced to suggest that rural communism indeed did hark back to

---

[15] Daniel Halévy, *Visites aux paysans du Centre, 1907–1934* (Paris, 1978), 182; Ernest Labrousse, "Géographie du socialisme," *La revue socialiste* 2 (1946): 137–48; "La montée du socialisme en France depuis un siècle, 1845–1945," *La revue socialiste* 1 (1946): 18–27; Goguel, *Géographie des élections françaises* and *Chroniques électorales: Les scrutins politiques en France de 1945 à nos jours*, (Paris, 1981–83). For the 1848 argument (votes for Raspail and Ledru-Rollin) see Frédéric Salmon, "Quelques remarques sur le vote communiste," *Communisme* 45–46 (1996): 161–75.

[16] Goguel, *Chroniques électorales*, 1:85.

[17] Examples are too numerous to cite, but see Goguel's works cited in n. 15 and Jacques Fauvet, *Histoire du parti communiste français* (Paris, 1964), 1:70–71, 187–88, 2:338–39; Annie Kriegel, *Les communistes français* (Paris, 1985), 105; Gérard Belloin, *Renaud Jean, le tribun des paysans* (Paris, 1993), 230–31; Jean-Paul Brunet, *Une histoire du PCF* (Paris, 1982), 39; Charles A. Micaud, *Communism and the French Left* (New York, 1963), 130; Philip M. Williams, *Politics in Post-War France* (London, 1954), 54; Jean-Marie Mayeur, *La vie politique sous la Troisième République* (Paris, 1984), 206, 322. Even Bon and Cheylan, in their methodologically sophisticated *La France qui vote*, 88, have recourse to tradition to explain communism's strength in Limousin.

Démoc-Soc and Radical roots? Why have scholars relied broadly on a socio-logical explanation (the presence of a large, organized working class) to ac-count for Communist strength in industrialized regions, but have dismissed such an approach for rural areas? By using the murky category of tradition to explain rural political behavior, observers have devalued Communist (and Socialist) voting in the countryside. Voters, they imply, backed leftist parties more out of habit than to express support for a particular social, political, and ideological agenda. In their eyes, rural communism was little more than a radicalized version of Radicalism. For one author, the PCF's support in ur-ban areas was a true Communist vote, while in the countryside it permitted the peasantry to affirm its oppositional stance while expressing its fidelity to republicanism.[18]

Communism in Corrèze did not adopt the geographical succession of the Montagne to any significant degree. Correlations between the Démoc-Soc, the Socialist (as of 1906), and the Communist vote fail to reveal any sus-tained relationship (see table 2.4).[19] Support for the Démocrates Socialistes was at best a fair predictor of future (seventy-five years later) voting for the Communist party. Only in 1924 and 1936 was there a slight similarity be-tween the cantonal ordering of Montagnard and Communist strength. When the Démocrate Socialiste geographical heritage did filter down to the twen-tieth century, it was not appropriated by any particular political group (save the 1919 Radicals), but instead was partly inherited by the left (table 2.4). By the 1930s, however, the left's implantation had lost what little locational heritage it had acquired from its Montagnard predecessors.[20]

In Creuse it is even more difficult to trace communism's geographical ori-gins back to the middle of the nineteenth century: there exists no association whatsoever between cantonal support for the Montagnards and backing for either the Communists, the Socialists, the Radicals, or the left (except in 1932) in the twentieth century (table 2.4). The influence of Martin Nadaud, Creuse's most famous political figure (to whom all left parties paid alle-giance) first elected deputy on the Démocrate Socialiste list in 1849, clearly was far more ideological than geographical.[21] Finally, in Haute-Vienne, a consistent link between Démoc-Soc voting and communism was equally lacking in the 1920s and 1930s. However, Montagnard voting was a better (if moderate) predictor of Socialist support between 1910 and 1919 in

---

[18] Jederman, *La "bolchévisation" du Parti Communiste Français, 1923–1928* (Paris, 1971), 107.

[19] 1849 election results are available only by canton. Compare with the map in Frédéric Salmon, "La gauche avancée aux élections législatives de 1849," *Communisme* 28 (1991): 69–82.

[20] Labrousse ("Géographie du socialisme") had called attention to the correspondence be-tween the Démoc-Soc and the joint Socialist-Communist map of support in the twentieth cen-tury. The correlations do not support this thesis in the three Limousin departments: in nine of twelve elections the correlation between the Démoc-Soc and the combined Socialist-Communist vote is actually lower than it is for the left as a whole.

[21] Martin Nadaud, *Mémoires de Léonard, ancien garçon maçon* (Bourganeuf, 1895).

Table 2.4. Correlation of percent Démocrate Socialiste vote, 1849, and Socialist, Communist, Radical, and all left vote, Limousin, 1906–1936, by canton (percent of valid votes cast)

	Démocrate Socialiste vote, 1849		
	Corrèze (N = 29)	Creuse (N = 25)	Haute-Vienne (N = 29)
Parti Socialiste			
1906	−.080		
1910	.250	.036	.324
1914	.077	.053	.200
1919	.159	.055	.362
1924		.077	.434
1936	.038	.181	.230
Parti Communiste			
1924	.310	.047	−.067
1928	.132	.155	.344
1932	.239	.078	.178
1936	.257	.077	.190
Radical candidates			
1919	.396	−.167	
Left parties			
1906	−.045		
1910	.320	.073	.000
1914	.348	−.215	.532
1919	.395	−.123	.362
1924	.433	.191	.378
1928	.349	.104	.360
1932	.250	.377	.414
1936	.005	−.138	.515

Sources: ADC 3M65 and table 2.1.

Note: In the few instances in which a party was not present in a given district, its vote has been set at zero. The effect on the coefficients is small.

Haute-Vienne than in Corrèze. It was no accident that this occurred where the SFIO was particularly strong and radicalism on the wane. More than in other Limousin departments, the Haute-Vienne left preserved and even strengthened a moderate geographical link with the Démocrates Socialistes well into the 1930s, thus once again demonstrating that when part of that heritage survived into the first decades of the twentieth century, it was inherited by the entire left rather than by any single political party (table 2.4).

The link between turn-of-the-century radicalism and the socialism and communism of later years is even more elusive. Communes that voted Radical in 1898 (Haute-Vienne), 1906 (Corrèze), 1910, and 1914 (Corrèze and Haute-Vienne) did not tend to support pre-Tours Socialist candidates or Communist candidates in the 1920s and 1930s (table 2.5). Indeed, the greater their earlier support for the Radicals, the fewer votes they cast for left parties in future decades.

Whereas communism inherited the SFIO's geographical patterns of sup-

Table 2.5. Correlation of percent of Radical vote with Socialist and Communist vote, and correlation of percent of all left votes, 1898–1936, Corrèze and Haute-Vienne (percent of registered voters)

	Radical votes					
	Corrèze			Haute-Vienne		
	1906 N = 290	1910 N = 290	1914 N = 290	1898 N = 203	1910 N = 186	1914 N = 205
Parti Socialiste						
1919	.049	−.072	−.076	.311	−.297	−.331
Parti Communiste						
1924	.053	−.031	−.085	.002	−.255	−.097
1928	.020	−.155	−.169	.179	−.296	−.047
1932	−.088	−.086	−.057	.170	−.356	−.078
1936	−.054	−.056	.029	.214	−.363	.002
	All left votes[a]					
1919	−.102	.026	.519	.426	.149	.406
1924	.136	.166	.468	.392	.282	.360
1928	−.183	−.020	.498	.260	.486	.397
1932	−.176	−.046	.345	.392	.445	.477
1936	−.079	−.280	.269	.474	.379	.514

Sources: For electoral results, see table 2.1.
[a]N = 205 for Haute-Vienne, 1910.

port in Limousin and Dordogne, it is far more difficult to trace this lineage back to the Radicals and the Démoc-Socs. Links between Montagnard voting and future Socialist or Communist support—as in Haute-Vienne—were, if anything, tentative and irregular. In Corrèze, and in other departments too, communes neither gradually nor consistently moved from radicalism to socialism or communism. Socialism in this area was not a radicalized form of radicalism (which is what the *toujours plus à gauche* interpretation implies) but a new political phenomenon which, in its early years, found a small yet dedicated electorate in communes where it, and later the Communist party, would continue to do well over the years.[22] Socialism did not continue an electoral tradition in this region, but instead created a new one that the Communists later appropriated.

The *toujours plus à gauche* thesis—communes voting in succession for the Démoc-Socs, the Radicals, the Socialists and the Communists—is far from convincing. Yet does this imply that a more general leftist electoral tradition was not operating in Limousin and Dordogne? In other words, did the geography of left support remain similar over time? Both Corrèze and especially Haute-Vienne cantons that backed the Démoc-Socs proved to be only

[22] Denis Faugeras argues that rural communism was nothing more than a second Radical party: "Recherches sur l'évolution politique de la Corrèze sous la Troisième République 1871–1946" (thèse de doctorat d'état en droit, Université de Limoges, 1986), 527–28.

moderately good predictors of what areas would vote on the left in the twentieth century, and in Creuse the relationship between Montagnard and leftist voting was virtually absent (table 2.4). Village level correlations show that turn-of-the-century leftist voting in Corrèze was only rarely associated with its interwar counterpart, while, in Haute-Vienne, leftist voting displayed greater geographical stability over the long term (table 2.5). There existed, then, the outlines of what one might term a *toujours à gauche* tradition in this region that dated back to the Montagnards, but it was neither as strong nor as consistent as has been commonly presumed.[23]

If the geographical evidence for the Montagnard-to-communism argument is slim, this is not to say that generations within given families did not cast their ballot in succession always further on the left—the grandfather for the Démoc-Socs and the Radicals, the father for the Socialists, and the son for the Communists. Both oral and written sources indicate that this was occasionally the case. The proponents of the *toujours plus à gauche* thesis have in large part transposed this type of evidence concerning the behavior of individuals to the electorate as a whole.

The Origins of the Communist Vote

The correlational analysis describes the voting behavior of communes and counties, not of individual voters. The strong geographical continuity between socialism and communism need not indicate that former Socialist voters supported the Communists; what is true of communes is not necessarily so of individuals. Who were the Communist voters and who had they supported in the past? Plotting the trajectory of voters in the pre- and postwar years is key to understanding the birth and development of communism in this region. How faithful would Communist electors remain to their party over the years to come? Ecological regression, which has been used, for example, to propose a profile of National Socialist voters, is a reliable, powerful technique for inferring individual-level behavior from aggregate electoral results.[24]

---

[23] For comments, based on visual comparisons, concerning the close association between the Montagnard vote and twentieth-century left support in other regions of France, see François Goguel, *La politique des partis sous la IIIᵉ République* (Paris, 1946), 19.

[24] The best introduction remains J. Morgan Kousser, "Ecological Regression and the Analysis of Past Politics," *JIH* 4 (1973): 237–62. See also Laura Irwin Langbein and Allan J. Lichtman, *Ecological Inference* (Beverly Hills and London, 1978), 50–60; idem, "Ecological Regression versus Homogeneous Units: A Specification Analysis," *Social Science History* 2 (1978): 172–93. On Germany, Jürgen W. Falter and Reinhard Zintl, "The Economic Crisis of the 1930s and the Nazi Vote," *JIH* 19 (1988): 55–85; and Jürgen W. Falter, *Hitlers Wähler* (Munich, 1991). The most up-to-date critique and discussion is Christopher H. Achen and W. Philipps Shively, *Cross-Level Inference* (Chicago, 1995). Their study was published after the statistical work for this book had been completed.

I have used ecological regression to compute voter transition tables between pairs of successive elections in Corrèze between 1906 and 1936. The analysis has been pushed back to 1906, fourteen years before the Communist Party's foundation, in order to trace the origins of Socialist and Communist voting. The transition tables provide us with *estimates* of voter behavior in the short term—they help us to gauge how those who voted in 1936, for example, had cast their ballots four years earlier—whereas the correlational analysis sheds light on longer-term geographical permanence (for additional details see the Appendix).

Socialism in Corrèze developed at a rapid pace in the years immediately preceding and following the Great War. In 1906, Socialist candidates, on the ballot in only two of the department's five electoral districts, polled a mere 0.4 percent of the votes cast, and between 1905 and 1911 the Socialist party lost members. By the eve of the war, however, Socialist candidates, present in three of Corrèze's electoral districts, received close to 8 percent of the vote. Socialism's original prewar supporters were a small, disparate lot of former nonvoters, Radicals, and, more surprising, conservatives (the transition table adds up to the total registered electorate in the bottom right-hand corner: table 2.6 estimates that 2.5 percent of the registered electorate voted Socialist in 1914 and had voted for the right in 1910; the columns indicate how those who had voted for the right in 1910 voted in 1914, and the rows show how voters for the right in 1914 had cast their ballots in the previous election). Indeed, an estimated 45 percent (divide 2.5 by 5.3 on line 1 of table 2.6) of those who supported the SFIO in 1914 had backed the right four years earlier, and in the Tulle-Sud electoral district, where the Socialists captured close to 11 percent of the vote, this proportion reached 60 percent. Part of this shift undoubtedly was linked to the practice of *la politique du pire* (voting primarily to defeat the Radicals); it also reflected, however, the radicalization of a fringe of the conservative electorate that refused to support the continued domination of political life by the Radical-Socialist Party. To draw a profile of Socialist supporters in 1914: they were unlikely to have voted Socialist in previous elections (in part because there had been few Socialists) and were, in the majority, not former Radical voters. Most voters who abandoned the Radical Party in that year cast their ballots for the right (table 2.6). The prewar Socialist electorate did not owe its existence to a leftist tradition characterized by voters who deserted the Radicals in order to support the party farthest to the left, as has often been presumed.

The strength of the Radicals derived from their grass-roots influence. The broad network of Radical-leaning municipal councilors, mayors, and *conseillers généraux* did their best to "guide" electors in their local and national political choices, and ensured that favors and services were, if necessary, rendered to them in return for their support. This practice was known as *le bras long* or more commonly in patois as *le plaçou* (from the verb *placer*), because one of a deputy's most important informal functions was to find his

Table 2.6. Estimated voter movements, Corrèze villages and towns 1910–1914 (percent) (*N* = 290)

1914 election	1910 election				Total
	Parti Socialiste	Radical candidates	Right parties	Non-voters	
Parti Socialiste	0.6%	1.2%	2.5%	1.0%	5.3%
Radical candidates	0.4	40.8	0.0	0.8	42.0
Right parties	0.0	6.3	15.5	0.0	21.8
Nonvoters	0.4	0.0	2.3	20.0	22.8
Ineligible	0.2	0.2	0.3	7.4	8.1
Total	1.6%	48.2%	20.6%	29.5%	100.0%

Sources: ADC 3M190, 3M192.
Note: Estimates that fall outside the 0–100% logical bounds have been set to their respective minimum or maximum, and the remaining cell entries have been adjusted by an iterative fitting procedure. Rows and columns do not always add up perfectly because of rounding.

constituents jobs in the state administration (the post office, for example) or even in private industry.[25] The war disrupted these relationships of patronage, and in so doing profoundly altered the local political landscape. Soldiers returned home with a transformed *mentalité*; a subprefect was prompted to write that "large numbers of them are liable to ignore the advice of their natural advisers, mayors, parents, groups leaders, and influential electors."[26] This situation worked to the detriment of the Radicals more than to any other political grouping. The young and ambitious leader of Corrèze's Radical Socialists, Henri Queuille, understood his party's predicament all too well—a predicament also linked to the Radical Party's disorganization and loss of identity at the national level during the postwar years—and realized that continued success necessitated new faces and policies; he thus eliminated the three outgoing Radical deputies from the 1919 Radical list and replaced them with younger left-leaning candidates.[27] While this strategy paid dividends in the long term, it probably accentuated the Radicals' defeat in 1919. Having dominated political life in the early years of the century, the Radicals now found themselves trailing the right and challenged by the Socialists. The Great War marked the end of an era for Corrèze radicalism.

The major downturn in radicalism's influence in the 1919 legislative elections benefited conservatives more than Socialists, in keeping with national trends in which the right emerged as the undisputed victor of the elections. Of those voters who deserted the Radicals in 1919, more cast their ballots

[25] Patronage was of considerable importance in a poor region such as Corrèze. A job within the administration guaranteed a secure income for a family.
[26] ADC 3M194, SP Ussel to PC, 3 September 1919.
[27] Gilles Le Beguec, "Henri Queuille: L'originalité d'un parcours politique," in *Henri Queuille et la Corrèze: Actes du Colloque de Tulle* (Limoges, 1986), 31–32.

Table 2.7. Estimated voter movements, Corrèze villages and towns, 1914–1919 (percent) (N = 290)[a]

	1919 election				
1914 election	Parti Socialiste	Radical candidates	Right parties	Non-voters	Total
Parti Socialiste	4.0%	1.8%	0.0%	0.1%	5.8%
Radical candidates	7.3	22.3	9.6	5.7	44.9
Right parties	0.5	0.4	18.4	3.6	22.8
Nonvoters	4.9	1.8	0.0	18.6	25.4
Ineligible	0.3	0.0	0.0	0.6	1.0
Total	17.0%	26.3%	27.9%	28.7%	100.0%

Sources: ADC 3M192, 3M194.
Note: See note to table 2.6.
[a]Weighted by registered electorate in 1919.

for the right than for the SFIO (see the row for Radical candidates in table 2.7). Nor was this a new trend: a quarter of those who voted for conservative parties in 1914 had cast their ballots for the Radicals four years earlier. Radical and conservative voters thus switched back and forth in important proportions. Still, former Radicals constituted over 40 percent of the 1919 Socialist electorate, and they were joined by most former Socialist voters as well as a solid contingent of those who had chosen not to cast ballots in 1914 (table 2.7). The new Socialists voters thus were of a different origin than those of the prewar years. Radicalized by the war, dissatisfied with the old political class, attracted by the local Socialist party's antimilitaristic discourse, sectors of the former Radical electorate, as well as some people who had abstained in the past, turned toward socialism. Because the Socialists were active in the area, held public meetings, organized party sections, and proposed a coherent and attractive policy to the peasantry, they filled much of the void left by the Radical Party's growing discredit. The SFIO's modern political organization (meetings, members, propaganda campaigns, and a newspaper), which contrasted favorably with the Radicals' often ephemeral presence between elections and their lack of political structures at the grass roots, clearly contributed to Socialist successes.[28] The presence of organized militants in the countryside enabled the Socialists to respond to the electorate in ways that the Radicals could not.

The Socialists were not the sole beneficiaries of radicalism's decline; to think of their growing strength as the consequence of a traditional *toujours plus à gauche* vote would be an error. That large numbers of Radicals jumped ship for conservative, not leftist, shores makes the leftist tradition

[28] On the difference between Radical and Socialist models of organization, Serge Berstein, "Les partis," in *Pour une histoire politique*, ed. René Rémond (Paris, 1988), 70–73.

theory all the more difficult to uphold. Those who came to socialism from radicalism did so for specific social and political reasons engendered by the war; theirs was not a vote of tradition but a mandate for local and national political change.

The Party of Fidelity

How did Socialists voters cast their ballots following the late 1920 Socialist split that gave birth to the Communist Party? Who were the first Communist voters, and who had they supported in the past? An estimated 60 percent of the young Communist Party's supporters in 1924 had backed the Socialists in 1919; in addition, the Party also captured support from former abstainers and some backing from Radical voters (table 2.8). But the new Communist Party received far from unanimous support from former Socialist voters: close to half of the 1919 Socialists either cast their ballots for the joint Radical-Socialist and Socialist Cartel des Gauches list (which included only one Socialist out of four candidates), decided not to vote, or disappeared from the registered electorate altogether (table 2.8). That some former Socialist voters backed the Cartel list was not surprising; if anything, it was surprising that so few did so. Others, dissatisfied with the alternative they faced between tepid reformism and Bolshevism, decided not to vote altogether.

Former Socialist voters nonetheless formed the backbone of the new Communist electorate. Once the division between Socialists and Communists was cemented, however, there would be little voter switching between the two parties. In 1928, when the Socialists ran for legislative office on their

Table 2.8. Estimated voter movements, Corrèze villages and towns, 1919–1924 (percent) (N = 290)[a]

1924 election	1919 election				
	Parti Socialiste	Radical candicates	Right parties	Non-voters	Total
Parti Communiste	9.6%	1.2%	0.0%	4.6%	15.4%
Radical list[b]	3.7	21.0	9.3	3.4	37.4
Right parties	0.0	0.0	18.6	2.6	21.2
Nonvoters	2.6	2.3	0.0	11.6	16.6
Ineligible	1.1	1.8	0.0	6.4	9.4
Total	17.0%	26.3%	27.9%	28.7%	100.0%

Sources: ADC 3M194, 3M196.
Note: See note to table 2.6.
[a]Weighted by registered electorate in 1919.
[b]Radical-led Cartel des Gauches list, which included one Socialist.

Table 2.9. Estimated voter movements, Corrèze villages and towns, 1924–1928 (percent) (N = 290)

	1924 election				
1928 election	Parti Communiste	Radical list[a]	Right parties	Non-voters	Total
Parti Communiste	11.7%	2.3%	0.4%	1.7%	16.1%
Parti Socialiste	0.9	6.4	0.6	0.0	8.0
Radical candidates	1.4	24.2	8.0	1.8	35.4
Right parties	0.2	6.5	13.9	0.2	20.8
Nonvoters	0.0	3.7	0.9	14.8	19.4
Ineligible	0.0	0.1	0.0	0.2	0.3
Total	14.2%	43.2%	23.8%	18.7%	100.0%

Sources: ADC 3M196, 3M197.
Note: See note to table 2.6.
[a]Radical-led Cartel des Gauches list, which included one Socialist.

own for the first time since the December 1920 Tours Congress, the overwhelming majority of their support came from those who had supported the Cartel des Gauches list in 1924 (table 2.9). Throughout the interwar years, voters seldom moved from socialism to communism, or vice versa. The Socialists would find new voters among former conservatives in the early 1930s and among previous Radicals at the time of the Popular Front (table 2.10), but rarely among previous Communist electors.[29]

The Communist electorate during the interwar period was remarkably stable. The majority of Communist voters in 1928, 1932, and 1936 had supported the Party in the preceding elections. Both in 1928 and at the time of the Popular Front, Communist gains came at the expense of the Radicals, and in 1928 these gains were confined to the department's villages, thus underlining the diverging behavior of rural and urban voters. In the late 1920s, rural Radical voters were more likely to switch their allegiance to the extreme left than were their urban counterparts.[30] The Communists also experienced some success (in 1928 and 1936) in convincing previous abstainers that their participation would be worthwhile (tables 2.9 and 2.10). The PCF's suicidal class-against-class tactic so discouraged its supporters that they deserted in large numbers in 1932, some to cast their ballots for the Radicals, others to boycott the polls altogether.

The Communists thus proved unsuccessful at luring large numbers of electors away from other parties. They met with difficulty in attempts to convert

[29] For the 1928–32 transition table see Boswell, "French Rural Communist Electorate," 739.
[30] A more detailed regression analysis shows that in 1928 the Communists received no support from former Radical voters in Corrèze's thirteen largest towns.

Table 2.10. Estimated voter movements, Corrèze villages and towns, 1932–1936 (percent) $(N = 290)^a$

1932 election	1936 election					
	Parti Communiste	Parti Socialiste	Radical candidates	Right parties	Non-voters	Total
Parti Communiste	10.7%	1.1%	0.0%	0.1%	0.1%	12.1
Parti Socialiste	1.0	11.4	0.0	2.7	0.3	15.4
Radical candidates	3.5	14.1	13.2	2.6	3.2	36.6
Right parties	0.0	1.4	2.1	9.9	2.1	15.5
Nonvoters	2.5	0.0	5.7	0.0	11.4	19.7
Ineligible	0.0	0.2	0.2	0.0	0.2	0.6
Total	17.9%	28.3%	21.1%	15.3%	17.3%	100.0%

Sources: ADC 3M200, AN C10045.
Note: See note to table 2.6.
^{a} Weighted by the registered electorate in 1936.

substantial numbers of Radical voters, and had even less success courting Socialists. That voter switching was both more common and more extensive between Communists and Radicals than between Communists and Socialists poignantly demonstrates how permanent and deep the split was between parties that had a common origin. That the Communists, despite their incessant efforts, were less able than Socialists to expand their electorate indicates the limits of the PCF's appeal in rural Corrèze.

The findings in this chapter call into question the commonly accepted idea that French political parties have geographical roots that reach far back in time.[31] If the locational instability of Limousin and Dordogne political parties (the Communists excluded) between 1849 and the Popular Front is any indication, the geographical implantation of mainstream political parties must be more fluid over the long term than generally is believed. Parties reinvent their geographical, and thus social, base on a regular basis. And while political traditions clearly exist on an ideological level, they are not necessarily as widespread on a geographical one. As a result, greater care needs to be exercised before speaking of voting traditions, and arguing that a given party is the recipient of a long-standing leftist or conservative voting tradition.

The PCF's success in the countryside comes not from leftist voting traditions—voters are more sophisticated than historians of the French countryside have suspected—but from the economic, social, and political developments of the first four decades of the twentieth century. The rural

[31] For a classic example of this thesis, Goguel, *La politique des partis*, 18–20.

Communist electorate's origin is different than generally has been argued. Communists, and their pre-1920 Socialists predecessors, did not benefit from a long-standing leftist tradition, nor did they fill the shoes of the Radicals. The absence of a *toujours plus à gauche* vote in one of the regions where it has been thought strongest places the Communist Party's achievements in new perspective. The coalition the Communists forged in the early 1920s remained remarkably faithful to a party that, after initial successes, experienced difficulty in substantially expanding both its electorate and its territorial base until after World War II. Throughout the interwar years the Communist vote proved to be a model of geographical stability.

3   The Patterns of Difference

Few people know Corrèze as well as François Monédière. His lifelong career as a militant and leader within Communist and noncommunist agricultural trade unions has brought him into contact with a wide range of *Corréziens* over the past seventy years. It was thanks to Monédière that the Communist Party gained influence within the largest agricultural trade union in the interwar Corrèze, the Radical-leaning Fédération Faure, and it was thanks to him that it managed to wrest control of this union after World War II. The son of a small peasant and miller, he was born and raised in the canton of Seilhac just north of Tulle, where the Communist Party established solid roots during the 1920s and 1930s. He is now retired on his small farm in the village of Beaumont (map 1).[1]

On my way to Monédière's farm in the midst of a July downpour I reflected on our first encounter, almost one year before, when I interviewed him along with the Communist president of the Conseil Général, Robert Bos, another old peasant, in the rather more imposing setting of the Prefecture in Tulle. Monédière had walked in late and sat down quietly opposite me. Though initially I thought I detected some reticence in his answers to my questions, I soon realized that this was not the case. Monédière may have been an unassuming and soft-spoken man, but here was a militant who knew Corrèze inside and out in a way that few others did. And this is what Robert Bos acknowledged when he turned to him on a few occasions and said, with a broad smile that accompanied his inimitable accent, "Go ahead, François, you can tell him better than I can!"[2]

One year later, having interviewed more than thirty old Party militants, I

[1] The Fédération Faure was known officially as the Fédération des Associations Agricoles Corréziennes. After World War II, Monédière was for many years the departmental president of the MODEF, which was closely linked to the PCF.

[2] Interview with Robert Bos, François Monédière, and Henri Peuch, Tulle, 24 August 1984.

was in a position to appreciate just how much Monédière knew. Here is a man who can answer some of my questions, I told myself as I tried to find my way through the low clouds that had settled on the rugged hills north of Tulle. If anyone could talk to me about the complex political geography of this region, perhaps it was François Monédière.

In the course of our conversation, Monédière, seventy-three years old in 1984, demonstrated a grasp of interwar rural problems and issues that few in the department could match. But when I asked him why the neighboring canton of Corrèze (the cantons are shown in map 8), hardly more than a stone's throw away from his property, had been one of a handful where the right had done consistently well throughout this century, Monédière looked out the window and paused to reflect. "I don't know," he answered after an extended silence, and he seemed genuinely puzzled. He found it difficult to explain why this canton, bordered on three sides by the reddest cantons in Corrèze (Seilhac to the east, Treignac and Bugeat to the north) and the nation, remained so refractory to the PCF. This was a problem that had preoccupied him, not to mention the Communist Party, for many long years and to which he had found no credible answer.[3]

If François Monédière had no ready-made solution to the puzzle, it was not for lack of information. He knew the canton of Corrèze well, having worked there within the agricultural trade union movement as well as having been the unsuccessful PCF candidate for *conseiller général* in 1937, when he obtained 16.4 percent of the vote, a more than honorable showing for a Communist in this area. With a twinkle in his eye he mused that his opponent, Lafarge, a well-established local doctor and notable, was the principal reason the canton remained such a right-wing stronghold: an expert in patronage politics, Lafarge did not hesitate to give his constituents free medical consultations, and this tactic paid off handsomely at the polls. But Monédière is the first to admit that he is far from satisfied with this partisan explanation. He can think of nothing that could explain Corrèze's peculiar political orientation; the structure of property is similar, the people neither richer nor poorer than in his native canton of Seilhac. The only perceptible difference is political tradition, and it is a difference that has perplexed local leaders to this day.[4]

My search for keys to Corrèze's political geography led me to Léon Champeix, the only important interwar Communist leader still alive in the mid-1980s. A short, balding man greeted me warmly at the door of the small house in Brive, where he had retired. Léon Champeix, seventy-three years of age in 1984, talked with ease and remembered his youth with great fond-

---

[3] In 1936, the right achieved its highest departmental score (47.3%) in this canton.

[4] For 1937 election results, ADC 3M316. Monédière did not mention religion as a potential factor. The Easter mass attendance in the canton of Corrèze differed considerably from that of neighboring cantons, and no convincing explanation has been found. See Louis Pérouas, *Refus d'une religion, religion d'un refus en Limousin rural, 1880–1940* (Paris, 1985). Interview with François Monédière, Beaumont, 31 July 1984.

Map 8. Limousin and Dordogne: cantons

ness. In response to my questions about his past, he stepped over to his bookcase and proudly removed his handwritten memoirs of the interwar years, exclaiming, "Here, everything is in there!"[5] His was a story worth writing. In the early 1930s, fresh out of Tulle's Ecole Normale, Champeix had taken up a position as a schoolteacher in Argentat, southwest of Tulle, and moved in 1935 to the small commercial center of Uzerche. Champeix joined the Party in 1934, and by 1937 had become treasurer of the Corrèze PCF. That same year he ran unsuccessfully for the Conseil Général in the canton of Uzerche.[6]

[5] Léon Champeix, "Souvenirs et libres propos d'un 'écrivain du dimanche,'" unpublished manuscript.

[6] *TC,* 27 November 1937; ADC 3M316.

I asked Champeix why the Communists had never established solid roots in the canton of Argentat, where he had taught earlier, and which bordered on PCF strongholds in southern Corrèze (the cantons of La Roche–Canillac and Lapleau). And, by the same token, how could he explain why voters rarely elected Communists to local office in the canton of Uzerche, where he had settled in the mid-1930s, whereas the nearby cantons of Bugeat, Seilhac, Sornac, and Treignac were solidly red? "That's difficult to explain," Champeix answered as he sat back and reflected for a moment. In the case of Uzerche, he felt it was primarily a question of personalities; the Socialists, led by Marcel Champeix, had always been strong there and it was impossible to dislodge them. In Argentat, the standard of living may have been higher, the notables more numerous and influential, and the church stronger; but that was by no means clear. In the end, Léon Champeix smiled, threw up his arms, and confessed that he was at a loss to provide a convincing explanation.[7]

Champeix had far less difficulty explaining the *tradition de gauche* on a larger scale. He had even written a short essay tracing the origins of the left's strength in Corrèze through past times—an undertaking that took him all the way back to the Gauls.[8] In the course of our discussion he attributed the department's progressive leanings to a wide variety of factors, ranging from temporary migrations and the influence of Limoges to the size of property holdings, poor working conditions, low salaries and levels of productivity, and a "widespread sentiment of equality and justice."[9] When asked why certain areas voted Communist and not others, he was unable to go beyond these general explanations.

Old militants were always ready to advance their own explanations of the map of Communist voting. They recalled that the Party had traditionally been well established in Haute-Corrèze (the northern part of the department), although they did have a tendency to forget that this was the case in other areas too. Invariably they advanced similar explanations: it was the temporary migrants, driven by economic necessity to leave their villages and work in Paris, Lyon, St-Etienne, and other urban areas, who returned and introduced communism to these poor, backward areas. As Léonard Leblanc, who worked long years in the Paris region construction industry, says: "It's certain that migration is what influenced Haute-Corrèze. There's no doubt about that. No doubt. The mentality is altogether different up on the plateau [of Millevaches], Bugeat, Tarnac, Peyrelevade, and up there, than it is if you go down toward Limoges, for example. Ah, it's completely different. . . . The Party took hold, I think, because of migrations in Haute-Corrèze. In my mind, there's no doubt about it."[10]

[7] Interviews with Léon Champeix, Brive, 30 July and 29 August 1984.
[8] Léon Champeix, "Bref aperçu historique de la Corrèze: luttes sociales et politiques," unpublished manuscript.
[9] Interview with Léon Champeix.
[10] Interview with Léonard Leblanc, Lacelle, 2 September 1983.

This opinion was expressed by many of those I interviewed. But when I asked old militants why the PCF did poorly in regions of southern Creuse where temporary migration rates were higher than in northern Corrèze but was successful in parts of Corrèze where temporary migration was nonexistent, they were unable to furnish an explanation that went beyond the claim that it was primarily a matter of personalities. If the Party failed to do well in certain communes and cantons, it was, in the words of Pierre Martin, because "it never found the men who were appropriate to the particular situation of those areas." [11] After crisscrossing Corrèze interviewing militants, I came up with numerous local, partial explanations. Even with the benefit of historical hindsight, however, those who knew the PCF and Corrèze best had difficulty formulating convincing explanations for the establishment of communism. Few things are so complex to untangle as political geography.

While it is difficult to explain the political geography of cantons and communes taken individually, it is possible, from a larger perspective that takes account of all villages in a department, to make sense of a region's political and social geography without doing undue violence to the evidence, and without generalizing unjustly from particular examples. This chapter proposes such an approach, from both cartographical and statistical points of view.

The Political Geography of Communism

The Communist Party established roots in distinct areas of Limousin and Dordogne, and this was critical to its achievements. Communism's support came overwhelmingly from the countryside; the PCF's performance was inconsistent among the few medium-sized towns parsimoniously sprinkled across the region. The Communists implanted themselves in a wide range of geographical environments in the countryside: in the poor, isolated Montagne; in hilly, often rugged terrain ill suited for agriculture; in richer *bocage*-type landscapes; and among some of the better-off agricultural areas where peasants grew tobacco and tended vineyards.

It is difficult to generalize with confidence about those rural areas where the Communist Party did best. In Limousin and northern Dordogne (Nontronnais) these regions were often hilly and "mountainous" (the geographic regions are shown in map 3).[12] The area in and around the Millevaches plateau (known as the Montagne by the local inhabitants) was at the heart of the Communist presence, though as one crossed over from Corrèze and Haute-Vienne to equally "mountainous" sectors of Creuse, the Party's strength diminished considerably. Some of these areas tended to be more iso-

---

[11] Interview with Pierre Martin, Argentat, 6 July 1984.

[12] Fifty-three percent of Corrèze is classified as "mountain territory" versus 31% for Creuse and 7% for Haute-Vienne. Guy Bouet and André Fel, *Atlas et géographie du Massif Central* (Paris, 1983), 306.

lated and economically disadvantaged than others, but by no means all of them. While zones of PCF strength such as the Millevaches plateau were located on the periphery of the region's few urban areas, other key regions of support could be found in the countryside near Tulle (Corrèze), St-Junien (Haute-Vienne), and Bergerac (Dordogne). And because of a long-standing tradition of out-migration, the isolated Millevaches plateau enjoyed far closer links to Paris, St-Etienne, and even Limoges than did most parts of Limousin. Relative isolation and distance from urban areas was not a critical, determining factor in rural communism's survival. Communist successes took place within entire regions that were cut off from the main axes of trade and communication.

It is equally difficult to generalize about the social and economic features of those cantons and villages where Communists found a receptive audience. Both Limousin and Dordogne ranked among the poorest agricultural regions in France. With a few exceptions, their soils and terrain did not allow for prosperous commercial farming. While the Communists scored well in some of the most disadvantaged areas (notably the Millevaches plateau) and poorly in richer agricultural zones such as the Brive Basin or the Basse Marche, no clear-cut association exists between communism and poverty in Limousin and Dordogne as a whole. The PCF did not do well in all economically backward areas, nor was it the only political party that was influential in such regions. Moreover, it gained a strong foothold in richer areas north of Tulle (Corrèze) and in the Bergeracois (Dordogne).

A Communist Bastion: The Montagne

Communism's regional electoral stronghold throughout the 1920s and 1930s was located in the Montagne Limousine, at the juncture of Corrèze, Creuse, and Haute-Vienne (maps 9 and 10 show how the Party fared among Limousin and Dordogne cantons in comparison with its regional average; the darker the shading, the higher the Communist Party's score over its regional mean). In few areas in France did one find villages so committed, unanimous, and faithful in their support of the Party. To any visitor, this high plateau, where the altitude ranges between 700 and 978 meters, must have looked forbidding during all but the summer months. Nature endowed this area with poor, shallow soils and a miserable climate. Large expanses of terrain were covered with heather and unfit for anything but pasture for sheep. Trees, which now cover large parts of the area, huddled around the scattered hamlets and villages.[13] A typical peasant might grow some rye (the soil was too poor for wheat and the general rule was that "good rye is bet-

---

[13] A. Demangeon, "La Montagne dans le Limousin," *Annales de géographie* 112 (1911): 316–37.

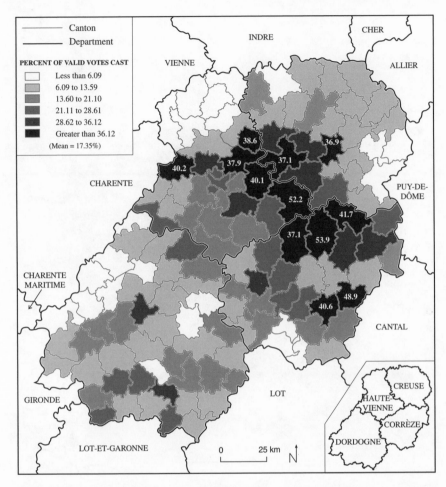

Map 9. Limousin and Dordogne: Communist vote, 1928 (by canton)

ter than bad wheat") buckwheat, potatoes, turnips, and the like, and raise some livestock and a few sheep. It was difficult for most people to scratch out much of a living on the bleak plateau. Maurice Bans, of the village of Viam (Corrèze), recalls that during the interwar years "we grew a little bit of everything and a little bit of nothing" in order to survive, and even at that, "we lived sparely." When he was a young boy, Maurice Bans's parents would ask him to purchase a *pain* on his way home from school on Saturdays, and he remembers being so hungry that "by the time I brought it home I had eaten almost half of it." [14] Faced with even more difficult material conditions, the nineteenth-century inhabitants of this region headed to Paris, Lyon, and

[14] Interview with Maurice Bans, Viam, 7 October 1983.

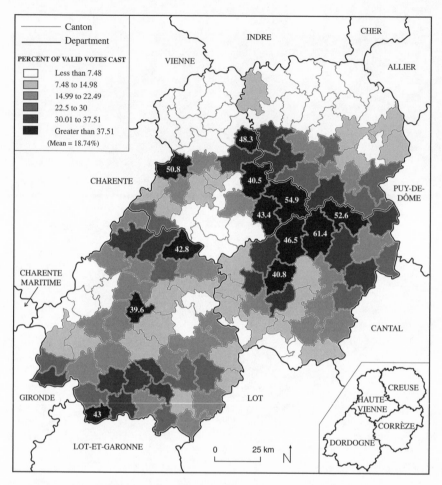

Map 10. Limousin and Dordogne: Communist vote, 1936 (by canton)

other large cities to work as masons and cabmen. By the twentieth century people were leaving with no thought of returning.

It was within such a context that socialism and later communism found durable support. By the mid-1930s, the Communists controlled numerous small municipalities in northern Corrèze, and a few around Eymoutiers in the southeastern corner of Haute-Vienne. In some villages they received the backing of over 75 percent of the voters. In 1928, the canton of Bugeat (Corrèze) ranked among the reddest cantons in France (53.9 percent of the vote); it was closely followed by the adjacent canton of Eymoutiers, communism's Haute-Vienne bastion (52.2 percent) (map 9). The PCF, however, did not enjoy a monopoly on this region. Until 1936, Communists in the Haute-Corrèze highlands faced successful competition from the Radicals. This was the stronghold of the influential Radical-Socialist deputy Henri Queuille, minister of agriculture for close to seven years in eleven interwar govern-ments, who represented the region in the Chamber of Deputies from 1914 to 1936.[15]

Communism's Strength in Disadvantaged Areas

Hilly terrain of mediocre agricultural value accounted for large expanses of Limousin and Dordogne. Life was little easier in these areas than on the Millevaches plateau. The southeastern plateaus of Corrèze (the cantons of La Roche–Canillac and Lapleau) are a good case in point (map 9). This was one of three significant centers of PCF strength in Corrèze, along with the plateaus to the northwest of Tulle and, of course, the Montagne in the north (maps 11 and 12). The Socialists had done well here before the 1920 split, and the Communist Party scored high in the 1920s before entering a period of relative decline in the next decade. In the cantons of La Roche–Canillac and Lapleau the Communists received, respectively, 40 and 48 percent of the vote in 1928; in villages such as Gros-Chastang and St-Hilaire-Foissac the figures rose above 60 percent. The terrain in the southeastern plateaus was abrupt, the soil of mediocre quality, cultivation difficult. Almost one-third of the land was occupied by heather and unfit for much besides grazing. From an agricultural point of view, this area was better off than the Montagne Limousine but certainly less favored than other regions in Corrèze.[16]

Similarly disadvantaged areas could also be found in neighboring Haute-Vienne. Outside the Montagne in the southwestern corner of the department (the canton of Eymoutiers), the bulk of the Communist Party's electoral sup-port came from villages alongside the Creuse border (the cantons of St-Léonard, Ambazac, Laurière, and Châteauneuf-la-Forêt). The better part of this region was hilly and rugged (the Monts d'Ambazac reach 700 meters), and the land, as in many other parts of Limousin, was poor and the climate unfavorable (map 13).[17] Precarious material conditions also characterized

---

[15] *Henri Queuille et la République*, Actes du Colloque de Paris (Limoges, 1987); *Henri Queuille et la Corrèze*, Actes du Colloque de Tulle (Limoges, 1986); Gilbert Beaubatie, "Henri Queuille: Un corrézien en République," *Historiens-Géographes* 316 (1987): 235–50; Isabel Boussard, *Les agriculteurs et la République* (Paris, 1990), 35–46; Francis de Tarr, *Henri Queuille en son temps, 1884–1970* (Paris, 1995).

[16] On Corrèze agriculture see Aimé Perpillou, *Cartographie du paysage rural limousin* (Chartres, 1940); Ministère de l'Agriculture, *Monographies agricoles départementales: La Cor-rèze* (Paris, 1959); C. E. Riedel, *La Corrèze agricole: Monographie réduite* (n.p., 1938); exten-sive reports in ADC 7M305 and 7M321.

[17] For Haute-Vienne agriculture, P. Dessalles, *Statistique agricole de la France: Annexe à l'en-quête de 1929: Monographie agricole du département de la Haute-Vienne* (Limoges, 1937); Alain Corbin, "Prélude au Front populaire: Etude de l'opinion publique dans le département de la Haute-Vienne, février 1934–mai 1936" (thèse de troisième cycle, Université de Poitiers, 1968).

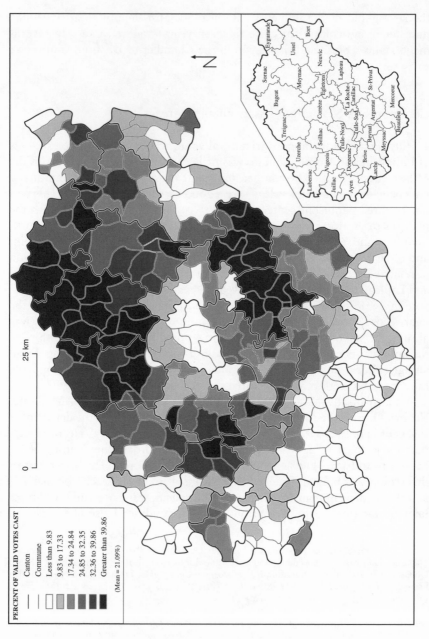

Map 11. Corrèze: Communist vote, 1928 (by commune)

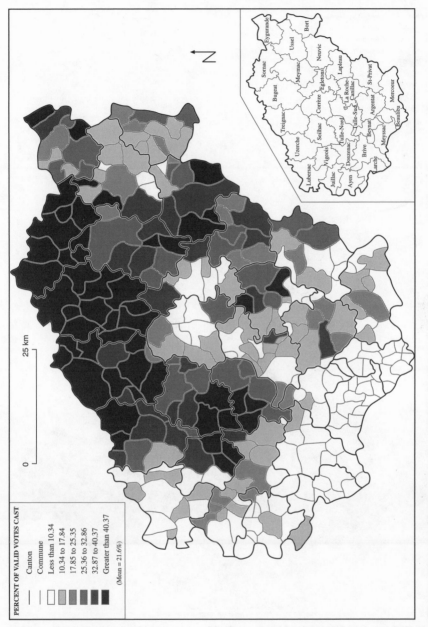

Map 12. Corrèze: Communist vote, 1936 (by commune)

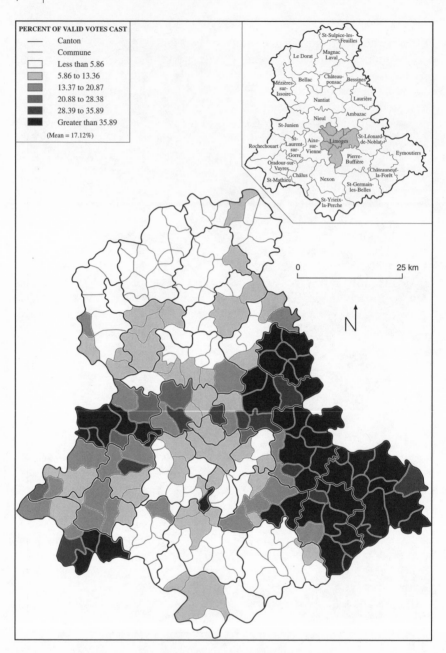

PERCENT OF VALID VOTES CAST
— Canton
— Commune
Less than 5.86
5.86 to 13.36
13.37 to 20.87
20.88 to 28.38
28.39 to 35.89
Greater than 35.89
(Mean = 17.12%)

Map 13. Haute-Vienne: Communist vote, 1936 (by commune)

large parts of Dordogne, and the PCF established a solid presence in some of them. The Nontronnais, just south of the Haute-Vienne border, remained a key center of Communist strength throughout the 1920s and 1930s. The low plateaus of the Nontronnais shared more in common with Limousin than with the rest of Dordogne. The rolling countryside was a patchwork of pastures, cultivated land, and woods. The soil lacked fertility (except in the canton of Lanouaille) and the area, one of the most backward in the department, had never been prosperous.[18] Polyculture with an emphasis on livestock (cattle, pigs) typified the region's agriculture.

In the southern half of Périgord the PCF's backers were scattered in the Dordogne valley, the Bergeracois, and, to a lesser extent, the Sarladais (also known as Périgord Noir) (map 10). The picturesque Dordogne valley, with its innumerable châteaus perched on nearby hills and its mosaic of fields near the river, could mislead the contemporary observer into thinking that this was a prosperous area. But a short drive inland reveals that the strip of fertile soil near the river is narrow indeed, especially in the Sarladais, one of Dordogne's least favored regions. Phylloxera had destroyed the vineyards of Périgord Noir in the late nineteenth century, thus spelling the end of viticulture. Cultivated land alternated with woods, pastures, and heather, which occupied close to one-quarter of the area. Polyculture reigned supreme. In some villages, peasants supplemented their incomes by selling nuts and truffles.

The PCF's Presence in More Prosperous Areas

The parallel between the relative strength of communism and the precariousness of living conditions can be overemphasized. There is little evidence that the poorer sectors of rural society backed the PCF in these areas. Neither did the Communists receive above-average scores in all disadvantaged areas: the better part of Creuse, Xaintrie in the southern Corrèze, Double, Landais, and Ribéracois in the western Périgord were all "missionary areas" for the Party. None of these regions differed markedly from similar, adjacent areas where the Communists established a solid base. Moreover, the PCF often had a substantial presence in some of Limousin and Périgord's more prosperous agricultural regions.

The region northwest of Tulle (Corrèze), known as the southwestern plateau, was one such better-off area. Mixed woodland and pastures (*bocage*) alternated with crops in the area's hilly landscape; small and medium-sized farms predominated, and the parceling out of the land (*morcellement*) was a barrier to agriculture. The richer soil made it possible to grow some

---

[18] ADD 1M82, SP Nontron to PD, 13 September 1933; "Journal de mobilisation agricole du département de la Dordogne" (1939) in ADD 7M99; "L'agriculture de la Dordogne," *Annales de l'office agricole régional du Sud-Ouest* 19 (1932).

wheat on a small scale. Subsistence agriculture coupled with small-scale live-stock raising was the norm. The PCF had initially done poorly in this area, but over time it established strength in St-Germain-les-Vergnes, St-Mexant, Chanteix, Lagraulière, and other small villages in the rolling countryside just to the north of Tulle, Corrèze's administrative capital. In 1936 the Communists received 56 to 69 percent of the vote in these villages, where peasants made up 75 to 94 percent of the registered voters (map 12). Without a doubt, some of the peasants in these villages cast their ballots in favor of Antoine Bourdarias, the Communist candidate. Tulle, where socialism first made its mark in Corrèze, was no longer one of the area's central left-wing bases. Many of communism's strongholds in this region, in contrast to those in the poorer Montagne, were not in communes that had a history of strong Socialist backing before 1920.

The Dordogne's richest agricultural region, the Bergeracois, was also one of the Communist Party's bastions during the Popular Front years. The Bergeracois had more in common with neighboring Agenais (Lot-et-Garonne) and Bordelais (Gironde) than with other *périgourdin* regions.[19] Wine (the most famous being Bergerac) was the region's principal agricultural product. Tobacco was grown in the Dordogne valley, and the region also produced some fruits. Properties, especially in wine and tobacco growing areas, tended to be smaller than in the rest of the department. The Communist Party's strength in the Bergeracois was located in rural areas of the Dordogne valley and near the Lot-et-Garonne border, where it obtained the majority of the votes in 1936 in small agricultural villages such as Sadillac (53 percent), St-Eulalie-d'Eymet (57 percent), and Singleyrac (81 percent) (map 10).[20]

An Uneven Presence in the Towns

Despite constant propaganda efforts, the Communist Party's establishment in urban areas was at best uneven. The PCF never was able to win the sympathy of much of the electorate in Limoges, Limousin's capital and largest city. In Brive, Corrèze's leading town, the Communists floundered after a strong showing their first time on the ballot. Less than thirty kilometers up the Corrèze River valley, in Tulle, the department's prefecture and the site of a sizable arms factory (Manufacture Nationale d'Armes), the Party did notably better, but not as well as in the surrounding countryside. Only in medium-sized Périgueux, Bergerac (both in the Dordogne), and St-Junien (Haute-Vienne) did the PCF score consistently well.

Périgueux, Dordogne's largest city (population 33,389 in 1926), was the center of Communist strength in the heart of the department. It was also

[19] Philippe Robert, *L'agriculture en Dordogne* (Bordeaux, 1958), 71.
[20] AN C10046.

Périgord's only major industrial town and the site of the Paris–Orléans railway yards and workshops, which employed 4,000 workers in early 1920. The bitter nationwide railway strike in May 1920 was closely followed in Périgueux, and the Socialist municipality, elected to office the year before, had actively supported the strikers. The strike's defeat and the subsequent firing of 2,300 striking railroad workers in Périgueux alone proved to be a severe political blow from which neither the town's working class nor the Socialist municipality ever fully recovered.[21] After the Tours Congress, the municipality turned Communist. Largely as a consequence of the 1920 strikes and of interminable squabbling in city hall, the Communists failed in their bid for reelection four years later. Communism in Périgueux, however, did retain a good part of its influence during the interwar period, and its urban character—railway and construction workers and public employees formed the bulk of the PCF's militants—distinguished it from its rural counterpart.[22]

St-Junien, Haute-Vienne's second-largest town (10,087 inhabitants in 1926), was the Communist Party's only true urban bastion in Limousin and Dordogne. The Communists received 27.5 percent of the vote here in 1924—an excellent showing by Haute-Vienne standards—and doubled their score four years later; by 1936, close to 64 percent of those who cast ballots did so in favor of the PCF. Thanks in large part to the political savoir faire of St-Junien's Communist mayor, Joseph Lasvergnas, the Party easily retained control of the municipality (they still did so in the mid-1990s) throughout the 1920s and 1930s. Glovemaking and related trades, along with paper mills, were the principal employers in this small, unattractive industrial town on the Vienne River. In 1929 the town's workshops and factories employed an estimated 2,850 men and women, of whom 1,200 worked in glovemaking alone. The peasant community within the town limits also contributed significantly to PCF successes.

Communist strength gradually spread from St-Junien to adjacent villages along the banks of the Vienne River, where, despite the presence of paper mills and textile manufacturing, the better part of the population was still occupied on the land. It is difficult to determine who was supporting the PCF here, peasants or workers, but considerable interaction existed between these groups both in St-Junien and in neighboring villages. Only in St-Junien did the Communists benefit from unusually strong support in an industrial town as well as in surrounding rural areas. It was no accident that the tension between the *ouvriéristes* (workerists) and those in the Party who under-

---

[21] AN F[7] 12982, PD to MI, 3 April 1920, and CS Périgueux, 11 June 1921. For the 1920 strikes see Annie Kriegel, *Aux origines du communisme français, 1914–1920* (Paris, 1964). The nationwide movement had originated with a victorious strike by Périgueux railway workers in January 1920.

[22] *PCTC*, 6 and 13 November 1921; *TCO*, 16 May 1925. Support for the Communists dropped from 39% in 1924 to 23% eight years later; it rose to 41.8% in 1936.

stood the importance of intelligent peasant propaganda was lower here than in other urban areas where the Communists found a receptive audience. Even in a highly agricultural society the interests of rural and urban Communists did not always merge. Towns did not always benefit from the PCF's rural strength, and close collaborative efforts between town and country proved to be the exception rather than the rule.

The maps confirm the Communist party's unique territorial permanence, and at the same time illustrate the chronological and geographical paths of the PCF's establishment. The Party's regional strength, which in 1924 had been largely restricted to the Montagne in Corrèze, the southeastern plateaus (La Roche-Canillac, Lapleau), and to a lesser extent the Nontronnais and the Bergeracois in Dordogne, expanded when the 1928 elections placed Creuse, and particularly Haute-Vienne, on the Communist map (map 9). The Party's newly found strength in these two departments was concentrated along their common border: from the canton of Eymoutiers in the southeastern corner of Haute-Vienne, one needed only to head north alongside the border separating Haute-Vienne from Creuse to find the PCF's principal zones of strength; the result was a marked imbalance in the Party's bases of support. But in that year, as in others, seas of indifference bordered PCF bastions (northern Creuse and Haute-Vienne; eastern and central Dordogne). In 1936, only in Dordogne, where the Communists increased their backing by 13 percentage points, did the Party make substantial inroads in areas where it had done poorly in the past. Not only did the Communists firm up their support in the northern part of the department, but they also expanded their base, both alongside the Dordogne River and in rural cantons of the Bergeracois (Eymet and Issigeac) on the Lot-et-Garonne border (map 10). In Corrèze, the Communists strengthened their support in the countryside northeast of Tulle, while losing voters in some of the bastions established earlier in the south-central regions, where the decline of temporary migrations and the disappearance of an earlier generation of PCF leaders slowly sapped the Party's strength (map 12).

Beyond Mapping

The PCF was successful in a variety of economic and geographic settings; without a detailed statistical study, however, it is impossible to discern precisely what these communes and cantons had in common. While a quantitative analysis will not explain why the Communists did well in some poor areas and not in others, it will help us determine if any common threads united villages favorable to the Party. Thus the next step is to see if relationships existed between communism and occupational, economic, demographic, or political factors. On this level, the maps are neither conclusive nor particularly suited to the task at hand.

It is never easy to speak in general terms about the relationship of electoral behavior and social and economic data without downplaying the complexity of the situation. In the case of Limousin, some observers have proposed that communism owed its strength to monoculture (livestock raising in the Montagne) and the existence of Communist-supported agricultural trade unions, while others have argued that migration or even family structure constituted the principal explanation.[23] But the evidence offered to support these propositions is not always convincing. Explaining why people make the political choices they do is a complex affair, and attributing these choices to any one dominating variable usually obfuscates more than it explains.

Numerous factors contributed to the growth of rural communism in Limousin, and we must acquire a sense of their importance. A statistical analysis should suggest a pattern and isolate those variables strongly associated with Communist voting. In this chapter, I first use ecological regression to provide estimates of the social composition of the Communist vote, then turn to a more classic multiple regression analysis of the links between political behavior and demography, population density, religion, and farm structure. Isolating the occupational profile of Communist voters and identifying what characterized those villages where the PCF did best will help establish the broader structure on which much of the subsequent analysis rests.

The Social Composition of Rural Communism

Who were the Communists voters? Did peasants, tenant farmers, sharecroppers, or agricultural workers constitute the Party's most faithful supporters? Did rural workers support the "party of the working class" in disproportionate numbers? Did temporary migrants, politicized during their urban sojourns, constitute a key element of the Communist electorate? In short, was the PCF's strong showing in rural Corrèze linked to its backing from any particular occupational group?

Complete data from voter registration lists on the occupations of all the 72,796 registered voters in 287 of Corrèze's communes in 1930 help provide an answer. Electoral lists, however, do not provide us with an entirely accurate picture of the occupational breakdown of those who worked the land.

---

[23] For the agricultural syndicalism and monoculture argument see Philippe Gratton, "Le communisme rural en Corrèze," in his *Les paysans français contre l'agrarisme* (Paris, 1972), 13–42; and for family structure, Hervé Le Bras and Emmanuel Todd, *L'invention de la France: Atlas anthropologique et politique* (Paris, 1981), 44–55.

When men registered to vote, they listed their age (at least twenty-one), place of birth, address, and occupation, and in the process some did not hesitate to use the opportunity to climb the social ladder on paper. In some villages peasant smallholders declared themselves to be *propriétaires* instead of less prestigious *cultivateurs*.[24] More troubling is the fact that sharecroppers, agricultural workers, and tenant farmers tended, understandably, to list themselves as *cultivateurs*, and are thus strongly underrepresented in the electoral lists. In place of these data, I substituted more trustworthy figures on sharecroppers and agricultural workers culled from a 1930 prefectoral survey, and statistics on tenant farmers from the village-level results of the 1929 agricultural census.[25]

The Corrèze's registered electorate in 1930 was overwhelmingly agricultural. Peasants alone constituted 63.8 percent of all registered voters, and this figure reached 78 percent with sharecroppers, agricultural workers, and tenant farmers (the landless). Others worked the land as well. It was not uncommon for artisans and shopkeepers (bakers, butchers, grocers, café owners) to cultivate a plot of land on the side. And those who, driven by poverty, migrated to the cities on a temporary basis to work as masons, stonecutters, and taxi drivers, returned to their native villages to tend their farms for three to six months a year. Portions of the rural electorate worked more than one trade at the same time, and the great majority had close ties to the agricultural economy. When the peasantry's income declined, the shopkeepers, artisans, small businessmen, and country doctors who served them suffered accordingly.

In 1928 the Communists found support among a relatively well spread-out cross section of the rural population: peasants, the landless, artisans, shopkeepers, and temporary migrants. Their electorate was more socially balanced than that of any other party. Those who worked the land accounted for two-thirds of the Party's electorate, and property-owning peasants alone made up one-third of the Communist Party's voters. An estimated 8 percent (divide 5 by 63.8 on line 1 of table 3.1) of the total peasant electorate cast their ballots for the PCF's candidates. This was a reasonable performance. The Communists, after all, gathered far more peasant votes than their Socialist archrivals, and the great majority of Corrèze peasants never ventured to the left of the Radical-Socialist party. But these results also show

[24] I have excluded Corrèze's two largest towns, Tulle and Brive, from this analysis. The voter registration lists I have used are in ADC 3M93–3M176. The electoral law required voters to submit documents proving their age and nationality, but required no proof of occupation. In general the voter's declaration of his profession was transcribed to the electoral list, although in some cases the committee in charge arbitrarily called all peasants *propriétaires*, or all those who worked the land *cultivateurs*.

[25] The figures concerning all other professions furnish a reliable picture of the occupational structure of Corrèze's voters. For data on sharecroppers and agricultural workers, see ADC 7M47; and for tenant farmers, the adjusted figures of the *enquête agricole* in ADC 7M306–7M318.

Table 3.1. Estimated voting behavior of social groups, Corrèze, 1928 (percent)

	Parti Commu- niste	Parti Socialiste	Radical candi- dates	Right parties	Non- voters	Total
Peasants[a]	5.0%	1.0%	29.0%	17.0%	11.0%	63.8
Landless[b]	6.0	5.0	0.0	0.0	3.0	14.4
Migrants[c]	1.0	0.0	1.0	0.0	1.0	2.4
Artisans and shopkeepers	3.0	2.0	0.0	2.0	2.0	8.8
Workers and employees	1.0	0.0	3.0	0.0	1.0	4.0
Other[d]	0.0	0.0	4.0	3.0	0.0	6.7
Total	16.2%	8.0%	36.3%	21.4%	18.1%	100.0%
Sharecroppers	0.0	0.9	0.0	1.9	0.6	3.5
Agricultural workers	1.6	1.6	2.1	0.2	0.7	6.3
Tenant farmers	2.7	1.6	0.0	0.0	0.4	4.7

Sources: ADC 3M197, 3M93–176, 7M47, 7M306–18.

Note: Controlling for lack of religious practice (percentage of civil burials, 1924–38), population change between 1931 and 1901, and population per km². See table 2.6 for note on rounding. $N = 282$.

[a] *Cultivateurs* and *propriétaires*.

[b] Sharecroppers, agricultural workers, tenant farmers. The figures for these three categories at the bottom of the table do not correspond exactly to the estimates for the landless because they are the result of separate regressions.

[c] Construction workers (masons, cement workers, plasterers, house painters, roofers, etc.) in migrant communes, taxi drivers, truck drivers, deliverymen, waiters, pit sawyers, cobblers, wine and cloth merchants, traveling salesmen, umbrella salesmen, tinsmiths.

[d] Merchants, entrepreneurs, schoolteachers, doctors, soldiers, students, rentiers, all other occupations, and unemployed.

the limits of communism's inroads among smallholding peasants, despite the Party's tireless propaganda campaigns geared toward them. The Communist Party's peasant votes were hard won. To gain additional peasant support, the Communists undertook a far more militant effort than did other parties. The fear—skillfully exploited by the Party's opponents—that the Communists, once in power, would split up the land (this was known as *le partageux*) clearly worked to the PCF's detriment.

The landless also formed a key component of the Communist electorate. The Party gathered close to half of the landless vote and, together with the Socialists, they virtually monopolized it. The more detailed breakdown of the landless vote (bottom half of table 3.1) is suggestive, although one should exercise care in interpreting estimates of the political behavior of small occupational categories. The Communist Party, which promised *la terre à celui qui la travaille* (land to the one who works it), found its strongest support among tenant farmers, failed to gain the support of sharecroppers, and split the vote of agricultural workers with the other two parties on the left. Of these three groups, tenant farmers were the closest to smallholding peasants, both in interests and in economic activity, and they clearly were seduced by the Party's promises to make everyone a *propriétaire* and its demands for higher prices for agricultural products.[26] Agricultural workers, usually employed in small numbers by better-off peasants (Corrèze was devoid of large, labor-intensive farms), recognized themselves less in propaganda directed at the small peasantry. The same was true of share-croppers, whose numbers had been consistently declining; by 1929 they worked only 6 percent of the farmland and accounted for 7.5 percent of those who tilled the soil.[27] Even in such a poor area, the interests of peas-ants, sharecroppers, and agricultural workers could clash; the Communists feared that by paying too close attention to the landless, they risked alienat-ing their primary constituents as well as their largest reservoir of potential voters, the peasants.

The Communists captured half of the migrant vote. Temporary migrations had been of considerable importance in parts of Limousin in the nineteenth and early twentieth centuries.[28] Driven by economic necessity, rural inhabi-tants from northern Haute-Vienne, the Monts d'Ambazac (the cantons of Laurière, Bessines, and Châteauponsac), and the better part of Creuse left their villages from March to November to work in the construction indus-try as masons, pavers, diggers, roofers, plasterers, and house painters in Paris, Lyon, St-Etienne, and other cities. Northern Corrèze (the cantons of Bugeat, Eygurande, Sornac, and Meymac) and the canton of La Courtine (Creuse) had fewer migrants in the construction field, but furnished Paris with large numbers of coachmen turned taxi drivers after the first decade of the century. *Scieurs de long* (pit sawyers) from the same area emigrated to varied destinations in rural France—especially the forests of Landes and Gironde—from October to June. Finally, in southeastern Corrèze (Xaintrie and the cantons of Lapleau, La Roche–Canillac, and Argentat), seasonal mi-grations took on a different character, with respect both to the migrants' destinations (Cantal and Auvergne) and to the trades involved (umbrella

[26] Virtually all tenant farmers listed themselves as *cultivateurs* on the electoral lists. Share-croppers and agricultural workers were far less likely to do so. Compare with Jacques Fauvet, who thought tenant farmers unlikely to back the PCF in the 1950s. See "La représentation poli-tique du monde paysan," in *Partis politiques et classes sociales en France*, ed. Maurice Duverger (Paris, 1955), 156–77.
[27] The regression overestimates the strength of the right among sharecroppers; calculated us-ing only those 211 communes where Conservative candidates were present, the regression in-dicates a more moderate relationship between sharecropping and the right. Corrèze had fewer sharecroppers than Dordogne (14.4% of those who farmed the land) or Haute-Vienne (18.2%). See Ministère de l'Agriculture, *Statistique agricole de la France: Résultats généraux de l'enquête de 1929* (Paris, 1936), 502–17.
[28] Alain Corbin, *Archaïsme et modernité en Limousin au XIXᵉ siècle, 1845–1880* (Paris, 1974), 1:177–225; "Migrations temporaires et société rurale au XIXᵉ siècle: Le cas du Limou-sin," *Revue historique* 246 (1971): 293–334; Pérouas, *Refus d'une religion*, 68–73. Tempo-rary migrations were not practiced on a large scale in Dordogne.

merchants, tinsmiths, traveling cobblers, but also large numbers of masons). Apart from those who worked in the construction trades, temporary migrants returned home during the summer months to help with haying and harvesting.

Seasonal migrations, which reached their apogee between 1845 and 1880, declined in the decade after World War I and reached symbolic levels in most communes by the end of World War II.[29] In Peyrelevade (Corrèze, the canton of Sornac) over 26 percent of registered voters in 1900 were temporary migrants, predominantly masons and coachmen. By 1920 this figure had declined to 18 percent, before dropping to 9 percent in 1939. Neighboring St-Rémy, which still counted close to 15 percent migrants in 1930, was left with almost no voters with migrant occupations by the eve of World War II.[30] In 1930, temporary migrants accounted for over 10 percent of the voters in nineteen Corrèze villages—and these were distributed equally between northern Corrèze and the more *cantalien*-type emigration practiced in the southeast. Fifty percent of all temporary migrants were masons, and together with others who worked in the construction field they constituted 75 percent of those who migrated to various parts of urban and rural France.

In the late 1920s migrants of all kinds returned to their home villages and supported the Communist Party in large numbers. Historians of Limousin have argued that many migrants turned toward revolutionary politics during their repeated sojourns in urban areas, and the evidence bears them out. In the 1920s and 1930s, authorities and Communist leaders alike thought that migrants played a critical role in the political education of the rural world, and the old militants I interviewed over fifty years later invariably pointed to migration as the most compelling explanation of PCF strength in this region.[31]

Historians generally have accepted this interpretation. They claim that similar maps of temporary migration and Communist voting reveal that migrants played a crucial role in disseminating left-wing ideologies in the countryside, and that temporary migrants were largely responsible for the growth of socialism and communism in some of the poorest, most isolated parts of Corrèze.[32] A detailed regression analysis, however, fails to support this theory. Neither peasants and the landless nor artisans and shopkeepers living in migrant villages were more likely to vote for the Communists than those who lived in other villages. Nor were they more likely to support the

[29] For the twentieth century, Marc Prival, *Les migrants de travail d'Auvergne et du Limousin au XX*^{e} *siècle* (Clermont-Ferrand, 1979).

[30] ADC 3M142, 3M161.

[31] *TT*, August–September 1924; *TCO*, 4 and 11 September 1926, 25 February 1933. Interview with Léonard Leblanc.

[32] Gratton, "Le communisme rural en Corrèze," 19–22. For Creuse, Georges Dauger, "Aux origines du Front populaire dans la Creuse: Contribution à une ethno-histoire des comportements politiques" (thèse de troisième cycle, Université de Paris I, 1983), 75.

Party if they lived in communes with a large percentage of migrant voters.[33] Migrants displayed political proclivities that distinguished them from their fellow villagers, but they did not play the influential role in spreading leftist ideas that some have ascribed to them. Even in migrant areas, rural communism was not "imported" from urban areas, but was an indigenous movement that owed its success to grass-roots organizing and to backing from a broad spectrum of occupational groups.

Artisans and shopkeepers, who occupied a central position in village communities, supported the Communists in significant proportions (table 3.1). Their propensity for left-wing politics—they cast over half of their ballots for Socialist and Communist candidates—is striking.[34] Artisans assumed key roles in the Communist Party, as cell secretaries in particular, because they were better placed to pass along the Party's watchwords. Peasants from outlying hamlets dropped by their shops in the village center to conduct business, catch up on the news, and perhaps have a drink at the local café. Rural depopulation, coupled with the agricultural crisis of the 1930s, hit artisans and shopkeepers hard. As their customers emigrated toward brighter shores, and as those who stayed cut back on their spending, blacksmiths, carpenters, and sabot makers, along with bakers, grocers, and café owners (to give a few examples), found that they, too, had trouble making ends meet. For most of these people, defense of their livelihood meant defense of the interests of their main clients, the peasants. This was particularly the case in small villages, where it was not uncommon for a shopkeeper or artisan to farm a small plot of land on the side. Less concerned about the threat of *le partage*, these people turned toward the left in an effort to find a solution to the agricultural crisis.

Preoccupied with their work among the peasantry, Corrèze Communists, not fully aware of the importance of artisans and shopkeepers within their electorate, rarely made sustained efforts to increase their support among these groups. In the mid-1920s, Léon Bossavy, one of the PCF's most gifted local leaders and known for his physical resemblance to Lenin, launched a one-man effort to bring artisans and shopkeepers throughout Corrèze over to the Party's views.[35] Bossavy's growing interest in these social groups eventually contributed to his separation from the PCF in the late 1920s. It was difficult enough, in the face of *ouvriériste* pressures, to campaign among the peasantry, but to go after the votes of what Bossavy termed the "middle

---

[33] See Laird Boswell, "The French Rural Communist Electorate," *JIH* 23 (1993): 745, table 10.

[34] The weighted regression suggests notably stronger conservative support among artisans and shopkeepers. Artisans and shopkeepers in ten of the department's largest towns (excluding Brive and Tulle) voted in large proportions for the right, demonstrating that artisans behaved differently in urban and rural settings.

[35] Bossavy, a self-employed mirror maker in Tulle, argued that artisans, shopkeepers, and peasants all belonged to the "middle classes" and could be won over to the cause of the proletariat. *TCO*, 19 November and 24 December 1927, 12 June 1926.

classes" posed even greater problems. Not until late 1937 did Corrèze Communists renew their attempts to increase their audience among artisans and shopkeepers.[36] That Communists nonetheless received significant support from these groups indicates that the propaganda they directed toward peasants also struck a chord with village blacksmiths, cobblers, carpenters, and grocers, whose fortunes were linked closely to those of the peasants.

The Communists thus found support in the countryside not among sharecroppers, rural workers, and employees but among a balanced mix of smallholding peasants, tenant farmers, agricultural workers, temporary migrants, artisans, and shopkeepers (table 3.1). Their electors shared close ties to the agricultural economy and were sensitive to its downturns and fluctuations. The Party did poorly among voters whose economic well-being depended less on the peasantry: workers and employees (who in the majority voted for the Radicals), along with members of other groups such as notables, merchants, businessmen, *rentiers*, students, and the retired, divided their allegiances between Radicals and conservatives.

These findings contrast with the results of previous investigations. In the 1920s and 1930s, both Corrèze Communists and prefects (who referred to the Party as *le parti communiste paysan* and to the movement as a whole as *le communisme agraire*) assumed by and large that the Party's members and voters alike were peasants.[37] For the historian Philippe Gratton, Communist support in Corrèze came from smallholding peasants and the Tulle working class.[38] The preceding account of voting behavior, however, illustrates how varied the Party's electorate was in a department composed largely of peasant voters, brings to light the role of artisans and shopkeepers, and suggests that rural workers were less sympathetic to the party of the working class than most observers have presumed.[39]

Demographic Downturn and Politics

The Limousin suffered from heavy and continuous population losses after its demographic high point in 1891: peasants, sharecroppers, tenant farmers, artisans, and shopkeepers permanently left in increasing numbers as their economic situations deteriorated and temporary migrations became

[36] *TC*, 13 November and 4 December 1937.
[37] ADC 7M22, 4M282, and 1M69; *TCO*, 28 April 1928.
[38] Gratton, "Le communisme rural en Corrèze," 33, 41. Gratton offers no evidence to show that Tulle workers supported the PCF. In 1928, the Communists received 23.4% of the vote in Tulle, and some of that support came from peasants who lived within the town's limits and from shopkeepers and artisans. The Communists met with consistent difficulty in organizing Tulle's working class. ADC 4M282 and AN F[7] 13120.
[39] Michel Cadé finds that in Pyrénées-Orientales shopkeepers and artisans accounted for 14.4% of the Party's members in 1937–38, but he does not analyze the role they played in the PCF's electorate. *Le parti des campagnes rouges: Histoire du Parti communiste dans les Pyrénées-Orientales, 1920–1939* (Vinça, 1988), 278.

less economically attractive.[40] Between 1901 and 1936 Creuse lost 27.3 percent of its inhabitants, Corrèze 17.4 percent, and Haute-Vienne 12.6 percent. Was there a connection, as some have suggested, between politics and demographic change? Did the Communists establish themselves in villages hardest hit by population losses?

A brief word on regression analysis is in order to place the remainder of this chapter in perspective. Regression analysis, which historians have come increasingly to adopt, is a far more powerful, informative, and flexible tool than straightforward correlation analysis. Put simply, a regression coefficient can help determine the percentage of change in the dependent variable (for instance, voting for the PCF) that could be expected from a 1 percent change in the explanatory variable (say civil burials). To take an example from Corrèze, a coefficient of .39 between the percentage of civil burials and Communist voting in 1924 means that for each 1 percent increase in civil burials the Communist vote increased 0.39 percent (table 3.5). In other words, a 10 percent increase in civil burials should lead to a 3.9 percent rise in the Communist vote. Lack of religiosity, however, clearly is not the only factor that explains Communist voting, and this is why regression equations are controlled for the effect of other variables, such as long-term population change, population per square kilometer, percentages of peasants and migrants, and farm size. Controlling helps us separate out the effect of civil burials from the influence of other independent variables held constant in the regression equation. To return to our example, the notable effect of civil burials on the Communist vote is *independent* of changes in population, farm size, or the percentage of peasants and migrants.[41]

The Limousin's dramatic population fall generally benefited neither the Communists nor their opponents. In both Corrèze and Haute-Vienne, long-term population change had no significant effect on Communist voting, and short-term population decline did so only in Haute-Vienne in 1936 (I have based my analysis on the figures that are statistically significant—see the Appendix for details) (table 3.2). The Corrèze figures (which are the most reliable, given the larger number of control variables included in the regression) are eloquent in this regard. What was true of the Communists was equally true of other political parties, with a few exceptions: the Corrèze right benefited moderately (in 1924 and 1936) from population losses, while Haute-Vienne Socialists, on the contrary, profited (in 1919, 1924, and 1936) from a lower rate of demographic decline and moderate population gains. In the first elections after the Great War a 10 percent decline in population losses could be expected to lead to a 2.4 percent increase in Haute-Vienne Socialist votes (table 3.2—find the regression coefficient [b] for the Parti Socialiste in 1919 [.24] and multiply it by 10).

[40] J. P. Larivière, *La population du Limousin* (Paris, 1975).
[41] The best introduction to regression is Michael S. Lewis Beck, *Applied Regression: An Introduction* (Beverly Hills and London, 1980).

Table 3.2. Influence of population change on Communist and Socialist vote, Limousin, 1919–1936, by commune (coefficients of regression [*b*] and determination [R^2])

	b	R^2
Corrèze		
Parti Communiste		
1936	.00	.32
1932	.02	.26
1928	.06	.29
1924	.13	.22
Parti Socialiste		
1919	.12	.22
Haute-Vienne		
Parti Communiste		
1936	−.20	.08
1936st	−.54 *	.10
1932	−.02	.13
1928	−.06	.09
1924	−.01	.11
Parti Socialiste		
1919	.24 *	.09
Creuse		
Parti Communiste		
1936	−.28 †	.16
1936st	−.26 *	.09
1932	−.05	.22
1928	−.08	.24
1928st	−.20 *	.26
1924	.00	.05
1924st	−.12 *	.07
1936 less 1924	−.28 †	.10
Parti Socialiste		
1919	−.05	.18

Source: ADC 6M106–8; "Corrèze: La population des communes aux divers recensements depuis 1846," *Données statistiques du Limousin* 4 (September 1978); "Creuse: La population des communes aux divers recensements depuis 1846," *Données statistiques du Limousin* 2 (May 1978); "Haute-Vienne: La population des communes aux divers recensements depuis 1846," *Données statistiques du Limousin* 1 (March 1978). For electoral results see table 2.1.

Note: For population change I have used 1901 as a base. The figure for 1936 thus indicates population change between 1936 and 1901. Controlling for percentages of civil burials, median delay between birth and baptism in 1900 (1910 for Corrèze), population per km² (Corrèze, Haute-Vienne), and, for Corrèze, percentages of migrants and peasants and mean farm size per commune. Corrèze N = 279; Haute-Vienne N = 201 for short-term and 203 for long-term change, 193 for 1924 (when cases with high residuals are removed); Creuse N = 250.

st = short-term population change, or the change since the previous census.

* Significant at .05 level.

† Significant at .01 level.

Creuse Communists followed the patterns of their Limousin neighbors in all elections except 1936, when a 10 percent reduction in population loss from one commune to another produced a 2.8 percent loss in PCF voting when variables gauging religious behavior are controlled for (table 3.2). In other words, the Party did best among those communes that suffered the greatest long-term population losses.[42] A variable measuring the difference between the Communists' scores in 1936 and 1924 shows that relative to Communist support in 1924, the 1936 Communist vote increased along with population losses (see the last line of table 3.2). When *Creusois* Communists, who had proved slow to establish a firm presence, finally made their mark on the political scene, they did so in those areas hardest hit by the demographic downturn. In 1924, 1928, and 1936, short-term population losses had likewise contributed to Communist strength, suggesting that in Creuse, more than elsewhere, the Party reaped the immediate benefits of the ravages of depopulation.

Since the decline in population was most acute in villages that experienced the greatest economic difficulties—indeed, these very difficulties were the root cause of migration—one might have expected these communes to be more responsive than others to Communist propaganda. But this clearly was not the case in Corrèze and Haute-Vienne, and not consistently so in Creuse. The massive rural exodus that began in the late nineteenth century had little effect on Limousin politics in the twentieth. Permanent out-migration destabilized village communities, families, and social life but had no uniform effect on political behavior.

Dispersed Habitat

Most of Limousin's and Dordogne's inhabitants resided not in the village center (called *le bourg* in Limousin) but in hamlets and on individual farms (referred to as *les villages* by the *Limousins*) scattered across the countryside. In 1936 a mean of 73 percent of Corrèze's population lived outside the village center. On the national level, many historians have underlined the links between patterns of settlement and politics: André Siegfried thought that in western France dispersed habitat favored the continued political domination of landed elites and of the clergy over the peasantry. In other areas—the Mediterranean, for instance—scholars have argued that the left benefited from the peasants' greater concentration in urban villages, where they came in contact with new political ideas. Hervé Le Bras has made the opposite argument for Limousin and proposed that red bastions corresponded to areas of dispersed habitat.[43] There is, however, no evidence to substantiate this

---

[42] I have plotted all these relationships in order to verify my interpretation. The population losses suffered by the great majority of communes give the coefficients a different significance.

[43] Hervé Le Bras, "Retour à l'origine," in *Autrement*, no. 122 (1991), 76. On the link between left-wing votes and agglomerated habitat, Raymond Long, *Les élections législatives en Côte-d'Or depuis 1870* (Paris, 1958), 216; Tony Judt, *Socialism in Provence, 1871–1914* (Cambridge, 1979), 108–9. On "protourbanization" and left politics in Aude, Laura Levine Frader, *Peasants and Protest: Agricultural Workers, Politics, and Unions in the Aude, 1850–1914* (Berkeley, 1991), 39–59. On the west, André Siegfried, *Tableau politique de la France de l'Ouest* (Paris, 1913), 381–85.

Table 3.3. Influence of percent of scattered and agglomerated population on Communist vote, Corrèze, 1936 and 1924 (coefficients of regression [*b*] and determination [R^2])[a]

	Scattered population		Agglomerated population	
	b	R^2	*b*	R^2
1936	.08	.32	−.08	.32
1924	.05	.22	−.05	.22

Source: ADC 6M106–8, 3M196, AN C10045.
[a]Controlling for long-term population change and for percentages of migrants, peasants, civil burials, median delay between birth and baptism in 1910, and mean farm size per commune. *N* = 279.

Table 3.4. Influence of population per square kilometer on Communist vote, Corrèze and Haute-Vienne, 1936 and 1924 (coefficients of regression [*b*] and determination [R^2])[a]

	Corrèze (N = 279)		Haute-Vienne (N = 199)	
	b	R^2	*b*	R^2
1936	.02	.32	.07	.08
1924	.03	.22	.02	.10

Sources: ADC 3M196, AN C10045; Institut national de la statistique et des études économiques, *Recensement de 1962: Population légale et statistiques communales complémentaires* (Paris, 1963).
Note: The Haute-Vienne towns of St-Junien and St-Sulpice Laurière, which had strong Communist support and high population densities, have been excluded from the analysis.
[a]Controlling for long-term population change, percentage of civil burials, median delay between birth and baptism, and (for Corrèze) percentages of migrants and peasants and mean farm size per commune.

claim. The PCF's performance in Corrèze was completely divorced from the structure of habitat: the percentage of agglomerated or scattered population per commune had no effect on the Party's score at the polls (table 3.3)—or on that of the Socialists (except in 1936), Radicals, or conservatives. In other words, whether people lived in small towns and village centers or in surrounding hamlets had no bearing on communism's electoral strength. Nor was population density among Corrèze and Haute-Vienne communes of any consequence to the Party's performance (table 3.4).[44] The Communists did equally well (or poorly) in sparsely and densely populated villages. Communist support was thus synonymous neither with geographical isolation nor

[44] Owing to lack of data, the towns of Tulle, Brive, and Limoges, all of which have high population densities, have been excluded from all the regressions in this chapter.

with urbanity. Nothing in the structure of habitat can help explain the PCF's rural successes in Corrèze.

Religion

Religious observance by both men and women was unusually low in large parts of Limousin. One-half of Creuse, along with northern Corrèze, central Haute-Vienne, and the Nontronnais in Dordogne, appeared as missionary areas on Fernand Boulard's map of *pascalisants* (those taking Easter communion), published after World War II. Only a thin strip of southern Corrèze and the southeastern part of Dordogne remained staunchly Catholic; the remainder of the region was at best lukewarm to the Church.[45] Religiosity had declined so dramatically by 1944 that the Catholic Church sent missionary priests to Limoges, and especially to rural regions of Limousin. In Creuse, which became the center of the rural missionary movement in the years after World War II, missionaries from the Oblats de Marie-Immaculée toured the countryside in horse-drawn caravans. Some priests in rural, anticlerical parishes chose to work part-time on farms, much on the model of the worker-priests, while others concentrated their efforts on establishing the Church's participation in local fêtes and popular commemorations. Whatever the method, there was no lack of proselytizing to do: of Creuse's 257 parishes, 214 had no resident priest; in 10 of the department's 25 cantons under 1 percent of the men attended church. While enthusiasm ran high, results over the long term proved disappointing. The missionary movement may have revitalized Church institutions and the local clergy, but it did little to reverse rural Limousin's ever-increasing indifference to Catholicism.[46]

Detachment from Catholic practice, which became marked from the late nineteenth century onward, did not manifest itself at the same time or with the same intensity in all of Limousin's villages. Considerable variation existed in religious observance among Limousin's cantons and communes, and particularly in Corrèze. Northern Corrèze, where it was not uncommon to find villages devoid of priests in the 1930s, was far more detached from Catholicism than was the south, and this trend persisted from the early years of the century well into the 1950s.[47] The question is whether a relationship

---

[45] See the map in Fernand Boulard, *Premiers itinéraires en sociologie religieuse* (Paris, 1954); idem, *Matériaux pour l'histoire religieuse du peuple français. XIXe–XXe siècle* (Paris, 1982); and François-André Isambert and Jean-Paul Terrenoire, *Atlas de la pratique religieuse des catholiques en France* (Paris, 1980).

[46] Louis Pérouas, "La Creuse, laboratoire de mission rurale, 1944–1960," *Revue d'histoire de l'église de France* 75 (1989): 359–70; idem, *Les Limousins: Leurs saints, leurs prêtres, du XVe au XXe siècle* (Paris, 1988), 207–8; idem, *Refus d'une religion*, 203.

[47] See the maps in Pérouas, *Refus d'une religion*, 24–25, 38–39. Following Pérouas, I use the expression "detachment from Catholicism" or "detachment from religious practice" instead of "dechristianization," which is a misleading expression. See his excellent discussion, 200–202.

existed between religiosity, or the lack of it, and political behavior in Limousin. This question has been asked only of Catholicism because the Protestant churches had only a minimal following in this area.[48]

Louis Pérouas argues convincingly that the median delay between birth and baptism is a far more precise indicator of detachment from religion than are the traditional measures of *pascalisants* and *messalisants* (those attending Sunday mass). In a nutshell, the longer parents waited beyond the three days accorded by the Church to baptize their children, the lower their level of religiosity.[49] The delay between birth and baptism remained a good indicator of religious inclinations through the first decade of the twentieth century. By the interwar years, however, the meaning of baptism had changed: it became a fête of childhood, and as a consequence tended to be pushed back in time. Moreover, with the drop in child mortality, it was no longer so urgent to baptize within three days after birth.[50]

A second measure of religiosity painstakingly compiled by Pérouas is the number of civil burials per commune during the interwar years. Civil burials and civil marriages (which are more difficult to track down) first appeared in Limousin in the 1880s, though it was not until 1905 that their numbers became significant. Sometimes organized under the aegis of the village chapter of the Libre Pensée, civil burials gave people the possibility of a dignified burial (with speeches, a procession, banners, flags, and so on) outside the Church. While the delay between birth and baptism measures the extent of detachment from religious practice, the percentage of civil burials provides us with an indicator of anti-Catholic sentiments. Unlike the increasing time lag between birth and baptism, which can be taken as reflecting growing religious indifference, a civil burial was a clear sign of marked opposition to the Catholic Church and especially to the local priest. The moderate correlations between civil burials and the delay between birth and baptism indicate that the two variables measure different aspects of religious behavior.[51]

---

[48] In 1922 only 6 of Corrèze's 289 communes had Protestant services. See *L'almanach annuaire de la Corrèze* (1922), and, for the nineteenth century, Pérouas, *Refus d'une religion*, 165–69. In the 1980s only 2% of Limousin's inhabitants claimed a Protestant faith: Pérouas, *Les Limousins*, 210.

[49] Pérouas, *Refus d'une religion*, 33–50. For a discussion of the method, see Claude Langlois, "Histoire d'un indice, indice d'une histoire: Le délai de baptême," in *Croyances, pouvoirs et société: Des Limousins aux Français: Etudes offertes à Louis Pérouas*, ed. Michel Cassan, Jean Boutier, and Nicole Lemaitre (Treignac, 1988).

[50] Gérard Cholvy questions whether the growing delay between birth and baptism measures declining religious convictions or a diminished fear of infant mortality. Pérouas shows that through 1910 the delay between birth and baptism provides us with an illustration of the geography of the decline in religious fervor—a geography that cannot be explained by differing rates in perinatal mortality. See Langlois, "Histoire d'un indice," 66; Pérouas, *Refus d'une religion*, 44n; Pérouas et al., *Léonard, Marie, Jean et les autres: Les prénoms en Limousin depuis un millénaire* (Paris, 1984), 183.

[51] The correlation between the percentage of civil burials and the median delay between birth and baptism is .477 for Corrèze, .528 for Creuse, and .503 for Haute-Vienne. A regression analysis shows that while both measures of religious practice are strongly and significantly re-

Detachment from Catholic Practice and Politics

More than for any other political party, religiosity (or the lack of it) had a profound effect on Communist voting. Throughout the interwar years, Limousin Communists consistently did best where anti-Catholic sentiments were strongest and, to a lesser extent, where detachment from religious practice was most pronounced. Independent of demographic, occupational, and economic factors, a 10 percent increase in civil burials would indicate an estimated 5.4 percent rise in the 1936 Corrèze Communist vote (table 3.5), and the figure was almost identical in Haute-Vienne (5.6 percent) (table 3.6). A hypothetical Corrèze commune where all burials were civil, for example, would be 54 percentage points more Communist than a village with no civil burials. Throughout the 1920s and 1930s hostility to religion consistently benefited the Communists, who met with success in villages with high rates of civil burial. This relationship was significant, though less important, in Creuse (table 3.6). Finally, in both Creuse and Haute-Vienne, the association between hostility to the Church and PCF support intensified over time: in relation to its performance in 1924, support for the Party at the time of the Popular Front increased as the number of civil burials likewise rose (see 1936 less 1924 in table 3.6).

Detachment from religious practice did not have as consistent an effect on Communist voting. Only in Corrèze (and Creuse in 1928) does a powerful and regular association between the median birth and baptism delay and Communist support appear. When one adjusts for the effect of civil burials and all the other independent variables, an increase of 100 days in the median delay between birth and baptism in 1936 leads to an estimated 5 percent increase in the Communist vote. Put another way, a village where the delay was 100 days longer than in a neighboring village should have 5 percent more PCF voters (table 3.5). Moreover, this relationship strengthened over time: in relation to Communist support in 1924, PCF backing in Corrèze in 1936 increased as the median delay between birth and baptism lengthened. In Haute-Vienne, however, the relationship between detachment from Catholicism and PCF voting was the opposite. From 1928 on, a greater median delay between birth and baptism contributed to a small but significant *decline* in Communist voting. In 1936 a 100-day increase in the median number of days until baptism led to an 18 percent drop in PCF voting (table 3.6). Haute-Vienne Communists benefited from anti-Catholic sentiments at the same time that they were penalized by marked detachment from religious practice.

---

lated (an increase in the time length between birth and baptism between villages leads to an increase in the percentage of civil burials), the percentage of variance explained is relatively low (the highest r^2 is .27 for Creuse). My thanks to Louis Pérouas for kindly providing me with the detailed data for both religious variables; maps based on these data are reproduced in less detail in his *Refus d'une religion*, 38–39, 54.

Table 3.5. Influence of religious practice on leftist vote, Corrèze, 1906–1936 (coefficients of regression [*b*] and determination [R^2])[a]

	Civil burials	Delay between birth and baptism, 1910	
	b	*b*	R^2
Parti Communiste			
1936	.54[†]	.05[†]	.32
1932	.41[†]	.03[*]	.26
1928	.35[†]	.03[*]	.28
1924	.39[†]	.03[*]	.21
1936 less 1924	.15	.03[*]	.16
Parti Socialiste			
1919	.33[*]	.02	.22
1914	.28[*]	.04[†]	.14
1910	.11	.01	.17
1906	.02	.00	.06
1936	−.07	−.04[*]	.15
1932	.06	−.04[*]	.10
1928	.03	.14[*]	.39
Radical candidates			
1936	−.40[*]	−.01	.08
1932	−.39	.01	.03
1928	−.48[*]	.04	.05
1924[b]	−.30[*]	.01	.12

Sources: Data on religion provided by Louis Pérouas. For electoral results see table 2.1.

[a] Controlling for percentages of migrants and peasants, population per km², long-term population change, percentage of civil burials, median delay between birth and baptism in 1910, and mean farm size per commune. For 1906–1914, controlling only for median delay between birth and baptism, civil burials, long-term population change, and population per km². N = 279; for Parti socialiste: 1906, 69; 1910, 121; 1914, 184; 1928, 148; for Radicals, 1936, 227.

[b] Cartel des Gauches list, which included one Socialist candidate.

[*] Significant at .05 level.

[†] Significant at .01 level.

Civil burials and the median delay between birth and baptism thus measure different aspects of religious behavior, and their effects on politics were far from identical. The more trustworthy Corrèze figures suggest that detachment from Catholicism and the growth of anti-Catholic sentiments consistently favored the Communists. Results from the other two Limousin departments also underline the key importance of civil burials, while in Haute-Vienne detachment from religion was not in itself a sine qua non of Communist successes. Why the difference? Part of the answer may lie in the differing regional significance of baptism. In northern Dordogne (Nontronnais) the delay between birth and baptism was low in relation to other indicators of religiosity largely owing to the importance of the cult of the dead in this area. Local inhabitants tended to follow Church teachings and bap-

Table 3.6. Influence of religious practice on leftist vote, Haute-Vienne and Creuse, 1898–1936 (coefficients of regression (*b*) and determination [R^2])[a]

| | Civil burials | Delay between birth and baptism, 1900 | |
	b	b	R^2
Haute-Vienne			
Parti Communiste			
1936	.56†	−.18*	.08
1932	.46†	−.11*	.13
1928	.46†	−.14*	.09
1924	.21†	−.06	.10
1936 less 1924	.35†	−.12	.05
Parti Socialiste			
1919	.40†	−.03	.09
1914	.29	.15	.04
1910	.37*	.04	.06
1898	.86†	−.26*	.26
1936	−.14	.03	.04
1932	−.12	.16*	.04
1928	.00	.07	.02
1924	.01	−.10	.05
Creuse			
Parti Communiste			
1936	.17†	.01	.16
1932	.13†	.01	.22
1928	.24†	.06†	.25
1924	.06*	.01	.05
1936 less 1924	.12*	−1.86	.10
Parti Socialiste			
1919	.21†	.03	.18

Sources: See table 3.5.

[a]Controlling for long-term population change, percentage of civil burials, and median delay between birth and baptism in 1900; for Haute-Vienne, also for population per km². Haute Vienne: *N* = 201; for Parti Socialiste: 1910, 1914, and 1919, 202; 1898, 62. Creuse: *N* = 250.

* Significant at .05 level.

† Significant at .01 level.

tize their newborn infants quickly; their Easter mass attendance, however, was among the lowest in the department.[52]

These findings should be interpreted with appropriate caution. The median delay between baptism and birth primarily reflects the religious behavior of women, who did not vote. The degree of religiosity among men was lower, but not necessarily uniformly so from commune to commune, so that the effect of religion on Communist voting may well have been different for

[52] Ralph Gibson, "Quantification and Explanation of Religious Practice: The Diocese of Périgueux in the 19th Century," in *Proceedings of the Fifth George Rudé Seminar in French History*, ed. Peter McPhee (Wellington, N.Z., 1986), 108.

men and women.[53] The connection between the religious behavior of women and the male political world was far from straightforward. The association between Communist voting and the median delay between birth and baptism thus should be viewed as indicating a general tendency (insofar as the religious tendencies of men were linked to those of women) more than a precise relationship. The percentage of civil burials provides a more faithful representation of the religious views of both women and men.

The link between declining religious fervor and the growing strength of the Communist Party can be placed in perspective by comparisons with other political parties. The early Socialist vote clearly bore the greatest resemblance to its future Communist successor. In 1919, on the eve of the Tours Congress, the Limousin Socialist vote increased in those communes with high rates of civil burials; this had also been the case, though less consistently, in the years preceding the Great War (in Corrèze in 1914 and Haute-Vienne in 1898 and 1910). The association between the pre-1920 Socialist vote and hostility to Catholicism was thus "inherited" by the Communists and not by any other political formation on the left. Detachment from religious practice, on the other hand, was of little consequence for pre-1920 socialism. Finally, the interwar Socialist vote in both Corrèze and Haute-Vienne was largely unaffected by religious behavior except during the 1930s, when Corrèze Socialists actually lost support in areas most detached from religious practice.

The case of the Radicals is instructive. This most anticlerical of political parties was unaffected by Limousin's growing religious indifference. The median delay between birth and baptism produced no sustained effect on Radical voting, although on two occasions in the prewar years (Corrèze in 1910 and Haute-Vienne in 1914) longer delays actually drove the Radical vote down. The percentage of civil burials had a more consistent influence on Radical voting: in the 1920s and 1930s Radical votes in Corrèze declined substantially in areas hostile to the Church—not what one would expect of a party unfriendly to the local clergy. In 1928 a 10 percent increase in civil burials from village to village led to an estimated 4.8 percent loss in Radical support when demographic and occupational variables are controlled for. How can we account for this finding? The Radicals did poorly in these regions precisely because their anticlerical platform found few supporters in areas where the Church's presence had hit rock bottom. In secularized villages, distinguished by large numbers of civil burials and an increasingly ephemeral Church presence, clericalism was no longer an issue. The Radicals needed a minimal amount of Church presence in order to survive; without it they lost part of their raison d'être. Local notables, few and far between in these areas to begin with, had less reason to set up a contre-pouvoir to the Church. These results place the relationship between religiosity and

[53] In 1911 Easter mass attendance in both Tulle cantons was 24.8% for men and 68.4% for women. By 1955 these figures had dropped respectively to 6.2% and 24.2%. Pérouas, Refus d'une religion, 64, 81–82.

radicalism on the national level in new perspective. It has often been argued that the Radicals were strongly established outside areas of high religious observance; but we can see that, in a region largely detached from Catholicism, the Radicals did not do best in villages where the Church's influence had declined most dramatically.[54]

The Communists, perhaps the least overtly anticlerical of all left parties in Limousin, established bastions in areas of religious indifference because major programs of social and revolutionary change (which the Catholic Church had consistently opposed) met with a positive response where the Church's power was restricted. The PCF established itself in secularized areas because there it faced little competition from the Radicals. And in such areas Church-related sociability—one of the few forms of sociability in the region's villages—was often nonexistent: the local priest was isolated, services were poorly attended, and churches were closed or abandoned. The Communists, as we will see in chapter 6, proved adept at filling in this gap by creating new networks of sociability and politics in the countryside. Such activities constituted one of the PCF's major appeals, and on this score the Radicals had little to offer.

These findings are consistent with what we know about the relationship between religion and politics: on the national level religion has been the variable that best "explains" left and particularly Communist voting.[55] Survey data from the 1950s and 1960s indicate that practicing Catholics were far less likely to vote for the Communists than for any other political party. In 1952 only 13 percent of PCF voters considered themselves to be devout Catholics, and in 1966 a mere 3 percent of all French Catholics cast their votes for the Communist Party.[56] A 1956 study by canton showed that the Corrèze Communist vote was negatively correlated with Sunday Mass attendance ($r = -.72$). This figure was lower in Creuse ($r = -.44$), Dordogne ($r = -.32$), and Haute-Vienne ($r = -.27$).[57] When we use more precise measures of detachment from religious practice, the same patterns emerge for interwar Limousin: correlations between PCF voting and both religious variables were strongest in Corrèze, somewhat less marked in Creuse, and weakest in Haute-Vienne (table 3.7).[58]

[54] For the nation as a whole, Serge Berstein, *Histoire du Parti radical* (Paris, 1980), 1:307.

[55] Daniel Derivry and Mattei Dogan, "Unité d'analyse et espace de référence en écologie politique: Le canton et le département français." *RFSP* 21 (1971): 551; Daniel Derivry, "L'analyse écologique du vote paysan," in Yves Tavernier et al., *L'univers politique des paysans dans la France contemporaine* (Paris, 1972), 131–62; François André Isambert, "Signification de quelques correspondances empiriques entre comportements politiques et religieux," *Archives de sociologie des religions* 33 (1972): 49–70.

[56] Jean-Marie Donegani, *La liberté de choisir: Pluralisme religieux et pluralisme politique dans le catholicisme français contemporain* (Paris, 1993), 53; François-André Isambert, "Comportement politique et attitude religieuse," in *Politique et foi* (Strasbourg, 1972), 36–40.

[57] These correlations are based only on rural cantons. Derivry and Dogan, "Unité d'analyse." For similar results, Isambert, "Comportement politique," 27.

[58] Given that coefficients based on cantonal data tend to be stronger than those based on communal data, the communal correlations between religion and communism for interwar Corrèze are comparable to those calculated on the basis of cantons twenty-odd years later.

Table 3.7. Correlation coefficient (*r*) between religious practice and Communist vote, Limousin, 1936, by commune

	Civil burials[a]	Delay between birth and baptism[b]
Corrèze	.397	.432
Creuse	.281	.178
Haute-Vienne	.209	.010

Sources: AN C10045, and see table 3.5.
[a]N = 283 (Corrèze), 257 (Creuse), 205 (Haute-Vienne).
[b]In 1910 for Corrèze; 1900 for Creuse and Haute-Vienne. N = 286 (Corrèze), 259 (Creuse), 204 (Haute-Vienne).

Farm Size and Communism

Observers of rural society have often tried to explain political behavior by examining property structure. Although this approach has taken many forms, all are based on the assumption that the close links between property and social structure have important consequences for politics. Siegfried was the first to propose the classic theory that regions dominated by small property holders tend to develop an egalitarian tradition, while sharecroppers, tenant farmers, and sometimes peasant smallholders in areas where there are large property holdings tend to come under the influence of prominent conservative landowners.[59] Was this the case in Limousin? It would seem unlikely in such an area, with few powerful landowners, but a larger question remains because the relationship between land structure and politics can take forms other than the exercise of political and social power by landholding elites. In Limousin and Dordogne, where social differences in the countryside were less marked than in many other regions, farm size may well have been a crucial factor.

The following analysis is based on the village results of the 1929 Corrèze agricultural census. This inquiry provides detailed information on the structure of the *exploitations* (farms); it tells us nothing, however, about the farm owners, and whether they farmed the land themselves, rented it out to tenants, or turned it over to sharecroppers. A farm might be made up of plots rented from several property owners, just as a landlord could lease land to several sharecroppers or tenant farmers. Given the absence of large, absentee landlords and the modest numbers of sharecroppers and tenant farm-

---

[59] This was not necessarily the case if these were absentee landlords. Siegfried, *Tableau politique*, 370–80. On land structure and politics, see Donald Sutherland, "Land and Power in the West of France, 1750–1914," in *Landownership and Power in Modern Europe*, ed. Ralph Gibson and Martin Blinkhorn (London, 1991); Alain de Vulpian, "Physionomie agraire et orientation politique dans le département des Côtes-du-Nord, 1928–1946," *RFSP* 1 (1951): 110–33.

ers in Corrèze, one can assume that farm size is a good proxy for property structure.

Small and medium-sized farms predominated in Limousin and Dordogne. The mean farm size in Corrèze corresponded to a medium-sized plot: 17.3 hectares, ranging from an average of 3 hectares in the southern village of Ligneyrac (canton of Meyssac) to 55 hectares in Lestards (canton of Bugeat) on the Millevaches plateau. A breakdown of farms according to size shows that 45 percent can be considered small farms (1 to 10 hectares) and 48 percent medium-sized farms (10 to 50 hectares). Large *exploitations*—above 50 hectares—were the exception (3.1 percent), and this was the case in the nineteenth century as well (see table 3.8). With one exception (fewer medium-sized farms), the same patterns were found in Haute-Vienne, Creuse, and Dordogne. The Corrèze's cultivated land was spread out among small and medium farms (23.8 percent and 63.9 percent, respectively of the total cultivated surface). Large estates did not account for an inordinate percentage of land under cultivation (table 3.8). Taken as a whole, Corrèze was an area of small to medium-sized farms par excellence.[60]

The definition of large, medium, and small farms depended on the fertility of the soil, the configuration of the land, the altitude and climate, and the type of agriculture that was practiced. In the Montagne Limousine, a peasant with fewer than 25 hectares was considered a small farmer, while in the richer Brive Basin to the south, a smallholder rarely cultivated more than 5 hectares. Larger farms, however, were not necessarily synonymous with prosperity: it was possible to do rather well working a small plot of fruits and vegetables in the Brive Basin, while peasants who cultivated considerably more land in other areas of Corrèze might struggle. Small farms tended to be concentrated in the south (the Brive area and the Lot border) and were characterized by the cultivation of fruits (nuts, apples, prunes, cherries, chestnuts) and young vegetables (peas, beans, melons); viniculture (though less than before the late nineteenth-century Phylloxera blight); and the raising of tobacco, corn, wheat, and some livestock. Brive and the Lot border were regions of both agricultural specialization and subsistence agriculture. On medium farms, located within a large central band crossing the department, peasants tended livestock and practiced polyculture. Finally, on large *exploitations* found especially among the poor soils of the Millevaches plateau and northern Corrèze, peasants grew some potatoes, rye, and buckwheat (for crêpes) and raised sheep. Heather (*landes*) and woods covered significant expanses of large farms.

Farm size had a considerable and consistent effect on Communist voting. Throughout the 1920s and 1930s an increase in the mean farm size per commune was associated with a rise in the Communist vote: in 1936 a 10 per-

---

[60] Plots of less than a hectare, which could rarely sustain a family, have not been included in the statistical analysis.

Table 3.8. Distribution of farms (*exploitations*) and cultivated land, Limousin and Dordogne, 1929, by size of farms (percent)

	Small			Medium		Large	
	<1 ha.	1–5 ha.	5–10 ha.	10–20 ha.	20–50 ha.	>50 ha.	N
Farms							
Corrèze	3.3%	15.4%	29.9%	33.8%	14.5%	3.1%	37,414
Creuse	19.4	20.9	20.4	20.8	15.3	3.2	39,168
Dordogne	14.2	20.1	23.7	23.9	15.4	2.6	66,511
Haute-Vienne	17.6	27.4	21.6	16.3	14.0	3.1	45,382
Cultivated Land							
Corrèze	0.3	5.0	18.8	36.5	27.4	12.0	
Creuse	0.9	5.9	12.3	24.9	39.0	17.0	
Dordogne	1.0	7.8	16.3	29.6	29.2	16.1	
Haute-Vienne	1.2	7.7	13.1	20.1	39.2	18.7	

Sources: Corrèze, according to the communal results of the agricultural inquiry in ADC 7M306–18; other departments, Ministère de l'Agriculture, *Statistique agricole de la France: Résultats généraux de l'enquête de 1929* (Paris, 1936).

cent increase in the mean farm size between communes contributed to an estimated 5.4 percent rise in PCF voting, when social, demographic, and religious variables are controlled for. This trend strengthened over time: relative to 1928, the Communist vote in 1936 increased as the average farm size per commune likewise rose (see 1936 less 1928 under Parti Communiste in table 3.9). A detailed analysis of the relationship between Communist voting and the percentages of small, medium, and large farms confirms these results. The Communists did poorly in regions of small farms—indeed, as the percentage of small farms rose, the PCF vote declined. On the other hand, the Communists implanted themselves most successfully in regions of medium and especially large farms (table 3.10). Given these regional differences, did the association between farm size and politics vary greatly among Corrèze's agricultural regions? An analysis that controls for regional differences shows this to be the case in the mid- and late 1930s. The existence of large farms in the north and east during that period had a positive effect on Communist voting, while, conversely, the presence of small farms produced the opposite result. Farm size had a more persistent impact on support for the PCF in northern Corrèze than in any other region.[61]

What of competing political parties? Here, as in other areas, conservatives were the mirror image of the Communists. The right saw its support increase as the mean farm size declined and as the percentage of small farms rose.

[61] I have used dummy variables to identify regional differences. This procedure is best explained in J. Morgan Kousser, "Must Historians Regress? An Answer to Lee Benson," *Historical Methods* 19 (1986): 66–70.

Table 3.9. Influence of mean farm size on voting, 1919–1936 (coefficients of regression [*b*] and determination [*R*])[a]

	b	R^2
Parti Communiste		
1936	.54[†]	.32
1932	.39[†]	.26
1928	.33[†]	.29
1924	.25[*]	.22
1936 less 1928	.23[†]	.11
Parti Socialiste		
1936	−.42[†]	.15
1932	−.27[*]	.10
1928	.68[†]	.39
1919	.24[*]	.22
Radical lists		
1936	.30[†]	.81
1932	.14	.03
1928	.46[*]	.05
1924[b]	−.45[†]	.12
1919	−.03	.03
Right lists		
1936	−.46[*]	.26
1932	−.50[†]	.23
1928	−.62[†]	.26
1924	−.05	.18
1919	−.59[†]	.33

Source: Farm size from ADC 7M306-18; voting results from ADC 3M194, 3M196–97, 3M200, AN C10045.

[a] Controlling for long-term population change, population per km², percentages of migrants, peasants, and civil burials, and median delay between birth and baptism. N = 279; for Parti Socialiste in 1928, 148; for Radicals in 1936, 227; for the right in 1936, 210.

[b] Radical-led Cartel des Gauches list, which included one Socialist candidate.

[*] Significant at .05 level.

[†] Significant at .01 level.

Conservatives did poorly in regions of medium and (along with the Socialists in the 1930s) large farms. The Radicals, the most influential political group in Corrèze, seem to have profited from higher mean farm sizes, though a more detailed breakdown indicates that the percentages of small, medium, and large farms had no effect on them during the interwar years. Farm structure had a consistent impact on one political party: the Communists.

Independent of other factors, the Communist Party scored highest in regions supporting medium and large farms, which is not to say that the medium and large peasantry voted for the PCF.[62] There was little paradox, however, in the fact that the PCF, which claimed to defend the smallholding

[62] Jean-Pierre Vaudon, "L'implantation du Parti communiste dans les milieux ruraux des arrondissements d'Issoire et de Thiers de 1920 à 1936," *Le mouvement social* 74 (1974): 93, argues that in Puy-de-Dôme, regions of medium-sized holdings proved the most hostile to communism.

Table 3.10. Influence of percent of small, medium, and large farms on Communist vote, Corrèze, 1924–1926 (coefficients of regression [*b*] and determination [R^2])[a]

	Small farms		Medium farms		Large farms	
	b	R^2	*b*	R^2	*b*	R^2
1936	−.18[†]	.30	.17[†]	.30	.61[†]	.31
1932	−.14[†]	.25	.13[†]	.25	.47[†]	.26
1928	−.09[*]	.27	.10[†]	.28	.38[†]	.28
1924	−.08[*]	.21	.07[*]	.22	.38[†]	.23

Sources: See table 3.9.

[a] Controlling for population per km², long-term population change, percentages of peasants, migrants, and civil burials, and median delay between birth and baptism. *N* = 279.

[*] Significant at .05 level.

[†] Significant at .01 level.

peasantry, did best as average farm size rose. The Communists (and most of their political opponents) considered the broad majority of Corrèze peasants to be *petits propriétaires* or *petits paysans* (literally, "small peasants"). Income disparities among those who farmed small and large plots tended to be minimal, and families that farmed larger plots of land were not necessarily richer than smallholders, nor did they exercise more influence in their communities. Wealth had more to do with the quality of the land and the nature of the crops than with farm size per se. The Party's strength in regions of medium and large farms, where relatively poor soils (and thus larger farms) gave way to polyculture, livestock, and sheep raising, increased after the agricultural crisis that struck the countryside in the early 1930s. What made these regions more prone to radical politics in times of economic downturns? Was there a relationship between voting and poorer types of soil structure?

An initial analysis indicates that such was the case: as the mean percentage of the total farm surface under cultivation increased, the PCF vote declined. A detailed breakdown, however, shows that this situation occurred only on small farms where a large percentage of the land was under cultivation. Put another way, the Party's fortunes declined in regions of small farms where little land was left untilled, and this trend grew stronger over time (table 3.11). The relatively fertile soils of the Brive basin, often parceled out into small fruit and vegetable farms, did not favor support for the Communists. What was true of small farms, however, did not apply to large ones. The Communists prospered where medium and large *exploitations* predominated, particularly in areas where the percentage of land under cultivation was high. In other words, the presence of large farms where the land was cultivated or turned over to pasture was more favorable to the PCF than similar areas where a significant percentage of the land was covered by ponds, forests, and heather (table 3.12).

Table 3.11. Influence of percentages of cultivated and wooded land on Communist vote, Corrèze, 1924–1936 (coefficients of regression [*b*] and determination [*R*])[a]

	Cultivated Land		Wooded Land	
	b	R^2	*b*	R^2
1936	−.16[†]	.28		
1932	−.08	.21	−.03	.21
1928	−.13[†]	.27	.02	.26
1924	.00	.20		

Sources: Farm size from ADC 7M306-18. Voting results from ADC 3M196-97, 3M200, AN C 10045.
[a]Controlling for population per km^2, long-term population change, percentages of peasants, migrants, and civil burials, and median delay between birth and baptism. N = 279.
[†]Significant at .01 level.

Table 3.12. Influence of percentage of cultivated land on Communist vote, Corrèze, 1924–1936, by size of farms (coefficients of regression [*b*] and determination [*R*])[a]

	Small farms		Medium farms		Large farms	
	b	R^2	*b*	R^2	*b*	R^2
1936	−.19[†]	.30	.07	.26	.23[†]	.29
1932	−.15[†]	.25	.05	.21	.18[†]	.24
1928	−.14[†]	.29	.06	.26	.15[†]	.28
1924	−.12[†]	.23	.03	.20	.17[†]	.23

Sources: See table 3.11.
[a]Controlling for population per km^2, long-term population change, percentages of peasants, migrants, and civil burials, and median delay between birth and baptism. N = 279.
[†]Significant at .01 level.

How should we interpret these findings? The Communists fared worst in areas of fertile small farms where peasants practiced polyculture and grew fruits and vegetables. More self-sufficient, less dependent on a single product to raise cash, these peasants raised crops that were not so badly hit by the Depression. Those who worked medium and large farms, however, relied on the sale of livestock (calves, cattle, sheep, pigs), and found themselves in a catastrophic situation when the prices of these products plunged. But dire economic circumstances are only part of the answer, because Communist support in regions of medium and large farms predated the agricultural crisis. Because they were more involved in the market, worked poorer soils, and lived in villages where the influences of Catholicism and prominent Radicals were greatly reduced, peasants were predisposed to heed the Party's watchwords. In the southern part of Corrèze, the PCF met with greater hostility for the opposite reasons. The agricultural crisis of the early 1930s only accentuated the growing split between the department's northern and southern regions.

Family Structure

In a departure from more conventional theories, Hervé Le Bras and Emmanuel Todd have argued that family structure is the key explanatory variable of contemporary French history, and of communism in particular.[63] Le Bras and Todd maintain that the geography of the three family structures present throughout French history corresponds to different political allegiances. Nuclear families, characterized by a desire for independence and isolation, tend to be unstable from a political point of view. Two types of extended family, which they name authoritarian and communitarian, are found in regions that respectively support the right and left. In authoritarian families, the parents delay the marriage of their heir as long as possible and prevent other children from marrying; these families tend to exhibit rigid right-wing tendencies. In communitarian families, in contrast, parents exercise no control over the age when their children marry; these families are typified by a desire for community and dependence.[64] Le Bras and Todd argue that the communitarian family was predominant in Limousin until the early nineteenth century, when its importance began to wane.

Le Bras and Todd claim that the destruction of the communitarian family in Limousin, as well as in Nord, Pas-de-Calais, Aisne, and Somme and along the Mediterranean coast, engendered profound psychological disturbances that led to the rise of the Communist Party. Communism was "a regression, in the psychoanalytical sense, toward the primitive family community," and in the minds of militants the Party cell replaced the old communitarian family.[65] Using census data, Le Bras and Todd assert that departments where early marriages were common (in 1955) and where a higher-than-average proportion of households encompassed more than one family (1.7 percent of all rural families in 1975) provide a good map of communitarian families and a sense of where they were strongly established in previous centuries. By comparing maps, Le Bras and Todd conclude that the rise of communism is inseparable from the decline of the communitarian family.[66] However, the presence of Communists in areas where communitarian families were nu-

---

[63] Le Bras and Todd, *L'invention de la France*. For good critiques, see Jean-René Tréanton, "Faut-il exhumer Le Play? ou Les héritiers abusifs," *Revue française de sociologie* 25 (1984): 458–83; Hughes Lagrange and Sebastian Roché, "Types familiaux et géographie politique en France," *RFSP* 38 (1988): 941–64; and Michel Vovelle, *La découverte de la politique: Géopolitique de la Révolution française* (Paris, 1993), 9–13.

[64] Le Bras and Todd, *L'invention de la France*, 30.

[65] Ibid., 86.

[66] Ibid., 49, and the pertinent comments of Lagrange and Roché, "Types familiaux." For a sympathetic account with regard to Dordogne see Gibson, "Quantification and Explanation."

merous in the past (and survive in small proportions today) hardly suggests that both factors are associated. One wonders how the presence of this family structure in Limousin actually translated into support for communism a century or more later. How can a family structure so marginal in the present exert such a disproportionate effect on people's political choices? And if the relationship the authors posit holds true, why did only a minority of voters in Limousin cast their ballots for the PCF?

Le Bras has since recognized that his "anthropological" approach raised more problems than it solved, and proposed that a combination of family structure, religion, and Parisian centralization is key to political orientation. In areas of Catholic influence, families adopted a more economically pragmatic and Malthusian attitude (i.e., late age at first marriage). The Limousin, on the other hand, was among those regions where Catholicism enjoyed no influence; deprived of the influence of the Church, families, left to themselves, failed to adapt economically to a changing world. The result was continuous social decline—accelerated by sharecropping (not the prevalent mode of tenure in Limousin, or, as we have seen, linked to communism)—because the lack of enough land or wealth to go around inevitably led to discontent, socialism, and communism.[67]

Le Bras and Todd's suggestive questions deserve attention, even though they could not resolve them successfully. Michel Vovelle has argued that a significant correlation exists between complex families and the strength of the left during the Revolution, but he is careful not to turn family structure into the key explanatory variable.[68] The relationship Le Bras and Todd have posited between the communitarian family and the later presence of a strong Communist movement in Limousin should not be discounted entirely. Such an association, however, is difficult to prove. Family structures in nineteenth-century Limousin were more complex than Le Bras and Todd admit.[69] Nuclear families lived side by side with extended families and multiple households, and there was considerable fluidity among all three. Nothing at present allows us to draw links between these types of family structures and future forms of political behavior.

This chapter has identified the patterns of difference that distinguished the Communists from their opponents. While it is never easy to explain a party's

Todd has pursued the argument on a larger scale in *La troisième planète: Structures familiales et systèmes idéologiques* (Paris, 1983) and *L'invention de l'Europe* (Paris, 1990).

[67] Hervé Le Bras, *Les trois France* (Paris, 1986), 120–31.

[68] His evidence, however, is ambiguous. Compare the figures in the text and the tables in *La découverte*, 307, 311.

[69] On family structure in Limousin, Jean-Claude Peyronnet, "Famille élargie ou famille nucléaire? L'exemple du Limousin au début du XIXe siècle," *Revue d'histoire moderne et contemporaine* 22 (1975): 568–82; Nicole Lemaitre, "Familles complexes en bas-limousin: Ussel au début du XIXe siècle," *Annales du Midi* 127 (1976): 220–24; Guy Perlier, "Recherches sur la structure familiale de la commune d'Eymoutiers au XIXe siècle" (mémoire de maîtrise, Université de Limoges, 1976).

social and geographical base of support, I have suggested that it is possible to go beyond visual correlations and, through a statistical analysis, give a clear sense of those factors that had the most powerful and consistent effect on voting behavior. The broader point of the last two chapters has been that, while particular factors clearly influenced people's political choices, their votes were neither shaped nor predetermined by larger invisible forces such as voting traditions and family structures. Communism differed radically from other political movements, those of the left included, both in its social basis and in the social, cultural, and economic elements that exerted the most powerful influence on its constituents.

To draw a profile of the Limousin and Dordogne Communist electorate: it originated (with a few exceptions) primarily in rural areas. Smallholding peasants, tenant farmers, agricultural workers, temporary migrants, village artisans, and shopkeepers closely tied to the agricultural economy formed the core of the Party's electorate; sharecroppers and rural workers, often considered a natural Communist constituency in rural areas, were less prone to cast their ballots for the party of the working class. Poverty was not a consistent feature of areas that backed PCF candidates, nor, for that matter, was relative economic well-being. Communist support was not a simple protest vote against difficult economic conditions in a poor rural area: the Party did not do best in those areas hardest hit by the rural exodus. Neither was communism linked to geographical isolation or family structure. The PCF electorate, however, was profoundly influenced by two factors: religion and farm size.

Low rates of religious practice, hostility to religion, and the absence of the Church on the local level all proved favorable to only one party in Limousin: the Communists. The Church's low profile, organizationally, socially, and spiritually, gave the Communists propitious grounds to advance their program of social change. In regions of medium and large farms where the Church was poorly established and Radicalism's influence was on the wane, the Communists found a receptive audience among peasants, tenant farmers, and agricultural workers (the latter two tended to be more numerous in these areas) who were vulnerable to the vicissitudes of the marketplace. The Communists filled a void in areas where the decline of religious practice and the discredit of the politics of patronage had robbed radicalism of a substantial part of its raison d'être. How they filled that void, and why they proved more successful in doing so than Socialists or Conservatives, is one focus of the chapters that follow.

4 Forging Communism in the Countryside, 1900–1920

Rural communism was molded by the circumstances surrounding its birth. The Great War, the Russian Revolution, and the social crisis of the postwar years had a deeply felt, though diverging, impact on the rural population of Limousin and Périgord. These events contributed to a changed political climate and to a radicalization of the Socialist Party's base. Even in remote rural areas of Limousin, the war had not left the social and political landscape unscathed. Radical notables lost their firm grip on power, while a new generation of men, marked and embittered by their experiences at the front, made their mark on politics and especially on socialism, and would continue to do so throughout the interwar decades. In the two years that followed the November 1918 armistice, Socialists successfully rebuilt and expanded their party, and debated many of the issues later critical to the Communist Party's success. The ruins of the war had given birth to a new discourse among Socialists, a discourse increasingly focused on antimilitarism, sympathy for the Russian Revolution and radical social change, antiparliamentarianism, and a sustained interest in the land issue. It was but one step to argue that a new political party was needed as well.

The birth of the Communist Party in Limousin and Dordogne had more to do with national and especially international matters (Lenin's desire to form a new International under Russian control) than with the practical details of local politics. But the new party established itself, and met with popular success, because (except in Haute-Vienne) it was able to tie the exigencies of international Communism to the concerns of rural militants and voters, and this was no minor accomplishment. In the eyes of militants, the young PCF both broke with the past and was a continuator of the new, more radical Socialist Party that had emerged from the war. In addition to continuing a tradition, the PCF best expressed the new demands of the postwar world.

The Communists could not escape their Socialist origins. Far from establishing itself in virgin territory, the Communist Party took root among towns and villages where Socialists already had been active for two decades. A majority of Communist voters in 1924 had cast their ballots for the SFIO five years earlier (chapter 2). Former Socialist militants formed the bulk of the PCF's members in the early 1920s. In Corrèze and Dordogne, the Communists gained control of the old Socialist organization and took over the SFIO newspapers; more often than not Socialist groups—then called sections—became Communist ones. The formation of an entirely new Communist Party, however, was a slow process. In the mid-1920s, Bolshevization brought the PCF's organization somewhat in line with the Russian model; the outcome of this campaign, however, was less visible in rural Corrèze than in the country's urban areas. The partial continuity that existed between socialism and communism in the electoral, organizational, and ideological realms diminished only gradually over the years. The Socialist movement's history in this region before and during the Great War is thus central to an understanding of the future success of communism in the countryside.

The Origins of Socialism

The history of socialism in Limousin and Dordogne since the late nineteenth century is complex, as it was on the national level.[1] The divisions between the various strands of French socialism—Guesdists, Allemanists, Vaillantists, and Reformists, to cite the most visible—in the years preceding French socialism's unification in 1905 are not critical to understanding the background to the Tours split in this region. Only in Haute-Vienne did Socialists achieve significant results, thanks in large part to their strength in Limoges la Rouge, where they controlled the town hall from 1895 to 1905; they recaptured the municipality in 1912, and, save for one major interruption between 1940 and 1947, have governed the city ever since.[2] The tensions between Guesdists (whose influence in Haute-Vienne has been overestimated) and Reformists gradually disappeared after 1905 as they began,

[1] On pre–World War I socialism, see Antoine Perrier, "Esquisse d'une sociologie du mouvement socialiste dans la Haute-Vienne et en Limousin," in *Actes du 87ᵉ congrès national des sociétés savantes: Section d'histoire moderne et contemporaine* (Paris, 1963), 377–98; Georges Verynaud, "Le mouvement ouvrier dans le Limousin contemporain," in *Histoire du Limousin et de la Marche*, ed. René Morichon (Limoges, 1972–76) 3:197–263; Georges Dauger, "Aux origines du syndicalisme et du socialisme en Limousin, 1830–1906," *Trames* (Limoges), 1986, 65–97; Pierre Vallin, "Aux origines du socialisme en Limousin, 1848–1914," in Louis Pérouas et al., *Les Limousins en quête de leur passé* (Limoges, 1986), 113–23; Pierre Cousteix, "Le mouvement ouvrier limousin de 1870 à 1939," *L'actualité de l'histoire* 20–21 (1957): 27–96.

[2] In 1945 the Communist resistance leader in Haute-Vienne, Georges Guingouin, was elected mayor of Limoges. He failed in his bid for reelection two years later.

together, to build a strong Socialist organization.[3] Adrien Pressemane and other leading Haute-Vienne Guesdists would team up later with reformist Socialists such as Léon Betoulle, Limoges's firmly entrenched mayor (1912 to 1940; 1947 to his death in 1956), to ensure the SFIO's continued success.

Both before and after World War I Haute-Vienne was the SFIO's regional stronghold. As early as the turn of the century, the Socialist militants Emile Teissonnière, Edouard Treich, and Emile Noël set out from Limoges to spread the Party gospel in the countryside. This approach was pursued and intensified after unification, as four future Socialist deputies—Jean Parvy, Sabinus Valière, Léon Betoulle, and particularly Adrien Pressemane—criss-crossed Haute-Vienne, often on foot, holding public meetings, establishing SFIO sections, and selling brochures and newspapers.[4] The tactic rapidly bore fruit. The speed with which large parts of rural Haute-Vienne turned to socialism was stunning. In 1906, Betoulle was elected deputy of Limoges 1, a district that encompassed Limoges proper and the surrounding rural areas, including the canton of Ambazac in the hills northeast of the city. By 1910, Haute-Vienne Socialists had captured 37.4 percent of the vote. Four years later, on the eve of the Great War, the Socialists did better in Haute-Vienne (55.5 percent) than in any other French department, and their candidates were elected to office in four of five districts. Support for Léon Betoulle, who faced no serious opposition, was close to unanimous (92.5 percent). Adrien Pressemane's performance was even more impressive: running in the rural district of Limoges 2, he obtained 61 percent of the vote and handily defeated the outgoing Radical deputy, Firmin Tarrade.

The strength of Socialist organization contributed to these results. Membership grew consistently, from 492 in 1905 to 2,700 in 1914 (see table 4.1) and these militants were grouped in 66 sections in 1912, compared to only 17 six years earlier.[5] We know little about rural militants, but if the example of Compreignac is any indication, the most active members tended to be artisans and shopkeepers rather than smallholding peasants.[6] The Party founded its own daily, *Le Populaire du Centre*, in 1905, and four years later introduced a biweekly, *Le Petit Limousin*, aimed at the countryside. By 1914, *Le Populaire*, with a printing of 10,000 copies, was the department's third largest daily, and *Le Petit Limousin* (6,000 copies) one of the most widely read biweeklies.[7]

---

[3] John Merriman places Haute-Vienne Guesdism in proper perspective in *The Red City: Limoges and the French Nineteenth Century* (New York, 1985), 194–201.

[4] Docteur [Jules] Fraisseix, *Au long de ma route: Propos anecdotiques d'un militant limousin* (Limoges, 1946), 59.

[5] *Encyclopédie socialiste, syndicale et coopérative de l'Internationale ouvrière: La France socialiste*, ed. A. Compère-Morel (Paris, 1913), 2:535–56.

[6] Pierre Vallin, *Paysans rouges du Limousin: Mentalités et comportement politique à Compreignac et dans le Nord de la Haute-Vienne, 1870–1914* (Paris, 1985), 289–90.

[7] ADHV 1T275. *Le Petit Limousin* sold some of its copies in Creuse.

Table 4.1. Membership in Parti Socialiste, Limousin and Dordogne, 1905–1920

	Corrèze	Creuse	Haute-Vienne	Dordogne
1905	232	199	492–800	400–477
1908	236	159–315	1,000	462
1911	147	238	1,600	637
1913	423	570	2,050	880
1914		700	2,700	
1918	270	195	775	800
1919	2,000	700	2,700	1,180
1920	3,000	1,200	4,300	1,900

Sources: *Encyclopédie socialiste, syndicale et coopérative de l'Internationale ouvrière: La France socialiste*, vol. 2, *Les fédérations socialistes*, ed. A. Compère-Morel (Paris, 1913); Georges Dauger, "Aux origines du Front populaire dans la Creuse: Contribution à une ethnohistoire des comportements politiques" (thèse de troisième cycle, Université de Paris I, 1983), 346–47, 344n; Pierre Cousteix, "Le mouvement ouvrier limousin de 1870 à 1939," *L'actualité de l'histoire* 20–21 (1957): 48; *Le Congrès de Tours* (Paris, 1980), 715; G. Decouty, "Introduction à l'étude de l'évolution de l'opinion publique dans le département de la Haute-Vienne" (thèse de L'institut d'études politiques, Paris, 1950), 275; Parti socialiste (SFIO), *XVIIᵉ congrès national tenu à Strasbourg: Compte rendu sténographique* (Paris, 1920), viiff.

The story of rural socialism in Haute-Vienne has been well told elsewhere, and one need only mention that the Socialists here were the first to give hard thought to their peasant policy on the regional level. After 1906, Socialist candidates increasingly deemphasized collectivization, and stressed instead that they would defend exploited small property owners. This realistic view was not shared by all Socialists, however, and in 1914 Sabinus Valière was elected deputy on a platform that stressed collectivization.[8] In neighboring Corrèze, the SFIO urged peasants in 1913 to support the Party if they wanted to preserve their holdings, and at the same time asked them to develop a "collectivist conception of production and property." Working small properties was an "inferior form of production," and peasants should organize cooperatives to defend themselves against capitalist expropriation.[9]

Socialism's strength in rural Haute-Vienne before the Great War was unmatched in the Corrèze, Creuse, or Dordogne countryside. These departments lacked the vigorous leadership and organization that gave the Haute-Vienne SFIO Federation much of its impetus, and they also were marked by distinct political contexts. In Haute-Vienne, growing Socialist activity had contributed to radicalism's collapse in the first decade of the century, whereas in the other three departments the Radicals remained a potent political force through the Great War and beyond. Large parts of the Haute-

[8] Vallin, *Paysans rouges*, 278–89, and "Aux origines du socialisme," 121.
[9] *TC*, 5 May and 12 December 1913.

Vienne countryside had turned to socialism before World War I; in Corrèze, radicalization was a consequence of the war.

Haute-Vienne Socialists enjoyed considerable influence in Creuse and Dordogne. The birth of organized socialism in Creuse in the closing years of the nineteenth century owed much to Haute-Vienne Guesdist militants; Socialist strength up to 1910 was located in the district of Bourganeuf, which was far less *Creusois* in character than it was influenced by Limoges. Close links also existed between Limoges and Dordogne. Militants from Haute-Vienne, and to a lesser extent Gironde, helped spread Socialist propaganda in Périgord in the early years of the century. The Dordogne Socialist Federation, founded in 1901 and affiliated with the Parti Ouvrier Français (the Guesdists), was led by Paul Faure.[10] A powerful orator and brilliant polemicist, Faure was instrumental in the development of *périgourdin* socialism. Although by 1913 the Federation counted close to 900 members (table 4.1) and the following year SFIO candidates received 10.1 percent of the vote, these results, particularly in rural areas, did not fulfill expectations. While socialism's strength was located principally in the Périgueux region, where Faure had campaigned energetically on three separate occasions, it also was making progress in the countryside, especially in poverty-stricken Nontronnais along the Limousin border. In 1913, Faure, future secretary general of the SFIO between 1920 and 1940, left Dordogne to assume new duties as editor in chief of *Le Populaire du Centre*, thus underscoring his close relationship with Haute-Vienne SFIO militants.

The Corrèze followed a course of its own. In the late nineteenth century Guesdist militants from Bordeaux launched a short-lived effort to establish the Parti Ouvrier Français. The followers of Edouard Vaillant had more success. The Parti Socialiste Révolutionnaire was founded in 1901 by Bernard Chambas, an employee of the Manufacture Nationale d'Armes in Tulle, who had become a Blanquist militant while working in Paris.[11] But progress, even after unification, was slow, and the Socialist Party lost militants between 1905 and 1911 (table 4.1) Only in the two years preceding the Great War did the Party make advances. The SFIO doubled the number of its militants and voters (to 7.9 percent), established thirty sections (most of them rural), and founded a weekly, *Le Travailleur de la Corrèze*, which counted 975 subscribers on the war's eve.[12]

Such was the state of *limousin* and *périgourdin* socialism before World War I. The influence of Limoges diminished rapidly as socialism took root in the countryside and a new generation of rural leaders and militants emerged.[13] The character acquired by socialism—and especially by commu-

---

[10] On Dordogne socialism see ADD 4M186 and *Encyclopédie socialiste*, 2:231–41. Paul Faure became *secrétaire fédéral* of the Dordogne Socialist Federation in 1904.

[11] *Encyclopédie socialiste*, 2:219–23.

[12] *TC*, 26 July 1914.

[13] For a different perspective, Vallin, *Paysans rouges*.

nism—in the countryside differed from its urban image. In parts of Limousin—the Montagne, to cite the most prominent example—Socialist ideas did not emerge from regional towns, but were brought back from Paris, St-Etienne, and Lyon by migrant workers. The exact path followed in the dissemination of political ideas in the countryside is difficult to plot, although the overall importance of Limoges, Périgueux, and Tulle in this process should not be overestimated.

The Impact of the Great War

The outbreak of hostilities in August 1914 marked the end of an era for French socialism, and within the SFIO it spelled the defeat of the antimilitaristic and pacifist policies central to socialism's identity in Haute-Vienne. In the first decades of the century Haute-Vienne Socialists had been at the forefront of antiwar campaigns. When the Briand government announced its intention to lengthen military service from two to three years in March 1913, the SFIO launched a nationwide protest campaign. Haute-Vienne Socialists organized large meetings in Limoges and circulated a petition against the three-year law. Rural inhabitants accounted for two-thirds of the 30,000 signatures collected, and in the village of Nieul three-fourths of the registered voters backed the petition. Despite impressive antiwar demonstrations in Limoges on July 28 and 31, Socialist opposition collapsed in the wake of Jean Jaurès's assassination and the sense of powerlessness that emerged from the ever-quickening pace of events.[14] When peace returned four years later, the political and social environment in the countryside had undergone profound changes.

The troop call-up was greeted with a mixture of surprise, stupefaction, and resignation in the countryside.[15] When prefects wrote that "calm, sangfroid, and determination" prevailed in Creuse and Haute-Vienne and "enthusiasm" in Corrèze, and that *périgourdins* were "very dignified, very calm, very resolved," they alluded to the towns more than the surrounding countryside, where the mobilization of peasants had disrupted the agricultural economy.[16] There was, however, no initial opposition to the war effort. By late August, the prefect of Haute-Vienne noted that the "spirit" of the peas-

[14] Vallin, *Paysans rouges*, 294; Merriman, *Red City*, 244–47.

[15] Jean-Jacques Becker, *1914: Comment les Français sont entrés dans la guerre* (Paris, 1977); see also by the same author, *Les Français dans la Grande Guerre* (Paris, 1980) and *La France en guerre, 1914–1918* (Brussels, 1988). The spirit in the Corrèze countryside at the outbreak of the war is captured in Martial Chaulanges's novel *Les rouges moissons*, vol. 3 of *La terre des autres* (Limoges, 1971–75).

[16] AN F⁷ 12937, P. Creuse to MI, 2 August 1914, and PC to MI, 2 August 1914; AN F⁷ 12939, PHV to MI, 2 August 1914. A few anti-German incidents took place in Tulle, Brive, Limoges, and Périgueux. AN F⁷ 12937, PC to MI, 4 August 1914; Merriman, *Red City*, 246; ADD 1M86, PD to MI, 5 August 1914.

antry was turning sour; warning of potential unrest, he called for increased surveillance of rural areas. The situation was more placid in Dordogne: in early September, reports indicated that the rural populations of the Sarladais were neither discouraged nor despondent; nonetheless, as a precaution, the prefect exhorted mayors to do their utmost to preserve favorable public opinion.[17]

Trouble never came to the countryside. As the war dragged on, men who had not been sent to the front grew increasingly resigned.[18] Prefects worried. They reported rumors that "backward" peasants along the Haute-Vienne and Dordogne border (cantons of St-Yrieix and Lanouaille), who held the priests and bourgeois responsible for the war's continuation, planned to destroy crops they did not need for their own consumption; without food, those in charge would have to negotiate and peace would be at hand. In northern Haute-Vienne, rumors of crop burning circulated.[19] While nothing of the sort happened, these rumors suggest that the *Union sacrée* had not brought social cohesion to the countryside, and small communities remained torn by enduring suspicions and feuds. Rumors underlined the deteriorating morale among the peasantry and fueled a growing fear of social conflict. One subprefect noted that peasants would contain their dissatisfaction as long as they could sell their products for the highest price, and as long as "agitators" did not capture their attention.[20]

The peasantry's situation during the war years was difficult, though not more so than in other areas of France. Large numbers of able-bodied men had been called up in August 1914 in the midst of the harvest, leaving women, children, and those men who remained to finish the task.[21] The number of men in rural areas decreased constantly throughout the conflict. Maurice Bans, whose father spent the entire war at the front, was twelve years old when hostilities broke out. "I took care of the farm with my mother," he recalls, "and I had a sister. We didn't have a very large herd at the time, perhaps ten head of cattle. Before I went to school in the morning I looked after the animals." From early April through late October, when there was too much work on the small family farm, Maurice Bans did not attend school at all, and by the time he was thirteen he had dropped out altogether.[22] In the face of these acute shortages of labor, women assumed an ever-increasing role in agriculture; in Dordogne they replaced one-third of

[17] AN F⁷ 12939, PHV to MI, 25 and 27 August 1914; ADD 1M86, SP Sarlat to PD, 5 September 1914, and PD to MI, 7 September 1914.

[18] ADC 1M66, SP Brive to PC, 2 February 1916.

[19] ADHV 4M174, CS Limoges to PHV, 1 July 1917. Similar rumors surfaced in Cher and Allier; Claude Pennetier, *Le socialisme dans le Cher, 1851–1921* (Paris and La Charité-sur-Loire, 1982), 174–75.

[20] ADD 4Z65, SP Ribérac to PD, 15 June 1917.

[21] An estimated two-fifths of the able-bodied men employed in agriculture had been called up by the fall of 1914. *Histoire de la France rurale*, ed. Georges Duby and Armand Wallon (Paris, 1976), 4:165.

[22] Interview with Maurice Bans, Bugeat, October 7, 1983.

the men employed on the land, and in other departments the figure was far higher. Women directed one out of every three farms nationwide during the war.[23] Village life was strangely quiet in the absence of large numbers of male peasants, blacksmiths, cobblers, bakers, and other artisans; local cafés had few clients. Social and political life came to a standstill. Each family lived in fear that one day the village mayor would knock at the door bearing terrible news.

Because most farms in Limousin and Dordogne practiced polyculture, they rarely suffered from food shortages. Those peasants more oriented toward a market economy, and thus not entirely self-sufficient, could usually purchase or barter for what they needed. The short supply and high price of labor hit the farms that employed agricultural workers hard. Equally troublesome was the lack of fertilizers and the requisitioning of draft animals and cattle. Yields, already low by national standards, declined, and those who worked the land had to switch to less labor-intensive and fertilizer-dependent farming (pastures instead of wheat, or letting land lie fallow).[24]

There has been some debate concerning peasant profiteering during World War I, but Creuse, Corrèze, Haute-Vienne, and Dordogne, with their predominantly autarkic agricultural economy, found themselves on the sidelines of such a trend.[25] If anything, the war encouraged the development of self-sufficiency among small farmers. Still, peasants did market their goods, and even within the war's inflationary context they could profit from the high prices commanded by products such as livestock. Some peasants qualified for state subsidies to soldiers permanently disabled by war wounds, orphans, war widows, and needy families with heads of household mobilized at the front. The latter received an *allocation* of 1.25 francs per day paid in cash, which contributed to the growth of a cash economy (by putting money in the hands of women who had rarely controlled the purse strings in the past) and to the preservation of morale.[26] By early 1918, Dordogne authorities claimed that savings were piling up in the countryside.[27] While the finan-

[23] Dordogne figure cited in Françoise Thébaud, *La femme au temps de la guerre de 14* (Paris, 1986), 149. For national trends, *Histoire de la France rurale*, ed. Duby and Wallon, 4:166. For a portrayal of Corrèze women during the war, Chaulanges, *Les rouges moissons*.

[24] Guy Avizou, *La vie des Creusois pendant la Grande Guerre* (Guéret, 1984); ADD 7M18.

[25] Despite the rise in agricultural prices, in innovative and market-oriented Vaucluse the peasantry's 1919 income reached only prewar levels. Claude Mesliand, *Paysans du Vaucluse, 1860–1939* (Aix-en-Provence, 1989), 1:352. On peasant gains during the war, see Michel Augé-Laribé, *Le paysan français après la guerre* (Paris, 1923); Pierre Barral, *Les agrariens Français de Méline à Pisani* (Paris, 1968), 186–91.

[26] Becker, *Les Français dans la Grande Guerre*, 22–25; *La France en guerre*, 89; Yves Lequin, "1914–1916, L'opinion publique en Haute-Savoie devant la guerre," *Revue Savoisienne*, 1967, 137–39; Pierre Barral, "La paysannerie française à l'arrière," in *Les sociétés européennes et la guerre de 1914–1918*, ed. Jean-Jacques Becker and Stéphane Audoin-Rouzeau (Nanterre, 1990), 241; P. J. Flood finds Isère villagers less likely to request an allocation, and argues that by early 1917 small farmers had not benefited from the war: *France, 1914–18: Public Opinion and the War Effort* (New York, 1990), 44–46, 136.

[27] ADD 4Z65, SP Ribérac to PD, 23 February 1918.

cial situation of the peasantry as a whole is difficult to measure, those peasants most engaged in the market economy did benefit; in the postwar years they would invest their savings in their farms, consolidate their landholdings, and repay their prewar loans under favorable terms.[28]

The war had a wide-ranging impact on Limousin and Dordogne agriculture. Peasants returning home found that farm machinery and buildings needed long-awaited repairs, land needed fertilizing, and livestock herds—the primary agricultural activity in Limousin—needed to be rebuilt.[29] But they also came back with new ideas, having interacted with other peasants at the front and, as their letters show, having keenly observed agricultural practices in northern and eastern France. As Henri Peuch explains, "They tried to use what they had observed there [in the north] to try to modernize a bit. . . . This was an important contribution to change." Peuch points out that in southern Corrèze the Great War marked the switch from the swing plow (*araire*) to the all-metal wheel plow (*brabant*).[30]

The immediate postwar years witnessed an increase in the percentage of small property owners in Limousin and Dordogne. Sharecroppers benefited from this trend. Some sharecroppers enjoyed the best financial situation they had ever known: if they left their *métairie* they could cash in on their share of the livestock, and this could amount to a handsome sum because livestock prices rose by 400 percent between 1914 and 1918. Depending on the capital at their disposal, better-off sharecroppers thus were able to purchase small or, particularly in Haute-Vienne, medium-sized plots of land. Sharecropping declined by 20 percent in both Haute-Vienne and Dordogne in the postwar period, but this figure also includes those who died during the war, migrated toward the cities, or became tenant farmers.[31] The ever-increasing importance of property holders did not go unnoticed among Socialist and, as of December 1920, Communist propagandists in the countryside, and enabled them to direct the bulk of their efforts toward small and medium peasants.

The most important consequences of the war were demographic. The *monuments aux morts*, prominent in most Limousin and Dordogne villages,

---

[28] Loan payments had been frozen between 1914 and 1920. When payments resumed, they did so at 1914 levels. Annie Moulin, *Les paysans dans la société française* (Paris, 1988), 176.

[29] Bégué, *L'organisation de la démobilisation et les conditions économiques d'après-guerre* (Limoges, 1918), 10; Paul Truc, *La Haute-Vienne pendant la guerre* (Limoges, 1918).

[30] Interview with Henri Peuch, Brive, 23 August 1983; Annick Cochet, "Les paysans sur le front en 1916," *Bulletin du centre d'histoire de la France contemporaine* 3 (1982), 45–46.

[31] Sharecroppers sometimes purchased land from the owners of the *métairie* they farmed. See Sally Sokoloff, "Land Tenure and Political Tendency in Rural France: The Case of Sharecropping," *European Studies Review* 10 (1980): 357–82, and her "Communism and the French peasantry with special reference to the Allier, 1919–1939" (Ph.D. thesis, London University, 1975), 130–35. For Haute-Vienne, P. Dessalles, *Statistique agricole de la France: Annexe à l'enquête de 1929: Monographie agricole du département de la Haute-Vienne* (Limoges, 1937), 349–54; ADD 7M18, PD to MI, 8 December 1936. ADHV 7M238, PHV to ministre de l'agriculture, 10 December 1936.

offer a chilling reminder of the high war toll. The small Corrèze village of Bellechassagne (population 273 in 1911) lost twenty-two of its men during the Great War. A total of 14,043 Corrèze soldiers (4.5 percent of the 1911 population) were killed during the war; in Haute-Vienne this figure reached 15,000 (3.9 percent) and in Creuse 10,941 (4.1 percent). Perhaps more telling, close to 20 percent of the men mobilized in Creuse died at the front, and the figure was nearly identical for the Limoges military region.[32] Principally as a result of war deaths and emigration, the generation of men born between 1891 and 1900 lost close to 40 percent of its members in Limousin between 1911 and 1921 (versus 15 to 20 percent nationwide) and this loss contributed heavily to the region's demographic decline during the 1920s and 1930s.[33]

Peasants constituted the majority of war victims. Cultivators and agricultural workers accounted for close to 64 percent of the dead in the district of Ussel (Corrèze), and if this is an indication of a department-wide trend, then some 9,000 Corrèze peasants never returned to their farms.[34] The Corrèze lost 20,000 peasants—one-fifth of the total number of those engaged in agriculture in 1911—through war deaths and the emigration of widows and injured soldiers. In Dordogne, the prefect numbered peasant losses at 9,800 (2.2 percent of the 1911 population), to which one could add 404 artisans who worked in agriculture.[35] That peasants had more than paid their share of the blood tax (*l'impôt du sang*) would be a recurring theme of organizations of all kind, the PCF foremost among them, during the interwar years. Indeed, men conscripted in rural areas suffered greater losses at the front than did their urban counterparts, in part because they were more likely to serve in the infantry, where casualties were highest. The Limoges military region was the third hardest hit in France.[36]

The war's human toll had a profound impact on rural communities, large and small. Male social life only slowly recovered its vitality in the absence of key members of the adult generation. The demographic losses among

[32] Gilles Quincy, "Les Corréziens morts au cours des guerres de 1914 à 1962 et les conséquences démographiques de la Première Guerre mondiale," *Lemouzi* 93 (1985): 3–7; Avizou, *La vie des Creusois*. The figure for Haute-Vienne is an estimate.

[33] Jean-Pierre Larivière, *La population du Limousin* (Paris, 1974), 2:383–84.

[34] Nationwide estimates of the number of peasants and agricultural workers who died vary between 538,000 and 673,000. *Histoire de la France rurale*, ed. Duby and Wallon, 4:169. These figures amount to 41–51% of all French war dead, a proportion that seems low. For a critique, see Antoine Prost, *Les anciens combattants et la société française, 1914–1939* (Paris, 1977), 2:4–5. ADC exhibit, "Les Corréziens et la Guerre, 1914–1918." The figure of 9,000 peasant dead is an estimate.

[35] ADC 7M26, directeur des services agricoles de la Corrèze to PC, 1920; ADC 7M37, Office agricole départemental de la Corrèze; ADD 7M18, "Enquête sur les vides causés par la guerre parmi les agriculteurs." The prefect's figures are low in comparison with those of Corrèze, which had a smaller population.

[36] Sauvy, *Histoire économique*, 1:374. The proportion of those mobilized who died of war injuries was 16.1% nationwide but 20.2% in the military region of Orléans and 19.6% in Limoges. It was lower in urban regions: 11.9% in Marseille, 10.5% in Paris.

men in the prime of life hit families, farms, and local institutions hard. The drop in the birth rate during the war years, the human losses at the front lines, and continued out-migration, all combined to hasten the aging of Limousin's population. The war contributed to older, more isolated rural communities marked by an imbalance among age groups and between men and women.[37] Put boldly, the conflict accelerated the social destabilization of the countryside.

The war was not just a memory: the ever-present wounded were living reminders. Some 33,700 *Corréziens* (12.3 percent of the 1921 population), 26,300 *Creusois* (11.5 percent), and 36,000 inhabitants of Haute-Vienne (10.2 percent) suffered wounds during the conflict, and even if a number of the wounded joined the large outflow of emigrants from Limousin, they still constituted an important percentage of the area's adult male population during the interwar years.[38] Prefectoral authorities estimated that close to 3,000 *périgourdin* peasants had been severely maimed (*mutilé*), and 539 of those abandoned agriculture on their return home, presumably because of their injuries. In St-Barthélémy-de-Bellegarde (Dordogne), ten of eleven *mutilé* peasants joined sixty-four demobilized soldiers in returning to their farms; close to 15 percent (112) of the total population had been called to the front, and thirty-seven never returned.[39] Most of the *mutilés* who chose to remain on the land were handicapped by their wounds. Pierre Darnetz, later a Communist militant in his home village of Gros-Chastang (Corrèze), was so badly wounded at Verdun in 1916 that doctors had to solder his thigh bone to his pelvis. Despite his injury, which made him a *grand blessé de guerre*, he continued to till the soil; his son, Marcel, remembers the difficulties involved: "It was a frightful infirmity, especially for the peasant's work he did, and he was always on one leg. His wounded leg was always an extension of his body, so it was behind him when he leaned forward. . . . And he stood on one leg. It's extraordinary when I think about it again. He did a peasant's work, hoeing, weeding, all these jobs one did by hand, and he was on one leg from morning till night."[40]

Pierre Darnetz, along with thousands of other Corrèze peasants, lived day in and day out with the war's physical and psychological legacy. Those who had made it through unscratched returned home to find that members of their family and their community had paid the war's heavy price. Although

[37] Larivière, *La population du Limousin*, 2:383–90.

[38] The numbers of wounded are estimates based on the national figures in Prost, *Les anciens combattants*, 2:3, 25. I have multiplied the number of dead by 2.4 in order to propose a figure for the number of wounded.

[39] ADD 7M18; ADD 4Z137, "Enquête sur les vides causés par la guerre parmi les agriculteurs."

[40] Interview with Marcel Darnetz, Gros-Chastang, 8 August 1984. Pierre Darnetz was awarded the *médaille militaire* for his actions as an infantry corporal in the war; the medal was confiscated in April 1940, some six months after the Communist Party was banned. See ADC 58W2145.

the postwar economy in the countryside was acceptable, war veterans had much reason for bitterness. Many turned to pacifism. In Limousin and Dordogne the Socialists, and later the Communists, successfully catered to veterans' antimilitaristic sentiments, and this was one reason for their growing popularity.

Socialism and the War

Socialists had not remained inactive during the war years. In May 1915, Haute-Vienne Socialists (including four deputies) criticized the SFIO's war policies in a report addressed to the Socialist leadership in Paris. It was not the Socialist Party's role, they wrote, "to push toward war to the bitter end, to adopt a bellicose attitude and close its ears to all rumors of peace." On the contrary, all peace proposals that did not question the territorial integrity of France and Belgium should be given a favorable hearing. The Haute-Vienne Socialists' proposition fell on deaf ears, however, as the SFIO reiterated its determination to pursue the war until the final defeat of Prussian militarism and imperialism.[41]

From 1915 on, Haute-Vienne remained at the forefront of opposition to the SFIO's war policies. Led by Adrien Pressemane, the four Haute-Vienne deputies played a central role alongside Jean Longuet within the *minoritaire* movement that opposed the SFIO's unconditional support of the *Union sacrée*'s war policy, and *Le Populaire du Centre* became an unofficial organ for their views. "The campaign against the war," reported a police source in September 1915, "has no center more active than Limoges," and a little over one year later the Haute-Vienne prefect noted the growing strength of pacifist propaganda. In June 1916, some 2,000 protesters in Limoges, many of them women, clashed with police and marched in support of two soldiers who had been reprimanded by their commanding officer. In St-Junien (Haute-Vienne), seven months later, the demonstration was far more pacifist than antimilitaristic in nature, as four hundred women gathered in front of the town hall to demand peace.[42] In Corrèze, Creuse, and Dordogne, opposition to the war was far less vocal, when it existed at all.

After the Armistice, Socialists in all four departments jumped on the pacifist and antimilitaristic bandwagon. It was, of course, much easier to wield lofty rhetoric against militarism in times of peace than in the midst of the conflict, so the wartime position of the Haute-Vienne Socialists had been remarkably courageous. The little we know about the exact state of Haute-

---

[41] *Encyclopédie socialiste*, 3:513, 516–23. See also AN F⁷ 13023.

[42] AN F⁷ 13023, Report to SG, September 1915 and PHV to MI, 11 November 1916. For Limoges, AN F⁷ 13023, commissaire de police Limoges to commissaire central, 18 June 1916. For St-Junien, Becker, *Les Français dans la Grande Guerre*, 188.

Vienne public opinion during World War I indicates that the SFIO's position reflected the views of a significant part of the Haute-Vienne peasantry.

Political activity returned only gradually to the countryside. Censorship remained in effect, public meetings were banned, and demobilization proceeded so slowly that the Socialists protested. In February 1919, Haute-Vienne Socialists urged militants to circumvent the prohibition on public meetings by holding private talks with groups of young sympathizers in the countryside.[43] By March—when political activity was again legal—the four Haute-Vienne deputies were crisscrossing their districts, reestablishing Socialist sections in one village and holding public meetings in the next. Corrèze SFIO leaders, displaying a degree of dedication and vigor they had not always shown before the war, soon followed in their path.

Large numbers of Socialist militants had been mobilized during the conflict, and their return was critical to bringing Socialist groups back to life. Nine-tenths of the Socialist militants in Châteauneuf-la-Forêt (Haute-Vienne) had been called to arms; how many made it back to the village remains unknown. A Dordogne leader, Paul Bouthonnier, complained in June 1919 that rural sections had been "decimated" by the war, and hinted that political and syndical action in the countryside was just getting off the ground.[44] The activity of Socialist sections and militants grew as demobilized soldiers came home in the spring, summer, and fall of 1919. A just-returned group of poilus organized the first meeting of the Panazol (Haute-Vienne) Socialist group in early March 1919—a pattern that would recur often in the small villages of Limousin and Dordogne. Socialist sections repeatedly called for the acceleration of demobilization: some soldiers were militants (or potential militants) and, moreover, they were needed in their home communities by their families and, during the summer months, on their farms.

Local authorities worried that returning soldiers, influenced by "Socialist and Bolshevik" propaganda, embittered by four years of physical and moral suffering, and upset by the slow rate of demobilization, would be a source of unrest. By September 1919, however, the subprefect of Ribérac (Dordogne) could report reassuringly that war veterans, having returned in a subversive state of mind, had calmed down after renewing their ties to family and village life.[45] While veterans' first desire was to reconstruct their shattered lives and live in peace, they were hardly devoid of political opinions. The subprefect of Sarlat (Dordogne) noted that poilus returned with the desire to use their vote to manifest both their political independence and their resentment of parliamentarianism. His colleague in Ussel (Corrèze) correctly predicted that Socialists would do well in rural communes with the support of young,

[43] *Pop C*, 19 January 1919; ADHV 1M167, CS Limoges to PHV, 27 February 1919.
[44] *Pop C*, 5 April 1919; *Prol D*, 1 June 1919.
[45] ADD 3M80, SP Ribérac to PD, 8 September 1919 and PD to MI, 10 September 1919.

dissatisfied war veterans. The Socialists, aware of the political importance of the poilus, rarely missed an opportunity to underline everything they had done in favor of veterans, *mutilés*, and the families of the war dead.[46] Throughout 1919 and 1920 Socialists proudly noted the presence of former soldiers in their sections and among the crowds that gathered in village squares to hear their speakers. The role of veterans was crucial because veterans, held in high esteem in their communities, often occupied leadership positions in municipalities or village SFIO groups. Those who had fought in the trenches were uniquely qualified to pass the pacifist and antimilitarist message of the Socialist and later Communist left on to the peasantry.

Rebuilding the SFIO

The war's end found the Socialist Party in an advanced state of disorganization. Membership had nosedived, sections had not met in years, newspapers had suspended publication, and part of a generation had died at the front. Militants and leaders set out to reconstruct the SFIO, and they did so in record time. In the year after the Armistice, rural Corrèze and Haute-Vienne witnessed an unprecedented wave of enthusiasm for socialism. In 1919 alone, Corrèze Socialists enlisted new members at a pace that neither they nor the Communists would ever duplicate: 1,000 members had joined by August, and in December they were 2,000 strong (table 4.1). The Socialists, who had recruited far beyond their initial expectations, were both surprised and elated by this continuous flow of new militants. The growth rate slowed noticeably in 1920, although on the eve of the December Tours Congress Socialist membership in Corrèze reached 3,000—the equivalent of 109 militants per 10,000 inhabitants—making it the ninth-largest federation in the country.[47] The postwar years marked the emergence of a new generation of militants whose life experiences and concerns differed considerably from those of their turn-of-the-century predecessors.

Corrèze Socialists did equally well at the polls. They skillfully capitalized on the gradual decline of the Radical Party, which lost its grip on local power during the war years. And, like their better-established Haute-Vienne counterparts, they intelligently catered to rural constituencies, sparing few efforts in doing so. While the nationwide results of the November 1919 legislative elections proved disappointing for the SFIO, Corrèze Socialists scored a major success with close to 23 percent of the vote—a 15 percent

[46] The subprefect of Sarlat reassured his superiors that veterans would nonetheless remain within the Republican camp. ADD 3M30, SP Sarlat to PD, 4 September 1919; ADC 3M194, SP Ussel to préfet Ussel, 3 September 1919. *Pop C*, November 1919 (special issue).

[47] *TC*, 10 August and 7 September 1919, 11 January 1920; *Pop C*, 11 September 1919. In 1913 Corrèze ranked 42d nationwide in membership.

gain over 1914—and elected to office François Aussoleil, a professor of rhetoric in Brive.[48] The SFIO, in contrast, managed only small gains in Creuse and Dordogne (table 2.1 in chapter 2 shows the electoral results). In Haute-Vienne, where radicalism had been virtually eliminated from the political scene before World War I, the Socialists continued to dominate local political life with over 50 percent of the vote, and this time managed to capture all five seats in the National Assembly. Throughout Limousin and Dordogne, the legislative elections provided the incentive to hold meetings (127 in Haute-Vienne alone), create sections, and reach out to large numbers of voters.

In Dordogne, Socialists failed to profit from radicalism's loss of influence after World War I. Less active in the countryside than their Corrèze and Haute-Vienne comrades, *périgourdin* Socialists concentrated much of their activity in the towns of Périgueux and Bergerac. One militant complained, "The tenant farmers, sharecroppers, and small property owners almost never hear about socialism. They read the bourgeois newspapers, which distort our ideals. The Socialist Party is represented as an organization of looters, assassins, and wreckers."[49] The Dordogne SFIO lacked leaders familiar with rural politics, men and women who understood the need to adapt their discourse to the peasantry and spread the Socialist message to the smallest villages. The report of an anonymous writer from Nontronnais exemplifies how the leading Socialist candidates from Périgueux and Bergerac spoke to rural audiences: "During the 1919 legislative elections, some candidates came to the little *bourg* where I live. They tried to explain socialism to an ignorant crowd. They had no success whatsoever. They were very cultivated and they developed their ideas in pure, elegant French, and our poor peasants didn't learn a thing. On the other hand, the candidates of the Bloc [National—the right] spoke the language of those who worked the land and appealed to their interests; they won an enormous majority."[50]

Such elementary political mistakes cost the Socialists dearly. Although two of the six candidates on the Socialist list were peasants—Edouard Blanchou and Marcel Poujol—they played second fiddle to urban leaders in the campaign, and did little electioneering outside their home districts. There was irony in the fact that in the department where the number of peasant Socialist office seekers was highest—Dordogne—the party was most insensitive to the rural world.

Périgourdin peasants who read the local Socialist papers in 1919–20 could not fail to notice that the SFIO's attitude toward the peasantry ranged from sympathetic to downright hostile, and a close reading of those articles

---

[48] Corrèze was one of only five departments where the SFIO progressed by more than 10% over its 1914 score. Annie Kriegel, *Aux origines du communisme français, 1914–1920* (Paris, 1964) 2:333.
[49] *Prol D*, 17 August 1919.
[50] *Pop C*, 15 February 1921.

relating to rural problems worried more than a few potential rural sympathizers. How could they help but entertain doubts after reading articles
about future state-run collective farms?[51] Granted, many contributors emphasized that small property owners would not be disturbed, but their words
differed subtly from similar articles in Corrèze and Haute-Vienne. Gabriel
Bouyon, a Périgueux schoolteacher and municipal councilor, wrote that Socialists would "*leave* the land to the one who works it," whereas in Limousin essentially the same sentence read that Socialists would *give* the land to
those who cultivated it.[52] The difference in tone was significant.

A difficult problem faced Dordogne Socialist militants in 1919. How
could they capitalize on a potentially revolutionary situation (confined, in
their eyes, to Périgueux, the site of working-class agitation and a newly
elected Socialist municipality) in an overwhelmingly rural department? It
was telling that the urban militants were the ones who spilled much ink de-
bating the revolutionary character of the peasantry. One writer justified the
party's efforts by arguing that the peasantry's collaboration was critical if the
working class did not want to go hungry after it seized power. The leader of
the Dordogne sfio, Paul Bouthonnier, adopted a moralistic tone when he
proposed that the "proletariat of the fields" would live in eternal shame if it
merely profited from the revolution without having participated in it.[53] Others wanted nothing whatever to do with the peasants. In March 1920, a
working-class militant asserted that the party's primary task was to intensify
its propaganda efforts among the urban working class, not the "petit bourgeois" peasantry. To claim that the revolution would be impossible without
the cooperation of the peasants amounted to saying that there would be no
revolution at all. The same militant, who clearly was no friend of the peasants, had earlier blamed the sfio's numerical weakness on Dordogne's rural
character.[54] Even those urban militants who favored propaganda efforts in
the countryside often demonstrated a profound ignorance of things rural.
Because peasants "lived in the midst of nature," wrote one well-intentioned
leader, "and had the opportunity to reflect in calm, pastoral settings, they
could consider and accept [Socialist ideas] more easily than factory workers, whose attention is monopolized by the machine of which they are the
slaves."[55] Such a romanticized understanding of rural politics did not serve
Dordogne Socialists well.

After the defeat of the 1920 railroad strikes in Périgueux, Socialist militants increasingly turned their attention to the countryside. But the tension
between urban and rural militants would last well into the Communist
Party's first years. In mid-1922, Paul Bouthonnier, then secretary of the Dor-

[51] *Justice* (Bergerac), 15 March 1919.
[52] *Prol D*, 16 November 1919.
[53] *Prol D*, 8 June 1919, 15 February 1920, and 11 July 1920.
[54] *Prol D*, 13 June 1920 and 29 February 1920.
[55] *Prol D*, 15 February 1920.

dogne Communist Federation, complained that too much emphasis was being placed on rural propaganda. Peasants, he claimed, were not revolutionary; for the forthcoming revolution (*le grand soir*), one could count only on the working class of the towns.[56]

Rural Socialism

Rural support was crucial to the development of socialism in Limousin and Périgord, and Dordogne leaders, with their *ouvriériste* leanings, clearly were on the wrong track. Their neighbors in Corrèze and Haute-Vienne, on the other hand, made a sustained, concerted effort to engage the rural world, and developed a coherent peasant policy, aptly summarized by the slogan (which the Communists lost no time in appropriating) *La terre à celui qui la travaille* (land to the one who works it). A small piece of property, militants argued, was to a peasant what a hammer was to a worker. The peasant's "small plot of land . . . is his tool," wrote *Le Populaire du Centre*. "It is clearly his and no one dreams of taking it away from him." [57] Socialists were at pains to reassure peasants that they would defend small property owners against capitalism, the state, and large landowners.

Limousin Socialists did not limit themselves to defending the smallholding peasantry; they also preached the virtues of association and, to a lesser extent, collectivization. Their emphasis on these themes, however, dwindled over time. Militants soon realized that articles and speeches describing the "iron laws of capitalism," which condemned small property holders to the dustbins of history, might be ideologically correct but were politically counterproductive. Socialists limited themselves to vague discussions of "developing collective property," while making it clear that property would not be collectivized at the expense of small peasants. They also sang the benefits of association that favored the production "of the greatest number of goods with the least effort." Short-term policies in defense of small property holders caught the peasantry's attention, and so did talk of redistributing large properties to those who needed land.[58] When militants from the small village of Bujaleuf (Haute-Vienne) wrote that "we want . . . to make everyone a *propriétaire* and ensure the well-being of the poor," they were expressing the opinion of a large majority of Socialists in the countryside who often equated social justice with the extension of private property to all.[59]

Socialist propaganda seduced large numbers of Limousin peasants in the

[56] ADD 4M192, CS Périgueux, 28 July 1922.

[57] *Pop C*, 16 September 1919.

[58] *Pop C*, 1 October 1919; *TC*, 28 September 1919. The Haute-Vienne Socialist leader, Adrien Pressemane, was reluctant to parcel out large properties to peasants. *Le Congrès de Tours* (Paris, 1980), 164.

[59] *Pop C*, 4 December 1919.

years after the Great War. One Corrèze leader, Jean Roumajon, claimed that peasants accounted for 75 percent of the Party's 2,000 militants in December 1919. Local militants proudly pointed out that rural Corrèze was among those departments where Socialist recruitment was strongest. In Dordogne, Socialists believed smallholders formed the great majority of the party's members outside Périgueux and Bergerac.[60] The sfio's electoral backing in the countryside was equally impressive. The Socialist deputy of Haute-Vienne, Jean Parvy, gauged that over 60 percent of his party's 1919 votes came from smallholding peasants, tenant farmers, sharecroppers, and agricultural workers; and in neighboring Corrèze, Jean Roumajon estimated the proportion at 80 percent.[61] Socialist leaders, however, did not detect the key importance of other rural groups—notably artisans and shopkeepers—within their electorate.

Unlike their counterparts in Dordogne, most Limousin Socialist militants saw the peasantry not as a mere appendage to the working class but as a decisive factor in the revolutionary movement. The Corrèze's Jean Roumajon expressed it well at the Congrès de Tours when he explained why his overwhelmingly peasant federation had voted unanimously in favor of joining the Third International: ". . . if it's a question of revolutionary talk, the peasant is perhaps behind certain elements from the towns, but if it's a question of revolutionary consciousness, of devotion to the Party, we say that the true apostles of socialism are over there, in the depths of the countryside . . . these comrades are the true revolutionaries, because they are anticapitalists and antimilitarists; they were anticlerical in the past, and they still are today; they are also antiparliamentarian."[62] While extolling the revolutionary nature of Corrèze peasants, Roumajon also put his finger on some of their principal political beliefs, two of which—anticapitalism and antimilitarism—had played an essential role in bringing peasants to socialism.

The first of their positions, which Roumajon described a bit strongly as "anticapitalism," was resistance to market forces. A program that promised to "consolidate small property and deliver it from all the parasites that feed on it" clearly attracted smallholders.[63] To those afraid of losing their meager landholdings, the Socialists promised aid and even land when they redistributed large holdings. To sharecroppers they promised major changes in the contracts that bound them to landowners. To all those who worked the land the party promised a wide range of reforms, ranging from the abolition of indirect taxation to lower prices for fertilizers and other essential goods. The Socialists presented a simplistic worldview to the peasantry in which the

---

[60] *TC*, 18 January 1920, 28 September 1919; *Prol D*, 21 November 1920.

[61] *VP*, 28 February 1920; *TC*, 18 January 1920. These figures are in keeping with the estimates of the agricultural composition of the 1928 Corrèze Communist vote (70%) presented in chapter 2.

[62] *Le Congrès de Tours*, 247.

[63] *Pop C*, 16 September 1919.

capitalist class, which was responsible for the war and expected the peasants to pay for it, was depicted as the principal enemy of peasants and their land.

The second factor was the antimilitaristic climate that prevailed among the peasantry. The Socialists successfully appealed to such sentiments, widespread among veterans, by claiming that those who had paid for the war in blood were also about to pay for it through taxes. The local SFIO harped on this theme in countless articles and speeches and did its best to convince peasants that their relative prosperity would soon be shattered by a huge rise in taxes. The bourgeois "will make you sweat to pay the enormous costs of the war," read one article, and "he'll lock up your children again for three to five years in his barracks, and he'll then get them killed waging a war somewhere."[64] After the 1919 elections, Socialist voters from Ambazac (Haute-Vienne) explained that "we had to avenge our dead . . . who fell in the horrible slaughter organized by capital, the Church, and militarism."[65] This opinion was shared by many rural inhabitants who cast their ballots for the SFIO.

There was, however, no direct relationship between the Great War and Socialist voting in 1919. Support for the SFIO proved unrelated to the casualty rates: the party's performance did not improve among villages that had suffered most from the war. An increase in the commune-to-commune percentage of war dead (which ranged from 0 to 9 percent of the 1911 population) had no effect on either Socialist, Radical, or conservative voting. Political allegiances were not associated with war losses at the village level. In this sense, the war was not directly responsible for the rise of the socialist movement in rural areas, but it certainly gave birth to a political and social climate favorable to socialism's rise.[66]

The Russian Revolution also played a part in the peasantry's radicalization. Peasants knew little about the actual turn of events in Russia. The local Socialist press published few instructive articles: The *Prolétaire de la Dordogne* left its readers in the dark until September 1920, when it cited the Bolshevik agrarian program for the first time.[67] The absence of reliable information did not prevent active Socialist sections from voting resolutions in support of the Russian Revolution, or party speakers from addressing the issue with rural audiences. In April 1919 the militants of St-Sulpice-Laurière (Haute-Vienne) ended their meeting to the cry of, "Long live socialism! Long live the soviets of Russia!" and marched out singing the "International."[68] Even if the exact mechanics of the revolutionary process lacked clarity, the

---

[64] *Pop C*, 23 October 1919. In their *profession de foi* for the 1919 elections, Haute-Vienne Socialists wrote that one of the major issues was "who would pay for the cost of the war." See ADHV 3M164.

[65] *Pop C*, 18 November 1919.

[66] See Parti Socialiste 1919 in Table 5.1.

[67] *Prol D*, 5 September 1920.

[68] *Pop C*, 5 April 1919.

Russian Revolution had, in the eyes of the peasantry, brought peace and redistributed land to those who worked it, and was worthy of support on these grounds alone.

There had been a revolution of sorts closer to home as well. Beginning in late June 1917, French military authorities confined rebellious Russian soldiers, who had been withdrawn from the front lines in Champagne, to an isolated army camp at La Courtine (Creuse), in the heart of the Millevaches plateau. Some 9,600 Russian troops mutinied in July 1917 and elected a soviet. Loyal Russian troops, backed by French ones, occupied the camp in mid-September of that year, causing numerous casualties. Covered up by military authorities, the Courtine insurrection was of little local political consequence; only in the nearby village of Tarnac does an oral memory of the event survive: here a carpenter, working in the seclusion of the woods, had told his young son of the revolt and indicated that this was the path to follow.[69] It was rumored that mutinous soldiers frequented the *auberges* in nearby villages and spread Bolshevik propaganda, but in view of the language barrier and the French Army's surveillance of the camp, this cannot have been a large-scale effort. Local Communists never publicly referred to the Courtine mutiny during the interwar years. Nor did the few Russian soldiers rumored to have married and settled in the region manifest any political activity.

Finally, a sense of social justice clearly imbued Socialist voters and militants. To join the fight against *les gros* was also to ensure greater equality for those who worked the land. Precisely because Limousin and Dordogne had few large landowners, the inequalities that did exist were all the more flagrant. And the absence of a large group of landed proprietors made it necessary to identify an enemy on the outside: the big capitalists who produced fertilizers and machinery, the middlemen who bought and sold agricultural produce, the state that taxed the peasants and gave them little in return. The search for an egalitarian society also dovetailed with a form of economic defensiveness. The ideal of the Socialist peasants was a regulated economy where price controls would guarantee that they could purchase goods cheaply and sell their own products at a high fixed price. They asked that their small plots of land be defended at all costs, and they entertained hopes of enlarging them at the expense of better-off neighbors. Small landholders whose farms were only marginally profitable sought protection from the free

[69] Interview with René Monzac, 3 August 1984. Pierre Poitevin estimates that 11 people were killed and 49 wounded, but others, citing witnesses who saw the army ship in lime to bury the dead, have proposed figures ranging from 200 to 600 mutinous troops killed. Poitevin, *Ce que la censure nous a caché pendant la guerre: Une bataille au centre de la France: La révolte des armées russes au camp de La Courtine* (Limoges, 1934) and *La mutinerie de La Courtine: Les régiments russes révoltés en 1917 au centre de la France* (Paris, 1938); Georges Dauger and Daniel Dayen, *Histoire du Limousin contemporain* (Limoges, 1988), 128–29; Laurent-Yves Giloux, "Le corps expéditionnaire russe en France pendant la Première Guerre mondiale et la mutinerie au camp de La Courtine," *MSSNAC* 42 (1984): 142–55.

market. And in the minds of many of them, the Socialists, and as of late 1920 the Communists, best represented this mixture of economic immobility and social justice that was theirs.

The Communist Party successfully catered to this *mentalité* throughout the 1920s and 1930s. Yet conditions had changed. The immediate postwar years had been a time of considerable social ferment. By the mid-1920s, however, many of the factors that had contributed to the peasantry's postwar radicalization had receded. The Communists found themselves appealing to peasants whose interest in radical social change had declined, and who were now preoccupied with shoring up their increasingly precarious material situation.

The Tours Congress and the Countryside

The Eighteenth Congress of the SFIO, held at Tours in December 1920, gave birth to the PCF, and had lasting consequences on the French political landscape. Some historians have seen the PCF as the result of important political tensions within the SFIO, while others have argued that the Communist Party's foundation did not correspond to a division between left and right, but was the product of historical circumstances. For Annie Kriegel, the Tours split took place after the Socialist Party's poor showing at the polls in 1919 and the defeat of the spring 1920 strike movement, but before the consequences of the Soviet setback in Poland brought an end to any hope of an imminent worldwide revolution.[70]

Delegates from Limousin and Périgord did not all share the same vision of the Socialist Party's future. Those from Corrèze and Dordogne cast their ballots in favor of joining the Third International, and the majority of their counterparts in Creuse, despite an active opposition, also supported the motion. Haute-Vienne militants swam against the tide: the majority found Moscow's twenty-one conditions unacceptable. The chain of events leading up to the split, as well as the exact breakdown between opponents and proponents of the Third International, had profound consequences on the development of communism. Where those in favor of the Third International held the upper hand (Corrèze, Dordogne), the Communists remained firmly entrenched throughout the interwar years.

The Third International found its strongest and most consistent supporters in Dordogne. The policy of the *périgourdin* leadership never wavered: the time had come to break with the reformism of the past and join forces with

[70] Kriegel, *Aux origines*; Robert Wohl, *French Communism in the Making, 1914–1924* (Stanford, 1966); Tony Judt, *La reconstruction du Parti socialiste, 1921–1926* (Paris, 1976), 3–12; Jean-Louis Robert, "Les origines du P.C.F.," in Roger Bourderon et al., *Le PCF étapes et problèmes, 1920–1972* (Paris, 1981), 13–39.

the Russian Revolution.[71] Dordogne Socialists had no kind words for those who wanted to reconstruct a new International, or who entertained doubts concerning the Russian Revolution. Even after the defeat of the May 1920 railroad strikes in Périgueux cooled their revolutionary euphoria, Dordogne leaders remained staunchly committed to their policy.

The Haute-Vienne, led by its five Socialist deputies, was a stronghold of opposition to the Cachin-Frossard movement to join the Third International. Adrien Pressemane and Jean Parvy, both well-seasoned leaders, believed the situation was far from revolutionary and resolutely opposed the twenty-one conditions. Pressemane's political ideas were irreconcilable with the Leninist concept of revolution; he was hostile to the dictatorship of the proletariat and the subordination of trade unions to the Communist Party. Having himself been a subject of Moscow's condemnation, he had little sympathy for the demand that Longuet and his friends be excluded from the new party. In early December 1920 he joined Léon Blum, Paul-Boncour, and others in forming the Comité de Résistance Socialiste, which led the opposition to the Third International.[72]

Corrèze militants shared some of their Haute-Vienne neighbors' doubts. After many months of hesitation, Corrèze Socialists, who had voted to "reconstruct" the International at the Congress of Strasbourg in February 1920, decided to back the Cachin-Frossard motion at their federal congress in October 1920.[73] With the backing of Ludovic Oscar Frossard, the future secretary general of the Communist Party, they expressed reservations to three of Moscow's twenty-one conditions: they asked in particular that Jean Longuet and his group be allowed to remain in the party, and noted that the subordination of trade unions to the party could not work in France.[74]

These choices did not reflect any clear-cut division between "reformists" and "revolutionaries," nor were they a consequence of stronger antimilitaristic or pro-Russian sentiments. The geography of the Tours split did not consistently correspond to a division between rural and urban areas. Rather, the deciding factor was the local Socialist leadership, which played a central role in guiding militants in their choices. Militants had few sources of information at their disposal to help them make up their minds. A reading of the

[71] *Prol D,* 1 June 1919.

[72] Pierre Cousteix, "Le Congrès de Tours vécu par une fédération socialiste: La Haute-Vienne," *Cahiers et revue de l'OURS* 121 (1981): 76–93; *Pop C,* 17 September and 21 October 1920; Wohl, *French Communism,* 182. Haute-Vienne delegates cast 61% of their votes at Tours for the *motion Pressemane,* which opposed the Third International.

[73] *TC,* 10 and 31 October 1920, 7 November 1920; Parti Socialiste, *17ᵉ congrès national tenu à Strasbourg, 25–29 Février 1920* (Paris, 1920), viiff. For an alternative explanation see Dauger and Dayen, *Histoire du Limousin,* 136–37.

[74] The situation in Creuse was more confused. The campaign to join the Third International was led by some of the old Guesdist militants (Julien Tixier, Jean Dufour), while some of the younger leaders—including at least three of the four candidates on the Socialist list in 1919—who often had more political clout, were opposed.

regional Socialist press kept them abreast of debates concerning proposed changes in the party's organization. They also received the visits of local leaders who passed through villages on speaking tours, and it was only natural to ask for their advice. In the end, however, Lenin's twenty-one conditions failed to elicit the kind of grass-roots interest historians have ascribed to them in retrospect. Militants focused their attention on issues that had an impact on their daily lives.

Thus the debate over the Third International in Limousin and Périgord was restricted to a small minority of Party activists. In principle, Socialist sections were to meet in the fall of 1920 to decide whether or not to join the new International. They also had to elect delegates for the departmental Socialist congresses where Moscow's twenty-one conditions would be put to a vote. There is little record, however, of any internal debate within sections before these federal congresses were held. Only three Socialist sections in both Dordogne and Haute-Vienne thought the matter important enough to publish their decision in the Party daily, and in Corrèze and Creuse no sections made their views public.[75] How many sections discussed the Cachin-Frossard motion, even in a cursory manner, and how many militants actually voted on the issue is open to question. Most Haute-Vienne delegates attended their federal congress without first having consulted the base, and the decision-making process bypassed party members. The future Haute-Vienne Communist leader Joseph Lasvergnas attributed this situation to the leadership's fear that peasants would support the twenty-one conditions.[76]

The period preceding the Tours Congress was one of great confusion for leaders and militants alike. The Socialist section of St-Priest-sous-Aixe (Haute-Vienne) thought (erroneously) that Moscow's twenty-one conditions were but a new edition of those for joining the Second International.[77] Many of the men who voted to join the Third International had only the vaguest knowledge of the strings attached. Some delegates left their villages with little indication from their fellow section members as to how they should cast their ballots. Smaller sections, unable to send a delegate to their federal congress, entrusted their mandates to local Socialist leaders, and a sizable minority were not represented at all.[78] To most militants, the debate was anything but crystal clear, and they looked to their leadership for advice and guidance.

In early 1921, sections met and ratified the choices their delegates had made. In the poor, isolated village of Murat (Corrèze), militants went out of their way to approve their delegate's vote at the federal congress and enthusiastically ended their meeting to the cry of "Long live the Third Interna-

---

[75] *Pop C*, 30 and 31 October 1920; *Prol D*, 14, 21 and 28 November 1920. Two of the Dordogne sections were peasant sections.
[76] *Le Congrès de Tours*, 322.
[77] *Pop C*, 8 October 1920.
[78] Thirty-five of Corrèze's 85 sections failed to send delegates to the Federal Congress.

tional!"[79] During late December 1920 and the first months 1921 a total of six-teen Corrèze sections and six Dordogne groups endorsed the decisions of their federations to join the new International. But these gestures of support were made after the important votes had been cast, and they only underlined the tendency of sections to follow the decisions of the local leadership. This was clearest in Dordogne and Corrèze, where both leaders and the base unani-mously supported the Third International. In Haute-Vienne, the division be-tween opponents and supporters of the new International corresponded to the differing allegiances of grass-roots Socialist leaders. The few Haute-Vienne backers of the Cachin-Frossard motion came exclusively from four cantons (Eymoutiers, Ambazac, St-Junien, and St-Mathieu) where the party leaders, who were also elected members of the Conseil Général, had pronounced themselves in favor of joining. Short-term tactical reasons, not larger social concerns, separated Jules Fraisseix and Jean Texier, two Haute-Vienne *con-seillers généraux* who supported the Cachin-Frossard motion, from Léon Be-toulle and Adrien Pressemane. Only later did major ideological differences take root.

Did young, rural, and peasant militants display greater enthusiasm for the new International, as Kriegel and others have suggested? In Haute-Vienne, the urban/rural division was not a sure guide to the party's future split. Haute-Vienne proponents of the Cachin-Frossard motion captured the sup-port of both militants in St-Junien and rural Socialists in the Monts d'Am-bazac, the Montagne (canton of Eymoutiers), and alongside the Dordogne border. Their opponents did well in Limoges, as well as in most of the countryside. No fundamental differences existed between the ten Haute-Vienne sections that joined the new Communist Party and the fifty-one sec-tions that remained in the old SFIO.

In Creuse, the majority of rural sections voted to join the Third Interna-tional, while militants from the department's principal industrial town, Aubusson, voted nay. When the breakup was formalized in the early weeks of 1921, however, at least seven rural sections, along with Aubusson and La Souterraine, remained loyal to the old Socialist Party. Still, Creuse Socialists followed the national pattern, in which small towns and villages joined the Communist Party and larger towns remained faithful to the SFIO.[80]

A Creuse delegate at the Tours Congress took these voting patterns to mean that "peasants and smallholders are . . . more revolutionary than in-dustrial [workers]."[81] Even the *ouvriériste* Dordogne leader, Marcel Dela-grange, was inclined to think so: "While workers are struggling to recover from the shock they suffered last May [in the railroad strikes in Périgueux], the peasants, in contrast, are preparing for a merciless struggle. Instinctively

[79] *TC*, 21 November 1920.
[80] *Le Congrès de Tours*, 249; *Pop C*, 26 and 29 January 1921. On national patterns, see Tony Judt, *Marxism and the French Left* (Oxford, 1986), 126.
[81] *Le Congrès de Tours*, 249.

attracted by the great Russian Revolution, aware of how they have been mis-led during and after the war, the rural masses, grouped in Socialist sections, have enthusiastically joined the Third International." [82]

This was quite a volte-face for one of the principal leaders of a Socialist federation that to date had been characterized by its hostility to rural mat-ters. If Dordogne peasants who joined the Third International en masse were not an anomaly but part of a nationwide trend, they deserved attention. Not all representatives of rural departments, however, believed that peasant sup-porters of the Cachin-Frossard motion were more revolutionary than other social groups, or had a clear sense of their objectives. One Creuse delegate thought not, and he made his opinion clear in no uncertain terms: it is an "illusion," he exclaimed, "to say that Creuse peasants are Communists. . . . The peasants are not yet familiar with Communist ideas." [83]

Rural grass-roots enthusiasm for the Third International was weaker than Creuse and Corrèze leaders claimed. The impetus to join did not originate from the Socialist base, but was intelligently engineered by local leaders who knew how to play up to the demands and needs of their militants. Joining the Third International was thus presented as a way of showing sympathy for the Russian Revolution, condemning the capitalist war, and expressing one's desire to break with the Socialist Party's past and its parliamentary em-phasis. This formulation reflected the peasants' actual state of mind, but the peasantry's radicalization did not necessarily lead to sympathy for Moscow's twenty-one conditions, as the case of Haute-Vienne clearly demonstrates: peasants in this department who remained in the old Socialist Party were just as "revolutionary" as their Corrèze counterparts who chose the Third International.

The Communist Party's Heritage

Even where Socialists had unanimously backed the Third International, the new Communist Party could not keep all the old Socialist members and leaders within its ranks. Militants, who had not always participated in the decision-making process, voted with their feet and abandoned the young Communist Party in droves. By late July 1922, the Corrèze Communists re-tained only 53 percent of the SFIO's December 1920 membership (a loss of 1,400 militants) and in Dordogne this figure dropped to 47 percent (a de-cline of 1,000 members). These considerable losses underscore how tentative the choices at Tours were, and how fragile they were in the face of a changed political situation and the cold reality of the Socialist Party's scission.

The militants' desertions disrupted the activity of Communist sections. In

[82] *Prol D*, 9 January 1921.
[83] *Le Congrès de Tours*, 340.

Viam (Corrèze), the dissident treasurer ran off with the accounting books, much to the chagrin of the remaining membership. The militants of Séran-don (Corrèze), deeply affected by the defection of key militants from "our dear and large family," nonetheless hoped that these stray sheep would re-turn home once the Communist Party had established a charter guaranteeing the rights of minorities. Smaller sections, such as that of Lafage-sur-Sombre (also Corrèze), did not survive the split, and village leaders acknowledged the damage, complaining that "the split has, as everywhere, caused disarray among our comrades. Some have left, discouraged." [84] The departure of one or two militants was sometimes enough to bring a section's activity to a com-plete standstill.

The leadership's defections were particularly marked in Corrèze. Jean Roumajon, who, despite deeply held reservations, had spoken at Tours in fa-vor of the Third International, left the new party in February 1921, and he was joined by Charles Spinasse, Frédéric Malaure, the secretary of the Cor-rèze SFIO, and Jules Vaysse, the administrator of *Le Travailleur de la Cor-rèze*. The fledgling Communist Party lost some of its most prominent lead-ers—Roumajon and Malaure had been on the Socialist list for the 1919 elections, and Spinasse, a first-rate speaker, had a solid grass-roots base—but this loss turned out to be less of a handicap than the faithful initially feared. The "dissidents" managed to take only a few Socialist sections with them, and over the next decade they would have to rebuild the SFIO on a largely new organizational, electoral, and political base.

The road to communism had not been straight. The Great War had pro-foundly altered the social and political fabric, and in doing so had provided an unexpected opening for Socialists. Four years of political vacuum, during which no elections were held and political activity remained dormant, had realigned local politics, and the Socialists, being less involved in the govern-ing structure, understood this situation earlier than most. The war radical-ized and reinvigorated rural Socialists, but radicalization did not systemati-cally lead to communism. In Haute-Vienne, where the Socialists benefited from a long-standing presence and a nationally known leadership, Socialists remained faithful to what Léon Blum had movingly called *la vieille maison*. If national and international contingencies were largely responsible for the Tours split, however, they played little part in the survival of the Commu-nist Party and its strong presence in parts of Limousin and Dordogne. The Communists quickly learned the lessons of the Socialist Party's postwar ac-complishments. They capitalized on the antimilitaristic and anticapitalistic discourse that was at the root of the SFIO's postwar success, and they ac-tively pursued propaganda efforts among rural constituencies. Although the young PCF survived the defections of militants and leaders, it soon faced

[84] *TC*, 30 January and 29 May 1921; *Prol C*, 24 February 1924.

more immediate and intractable difficulties. The sociopolitical crisis that gave rise to postwar interest in leftist politics declined after 1920. Not until the Depression would such an opportunity again present itself.

The new Communist Party had inherited the old SFIO's geography of support, and in Corrèze the majority of Communist voters had previously voted for the SFIO. How can we explain this continuity? In Corrèze and Dordogne, most of the old Socialist Party leaders went over to the newly founded PCF and brought with them the SFIO's organizational infrastructure. But this explanation is less compelling in the other two Limousin departments. In Haute-Vienne, the Communists preserved the better part of the Socialists' geographical heritage, despite the fact that the Socialists had left the Tours Congress along with the majority of their militants and the party apparatus.

Flanked by a rival on the left, the Socialists had great difficulty reaping the heritage of the postwar crisis, even in Haute-Vienne, where they were strong and adopted a leftist discourse. During the interwar years the Socialists would rebuild the SFIO on a largely new geographical and electoral basis, both urban and rural. The Communists, on the other hand, while claiming to break with the past, nonetheless would pursue some of the policies and tactics that had contributed heavily to the successes of the old Socialist Party. Voters perceived the Communists as continuators of the SFIO, and the presence of former Socialist militants within the new Communist Party helped perpetuate the "confusion" between the two parties. In the mental representation of the electorate, pre-Tours socialism and communism shared traits that distinguished them from other political parties; hence their common territorial stability. Seen in this light, the history of socialism before December 1920 provides more than traditional background material; it is the foundation on which rural communism's success was built during and after the interwar years.

5 Rural Society and Communism

Even to contemporary observers, rural communism was a contradiction in terms. A working-class party that, it was thought, backed collectivism and the Soviet example yet successfully appealed to "conservative" property-owning peasants made little sense. This is why tradition, be it red or republican, was often invoked to explain the Party's baffling presence in parts of the countryside. Had the PCF's policy been so sectarian and ill adapted, however, and had the Communists imposed their program from the top down, rural communism would have been a dismal failure. But the Communists proved responsive to pressures and demands from below. Their enduring implantation owed much to the judiciously balanced program they presented to rural inhabitants.

In the aftermath of the Great War, sectors of rural society found in the Communist Party an outlet to express their views. In the villages of Limousin and Dordogne, the Russian Revolution captured the imagination because it symbolized the victory of *les petits* against *les gros* (the rich). The Revolution was perceived as bringing peace and ushering in a new era of social justice. The concern for peace after the butchery of World War I also brought strong antimilitaristic sentiments to the countryside. The Communists adroitly proclaimed the dual theme of the Russian Revolution and antimilitarism as they crisscrossed the hinterlands in search of new militants, sympathizers, and voters. Thanks to these persistent campaigns, peasants, artisans, and others listened to what PCF speakers had to say on agricultural matters. The Communists successfully portrayed themselves as the best defenders of small property owners. They remained keenly attentive to the views of the base, which was often torn between sympathy for the Russian Revolution, a commitment to social justice, a deeply ingrained economic defensiveness, and a strong sense of individualism. From such contradictory elements the Communists forged a cohesive worldview.

A Founding Myth: the Russian Revolution

In the fall of 1921 the Communist Party (with the Soviet government's green light) launched a nationwide campaign to help the Russian regime cope with a massive famine. "Peasant Communists," wrote Renaud Jean, the Party's leading spokesman on peasant matters, "your duty is simple. Go from farm to farm with a pack on your back. Tell your comrades of the plow that children are dying in Russia. You will sometimes be poorly received. But usually you will be understood, and a generous shovelful [of wheat, rye, etc.] will make your load heavier." In Haute-Vienne the *camarades* were asked to donate one day's salary to save Russian children, and were reminded that a "great people is suffering at this time, for you, for your total emancipation."[1]

Though the campaign in favor of the Russian people was anything but a success at the national level and received mixed results in Limousin and Dordogne, the rural inhabitants of two areas of PCF strength in Corrèze, the cantons of Seilhac and especially Haute-Corrèze, demonstrated their sympathy in large numbers. Communists in the red canton of Bugeat printed a poster addressed to "people with a heart," painting a grim picture of the Russian situation: the country lacked bread, clothing, tools, and pharmaceuticals; factories stood idle and the inhabitants were dying of "misery, sickness, and cold." It was up to some of the poorest inhabitants of Limousin to

> save the Russians, guilty only of wanting to establish a regime of justice and liberty. Is this a crime for us French, sons of the Revolution of 1789?
> Let us send the Russians all the material help we can possibly give. Let us levy the tithe not only on the superfluous but also on what we need. Wheat, canned goods, pasta, rice, chocolate, clothing, shoes, thread, needles, wool . . . the smallest everyday objects will be gratefully received. Peasant, give us your bushel of wheat![2]

The rural inhabitants of the poor highlands responded, at times generously, to this call for solidarity. In the village of Sornac, the peasant members of the Communist cell decided to send 300 kilograms of rye to their "Russian comrades." The cell of Sérandon congratulated Jean Laussine, father of a large family, who donated 5 francs.[3] High on the Millevaches plateau, 15 percent of Toy-Viam's inhabitants (population 225 in 1921) participated

---

[1] *VP*, 29 July 1922; ADHV 1M168; see also *TT*, July–August 1921. On an international level, much of the humanitarian aid for Russia was supplied by the American Relief Administration.

[2] 1922 poster, Bibliothèque Nationale, packet 1497.

[3] *PCTC*, 19 and 26 February 1922.

in the gift-giving effort; solidarity was equally important in nearby villages: 102 of Tarnac's residents (close to 8 percent of the population) responded to the Communist Party's call, and proportions were similar in bordering Bugeat (6.7 percent) and Viam (7 percent). Tarnac's Communist municipality joined in the effort by pledging 200 francs to the Comité de Secours aux Russes Affamés.[4]

The majority of all donations were monetary; in Tarnac they averaged over 4 francs per person. People who lived in isolated hamlets, however, proved less inclined to give a few francs than the more socially diverse inhabitants of the village center. Instead, the overwhelmingly peasant population of the hamlets contributed bundles of used clothing, shoes, sheets, school supplies, and grain sacks. Peasants also donated rye and, exceptionally (for the soil in Haute-Corrèze was poor), wheat. These contributions in kind, often of modest proportions (one decaliter of rye, for example), were important for, as one old militant told me, "properties were small and, you know, rye is bread. We only ate rye bread at the time. White bread was on Sundays."[5] Some peasants displayed more generosity than others: in Toy-Viam, P. Poulet led the way by donating four *boisseaux* (decaliters) of rye, one sack to store grain, one pair of shoes, and some used clothes; the largest contribution on record, one hectoliter of rye, was made by Léger Peyrot of Bugeat.

The gestures of support by the villagers of the Millevaches plateau were touching and politically revealing. Of course, we should not confuse a form of solidarity with deep roots in peasant culture (*l'entraide paysanne*) with an ideological conversion, but it is clear that these contributions were not devoid of political significance. Party members and sympathizers accounted for perhaps half the gift givers, and oral sources indicate that most other donations came from the left. More than simple charity was involved: there is no record of any donations to the Russian people in nearby villages dominated by conservatives and Radicals.

The Communist party has undertaken countless solidarity campaigns in the many years since the campaign to help the Russian people, but when I asked Jean Lalanne, born and raised in Sornac and twenty-seven years old in 1921, whether people in his home village had been struck by the Russian Revolution, the first thing that came to his mind was the charity drive for Russia. "Yes," he answered, "many people collected wheat and other things to send there [to Russia]. There was a large movement [in favor of the Russian Revolution]."[6] Clearly, this was not just another Party fund-raising

---

[4] ADC 2 O Tarnac 3, February 1922 and lists of donators in *PCTC*, 26 March; 2, 9 and 23 April; 7 and 21 May; and 4 June 1922. Money, clothes and food were also gathered in the villages of Lagraulière, Chanteix, and St-Salvadour in the hills north of Tulle.

[5] Interview with Marcelle Etienne, Toy-Viam, 2 July 1984.

[6] Interview with Jean Lalanne, Mestes, 7 October 1983.

scheme: in Sornac and elsewhere it corresponded to a wave of sympathy and solidarity with the Bolshevik Revolution. On the bleak and forlorn Mille-vaches plateau, and elsewhere in Corrèze, the gift-giving campaigns helped cement new forms of solidarity and militancy that would anchor Communist successes. These campaigns also gave the peasants a chance to extend concrete support to a revolution of which they had only a mythic image. Rural inhabitants acquired a sense of participating in a worldwide enterprise at a time when their physical isolation became increasingly difficult to bear, and when short-term prospects of radical social change in France had vanished.

In future years, the absence of fund-raising campaigns made sympathy for the Russian Revolution far more difficult to measure. The Communist Party could hardly cite the agricultural achievements of the Revolution as an example to Limousin peasants while at the same time asking them to reach into their pockets for a donation to the struggling Russian peasants. Even in 1921–22, the huge scale of the Russian famine (5 million dead) was never discussed. The utopian descriptions of the Soviet countryside that began to appear regularly in the regional Communist press in the mid-1920s ruled out any solidarity drives in the Limousin countryside.

The Russian Revolution's positive image in the postwar period was a product of the rural world's longing for peace and social justice in the aftermath of the Great War. Few militants and sympathizers knew much about events in Russia; what struck them—and younger people who had not directly experienced the war as well—was that the Russian Revolution had brought peace, and few things were more important in a country that had been ravaged by war. "Well, I came to the Communist Party," Robert Bos explained, "because I was born just before the First World War [in 1911], and in my family everyone was called up, and when the October Revolution took place, the first thing Lenin did was to offer peace to the world. . . . The soldiers brought the news back right away, right away. And I think the news spread like an oil stain. We were fighting not for the people but for capitalism. We spoke of Lenin as a man who wanted peace."[7] And Léon Champeix, the former treasurer of the Communist Party in Corrèze, added, "At the beginning of communism in Corrèze there was pacifism, there was the desire for peace. We were sick of the war of 1914–18, the costs had been too high."[8]

The Limousin and Dordogne Communists capitalized on these sentiments and effectively positioned themselves in the countryside as the party that would bring social reform and an end to all wars. "For my father," said Marcel Darnetz, "the Communist Party would bring peace. For him this war

[7] Interviews with Robert Bos, Tulle, 24 August 1983 and 30 July 1984.
[8] Interviews with Léon Champeix, Brive, 30 July and 29 August 1984.

was really the big event that had marked him, and the Communists were to bring a new, more just society." [9]

The PCF was fully conscious that first-generation Communist militants often shared these experiences. In their 1921 agrarian program, the Communists recognized that the "rural populations, which in some areas have turned toward the Communist Party, seek above all in the Revolution a haven against war." [10] In numerous Limousin and Dordogne villages a kernel of pacifist war veterans, revolted by the war, influenced by Socialist and later Communist propaganda, and impressed by the Russian Revolution, played a key role in the establishment of the Communist Party. But the Russian Revolution represented more than just pacifism; in the often dualistic worldview of the peasantry it also represented the victory of *les petits* against *les gros*. "Even if people weren't educated," said André Plazanet, "they thought it was great the way that . . . It didn't happen all by itself, but they got rid of the lords [*ils ont foutu les châtelains en l'air*]. Even without knowing how things were going over there, the attraction [for the Revolution] remained." [11] It mattered little to struggling peasants that postwar Limousin was home to few lords and large property holders; they liked to hear that small peasants elsewhere had defended their rights against more powerful social forces.

The Revolution signified different things to different people. For some it represented socialism; for others, who saw things in French terms, it meant a radical republic; and for others, of course, socialism *was* the republic—the *république sociale*. This was the view of Jean Lalanne: "Well, for those who were like me, and many others who knew what a revolution was, socialism was coming. Socialism, that was what they wanted, the republic!" [12] Some militants made sense of the Russian Revolution by incorporating it into the French revolutionary and republican tradition. This fitted in nicely with the contemporary Socialist view that the Russian Revolution was but an extension of its French predecessor. [13]

Thus the Bolshevik Revolution was initially viewed with considerable spontaneous sympathy in parts of Limousin and Périgord. The Revolution provided an outlet for the utopian needs of a rural society traumatized by war. Peasants and other rural inhabitants knew little about the course of events in Russia; in any case, they paid attention only to what they wanted to hear, and to those elements that confirmed their views. In their eyes, the

---

[9] Interview with Marcel Darnetz, Gros-Chastang, 8 August 1984.

[10] "Thèse sur la question agraire du Parti communiste français," in *Le Parti communiste et la question paysanne* (Paris, 1947), 32.

[11] Interview with André Plazanet, St-Clément, 1 September 1984.

[12] Interview with Jean Lalanne.

[13] See François Furet, *Le passé d'une illusion: Essai sur l'idée communiste au XXᵉ siècle* (Paris, 1995), 79–120; Gérard Belloin, *Entendez-vous dans nos mémoires . . . ? Les Français et leur Révolution* (Paris, 1988), 185–87.

Revolution proved that it was simultaneously possible to undertake massive social change, defend small property, distribute land to the landless, and defend peace. This was a reassuring vision of social change, directed largely at outsiders (the rich bourgeois, *les gros*, and city dwellers) whom they held responsible for the difficulties of rural communities.

The myth of the Russian Revolution was not shared by all in the countryside. By the mid-1920s, denunciation of the peasants' situation in the Soviet Union had become the central theme of all anticommunist discourse, whether Socialist, Radical, or conservative. The PCF was Moscow's servant; the Soviet regime was chaotic and oppressive, and had reduced a former grain-exporting nation to famine.[14]

The Campaign against the War

The desire for peace, which had fueled sympathy for the Russian Revolution, was also linked to the popularity of the Communist Party's antimilitaristic rhetoric. The PCF's continuous, aggressive campaign against war was at the heart of its success. The Great War had created fertile ground for the development of communism, and the Party was quick to take advantage of the opportunity by appealing to widespread antimilitarist and pacifist sympathies in rural areas. To war veterans who had returned to their villages embittered by years at the front, and to all those who had suffered from the conflict, the Communists proposed a straightforward explanation of the Great War's causes: capitalism resorted to war in order to resolve its contradictions, and big capitalists perniciously used the war to enrich themselves.[15] As Marcel Darnetz explains:

> "On returning to Gros-Chastang and learning of requisitions here, requisitions there, and that families whose children were already at war and had been killed had been harmed, [my father was] filled with a profound feeling of injustice. And in that state of mind he encountered the Communists, who told him, "The war? But, my poor friend, it is capitalist society that engenders it. The war? But it is the capitalist world that seeks to resolve its crises, these capitalists who enrich themselves in order to conquer, and so on—*there* is the cause of the war." And they told him, "But there is something else, there is the Russian Revolution, there are the Russian Communists. They want to do away with the war, and with them there will be no war."[16]

The Communists hammered away at these popular explanations throughout the 1920s and 1930s, and their success had much to do with the sim-

[14] Vigeois, 1929 Socialist leaflet, ADC 3M466.
[15] Daniel Halévy found the Communists raising the same themes in Allier in 1934: *Visites aux paysans du Centre* (Paris, 1978), 327–28.
[16] Interview with Marcel Darnetz.

plicity of their arguments. The culprit they designated—the capitalist class—was also, in their eyes, responsible for the difficult situation of those who worked the land. The Party never lacked opportunities to raise its opposition to the war, or men, particularly veterans, to undertake propaganda campaigns on the issue. When a militant died of war-related wounds, when communes erected war monuments, when young men were drafted, when the government contemplated extending the length of military service, and when the Communists ran for office, the PCF was ready to denounce the warmakers.

Antimilitaristic rhetoric occupied a prominent position in the Communist Party's electoral campaigns. While most of the Party's opponents in cantonal elections emphasized purely local themes (roads, electrification, bus service), Communist candidates took a more political approach and portrayed themselves as the best bulwark against a future war. In the 1922 cantonal elections, virtually all the programs of Corrèze Communists gave prominence to the antiwar struggle; PCF candidates promised to abolish militarism, and some proclaimed in block letters, "Not a sou, not a man to imperialism, militarism, and other works of death," before urging voters to go to the polls "to the cry of 'down with the war.'" [17] The antimilitaristic theme remained at the center of Communist discourse throughout the interwar years—both during the class-against-class period, when the Party warned voters that capitalist countries were preparing for war against the Soviet Union, and beginning in 1934, when the emphasis switched to the danger that fascism represented for world peace.[18] In all circumstances, the Party played upon pacifism in the countryside, and this policy paid dividends.

The Communist Party's antimilitarism brought in votes. Backing for the 1919 Socialists was unrelated to variations in a commune's percentage of war dead (see chapter 4), but such was not the case for the Corrèze Communists. In two of four interwar elections, the Communist vote was clearly affected by the percentage of men who died at the front: In 1924, a 1 percent rise in the percentage of war dead from one commune to another produced an estimated 1.45 percent increase in the PCF vote (table 5.1).[19] The Communists scored well in villages hard hit by the war, largely because their antimilitaristic propaganda found a receptive audience among the families and friends of those who died at the front. No other political party exploited the war issue with such skill, and it was a central issue in those small villages disproportionately struck by the war's heavy toll. In 1936, five voters in St-Saud-Lacoussière (Dordogne) chose to explain their vote for Gustave Saussot, the successful Communist candidate for deputy, by marking "Long

[17] ADC 3M298, program of peasant militant Jean-Baptiste Leblanc. See also ADC 3M296, ADD 3M128, and ADHV 3M321.

[18] See numerous leaflets in ADC 3M304, 3M309–312.

[19] War losses did not affect other political parties—save the 1932 Radicals, who actually lost votes as the percentage of war dead increased.

Table 5.1. Influence of war losses on Socialist and Communist vote, Corrèze, 1919–1936 (Coefficients of regression [b] and determination [R^2])[a]

	b	R^2
Parti Socialiste		
1919	.18	.22
Parti Communiste		
1924	1.45[†]	.24
1928	.93	.29
1932	1.22[*]	.27
1936	1.01	.32

Sources: Gilles Quincy, "Les Corréziens morts au cours des guerres de 1914 à 1962 et les conséquences démographiques de la Première Guerre mondiale," *Lemouzi* 93 (1985): 3–7; ADC 3M194, 3M196–97, 3M200, AN C10045.
[a] Controlling for percentage of long-term population change, percentages of migrants and peasants, population per km², percentage of civil burials, mean delay between birth and baptism in 1910, and mean farm size per commune. N = 279.
[*] Significant at .05 level.
[†] Significant at .01 level.

live peace. Down with war" on the preprinted ballots bearing the candidate's name.[20]

The Great War had marked an entire generation, and from that generation the PCF recruited some of its most dedicated followers. The success of the Party's antimilitaristic line owed much to its militants, many of them former soldiers. Veterans attracted by the PCF's pacifist and antimilitaristic rhetoric figured prominently among those who established and directed Party cells—the cell secretary in Domme (Dordogne) was a 100-percent-disabled ex-serviceman[21]—and they played key roles in Communist municipalities.

PCF veterans made sure that memories of the war did not fade in the countryside. How could the war be forgotten by those who lived with its scars and those whose loved ones had not returned? Paul Loubradou, elected Communist deputy of Dordogne in 1936, wrote a strongly antimilitaristic memoir of the war years, and doubtless much of what he expressed in print reappeared in his propaganda.[22] And the war continued to take its toll. It was not uncommon to read in the Communist paper obituaries of militants who had died of war-related wounds and diseases, and their deaths only served to reinforce antimilitaristic sentiments. In 1926, Jean Luc, a PCF member from Peyrelevade (Corrèze), high on the Millevaches plateau, died

[20] As a result, their votes were declared void. AN C12582.
[21] AN F⁷ 13096, CS Périgueux to SG, 14 January 1926.
[22] Paul Loubradou, *Les cahiers de Jean Lascar, 1914–1918* (Paris, 1934).

of the injuries he had sustained at the front. At his funeral, the militant and *mutilé de guerre* François Dubayle, owner of a café-hotel in nearby Bugeat (Corrèze), delivered a strongly worded speech against the war in which he described the horrors of the battlefield and promised that Luc's comrades and friends would do their best to prevent "capitalist imperialism" from starting another armed conflict. Two years later, thirty-eight-year-old Amédée Jouannaud, secretary of the Communist cell of Fransèches (Creuse), died of a "long and painful illness that he had caught in the trenches during the Great War." His village comrade Romanet, a retired schoolteacher, pronounced a eulogy at his grave, as did a militant from a neighboring village.[23] Grass-roots PCF militants astutely used funeral processions for preaching to both the faithful and the unconverted. And their invariable message—the Communist Party's hostility to war and the capitalist system's responsibility for it—was popular in the countryside.

The war also marked younger generations. Henri Peuch, who was only a small boy when the war ended, would hear all about it during the next decade from his father and his nine uncles, all war veterans. When his family met on Sundays in his village of Albussac, there was one principal subject of conversation: the war. Two of Peuch's uncles joined the Communist Party early on, and Peuch claims to have been influenced by one who had mutinied at the Chemins des Dames (April 1917) and whose death sentence had been commuted so that he could be sent to Verdun. Brought up in such an environment, many men of Peuch's generation were profoundly marked by the war they had been too young to experience directly and were sympathetic to the Communist Party's stance.[24] Hatred of the war was not limited to those who had fought at the front; it was shared by men and women of all generations, and it quickly became one of the defining features of the *mentalité* in rural areas.

One of the principal aspects of the Party's campaign against the war centered on commemoration of the war dead. Opposition to war memorials by Socialists (through 1920 and sometimes beyond) and Communists was scattered and poorly organized. In 1919 the Haute-Vienne Socialist daily called upon readers to oppose the erection of war memorials; if a monument was nonetheless built, militants and sympathizers were to demand that the following words be chiseled in the stone: "The war, the work of capitalism, militarism, and stupidity, has killed our brothers who wanted to live. Remember!"[25] These suggestions, however, did not become official policy. Only one Socialist commune, Gentioux (Creuse), in the heart of the Millevaches plateau, erected (in 1920) a vigorously antimilitaristic monument: it depicts a young, clog-wearing orphan whose raised fist points to the list of sixty-

[23] *TCO*, 11 September 1926, 28 January 1928, and for examples from Chamberet (Corrèze), 23 February 1929 and 15 May 1926.
[24] Interview with Henri Peuch, Brive, 23 August 1983.
[25] *Pop C*, 26 December 1919.

three names carved in the stone. Underneath, the moving inscription reads "Damned be war" ("*Maudite soit la guerre.*")[26]

It was no accident that Communists headed both Corrèze villages—Lagraulière and Toy-Viam—that built no *monument aux morts* during the interwar years. To this day, Toy-Viam has no monument to the war dead, and when Lagraulière's Communist mayor finally erected a monument in the 1970s to honor all the war dead of the twentieth century, he could not avoid reopening an uncommonly bitter dispute. In both villages, opposition to the monuments was overtly political. This was equally the case in industrial St-Junien (Haute-Vienne), where the Communist municipality, in control of the town hall since 1920, adamantly refused to commemorate the "big capitalist massacre," and still had not commissioned a monument by 1930.[27] Those Communist villages that did build monuments carefully selected their location and form. In Tarnac and Chanteix, the PCF municipalities chose simple stelae, more neutral than monuments denoting victory or grief; Tarnac's municipality, under pressure from sixty-seven families who lost loved ones in the war, placed the memorial in the cemetery, where the families claimed it would be better respected.[28]

War memorials were as hotly debated in Limousin's small communes as they were elsewhere throughout the nation. Opposition to monuments, often fueled by a group of well-entrenched pacifist war veterans who organized counterdemonstrations and protest banquets when memorials were inaugurated, helped forge a sense of Communist identity while demonstrating the depth of the Party's antimilitaristic sentiments.[29] Over time, however, Communists realized that antimilitarism was a double-edged sword. Better a sober monument than a hard-line stance. Militants were keenly conscious that opposition to memorials would be seen as unpatriotic in villages where the Party's message was poorly received. By the late 1930s, the Party had changed its stance on the issue. In 1937 the tireless Communist deputy Marius Vazeilles, dedicating Chaveroche's (Corrèze) monument, "saluted the victims of the war and condemned international fascism, which is trying to provoke a new conflict."[30]

---

[26] The Gentioux monument was boycotted by state representatives for sixty-five years. Not until 1985 did the Creuse prefect participate in a wreath-laying ceremony at the monument on Armistice Day.

[27] *TCO*, 17 May 1930.

[28] ADC 2 O Tarnac 4. On war monuments see Antoine Prost, *Les anciens combattants et la société française* (Paris, 1977) and "Les monuments aux morts: Culte républicain? culte civique? culte patriotique?" in *Les lieux de mémoire*, vol. 1, *La république*, ed. Pierre Nora (Paris, 1984), 195–225; Annette Becker, *Les monuments aux morts: Mémoire de la Grande Guerre* (Paris, 1988); Daniel Sherman, "The Nation: In What Community? The Politics of Commemoration in Postwar France," in *Ideas and Ideals: Essays on Politics in Honor of Stanley Hoffmann*, ed. Linda B. Miller and Michael Joseph Smith (Boulder, Colo., 1993), 277–95.

[29] For examples see *TCO*, 13 September 1924, 23 January 1926.

[30] *TC*, 25 September 1937.

Antimilitarism had its own internal dynamic at the grass roots; from the beginning, militants and sympathizers needed no prodding from Party headquarters to raise the issue. In 1926 a group of Chamberet (Corrèze) Communists, chanting the "International" and crying, "Long live the Soviets!" joined the procession of the agricultural association's yearly fête. They reached the stage, located in front of the *monument aux morts*, before the band, and their leader proceeded to harangue the crowd on the subject of the Great War.[31] The choice of the topic was significant, and Chamberet's militants were astute in taking advantage of this ready-made forum to express their views.

Beginning in the mid-1920s, the Party, helped by the Jeunesses Communistes, sponsored demonstrations of young conscripts to protest against the "bourgeois army." In 1926 the draftees of Magnat-L'Etrange (Creuse), sporting red rosettes, marched down the village's main street chanting the "International" and the "Jeune Garde"; they stopped before the war memorial and listened to a speech by a young militant who claimed that the village's soldiers had died defending a cause that was not theirs. The protests of young conscripts gathered strength in the 1930s, and in numerous villages the PCF organized demonstrations against the proposed extension of military service to two years.[32] The movement reached a high point on June 3, 1935, when the draft review board in Seilhac (Corrèze) called up draftees. The PCF trucked in militants and sympathizers from the Party-run villages of Chanteix and Lagraulière, and by early morning a few hundred young people massed in front of the town hall; all were "known Communists or sympathizers, and all belong to peasant families." The 250 protesters who managed to squeeze into the hearing room were promptly ejected by the police for disrupting the proceedings. When the prefect arrived from Tulle, he was greeted with red flags and calls of "Soviets everywhere!" "Down with war!" and "Down with the two years!"[33] These actions, the work of peasant Communists in an entirely rural canton, were in tune with shifting public opinion in the countryside north of Tulle. It was telling that in Favars (Corrèze), a commune dominated by the Radicals, 116 inhabitants (23 percent of the population) signed, in March 1935, a petition on the town hall's letterhead that read, "We are against any increase in the length of military service because we don't want war." Two months later, a joint Socialist-Communist list of candidates emerged victorious from the Favars municipal elections, and a Communist mayor gained office.[34]

[31] *TCO*, 2 October 1926.
[32] AN F[7] 13096, préfet Creuse to MI, 1 February 1926. The "Jeune Garde" was the song of the Jeunesse Communiste. See the protest meeting in La Roche–Canillac (Corrèze) held on 24 March 1934 (ADC 1M76) and the antimilitaristic demonstration in Lagraulière one week later (ADC 1M68).
[33] ADC 1M68, CS Tulle to PC, 3 June 1935, emphasis mine; *TCO*, 8 June 1935.
[34] See ADC 1M68, 3M384, 3M345.

The severe agricultural crisis that struck in the early 1930s had only aggravated the mood in rural areas, and the proposed increase in the length of military service gave new life to antimilitarism. Limousin and Dordogne had long been centers of resistance to recruitment. Turgot himself had complained of this in the mid–eighteenth century, and from the the mid-1790s until well into the next century Corrèze had one of the highest desertion rates in the nation.[35] In isolated, mountainous rural communities, villagers mobilized to defend deserters and hide draft evaders. The Great War, with its trail of misery and suffering, rekindled an underlying hostility to the military, and by the 1930s the draft itself was criticized openly. But whereas in past centuries draft resistance was a traditional defense of the peasantry's mode of life, in the twentieth century it was far more political in nature, linked to a rural pacifism that the Communists adroitly encouraged. Here, as in other areas, the Communists embodied more contemporary forms of political action.

Rural society displayed far less enthusiasm toward the PCF-affiliated organizations that, in theory at least, were to have been at the forefront of the struggle against militarism. Neither the Jeunesse Communiste nor the Association Républicaine des Anciens Combattants (ARAC), a veterans' group closely linked to the Party, ever got off the ground in Limousin and Dordogne.[36] Antimilitarism and pacifism alone were not enough; only when they formed part of a larger political and social agenda did they attract voters and sympathizers.

Courting the Peasantry

The changed political situation that grew out of the war, growing sympathy for the Russian Revolution, and a firmly anchored antimilitarism all provided openings that the Communists deftly exploited. But militants and sympathizers knew that the PCF's continuing success in the countryside would depend on its everyday practice, on its political flexibility and openness to peasant demands. It was one thing to group together disgruntled war veterans, smallholding peasants, tenant farmers, rural artisans, and shopkeepers clamoring for social justice, but it was quite another to preserve and expand this base. To this end, the Communists concentrated the bulk of their propaganda on rural issues. Militants might begin speeches with a discussion of the Party's stance on the war, but inevitably they would move on to discuss village politics and argue that the PCF was best placed to defend the

---

[35] Jean Boutier, *Campagnes en émoi: Révoltes et révolution en Bas-Limousin, 1789–1800* (Treignac, 1987), 211–16; Alan Forrest, *Conscripts and Deserters: The Army and French Society during the Revolution and Empire* (New York, 1989), map p. 2.
[36] On the ARAC see ADC 4M282, AN F⁷ 13128, ADHV 1M175.

peasantry's interests. The Communists criticized the big capitalists who exploited small peasants and the state that refused to intervene in their favor. But they went further than mere protest by proposing both short- and long-term programs, and they also made important efforts to organize Communist agricultural trade unions. Their consistent defense of "small owners" (*petits propriétaires, petits paysans*) was in fact a defense of all peasants. In the Communist vocabulary, the small peasants were defined more by their income than by the size of their property. In the PCF's view, the vast majority of Limousin and Dordogne peasants were "small owners." [37]

Louis Freyssinet, following in the footsteps of his father, was Communist mayor of the small Haute-Corrèze village of St-Germain-Lavolps until depopulation forced the closing of the school where his wife was employed. The Freyssinet family then left St-Germain-Lavolps to seek employment in the Tulle region. An able politician, Freyssinet was soon elected mayor of Ste-Fortunade, a larger and more prosperous bourg 10 kilometers south of Tulle, where I interviewed him in what is surely one of Corrèze's most beautiful *mairies*. Freyssinet speaks with great ease and fondness of his native Haute-Corrèze. When I questioned him about the Party's past rural policy, he answered by recounting a humorous incident that aptly illustrates the Party's rural propaganda and its limits:

> Ah! There were things that were incredible! For example, one of the guys in our cell [in St-Germain-Lavolps] said to a very small[holding] peasant one day—he was on top of a hill and he pointed to the farm of a big peasant who owned three hundred hectares and he exclaimed, "You see, if we're elected, well, all that," he said, pointing to the vast expanse of land on the horizon, "all that will be yours!" "Ah, that would be great," the peasant enthusiastically replied, "that would be really great. But you know," he went on after some thought, "I think there's just a little bit too much!" [38]

There is a kernel of truth to this story, which incidentally shows that Communists were far from being devoid of a sense of humor about themselves, their past, and their policies. After all, the Party's motto, *La terre à celui qui la travaille*, implied a redistribution of land in favor of those whose properties were not economically viable. It was obviously more popular to guarantee and perhaps expand a peasant's plot of land than it was to discuss collectivization, just as short-term demands such as an increase in prices were more likely to mobilize people than were long-term dreams of agricultural restructuring. The result was a permanent tension between short- and long-

---

[37] There is thus no contradiction between the PCF's appeal to "small owners" and the fact that it did best as average farm size rose (see chapter 3) because all these peasants had similar incomes. For the PCF, a large property owner employed more than one agricultural worker.

[38] Interview with Louis Freyssinet, Ste-Fortunade, 1 September 1983 and 30 June 1984.

term demands, between solutions based on pragmatism and those based on ideology, between militants who saw the peasants as a revolutionary class and those who thought they should play second fiddle to the workers, between peasant policy at the national level and that at the local level. The relative strength of these various elements depended highly on personalities and the political climate. The emphasis at a rural meeting depended considerably on whether the speaker was a Corrèze peasant militant or an *ouvriériste* leader from Dordogne. In short, what appeared to be a unified peasant policy at the national level had significantly different local variants. And the Party's rural policy was constantly adjusted, refined, and modified to stay abreast of public opinion and of social and economic changes in the countryside.

How did peasants perceive the Communist Party's program? On this question we have precious little information save what can be culled from oral interviews. The Limousin and Dordogne Communist press published countless articles on the peasant question. Despite constant encouragement, few peasants who were not active in the Party's leadership submitted written work. And when they did, their pieces had more to do with parish-pump politics than with agricultural matters per se. This was a disappointment to editors on the lookout for articles written in "peasant style," in the hope that such pieces would increase readership in the countryside.

The Communist weekly *Le Travailleur de la Corrèze* solved the problem in 1935 by publishing a regular piece by a "small peasant" (signed "Lionardou, paysan corrézien") whose down-to-earth reasoning proved popular. Lionardou was even congratulated by a group of St-Yrieix-le-Déjalat (Corrèze) peasants who noted with much satisfaction that his views fully corresponded with their own. In fact, unbeknownst to most readers, the highly successful column was written by Clément Chausson, the director of the newspaper (and of a profitable sawmill) and one of the PCF's most popular leaders in Corrèze.[39] A few years later Chausson published another column purportedly by a hardworking peasant woman who complained about high prices and the sorry state of agriculture. Chausson's approach was not unusual: the local Party leadership composed most "peasant-style" pieces, and here we glimpse the difficulty of mobilizing active and engaged militants at the grass roots. Writing a weekly or even monthly column was an activity reserved for those who were at least half-time militants: only they had the time, the dedication, the political knowledge, and the educational background to carry out such a task.

Peasants rarely wrote about agricultural matters or formulated rural policies. Those who worked the land authored only 6.4 percent of some 450 articles concerned with things rural and published in the regional PCF press

[39] *TC*, 29 February 1936; interview with Léon Champeix.

during the interwar years, and half of those were written in 1937–38 by one Haute-Vienne militant, Léon Pagnoux, who had been trained at the Communist Party's *école centrale*. In contrast, close to 36 percent of the articles were composed by full-time militants, schoolteachers, artisans, and people employed in agriculture-related fields. Marius Vazeilles, the indefatigable Haute-Corrèze nursery gardener and influential PCF expert on the rural world, alone authored 10 percent of all signed articles on the peasant question during the interwar years, far more than were written by the peasants themselves.

Analysis of the rural Party leadership does shed light on the peasantry's state of mind, however. Grass-roots leaders, constantly in touch with their constituents, displayed a keen awareness of what they could tell the peasantry, and carefully tailored their discourse accordingly. It was not unusual for a Communist representative to tone down or ignore national peasant policy that he felt was ill adapted to his region and posed a threat to his own (and the Party's) political base. Peasants influenced the formation of policy at the local level. Largely because the PCF was not preoccupied with peasant matters, rural leaders and militants enjoyed more independence than other Party members, although they always walked a fine line to avoid political problems with PCF headquarters in Paris.

Much of grass-roots propaganda was, of course, modeled on national policy. The Communist Party's official rural program, adopted at the 1921 Congrès de Marseille and approved (with a few minor criticisms) by Lenin, remained in effect until the early 1960s.[40] Drafted by the Party's leading peasant experts—Ernest Girault, J. Castel, and especially Renaud Jean and Marius Vazeilles—the agrarian platform distinguished among large capitalist property owners who employed agricultural wage labor, those whose land was farmed by sharecroppers and tenant farmers, and smallholding peasants who cultivated their own plots. After the Revolution, all large landholdings would be expropriated without compensation. Properties that had been farmed by agricultural workers would be turned into cooperatives. Sharecroppers and tenant farmers could farm the land they had cultivated in the past. Small peasants were to be left untouched, and if their plots were too small, they would gain land that had belonged to large landholders. For the peasantry the major difference between the new and old regimes would be juridical: small peasants would no longer own their land, but they could use

[40] "Thèse sur la question agraire." Lenin's commentary is also reprinted in this volume. The *thèse* did not represent a major break with the peasant policy of the pre-1920 Socialist party. For an alternative view of the PCF's agrarian policy, see Gérard Belloin, *Renaud Jean, le tribun des paysans* (Paris, 1993), 71–82, and for an orthodox position, Jean Gacon, "La politique paysanne du Parti communiste français de 1921 à 1939," *Cahiers de l'Institut Maurice Thorez* 24 (1971): 33–44.

and freely profit from it throughout their lifetimes (what the Party termed "the absolute and perpetual enjoyment [*jouissance*] of their property"). Finally, the Communists acknowledged that the profit motive was the principal moving force of peasant activity, and they guaranteed that peasants would be free to dispose of their gains as they pleased.

The Communists proposed a tactically intelligent postrevolutionary rural program. The PCF's principal concern was not to alienate the smallholding peasants, tenant farmers, and sharecroppers whose backing (or at least neutrality) they needed in order to gain and preserve power.[41] Collectivization, although recognized as a superior form of cultivation, was relegated to the distant future, and even then peasants would join cooperatives on a purely voluntary basis. The Revolution promised peasants retirement benefits, health insurance, electrification, fertilizers, and modern machinery. The abolition of private property was more difficult to explain in the countryside, and peasant leaders, in their popularizations of the Marseille program, were at pains to emphasize that the notoriously ambiguous term *jouissance* (use, enjoyment) gave one all the advantages (and more) of property ownership with none of the drawbacks.[42] Rural militants soon realized, however, that this theme was not to their advantage, and within a few years they backtracked and affirmed to all who listened that after the Revolution small peasants would keep their land and be allowed to pass it on to their children; they would also be freed of all debts and mortgages.[43] The new regime, on the other hand, would expropriate large holdings and award the land free of charge to the people who cultivated it. In the opinion of Corrèze's Marius Vazeilles, defending and expanding family property was a political and tactical necessity, even if the ensuing parceling out (*morcellement*) of the land (because of inheritance) had numerous unfavorable consequences. The end, in his words, justified the means: the point was to take power, not to follow an ideologically pure (and suicidal) line advocating the development of collective property. As Renaud Jean wrote, "our Party—and all peasants must know this—is the Party of land for the peasants."[44]

This was precisely the central theme at which Limousin and Dordogne rural militants hammered away for most of the interwar years. In countless speeches, slogans, electoral leaflets, posters, and newspaper articles, Com-

---

[41] The delegate Ilbert declared to the PCF's 1925 congress: "The Revolution will be commanded to a certain degree by the peasants. If the Revolution is not supplied with wheat and agricultural products, it will, despite all the sacrifices of the proletariat of the towns, be condemned to failure." Parti communiste, "4ᵉᵐᵉ Congrès national tenu à Clichy les 17, 18, 19, 20 et 21 janvier 1925," typescript, Bibliothèque Nationale, 1259.

[42] For example, peasants could no longer lose their land to creditors of all kinds. Renaud Jean, *Entre paysans: Commentaire du programme agraire du Parti communiste* (Paris, 1922), 18–19; *VP*, 7 January 1922; Duchatel, *Le communisme aux champs* (Sens, 1922), 10–11.

[43] *Aux travailleurs des champs* (Paris, 1932), 15; *La misère au village* (Paris, 1935), 28.

[44] Marius Vazeilles, *L'action communiste dans les campagnes* (Paris, 1925), 18; Renaud Jean, *L'union des paysans de France* (Paris, 1936), 51.

munist militants stressed that they were the friends and defenders of small-holders and of those, less fortunate, who aspired to their own plot of land. Even during the PCF's first years, village militants rarely entered into subtle debates concerning *jouissance*, and instead stated loudly and clearly that they considered peasant property to be the tool (*l'outil de travail*) of those who cultivated it.[45] Any form of expropriation was excluded. When inept Creuse militants swam against the tide in 1924 and denounced the right to private property in front of peasant audiences, the results were disastrous; that experience was not repeated.[46]

The land issue was important in this region, though perhaps less so than in other areas of France where the proportion of owners was not so impor-tant. Whatever the region, those who worked the soil were extremely sensi-tive to property matters. It could only prove popular to propose, as Haute-Vienne militants did in early 1921, to help small peasants keep their land and help the landless to acquire some. It was equally popular to denounce large property owners (and assimilate them to the nobility by calling them *hobereaux*) whose holdings lay fallow while small peasants nearby could barely make ends meet.[47] And it was even more popular to suggest that small peasants who needed land would benefit from land redistribution. What small peasant, after all, could not imagine that he could make a good case for deserving more land? One enthusiastic PCF voter in Servières-le-Château (Corrèze) scribbled on his ballot that it was time to "take the mayor's land and Lathieyre's titles and give them to those who have none. Long live Lenin!"[48]

Militants in the countryside portrayed the PCF as the defender of small property owners, arguing that only under communism would small peasants be fully free. In the words of François Aussoleil, "Small property is only an illusion. Only communism can turn it into reality." Land, the Communists emphasized, should belong only to those who worked it; the PCF's role was to protect smallholders from gradual expropriation by large landholders. Gustave Saussot asked rhetorically in his 1936 electoral program, "Who is depriving the great majority of peasants of individual property, if not the big monopolists, the big speculators and financiers?"[49] By the late 1930s, Com-munist propagandists were guaranteeing that middling peasants would be

---

[45] Marius Vazeilles was one of the few who discussed the problem of *jouissance* in his cam-paign literature for the Conseil Général in 1922. Other candidates avoided the issue altogether, probably to their advantage. See ADC 3M296, 3M298, ADD 3M128, ADHV 3M231; *TT*, Jan-uary 1923.

[46] *TCO*, 17 May 1924.

[47] ADHV 1M168. The *hobereaux* theme was a favorite of the regional Communist press. In the PCF's local language, *hobereaux* designated lords in general, and not less fortunate landed nobles. See *TCO*, 13 November 1926, and the article by a peasant correspondent from Agonac (Dordogne), 6 August 1932.

[48] AN C 10705.

[49] *PCTC*, 1 January 1922; *TCO*, 21 April 1928; Saussot electoral leaflet, ADD 3M91.

entitled to keep their holdings—regardless of size—and explained that the Party's role was to help peasants realize maximum profit from the land they cherished, the land their families had paid for with generations of hard work.[50]

Collectivism?

Rural militants tirelessly reassured their audience that the Party was no enemy of small landholders, for even in politically "advanced" areas such as Limousin and Périgord the fear of *le partageux* had not fully disappeared. *Partageux* (from the verb *partager*, to split up, divide), an old term used in the countryside, referred to the Socialists and, between the wars, to the Communists, who, it was rumored, angled to divide up wealth, land, cows, and women once they reached power. The PCF's right-wing opponents rarely missed an occasion to insist that the Communists would conduct a *partage* at the expense of the small peasants. They teased Communist candidates by asking them to put their ideology into practice before the Revolution, and share their potatoes, chestnuts, and rye with their neighbors.[51] The fear of the *partageux*, fueled by ever-present rumors, was at the heart of anticommunist discourse, and the claim that the PCF would "split up the cows" hit home in a region where the size of a farm was often described in terms of the number of cows it could sustain ("a ten-cow farm").

The Communists, troubled by these attacks, did their best to contest their ill-founded reputation: rural cells wrote to the newspaper to claim that the Communists were not *les partageux*, militants stressed the theme in their speeches, and candidates almost always raised the issue in their electoral propaganda. In the 1936 elections, Marius Vazeilles, who had spent the better part of sixteen years traveling through the Corrèze highlands, found it necessary to stress once again that the PCF had no intention of splitting up the peasants' cows or land. One candidate candidly admitted that the Party did not believe in *le partage* because it was impossible to split things up equally.[52] Joseph Biaugeaud was more representative of the Communist tone when he reassured peasants that "our party does not want to split up your properties. This is a childish fable that is told to you, just as one frightens children with the bogeyman [*croquemitaine*]," and he went on to argue that if small peasants no longer wanted to share (*partager*) their wealth with the bourgeoisie, they should vote for the Communist Party.[53] A young peasant from Neuville (Corrèze) turned the tables and proposed that the true

[50] *TCHV*, 5 February 1937.

[51] *La Croix de la Corrèze*, 18 November 1934.

[52] See the article signed by the cell of Ste-Féréole (Corrèze), *TCO*, 31 March 1928; on Vazeilles, ADC 3M302.

[53] *TCCHV*, 20 April 1936.

partageux were the banks, "which steal your savings," and the state, "which takes your money for taxes." There was nothing to fear from the Bolsheviks, argued the regional PCF paper, for they had "created" small property in Russia where none had existed before.[54]

The fear of the *partageux* was strongest among older people, especially in areas where the PCF's opponents had an important presence. In the Haute-Corrèze bastion, militants recall that few believed the stories concerning the *partageux*. "In the past we were blamed for wanting to strangle people and divide everything up," complained Maurice Bans. "They told our local peasants, for example, 'You have a cow, but the Communist party is going to split it up, and then you'll no longer be able to plow because you'll only have half a cow!' People didn't believe this. Just as they said, for example—and I don't think it was true—that in Russia children were turned into sausage."[55] This opinion was confirmed by Jean-Baptiste Vars, from the nearby village of Pérols-sur-Vézère, who put his finger on another reason why the inhabitants of the Montagne remained unconcerned by *le partageux*: "I remember that we used to say, 'They'd better come fast if they want to *partager* because before long there won't be anything left to split up!'" He laughed. "But it's true! When you see entire villages that have disappeared, entire villages!"[56] In the poverty-stricken, depopulated Corrèze highlands, peasants, who had little to lose, showed little apprehension that the Communists would split up their land and possessions. A militant in the Tulle area remarked ironically that the Radical deputy was wasting his time warning the peasants that the Communists would expropriate their land, for large numbers of small and middling peasants were already abandoning their plots in the hope of finding a better future elsewhere.[57] In southern Corrèze, in and around Albussac (canton of Argentat), fear of the *partageux* was more common, but the presence of a "large" landholder, Jean Terrade, among the PCF's more active militants was a reassuring signal to Henry Peuch:

> Terrade was a rather important peasant, and at the time he was criticized by lots of peasants . . . [The Party used Terrade as an example] "You want the *partageux*? You want to *partager*? You want to *partager* his [Terrade's] large property?" It was an advantage for the Party to have a big property owner among its members—he was considered to be a large *propriétaire*, he had a property of forty or fifty hectares. Moreover, we knew that these were well-established people who had financial means, because in the countryside we all knew each other, we knew the houses where there was money, old money, and the houses where there was no money. Now it was considered that Terrade's was a house that had

[54] *TCO*, 3 February and 3 March 1935. On the *partageux* see also Ernest Girault, *Paysans! A bas les partageux!* (Paris, n.p., n.d.).
[55] Interview with Maurice Bans, Bugeat, 7 October 1983.
[56] Interview with Jean-Baptiste Vars, Meymac, 3 October 1983.
[57] *TCO*, 28 December 1935.

money—and this helped us, maybe, to attract the sympathy of people who were not Communists but who knew that Terrade was a Party militant and leader, and that he was very intelligent and very esteemed, and many people came closer to us even if they didn't join the Party.[58]

How did militants respond if a small peasant accused the Communists of being *partageux*? Maurice Bans, a smallholding peasant elected mayor of Viam (Corrèze) in 1935, explains: "I'd say, 'No, we don't want to split things up; on the contrary, we'd like to give you some [land]! Don't you see that your neighbor has too much there? You, you've got two or three cows, he's got fifty, he should give you a little so you'd have at least ten!'" He laughed.

"In other words," I probed, "we'll defend you, we'll defend your . . ."

". . . your property, your small property, and we'll try to enlarge it if we can."[59]

The defense of small property stood squarely at the center of rural Communist propaganda, and militants did not emphasize collectivization or how the agricultural world would be organized under a Socialist regime. At best, a candidate such as Guillaume Brousse, the Communist mayor of Lagraulière (Corrèze), might explain that the Party had no plans to touch the peasants' land, but wanted them to unite their efforts and work together with machines provided by the state.[60] These suggestions, however, proved too bold. PCF members at all levels acknowledged that speaking of collectivism (or even work in common) could only be counterproductive. "Collectivism" remained a pejorative term in the countryside, and in the opinion of all the old militants I interviewed, it was advisable to avoid the issue. When I asked Jean-Baptiste Vars, "Did one speak to the peasants of collectivization?" he answered, "Of collectivization, no. It would have been a major blunder to do so."

"At the time, do you think one could have successfully spoken of collectivization, of putting things in common?"

"No, no, one shouldn't have spoken of that."

"The peasants were too individualistic?"

"Too individualistic, too attached to their plot of land."[61]

Henri Peuch agreed that they had little to gain by raising the issue: "We never went so far as to discuss collectivization—we thought the matter should be freely decided [by the peasants]. We spoke of sharing large machinery. We were very flexible."[62]

[58] Interview with Henri Peuch.
[59] Interview with Maurice Bans.
[60] See his *profession de foi* for the elections to the Conseil Géneral in the canton of Seilhac in May 1922, ADC 3M296.
[61] Interview with Jean-Baptiste Vars.
[62] Interview with Henri Peuch.

Joseph Masdupuy concurred. "No, we never spoke of collectivization. And I never believed in it."[63]

Even those militants who supported collectivization conceded that their potential supporters were hardly receptive to such ideas. Léger Peyraut, an active Party militant and small peasant turned wine merchant in Lamazière-Basse (Corrèze), favored collectivization but recognized that it was a touchy issue in his village: "We spoke about it [collectivization], but it was a very complicated problem. To collectivize was great, but to make people understand what it would entail [was another matter].

"But in principle," I asked him, "you were for?"

"Ah, me? I was for!"

"But a lot of people in the Party didn't agree with you?"

"There were many who were unsure, who didn't know much about it, but in principle peasants like to own their own land. To change that would be complicated."

"But the Party's watchword," I reminded him, "was 'land to the one who works it.'"

"In the end, it's the same thing. But to get good results, the collectivity [is best]."

Moving on to the question of recruiting, I asked, "When you went to speak to someone to try to tell him, 'Listen, come to the Party' or 'Come to our cell meeting,' did you talk to him about collectivization?"

"No. First of all, that wasn't the issue. It wasn't discussed at all. I spoke mainly of the material concerns that people might have."[64]

Similarly, André Plazanet, a smallholding peasant in St-Clément (Corrèze), claimed that collectivization would not have bothered him or his fellow militants, but he admitted that he never raised the issue on speaking tours in the countryside.[65]

While militants rarely spoke of collectivization in their daily propaganda, there were occasions—during the Party's early years and especially in 1932, in the midst of the class-against-class period—when the issue was addressed in the columns of the PCF paper. At first, militants tried to convince peasants that, contrary to what they might have thought, communism was not something foreign to them. In May 1921, an idealistic Dordogne militant maintained that the peasants of Les Farges (Dordogne), where the Party cell was twenty-five members strong, did not fear collective property; after all, they already shared some tools and occasionally worked together in the fields. A similar theme was raised in 1936 by an overenthusiastic Corrèze émigré who cited his home commune as an example of collectivism; in fact, villagers, in a classic case of agricultural cooperation, had joined together to

[63] Interview with Joseph Masdupuy, Gros-Chastang, 3 September 1984.
[64] Interview with Léger Peyraut, Lamazière-Basse, 1 September 1984.
[65] Interview with André Plazanet.

purchase a thresher and a saw. In both cases the argument was that communal solidarity was an elementary form of communism. Peasants practiced communism without knowing it.[66] It followed that their hostility to communism was unfounded.

The whole issue of collectivization was linked to events in the Russian countryside, and while articles glorifying that country abounded in the local Communist press, few authors ventured to discuss in detail what was happening there. Their rehashed versions of Soviet propaganda, however, were reason enough to worry peasant readers and gave headaches to more than one rural militant.[67] The principal, though unavowed, reason militants did not speak of collectivization in small villages was that it evoked the Russian situation. Léon Champeix told me, "No, no. We didn't speak of it at all. We knew collectivization was being carried out in Russia, but we didn't talk about it." I asked him if the peasants knew, and he said, "Oh, yes, the peasants knew!" When I asked him what they thought of it, he replied, "Well, the peasants paid attention to what was happening. They were waiting to see what the end result would be, that's all."[68]

Collectivization, which received bad press outside Communist circles, was a subject of concern for the peasantry. But accurate information was hard to come by, and little was known outside Russia concerning the appalling human toll (some 6 to 11 million dead) of forced collectivization and the ensuing famine in 1932–33.[69] Save for a few *ouvrièristes* leaders in Dordogne and Haute-Vienne, militants saw little reason to spend their political capital defending the record of Soviet collectivization while claiming that similar methods would not be applied in France.

Militants walked a tightrope between their commitment to the Revolution and the political realities in their villages. While the myth of the Russian Revolution remained very much alive among segments of the Limousin and Dordogne rural population, peasants and militants by no means agreed that Soviet rural policy should be transposed to France. When a group of Tarnac (Corrèze) militants wrote that "we want the land to belong to those who work it," and added, "our horizon is the same as in the land of the Soviets and we are advancing toward it, toward happiness," they were defending their right to own land and at the same time proclaiming their allegiance to the Russian Revolution. Similarly, the cell of Le Bugue (Dordogne) put its own spin on the Russian experience when it wrote, "We must proclaim, just as in Soviet Russia, expropriation of the rural lords and of rich landed prop-

[66] *Prol C*, 8 May 1921; *TCCHV*, 13 June 1936. See also Paul Vaillant-Couturier, *A ceux des champs* (Paris, 1920), 55–56; Girault, *Paysans! A bas les partageux!* 26.

[67] *TCO*, 19 and 26 November 1927, 8 and 29 March 1930, 30 May 1930, 14 November 1931, 9 July 1932; *TCHV*, 12 October 1937.

[68] Interview with Léon Champeix.

[69] Robert Conquest, *The Harvest of Sorrow: Soviet Collectivization and the Terror-Famine* (Oxford, 1986), 306.

erty owners. Land to the one who works it."[70] Collectivization was simply not envisaged. In France, as in other parts of rural Europe where Communists did well, there was an underlying and persistent hostility to collectivist solutions. In post–World War II southern Italy, the redistribution of some large landed estates provided an opportunity to establish cooperatives (hampered, it is true, by land of poor quality and too many members) and encourage collective work. Though the Communists had gained rural strength in the region, Fausto Gullo, the Communist minister in charge, met with opposition on both fronts—80 percent of redistributed land was cultivated individually, not collectively. In 1949, peasants who occupied the great estates in Marineo (Sicily) immediately proceeded to parcel out the land to individuals. As Paul Ginsborg notes, abstract appeals to collectivism carried little weight in the face of "the deep-rooted individualism of southern peasant culture."[71]

Collectivism divided rural militants more than it did the PCF's electorate. The majority of the PCF's militants in agricultural areas had only the vaguest notion of collectivization, and it was not the moving force behind their political commitment. Others—a minority—favored collectivization and state control in the long term. Two such examples are worth citing because they vividly illustrate the tensions and limits of Communist agricultural policy.

In the fall of 1933 the Corrèze Communists launched a fund-raising campaign to send a peasant for a month-long pilgrimage to the Soviet Union.[72] For obvious propaganda purposes they selected someone who had Communist sympathies but was not a Party member—much to the chagrin of a few dedicated peasant Communists who hoped to be the chosen ones, and to this day regret that they were not. At the urging of their *conseiller général*, Antoine Bourdarias, Party leaders finally picked A. Paucard, a peasant smallholder—he owned five hectares of land—from the village of St-Salvadour (Corrèze). Paucard was a self-taught man with uncommon writing skills for someone with only a primary school education. Militants looked forward to Paucard's articles for their newspaper, and even to a future book.[73]

Paucard's *Un mois en Russie par un paysan de la Corrèze*, published shortly after his return, was not the book the Party was hoping for. Im-

[70] *TCO*, 23 March 1935; *Le Travailleur de la Dordogne*, 30 December 1933.

[71] Marc Lazar, *Maisons rouges: Les Partis communistes français et italien de la Libération à nos jours* (Paris, 1992), 205; Paul Ginsborg, *A History of Contemporary Italy: Society and Politics, 1943–1988* (London, 1990), 3, 106–8, 122–29.

[72] Dordogne Communists had sent a small peasant and municipal councillor from the village of Faux to Russia in 1927. See AN F[7] 13109. On the voyage to the Soviet Union, Fred Kupferman, *Au pays des Soviets: Le voyage français en Union soviétique, 1917–1939* (Paris, 1979).

[73] Paucard was one of six members of a PCF-sponsored "peasant delegation." Upon its return, the delegation published an idyllic statement denying the existence of famine in Russia, claiming collectivization was not being carried out by force, and declaring that their Russian comrades were "happy and in good health, and seem to have a physical and moral balance that is unknown in capitalist countries." *TCO*, 16 December 1933.

pressed by what he had seen in Soviet Russia, Paucard returned home an out-and-out collectivist—too much so for the local political climate. Paucard lacked the political finesse of a seasoned militant, and did not hesitate to put into print what other militants might admit only in private, if at all. In his often rambling book, Paucard predictably sang the praises of the Soviet agricultural system (he was in good company; Edouard Herriot, the leader of the Radical party, had done the same), but he also criticized his overly individualistic fellow Corrèze peasants, who were unreceptive to any form of solidarity. The Corrèze peasant, Paucard argued, has a "savagely individualistic mentality," and "his mind [is] stubbornly closed to any idea of solidarity and collectivism." Touring through a "kulak" area refractory to collectivization, Paucard noted:

> This reminds me a bit of my country. This old part of Corrèze where I was born, where people are bent on gains and unfortunately closed to generous ideas of solidarity; where jealousy does so much to imprison the poor, miserable life of the humble who are faced with the difficulties of existence. And the state . . . lets these miserable individualists believe that they enjoy a true godsend with this liberty from which one pretends happiness is born.
>   Oh! Men of goodwill, when will you understand the stupidity of your desire for possession [of property]? [74]

Paucard, who later joined the Communist Party, was a maverick and few in the Corrèze shared his enthusiasm for collectivism. As one old peasant militant told me, "Paucard had four or five hectares of land, so it didn't bother him in the least to collectivize!" [75] Even though Paucard's book also was a veiled criticism of Corrèze Communists, who were no less individualistic and attached to their property than other peasants, the Party organized a speaking tour and helped sell the book in the countryside. Bourdarias, who had been instrumental in sending Paucard to Russia, noted that, despite some misunderstandings, the book was a good guide to the situation in the Soviet Union. [76]

Paucard was one of the few who openly manifested his sympathy for collectivism and his contempt for those who remained attached to their property. But others within the Party believed that state control of the land would, in the words of André Plazanet, guarantee the "stable employment, retirement, and paid vacation that those employed in agriculture enjoyed in the Soviet Union." [77] When a tenant farmer in Combressol (Corrèze) asked

---

[74] A. Paucard, *Un mois en Russie par un paysan de la Corrèze* (St-Salvadour, 1934), 105, 96–97. For an account from a different region of France, Charles-Henri Martin, *Un paysan au pays des Soviets* (Paris, 1935).

[75] Interview with André Plazanet.

[76] *TCO*, 8 September 1934. Paucard insisted on printing his book himself and refused to correct certain "errors" that Communist militants had found in his manuscript. Interview with François Monédière, Beaumont, 31 July 1984.

[77] Interview with André Plazanet.

if peasants like himself, who worked from dawn to dusk to feed the people, were not civil servants (*fonctionnaires*), he was expressing a sentiment not all that foreign to the peasantry's mentality. Many a peasant struggling to make ends meet dreamed of migrating to the city to become a civil servant. Thanks to the intervention of local dignitaries with connections in Paris, this remained one of the rare opportunities for social mobility in the region.[78] Becoming a *fonctionnaire* was also the dream of some Communist peasant militants. When I asked Maurice Bans, "How did you envisage that agriculture would be organized under a Socialist society? Did you speak of collectivism?" he replied, "Well, we thought, I thought that we would become *fonctionnaires*. Why not?"

"in other words, the land would be . . ."

"Would belong to the state, and we would be *fonctionnaires*."

"So you weren't particularly committed to preserving your land?"

"Not at all, not at all! What's our small plot of land? It's a tool, just like the mason's hammer and trowel, and a tool that makes you starve to death is even worse. They spoke to us often of the *fonctionnaires* of the educational system who were privileged and had nothing to worry about. So why shouldn't we become *fonctionnaires*, since they're so well off?"[79]

There was, of course, nothing terribly revolutionary about wanting to become a *fonctionnaire*. Collective property, in this case, was but a means to status and job security, two domains where peasants felt particularly vulnerable. For a peasant who could barely stay afloat, collective property and guaranteed employment might be seen as the only means of staying on the land and avoiding the uncertainties of searching for employment in the city.

Bread-and-Butter Issues

The whole discussion centering on property was critical to a party suspected of having an eye on the peasantry's land. Having reassured its potential backers, the PCF needed to convince them through its positions on bread-and-butter issues. Peasants were interested primarily in the PCF's short-term proposals. François Monédière explained: "At the time we considered short-term demands necessary and mobilized people, and we're still following the same orientation today. It's not tomorrow's perspectives that mobilize people but what they need, what's necessary for them, the urgency of their need. You have to appeal to their needs."

"So people could agree on their immediate demands without necessarily agreeing on what would happen in the future?"

[78] *TC*, 9 October 1937. "It is undeniable," wrote the *TCO* on 5 May 1934, "that the young peasant has his eyes increasingly turned toward the city. He would like to be a *fonctionnaire* and have his future assured."

[79] Interview with Maurice Bans.

"Yes, that's at the basis of mass organizations. In the [agricultural] union, just as in the working class, what brings people together is their need, their immediate needs. We have to follow those needs as they change so we can take advantage of them to mobilize people." [80]

The Communists tirelessly emphasized their short-term platform, which appealed to a large spectrum of the rural population. Their principal demands, which remained unchanged throughout the 1920s and 1930s, included:

- Higher prices for produce and livestock.
- Lower prices for fertilizers, seeds, and agricultural machinery.
- Suppression of all taxes for small peasants. [81]
- Limitation on agricultural debts (reduced interest rates; payment delays; some proposed the suppression of mortgages).
- Wide-ranging cheap credits for small peasants.
- Retirement at age 60 for those who worked the land.
- Health insurance and family allowances.
- Insurance protection against agricultural calamities.
- Lower transport costs for agricultural goods.
- Nationalization of fertilizer production.
- Rural electrification.
- Reform of tenant farming (nine-year leases, improved lodging, compensation for improvements by tenant farmers).
- Reform of sharecropping (two-thirds of the crop for the sharecropper, suppression of dues in kind, compensation for agricultural improvements). [82]
- Expropriation of uncultivated land and its distribution to sharecroppers and tenant farmers free of charge. [83]

There was a bit of everything for the Party's targeted constituents in these proposals. The Communist platform judiciously appealed both to the peasants' pocketbooks and to their sense of social justice. What peasant, after all, did not dream of doing away with taxes and benefiting from lower interest rates, while selling his produce at a higher price and purchasing machinery, grain, and fertilizers at reduced cost? This program attracted peasants be-

[80] Interview with François Monédière.

[81] The measure was intended for the small farmer who worked the land with family members, but some extended this future tax break to all peasants, even if they employed some labor. At other times militants claimed that peasants who earned more than a specified figure would be taxable. *TCO*, 10 January 1925, 12 November 1927.

[82] The demand for two-thirds of the crop appeared in the 1930s. See Renaud Jean, *Métayers, défendez-vous!!! Luttez pour les deux tiers* (Paris, circa 1931–32). In preceding years, the Communists asked that the sharecropper be allowed to put aside what he needed to feed his family before the crop was split in two equal shares.

[83] All these demands were put forward in the Limousin and Dordogne Communist press. See also J. Castels, *Le prolétariat et les paysans* (Paris, 1925); J. Desnots, *La lutte des classes au village: Pour le pain, la paix et la terre* (Paris, 1932); *Aux travailleurs des champs*; *Les communistes défendent les paysans* (Bourges, 1935).

cause it sheltered them from the perils of the marketplace, protecting them against overzealous creditors and important price fluctuations. In this sense, the Communist Party, which in the words of Renaud Jean was "ready to do anything in order to save [the peasants]," [84] was perceived by a significant segment of the Limousin and Dordogne peasants as their best rampart against economic change. The Communists' proposals—to set up a protected agricultural economy (price controls) and to carry out a program of social justice for the disadvantaged—corresponded to the views of peasants who were both politically advanced and economically defensive.

Communism's influence dipped considerably in the countryside during the early 1930s, when the Party's pragmatic short-term program became tainted by ideological issues. But there were limits to how far one could go, as René Fromage (alias Fronsac), the secretary of the Limousin Communist Party, learned in 1932. Fronsac, a Party cadre who was of neither peasant nor Limousin origin, denounced reforms proposed by rural militants—higher prices for agricultural produce, loans for peasants, compensation for price drops. These demands, Fronsac claimed, prejudiced the Party's long-term goals by turning poor peasants away from the class struggle. Within two weeks, under strong pressure from Corrèze rural militants appalled by his lack of political realism, Fronsac had publicly retracted his views.[85] Such a humiliating exercise clearly demonstrated the influence rural militants preserved in the face of leaders designated by the urban Party hierarchy, even at the height of the sectarian class-versus-class period.

In order to sustain rural society's interest in their short-term program, the Communists constantly reassured questioning peasants about their long-run objectives. Even the most hard line of militants recognized that the Party's progressive supporters in the countryside did not take to collectivism. Peasants might donate grain to starving Russians, protest against the war, and applaud anticapitalist rhetoric directed against the trusts, the intermediaries, and the state, but they were also concerned with preserving their way of life and their property in the face of changing economic conditions.

The encounter between communism and rural society was not a one-way street. The PCF's rural policy reflected an informal negotiation between militants and the electorate at large. More than competing political parties, the Communists offered the peasantry a platform to express their views. Behind the ever-present stereotypical language (*langue de bois*) lay a party that was

---

[84] According to Renaud Jean: "Our party . . . is the party of less arduous and shorter work, the party of easy and prosperous peasant life, but it is above all the party of higher prices for agricultural products, of defense of agricultural property, the party of [family] allowances, credits, and a moratorium on debts; in a word, the party that, when all over France the peasant is crying out in distress and calling for help, is ready to do anything to save him." *L'union des paysans de France* (Paris, 1936), 51; *Le Travailleur de la Dordogne*, 25 April 1936.

[85] TCO, 23 October 1932, 5 November 1932.

responsive and attentive to rural concerns. In the end, rural communism was defined as much by perceptions from below as by policies, however watered down, elaborated from above. The Communists best embodied (and exploited) the suspicion of the state, the hatred of *les gros* and *les bourgeois*, and the dream of an egalitarian society of small property holders dear to sectors of the Limousin and Dordogne peasantry. The peasants did not so much subscribe to a forward-looking ideology as see in the Communist Party a leader in their struggle against change. For them, economic immobility also was a form of social justice.

6 Militancy and Sociability

The French Communist Party distinguished itself from its principal opponents both by its objectives (to take power by any means)—even if they were rarely stated explicitly in rural areas—and by its organization. In the Limousin and Dordogne countryside the PCF was often the only political party that remained active and mobilized outside election periods.[1] The Party's endurance in rural areas was the result not only of intelligently targeted policies but equally of an impressive network of rural militants, leaders, and cells. The PCF established cells, sponsored dances, and brought speakers to the region's smallest villages and hamlets, and in doing so altered forms of sociability and the shape of local politics. The Communists were better placed to respond to changes in political, social, and economic environments where they were strong. The presence of capable, dedicated militants in rural areas was essential to winning the peasantry's confidence and support.

Leaders and Candidates

The Party's results at the polls depended largely on its ability to present popular, trustworthy, and well-established candidates. To Léon Champeix, a small-town schoolteacher and former PCF candidate in a rural canton, "the value of a militant who undertakes political propaganda, his personal value, sometimes counts more than the ideology itself. You may have greater confidence in a man—whether he's on the right or on the left—if he is respected, if he's sincere, if he's honest. You may have more confidence in him than in his ideology. The propagandist's personality counts as much as his doctrine in the success of a propaganda campaign."[2]

[1] This was also true of Haute-Vienne Socialists.
[2] Interview with Léon Champeix, Brive, 30 July and 29 August 1984; Léon Champeix, "Souvenirs et libres propos d'un 'écrivain du dimanche,'" unpublished manuscript, 37.

The Communists met with disappointing, even catastrophic results when they ran little-known apparatchiks for office. A good militant was not necessarily a good candidate. Armand Soleilhavoup, Communist mayor of Lagraulière (Corrèze) in 1984 and *conseiller général* of the canton of Seilhac, who had considerable experience as a Party candidate, explained: "There is the militant, and there is the candidate, and they don't coincide. I would say that a militant, the perfect militant, rarely makes a good candidate. In the countryside, the most active and exemplary militant rarely makes a good candidate. So it boils down to personalities."[3] There were, of course, exceptions. Marius Vazeilles and Clément Chausson, both good militants and excellent candidates, were gently pushed aside by the Party's leadership in the 1930s and replaced by more politically malleable Party-trained militants. As Léon Champeix put it, "The Revolution is too serious an affair to entrust it to amateurs."[4]

A good speaker, both known and appreciated in the countryside, could often gain sympathetic ears among voters who had no initial predisposition toward communism. Rural militants in northern Dordogne argued that it was better "to keep peasant leaders who speak the language of the land" than to bring in Périgueux workers who "don't understand the peasant mentality" and would only "strike a mortal blow to communism in the countryside."[5] Jules Fraisseix, doctor and Communist deputy of Haute-Vienne, strongly opposed the running of working-class candidates for legislative office, because they lacked the skills essential for campaigning in the countryside.[6] The Party's rural militants knew that peasants were best approached by fellow peasants or by those who knew their problems well. Léon Champeix recalled:

> In general, everything depended on the propagandists. . . . The peasant is a very different person from the city dweller. What interests the peasant is his land, to live by the rhythm of the seasons, his fields, his animals, and he's always more or less suspicious of everything that comes from the city. He's distrustful because to him the city is a site of parasitism. It's an old mentality that still exists. And he's the one who works so that all that [the city] can live. So he's totally distrustful. But propaganda, when it's carried out by people of his own background, it's well, very successful. Propaganda among Corrèze Communist peasants was carried out by peasant Communists or by people who were not peasants but were known and respected in the countryside. These were people you saw at work every day, and they were well regarded. And of course what they said brought results, because the peasant, he'll read his newspaper or you'll tell

---

[3] Interview with Armand Soleilhavoup, Lagraulière, 5 July 1984.
[4] In 1937 the Corrèze Communist Federation was taken over by Clovis Chirin, a worker at the Manufacture Nationale d'Armes in Tulle. Champeix, "Souvenirs," 17.
[5] AN F⁷ 13109, CS Périgueux to SG, 21 March 1927.
[6] ADHV 1M168, CS to PHV, 17 September 1923.

him something, well, and so when he's working in his field or at home—he's isolated, especially in Corrèze, where villages and farms are quite isolated—and he'll think about what he's read or what he's been told. He turns all that around in his head—since he doesn't talk much and he doesn't see many people—or he'll see a neighbor and he'll talk to him about it. He's much more impressed by the propaganda that's aimed at him, and it leaves lasting marks.[7]

Communist militants spent much time in the field going after rural and peasant support. They pressed the flesh at fairs and markets, attended public meetings held by other political parties to give *la contradiction* and make their views known, held assemblies with the help of a few militants, and attended cell gatherings. André Plazanet, a local Communist official who also worked for the Party-sponsored peasant unions, held countless "peasant meetings" in Corrèze during the 1930s, "and everywhere I was well received. Note that I didn't put a gun to people's heads!"[8] And Henri Peuch added: "I think the leaders of my day were much closer to them [the peasants]. We lived much less in offices than we do today, and much more on the fairgrounds, much more in the villages. It was much harder to be a militant then."[9]

Marius Vazeilles and other leaders walked countless kilometers to hold meetings in the desolate villages and hamlets of Haute-Corrèze. Georges Lacassagne recalls how François Aussoleil, Communist deputy of Corrèze, arrived by bus in the village of Gros-Chastang in the early 1920s to give a speech. Aussoleil, who was over sixty years of age at the time, then climbed up a steep ravine to neighboring La Roche–Canillac, where he held another meeting at 2:00 P.M., before trudging off to give a final talk in Champagnac-la-Prune.[10] Campaigning was hard work. Léon Champeix, who in 1937 ran for the Conseil Général in Uzerche, would set off on foot to hold village meetings after teaching his classes:

Eight days ahead of time I'd ask the mayor to let me use a room or the covered part of the school playground [*préau*]. I'd have local comrades put up posters announcing a meeting on such-and-such a date, at such-and-such a time. And then I'd often set off on foot. I'd sometimes leave on foot around four or five o'clock in the afternoon, a pack on my back. I didn't have a car, I didn't have anything. I did it on foot; I had merit. So I'd go speak to them. Sometimes I had [an audience of] ten or a dozen, sometimes thirty, forty, or fifty. And so we'd talk like that, among pals. I outlined peasant demands to them, I talked a bit about generalities, about peace and so on, and then about our agenda at the moment. I developed the themes that we [the Party] developed at that time. And

[7] Interview with Léon Champeix.
[8] Interview with André Plazanet, St-Clément, 1 September 1984.
[9] Interview with Henri Peuch, Brive, 23 August 1983.
[10] Interview with Georges Lacassagne, Gros-Chastang, 3 July 1984.

then the meeting would break up and we'd go have a drink. Very little debate and opposition, very little, very little.[11]

The stonecutter Albert Coucaud, who ran for the Creuse Conseil Général the same year, was slightly better off; he used a bicycle to campaign on Sundays and after work, and sold picture postcards of himself to raise funds for his shoestring campaign.[12] By the late 1920s some of the more well-to-do Corrèze militants, such as Joseph Biaugeaud and Clément Chausson, owned cars, and occasionally they lent them to their comrades, but the better part of the Party's candidates used public transport, rode bicycles, or walked.

In the countryside it was imperative to preserve and cultivate personal relations with electors and militants. The PCF's most effective leaders worked at occupations that brought them into constant contact with rural society. As a country doctor, Jules Fraisseix called upon large numbers of households in the Eymoutiers region, and this no doubt contributed to his election as mayor and *conseiller général* of Eymoutiers and deputy of Haute-Vienne in 1928. Clément Chausson, an excellent peasant propagandist and financially comfortable sawmill owner in Egletons (Corrèze), visited suppliers and clients in surrounding areas. Joseph Biaugeaud, a traveling merchant and son of a Dordogne sharecropper, was equally well acquainted with things rural. Léger Peyraut sold and delivered wine in and around Lamazière-Basse (Corrèze) and did not hesitate to talk politics when it seemed appropriate. "When you sell wine," he explained, "you see people and you talk about everything. If you know how to handle the situation, you can bring some over [to the Communist Party]."[13] This is precisely what Peyraut did in the 1935 municipal elections in Lamazière-Basse, which saw the Communists gain control of the town hall. Antoine Bourdarias, a leader of Corrèze peasant protests in the mid-1930s and *conseiller général* of Seilhac in 1934, earned a meager living going from farm to farm collecting rags and rabbit skins. Though this was considered a shabby way to make a living, it enabled Bourdarias to establish valuable personal contacts and keep abreast of the way the peasants were thinking. Armand Soleilhavoup commented:

Bourdarias's work was a bit of an embarrassment because when he was elected [to the Conseil Général] he was what we called a ragpicker, and he wasn't much to look at. He collected rabbit skins and all that. Well, there's nothing shameful about it, they were needed at the time . . . that's how he lived. And in fact, that was precisely his strength, because he was known in the canton, he'd go to all the houses. You wouldn't think it, but before the war they came through regularly, we'd hear them cry, "Rags! Rabbit skins!" . . . In general he had a rather shabby appearance. To sort through those rags that were often filthy and

[11] Interview with Léon Champeix.
[12] Gabrielle Thévenot, *Une vie de Creusois à travers le siècle . . . à travers la France* (Guéret, 1981), 175.
[13] Interview with Léger Peyraut, Lamazière-Basse, 1 September 1984.

all that, you couldn't be . . . Well! But just the same he was very much appreciated, and if he was elected, it wasn't without good reason. He had made himself popular. He was very intelligent, very sharp.[14]

François Monédière commented, "He decided to collect rags and be a ragman. And people weren't pleased about that. It seemed demeaning for a man of his character, even though he was intelligent and was a good militant."[15]

Bourdarias's occupation was a handicap, for rural inhabitants proved far from indifferent to the social status of a candidate for office: he *had* to be respectable, and if he was a peasant, it was important that he cultivate his land well, even at the expense of political activity. But Bourdarias managed to overcome the electorate's prejudices by his hard work, his talent as a propagandist, his political finesse, and his personal contact with voters, and he established a solid base in the area northwest of Tulle. By the late 1930s he had been named editor in chief of the *Travailleur de la Corrèze* and was employed as a full-time propagandist (*permanent*) by the Communist Party.[16]

Marius Vazeilles, one of the PCF's two experts on rural issues, is the best example of a militant who forged close ties with the peasantry. Vazeilles's occupation as a nursery gardener (*pépiniériste*) and forestry expert and his lifelong campaign for the reforestation of the Millevaches plateau, not to mention his passion for archeology, brought him often to the highland's most isolated villages. "Vazeilles," wrote an enthusiastic Central Committee envoy in late 1921, "is really the life and soul of the organization, always ready to set to work, keeping sections gasping for breath and setting a fire under everyone. It's not money our Party needs to make great strides, it's men of that sort."[17] His archaeological interests earned him lyrical praise from Maurice Thorez, secretary general of the Communist Party, in the 1937 edition of his autobiography, *Fils du peuple*.[18] Vazeilles—whose bushy beard became a trademark on the plateau—was widely known and respected by supporters and political adversaries alike for his efforts to reforest large parts of the region with Douglas pine and other conifers. Jean-Baptiste Vars recalls how "he'd come and sit down and have a bite to eat at our house with my grandfather, who didn't share his political opinions; but he was still Monsieur Vazeilles."[19] Vazeilles, who was neither from Corrèze nor of peasant origins (his father was a forest ranger in Allier), became well integrated

[14] Interview with Armand Soleilhavoup. Rabbit skins were used, among other purposes, for boot linings. Rabbit skin gatherers disappeared after World War II.

[15] Interview with François Monédière, Beaumont, 31 July 1984.

[16] *TC*, 5 February 1938; Parti Communiste Français, Région de la Corrèze, *Conférence régionale des 10 et 11 décembre 1938 à Tulle* (n.p., n.d.), 6.

[17] *PCTC*, 25 December 1921.

[18] Maurice Thorez, *Fils du peuple* (Paris, 1937), 206. Vazeilles, who broke off from the Party after the Nazi-Soviet pact, was no longer mentioned in postwar editions of the book.

[19] Interview with Jean-Baptiste Vars, Meymac, 3 October 1983. Vazeilles published a book and numerous articles on the reforestation of the plateau. See his *Mise en valeur du plateau de Millevaches* (Ussel, 1931).

in the rural community in the years after his nomination as forest warden for the Millevaches plateau in 1913.[20] Jean-Baptiste Vars remembered him as "an honest man, a simple man, who had class. You know, in comparison with others, he was an above-average man. Still, he remained an honest man [*brave homme*]. He'd arrive in Meymac, sit down, and drink a bowl of milk with the peasants. It wasn't put on, it was his temperament. He felt at home and he said so. Though his own family was slightly bourgeois, he felt much more comfortable with the peasants. Even those who had voted against him came to see him afterward for advice—he was a *pépiniériste*, a man of the woods."[21]

Vazeilles's work as a forestry and agricultural expert on the Millevaches plateau gained him much sympathy in the countryside. His politics matched his gracious, warm, and open personality: he was neither dogmatic nor sectarian ("He didn't have the *théorie terrible* that you found in Paris," said his daughter), and in this respect he was representative of most Corrèze rural militants. Theoretical issues were, in the end, of secondary importance to him. Vazeilles remained moderate and down to earth in his discussions with peasants. He was an excellent orator, "a popular man, a great guy who never spoke from a platform but climbed up on a table in the middle of the crowd."[22] Vazeilles was no ideologue: he outlined ideas that were simple, straightforward, full of common sense, and easy to understand. Hardworking, persistent (he was elected deputy on his fifth attempt, and ran in countless local electoral contests), extremely well versed in agricultural matters (Thorez had considered him for minister of agriculture if the PCF were to join the Popular Front government),[23] keenly aware of the complexity of the rural world, and always ready to water down the Party's ideology when necessary, Vazeilles was the model rural Communist militant. In politics as in forestry and agriculture, Vazeilles was no theoretician but a first-class popularizer.

The PCF's most accomplished Limousin and Dordogne leaders shared a deep concern for rural society. The same could not always be said of the Party hierarchy—working-class militants often dominated Haute-Vienne and Dordogne federations—but at election time, under pressure from the base and peasant militants, the PCF's lists of candidates favored the countryside. The eighty-three Communist candidates who ran for legislative office

---

[20] Vazeilles quit the Eaux et Forêts in 1920 after the administration named him to a new position in Bar-le-Duc (Meuse). The Socialists, and later the Communists, claimed that Vazeilles's transfer had been politically motivated. ADC 3M195 and *PCTC*, 24 September 1922.

[21] Interview with Jean-Baptiste Vars. See also the interview of Vazeilles's daughter, Marguerite, in Guillaume Bourgeois, "Le groupe parlementaire communiste d'août 1939 à janvier 1940: La question des démissionnaires" (mémoire de maîtrise, Université de Lille III, 1978–79), A149.

[22] Interview with Henri Peuch.

[23] Guillaume Bourgeois, "Communistes et anti-communistes pendant la drôle de guerre" (thèse de troisième cycle, Université de Paris X, 1983), 183n.

in Limousin and Périgord between the wars included twenty-two workers, fourteen peasants, ten artisans, ten employees, five shopkeepers, and four merchants. While the PCF apparatus exerted considerable pressure for a minimum number of working-class candidates, the Communist Party's most serious candidates were those who had the closest links to the countryside. Local leaders tactfully sent urban workers and employees to districts where they stood no chance of being elected; their candidacies were largely symbolic and did little to improve the Communist Party's standing in areas where it was already poorly established. The four Communists elected to the Chamber of Deputies during the interwar years all enjoyed close ties with the rural world: Jules Fraisseix, who gained office in 1928, lived in Eymoutiers and practiced medicine in the poor rural regions of southeastern Haute-Vienne; Gustave Saussot, elected in Dordogne in 1936, owned a small automobile and agricultural machinery repair shop in the *bourg* of La Coquille; Paul Loubradou, also elected in Dordogne that year, was a painter of sorts, and as leader of the Communists in Bergerac he played a key role in establishing the Party in the southwestern corner of Dordogne; and Marius Vazeilles was widely known throughout the Corrèze highlands.[24]

The number of peasant candidates was higher in local elections, in keeping with the PCF's tendency to restrict their participation to less significant contests. In interwar Corrèze, peasants accounted for 44.3 percent of all Party candidates for the Conseil Général and the Conseils d'Arrondissement combined; they were far more numerous than artisans (18.8 percent), merchants (8.5 percent), and workers (4.7 percent). Militants enjoyed more freedom to select local candidates than national ones. In the countryside it was simply bad politics to nominate an outsider unknown in the region. Peasants, moreover, proved more willing (and able) to run for local political office than for the post of deputy: cantonal and municipal elections did not consume a great deal of time, but a serious legislative campaign—especially during the spring, when most elections were held—posed great difficulties. It was the campaigns of popular rural militants for local office that familiarized many voters with the Party's basic demands and with a vulgarized version of Communist ideology.

The Party's grass-roots candidates were a mixed lot. Some proved to be talented campaigners, and in the mid-1930s a few attended short PCF training schools (*écoles du Parti; écoles paysannes*). The Party federation helped them print their electoral program (when it did not supply them with one) but usually left them to campaign on their own. Many candidates had little experience speaking in public, and their ideological grounding was often limited. Some had only a meager education and were ill prepared to take on positions that assumed more than minimal literacy. François Chansiaud,

---

[24] François Aussoleil, Corrèze Communist deputy from 1921 to 1924, was first elected on the Socialist ticket in 1919. He joined the Communist Party after the Tours Congress.

who ran a small sawmill and a harvesting business, declared his candidacy for the Conseil Général of the canton of Vigeois (Corrèze) in 1928 in the following terms: "J'ais l'ônneur de vous prévenire que je pôsse mas Candidature au Eletion Cantonal a Vigois. Candidat du Bloque ouvriére et pezson di Communistte. Resevais M^er le Préfet mais sinseire salutation."[25] His fellow Party member Iréné Pradier, whose spelling was equally idiosyncratic, informed the Dordogne prefect that he was running for the Conseil d'Arrondissement as a candidate of the "partît Comuniste Moderée"[26] Neither candidate, then, could spell the name of the party on whose platform he was running, and one thought the Communists to be "moderate." Neither Chansiaud nor Pradier, however, conducted anything resembling an electoral campaign, and in this they were not representative of Party candidates. In parts of the countryside where the Communists were weak, they sometimes turned to candidates who had limited educational and ideological knowledge.

The PCF's strong presence in the countryside owed much to the hard work and dedication of popular, trusted, well-established militants and leaders. The Party's success, however, was also a function of its program. Support for the Communist Party had more to do with bread-and-butter politics than with prominent personalities. A number of the Communist Party's interwar militants and leaders disappeared from its ranks after World War II. Some had died during the conflict, others had moved, and yet others had parted with the Communists for political reasons. The region's three Communist deputies were disillusioned by the Nazi-Soviet pact: Gustave Saussot and Paul Loubradou were among the first, in late August 1939, to resign from the Party and its parliamentary group; and Marius Vazeilles, who appealed from prison to his Radical rival Henri Queuille, disassociated himself in early 1940; in Vazeilles's case the motivations appear to have been both financial (he wanted to avoid selling his landholdings, especially his tree farm, to pay the heavy fines levied by the judicial system) and political. After the war, Vazeilles was expelled from the PCF and denounced as a traitor; in classic Stalinist fashion, he disappeared from old PCF photographs, and when his face remained visible, his name was omitted from the caption.[27] Joseph Biaugeaud left for Bordeaux in 1945, and Antoine Bourdarias handed in his Party card shortly thereafter. But the loss of the Communist Party's most popular rural leaders (and some of its founders) had no impact on the PCF's score at the polls or on its political geography. On the contrary,

---

[25] ADC 3M304, letter to PC, 9 October 1928. Chansiaud was elected deputy mayor of St-Bonnet-L'Enfantier in 1935: ADC 3M344–45.

[26] ADD 3M131, letter to PD, 30 September 1934.

[27] Bourgeois, "Le groupe parlementaire"; "Communistes et anti-communistes"; and Vazeilles's biography in the *Dictionnaire biographique du mouvement ouvrier français*, vol. 43 (Paris, 1993); Francis de Tarr, *Henri Queuille en son temps, 1884–1970* (Paris, 1995), 271–74. On photographs, Gérard Belloin, *Renaud Jean, le tribun des paysans* (Paris, 1993), 317.

the Communists, led by a new generation of militants trained during the war, capitalized on their leading role in the Resistance and brought in new members and voters in record numbers.

The Party's ability to survive the defections of its leading interwar peasant militants helps place the role of leadership in proper perspective. The central reasons that people turned to communism had not changed. The PCF's program, which had gained credibility by its association with the Resistance, was more attractive than ever. Communist militants, old and new, filled the gap left by Vazeilles and others, and what they lacked in charisma they made up with hard work and dedication. They also benefited from a proportional electoral system that gave more weight to political parties than to personalities.

Personalities played an important role in communism's implantation, of course, but the Party was not as dependent on its leaders as other parties were on theirs. A comparison with the Radical party is instructive in this regard. In 1936, Henri Queuille, Corrèze's leading Radical politician during the interwar period, decided not to seek reelection, and the Communist Marius Vazeilles was elected to office. The strength of radicalism in Haute-Corrèze owed much to the personality of Henry Queuille, and when he pulled out, the Radicals, who had no organization whatever, collapsed. The Communists were the mirror opposite of the Radicals: their extensive grass-roots organization was unmatched by any other party, and they also had a clear, coherent program. Dissatisfied leaders, militants, and voters could (and did) abandon ship, but the PCF was well equipped to weather political storms. The Party's structure made it possible to develop interchangeable militants and leaders at the local level. Other parties—Radicals and conservatives in particular—proved more dependent on notables and other self-selected individuals whose positions and base of support became increasingly precarious. In many ways the Communists were an island of stability in an ever-changing political environment.

Members

The Communist Party's membership varied widely among departments and time periods (table 6.1). The Corrèze furnished the largest, most consistent membership contingent: the Communists counted 2,000 militants in 1921, making it the twelfth largest federation in the country; this figure dropped rapidly in the following years, although at no time did the PCF dip under 500 members.[28] Growth resumed in 1935 and accelerated with the Popular Front, and the Party reached close to 3,000 members in the late 1930s. This pattern was repeated in the other three departments: the relative

[28] *PCTC,* 25 December 1921.

Table 6.1. Membership in Parti Communiste, Limousin and Dordogne, 1921–1939

	Corrèze	Creuse	Haute-Vienne	Dordogne
1921	2,000	900	1,000	1,449
1922	1,600	600	700	900
1923	773		885	610
1924	676		765	350
1925			622	
1926	750		500	350
1927				748
1928	843	475	601	675
1929	500	350	593	680
1930	670	350	706	565
1931				450
1932			505	370
1933				418
1934				398
1935	1,002		636[a]	838
1936	1,744		2,782[a]	2,152
1937	2,650	1,270	2,930	2,850
1938	2,606		4,000[a]	2,630
1939	>3,000	1,270	1,829	2,630

Sources: ADC: 1M70, 4M282; ADD: 4M192–95; ADHV: 1M165, 1M168–70, 1M172, 1M175, 4M174; AN: F[7] 13097, F[7] 13115, F[7] 13118, F[7] 13130; regional Communist party press; PCF congresses.

[a] Creuse and Haute-Vienne combined.

strength of the first years soon gave way to important losses during the adaptation period that followed the Party's birth, and membership stabilized at relatively low levels before growth resumed in the mid-1930s. In Dordogne and Haute-Vienne the Communists had mixed success, and not until the emergence of the Popular Front did they establish a solid organization. Finally, the Party never recruited militants on the same scale in Creuse as in the rest of Limousin or in Dordogne. In 1937, when membership reached its peak, the Communists counted close to 10,000 militants in Limousin and Périgord, twice as many as in 1921. The Party's membership, however, never represented more than a small portion of the Communist vote (12 percent of the electorate in Corrèze and Haute-Vienne in 1936).

We can place these figures in perspective by calculating the density of Communist militants per 10,000 inhabitants (table 6.2). Throughout the interwar years, Corrèze boasted one of the highest densities of PCF members in France. In 1921 this department counted more militants per 10,000 inhabitants than the entire Paris region, and it ranked fifth in the nation, behind Seine-et-Oise, Vaucluse, Aube, and Seine-et-Marne. In the following year, Corrèze leaders proudly noted that their federation, the eighth largest in the country, placed third in terms of the number of militants per 10,000 inhabitants.[29] Under the Popular Front, Corrèze trailed only the Paris area

[29] *PCTC*, 25 December 1921, 1 October 1922.

Table 6.2. Number of Parti Communiste members per 10,000 inhabitants, 1921–1939

	Corrèze	Creuse	Haute-Vienne	Dordogne	France	Provinces	Paris region
1921	73	39	28	36	27	25	39
1922	58	26	19	22			
1928	31	21	17	17			
1930	25	16	20	14			
1935	38			21	24[a]		
1936	66			55			
1937	100	62	87	73	64[a]–77	58	152
1939	114	62	54	67			

Sources: Membership data for France, the Paris region, and the provinces from Annie Four-caut, *Bobigny, banlieue rouge* (Paris, 1986), 26. Mean density figures from Philippe Buton, *Les lendemains qui déchantent: Le Parti communiste français à la Libération* (Paris, 1993), 272–73. For Limousin and Dordogne, see table 6.1. I have used the population figures for 1921, 1926, 1931, and 1936.
[a]Mean density for all departments.

and a few industrial departments in the north and east. The strength of the Communist movement was also notable in Dordogne and Haute-Vienne: the density of militants in these two departments was close to the national figure and consistently higher than the provincial average.

These were positive results for overwhelmingly rural departments. It was far more difficult, after all, to recruit members in rural areas than in urban ones. Peasants were less inclined to join political organizations and had less time at their disposal, particularly in summer, to attend meetings, sell news-papers, and enlist new members. Large numbers of Limousin and Périgord militants left the PCF's ranks in the early 1920s; their disillusionment with militancy was not peculiar to the countryside but part of a nationwide phe-nomenon. Moreover, the decline and stagnation of the Communist mem-bership had no consistent effect on the Party's success at the polls.

Who were the Party's members? Communist militants and police author-ities agreed on at least one thing: the Party's membership was overwhelm-ingly rural and peasant. PCF leaders in neighboring departments concurred: "Our federation," wrote a Creuse militant, "is almost entirely composed of small property owners"; and in Dordogne, Gabriel Bouyon noted in 1921 that peasant smallholders predominated in the most active and successful cells.[30]

Reports from the Communist hierarchy did not always confirm the Party's rural character. A 1929 survey based on 37 percent of Limousin and Péri-gord's 1,893 members concluded that peasants (46.7 percent) and workers

[30] AN F[7] 13096, MI to PC, 26 January 1925. For Creuse, *TCO*, 13 September 1924; and for Dordogne, *Prol C*, 8 May 1921.

(44.7 percent) accounted for similar proportions of all Party members.[31] The survey's reliability, however, is open to question: the number of "workers" seems out of all proportion to what we know from other sources, and, though none were listed, must have included a large number of both rural and urban artisans and small shopkeepers. Moreover, 55 of the 177 cells that did respond were more likely to be located in towns or large *bourgs* than in villages, and this skewed the final result. Taken at the height of the sectarian class-against-class tactic, the survey reveals more about the PCF's desire to represent itself as a party of workers than about the actual rural membership.

A more in-depth knowledge of the Communist Party's social composition can be established, however. Complete lists of Party members are rare, but it is possible to reconstruct the membership by using a broad range of sources, and I have done so for interwar Corrèze. The prefectoral administration, helped by the police, kept close tabs on the Communist Party throughout the 1920s and 1930s, and periodically attempted to identify cells and militants. When the government banned the PCF in late September 1939, after the Nazi-Soviet pact, the Corrèze gendarmerie compiled extensive lists of Party members, and in June 1940 it used them to confiscate the Legion of Honor and the *médaille militaire* from PCF militants. This work was continued by Vichy, which withdrew hunting licenses from suspected Communists. I have used these police lists with caution, for they are never complete or devoid of inaccuracies. Local Communist newspapers also provide crucial information on membership: rural cells often reported on their meetings, listed names of some members, and mentioned those elected to the posts of cell secretary and treasurer. Finally, large numbers of PCF militants ran for municipal, departmental, and national political office. Insofar as possible, I have compared and confronted these sources and eliminated dubious cases. I then cross-checked the resulting roster of 1,925 militants with voter registration rolls to verify occupational status. If anything, the following analysis underestimates the importance of the rural element within the Party's ranks. Members mentioned in the Communist press and in police reports tended to be more active than others. Authorities knew more about militants who lived in towns or in the village center—where artisans and small shopkeepers settled—than about those who lived in the surrounding hamlets.

The Corrèze PCF was primarily a peasant party. Smallholding peasants composed the majority (57 percent) of the 1,420 Communist militants whose occupations have been identified (table 6.3).[32] Artisans (16.8 percent) and shopkeepers (6 percent) also joined the Party in significant numbers; car-

[31] AN F[7] 13118, "Parti communiste français: Région limousine: Rapport moral, 1929."

[32] Because of their small number, I have included the three sharecroppers, eight tenant farmers, and seven agricultural workers among peasants. The number of tenant farmers is underestimated because they tended to declare themselves as *cultivateurs* on voter registration lists.

Table 6.3. Social composition of Communist membership, Corrèze, 1920–1939[a]

	All members		Cell secretaries	
	N	%	N	%
Peasants	814	57.3%	53	38.7%
Artisans	239	16.8	40	29.2
Shopkeepers	92	6.5	17	12.4
Masons	77	5.4	9	6.6
Workers	63	4.4	2	1.5
Employees	35	2.5	3	2.2
Retired	26	1.8	5	3.5
Merchants, entrepreneurs	24	1.7	2	1.5
Other	19	1.3	4	2.9
Teachers	14	1.0	2	1.5
Other migrants	9	0.6		
No profession	8	0.6		
	1,420	99.9%	137	100.0%

Sources: Regional Communist press: ADC 1M70–73, 4M282–85, 58W2145, and numerous other police reports and election files in ADC (1M, 3M, and 4M series) and AN (F¹ CIII and F⁷ series). The voter registration lists I used are in ADC 3M93-176.

[a]The towns of Tulle and Brive are not included.

penters and blacksmiths, bakers and café owners had much in common, socially and politically, with their best clients, the peasants. Masons and other temporary migrants, who often farmed plots of land on a part-time basis, accounted for close to 6 percent of PCF members. Broadly put, the structure of the Party membership paralleled that of its electorate: a strong agricultural component associated with a smaller number of artisans, shopkeepers, and temporary migrants. Workers and employees, who were the objects of countless recruitment drives, failed to account for a significant percentage of militants. This was a party of the working class, largely devoid of anything resembling an urban or rural proletariat. More than any other political movement in the region, the Communists successfully forged a strong membership base in the rural world. Placed in a national context, these figures underscore PCF successes outside what are considered to be its traditional constituencies. In urban areas, as Annie Fourcaut and Michel Hastings have shown, the Communist militant was not necessarily a skilled worker employed in a large factory; and in the countryside he was neither the most exploited nor the most proletarianized of society's members.[33]

Over time, the Communist Party became increasingly ruralized. The number of artisans and shopkeepers declined in many small communes during the interwar years, and the growing peasant character of the population had

[33] Annie Fourcaut, *Bobigny, banlieue rouge* (Paris, 1986), 104; Michel Hastings, *Halluin la Rouge, 1919–1939: Aspects d'un communisme identitaire* (Lille, 1991), 222–23.

an impact on the social composition of the Party's membership. By 1947, peasants accounted for 70 percent of Dordogne's 14,188 militants.[34] The Communists lost some of their best militants when artisans deserted small villages in search of employment, and in the long run the Party increasingly relied for support on those directly engaged in agricultural endeavors.

The occupational makeup of cells did not consistently reflect the population's social composition. Artisans might play an important role in villages where most people were peasants and be underrepresented in bourgs where their presence was more important. St-Sulpice-Laurière (Haute-Vienne) was an important railroad juncture, but if one believes the police reports, the most active cell members in 1930 were peasants, not railroad workers.[35] In general, however, peasants made up the majority of cell members in villages. This was the case in Beauregard (Dordogne), where 8 of 11 known members worked the land, and also in Corrèze villages such as Albussac (30 of 42 militants were *cultivateurs* and 6 were migrating masons), St-Clément (peasants accounted for all 26 militants), and Viam (13 peasants out of 16 members). Could it have been otherwise when, to take but one example, peasants accounted for 81 percent of Viam's 174 registered voters in 1930?[36]

In keeping with national trends, the Communist Party's membership was overwhelmingly male. Few women joined the Party, nor did the Communists make any serious effort to recruit them. The rare steps in this direction met with indifference or hostility in rural areas, and since women could not vote, there was little incentive to prod the Party into action.[37] Unlike Communists in the Paris suburbs or in Nord (Halluin), the militants of Limousin and Dordogne never symbolically put women up for local political office. In Corrèze, women constituted a mere 1.1 percent of the total number of militants.[38] The 22 women, 6 of whom lived in the towns of Bort and Ussel, included 5 peasants, 2 railroad and tramway workers, 2 seamstresses, 5 widows, and 3 cell secretaries, but only one housewife. Some of these women were the daughters or spouses of militants; others, war widows in particular, enjoyed prominent status in village communities. In the late 1930s the Party organized women in the Comité Mondial des Femmes contre la Guerre et le Fascisme, and young women in the Union des Jeunes Filles de France (seventy mem-

---

[34] Parti Communiste Français, Fédération de la Dordogne, *Conférence fédérale des 7–8 juin 1947: Rapport politique présenté . . . par Lucien Dutard* (n.p., n.d.). The *percentage* of peasant members declined in the 1960s and 1970s: 27.5% of Corrèze's militants in 1970 were peasants. G. Lord, "Le PCF, structures et organisation d'une fédération départementale," paper delivered at the European Consortium for Political Research, Paris, 1973, 11.

[35] AN F[7] 13123, CS Limoges to SG, 4 February 1930.

[36] For Beauregard, AN F[7] 13098, CS to PD, 2 September 1932; for Albussac, ADC 1M71, ADC 58W2145, interview with Henri Peuch; for St-Clément, interview with André Plazanet; for Viam, ADC 3M175, interview with Maurice Bans, Viam, 7 October 1983.

[37] Only a few articles denounced the Party's lack of propaganda among women and outlined the harsh working conditions of peasant women. *Prol C*, 25 March 1923; *TCO*, 9 May 1925.

[38] Nationwide fewer than 5% of PCF members were women. Interview with Marie Chassagne, Brive, 8 September 1984.

bers in Corrèze in 1938). The Comité, which sponsored speaking tours against fascism in larger towns, failed to foster greater participation of women in PCF politics.

The PCF counted even fewer schoolteachers within its ranks (1 percent). The Communists, who worked hard to enlist teachers, succeeded only in arousing the curiosity of the authorities. Prefects and zealous gendarmes were quick to exaggerate the role of schoolteachers in the propagation of the PCF's ideology. Those few rural *instituteurs* affiliated with the PCF did not enjoy undue influence among their students.[39] The treasurer of the Corrèze Communists, Léon Champeix, a teacher in Uzerche, recalls that few of his colleagues ever took out a Party card. Those who did, however, often occupied positions of importance. Antoine Perrier, *professeur* at the lycée of Tulle (Corrèze), headed the PCF in that town for a few years and was federal secretary of the Corrèze Communists in 1930; the first Communist deputy of Corrèze, François Aussoleil, taught in Brive. Two of the more active Communist militants in Haute-Vienne, Georges Guingouin (the future Resistance leader) and Marcel Lenoble, both worked as village schoolteachers, and together they waged a vigorous campaign for legislative office in the rural district of Limoges 2 in 1936.[40]

The social profile of the PCF's village leadership paralleled that of the base. Peasants headed close to 40 percent of all cells, followed by artisans (29 percent), shopkeepers, and masons. Those who worked the land exercised even firmer control over cell treasuries. PCF cells counted very few workers (a total of two), employees, and schoolteachers among their leaders (table 6.3). Rural artisans played a prominent part in cell leadership throughout the interwar years. The cartwright, carpenter, sabot maker, baker, or café owner established in the village center had more extensive contacts than the average peasant and was well positioned to disseminate the Party's watchwords. In workshops, small stores, and, of course, bistros, owners and clients met informally and discussed politics. During the busy summer months, artisans could devote more time to Party business than peasants. That artisans were overrepresented as cell secretaries had much to do with their role as vectors of sociability and exchange in the village community.

Migrants

Temporary migrants, more numerous in the PCF than in the electorate as a whole, deserve special consideration because commentators and PCF lead-

---

[39] Authorities overestimated PCF strength among schoolteachers. See AN F⁷ 13091 (Dordogne), AN F⁷ 13106 (Creuse), AN F1 CᴵᴵᴵI 1127 (Dordogne); ADC 1M70–71; ADD 4M193; ADHV 1M171–172. Guy Georgy, *La folle avoine* (Paris, 1991), 124, 181–82.

[40] Interview with Léon Champeix. For Perrier, AN F⁷ 13098.

ers from Secretary General Maurice Thorez on down believed they played a critical role in rural communism's development.[41] Those who worked in the cities came home with new ideas and a more in-depth knowledge of politics. Migrants—even those who settled for twenty years in the Paris region—remained profoundly attached to their native villages; many lived in the expectation of returning home for good and buying a small plot of land. For close to two decades Jean Lalanne drove a taxi in Paris, going back to his native Sornac (Corrèze) for two or three weeks each year. He joined the Socialist—and later the Communist—Party in Sornac, and throughout the interwar years bought his Party card in his home village, not in the capital city. In 1939 he packed his bags and bought a small farm in Mestes (Corrèze), where he settled and became active in Communist politics in the years after World War II.[42]

Some migrants took up key positions in their home communities. Alfred Freyssinet returned to his native St-Germain-Lavolps (Corrèze) in the mid-1920s after many years as a taxi driver in Paris. Elected as a Radical municipal councillor in 1925, he joined the PCF before the end of the decade and became mayor of his tiny village in 1932. Returning migrants kept a low profile; though some were elected mayors of small villages, few ever held electoral offices of higher rank or assumed major responsibilities in the Communist Party.

Like many other Limousin natives who had settled more or less permanently in the Paris region, migrants from Corrèze formed an association, Les Originaires de la Corrèze, and published a short-lived monthly newspaper, *Di Lou Cantou*, in the late 1930s. The Originaires were politically diversified, but the organization was firmly in the hands of Communist militants. They held meetings, arranged a yearly banquet, and encouraged their members to subscribe to the Limousin Communist press and assist their village cells when they returned home. The association's initial goal was to put an end to the "plague" of emigration by working to improve agricultural productivity in migrant areas of Corrèze. The task proved far too ambitious for such a small group. In practice, the Originaires limited themselves to sustaining their cultural and social well-being and to informing *Corréziens* back home of the harsh realities of work in the capital.[43] Migrants from the large villages of Chamberet, Peyrelevade, and Sornac (all in Corrèze) founded their own association, which played an active part in Communist politics. In 1926, the *originaires* of Peyrelevade and Sornac gave their respective cells red flags embroidered with the hammer and sickle at banquets attended by

---

[41] Thorez argued that migrants were partially responsible for the politically advanced character of the Creuse. *Fils du peuple,* 27.

[42] Interview with Jean Lalanne, Mestes, 7 October 1983.

[43] *TCO,* 30 July 1927, 25 February 1933; *Di Lou Cantou,* April–May 1937, February 1938. The *TCO* had 200 subscribers in the Paris region in 1927. See as well *Limousins de Paris: Les sociétés d'originaires du Limousin sous la IIIème République* (Limoges, n.d.).

large numbers of migrants. Sornac migrants "living temporarily in Paris" printed a poster supporting Communist candidates in the 1925 municipal elections.[44]

Today old Communist militants recall that the return of migrants provided a propitious occasion to discuss politics. Louis Freyssinet's uncles "came back to hay for eight or ten days, and we'd have discussions in the fields, in the house. . . . We'd talk politics in the shade of an oak tree when we'd stop mowing to have a bite to eat. . . . Things were very clear, the discussions were good because they were not artificial. People quickly became aware of the problems involved." [45]

Migrants had a qualitatively different experience of politics in the cities, and they shared their thoughts, orally and through letters, with their families and fellow villagers. Their dual positions as peasants and workers, property owners and salaried employees, *campagnards* and city dwellers, gave them a unique outlook on political life. Some had been involved in trade unions and had taken part in strikes. Maurice Bans from Viam recalled that "people from my commune were flexible [*polyvalent*], they were at home in the city and the country, they would go spend the winter in Paris or Lyon. There were perhaps forty of them—young people—and when they returned they'd bring back things and ideas, and they had joined unions in the cities. What was there here? There was nothing. Even today there is nothing. . . . [The migrants] came back from the city and brought ideas that they passed on to the peasants." [46]

Jean-Baptiste Vars added, "All those who returned, they were the ones who were the precursors of political change." [47]

Viam and other small villages in migrant regions enjoyed closer links to Paris and Lyon than to Limoges, Tulle, or Brive, and for some small peasants such as Maurice Bans, who never migrated, the attraction of the city is still strong. But while the migrants' experiences differed from those of villagers who remained on the barren Millevaches plateau, it is not clear that they actually knew more about politics than the stay-at-homes or that they were responsible—as prefects, Communist leaders, and old militants were inclined to think—for the growth of left-wing ideas in their home communities.

Migrants of all kinds reinforced preexisting ideas and political convictions. Asked whether "new ideas" emerged in Viam and whether migrants' views colored their development, Maurice Bans said, "Yes, of course the esprit was already there." [48] The presence of migrants in any given commune gave communism a character it did not have in other areas of Limousin and

---

[44] *TCO*, 29 August, 4 and 11 September 1926; poster, Bibliothèque Nationale, packet 1722.
[45] Interviews with Louis Freyssinet, Ste-Fortunade, 1 September 1983 and 30 June 1984.
[46] Interview with Maurice Bans.
[47] Interview with Jean-Baptiste Vars.
[48] Interview with Maurice Bans.

Dordogne, but the migrants were not of central importance to the Party's strength. Many migrant villages in Creuse, Haute-Vienne, and even Corrèze had no significant PCF presence. Nothing differentiated migrants from these villages from those of Communist-leaning ones. The difference between communes was essentially a matter of political allegiance.

Ouvriérisme

The Party's social composition gave regional leaders mixed satisfaction. Those who favored work among the peasantry obviously had good reason to be pleased. Peasants, they noted, were "more accessible to Communist ideas than many workers in industrial centers." Jules Fraisseix wrote admiringly of the poor Limousin peasants, whose commitment to communism equaled that of workers in major industrial centers and in Paris. "The development of class consciousness is advancing well," wrote one Party observer, "and we can say that Corrèze peasants are a revolutionary force with which the bourgeoisie must contend."[49] A leader from Dordogne concurred when he remarked that one could make conscious revolutionaries out of "our honest peasants," and in nearby Corrèze the Party was proud to see "peasants setting an example for workers." Some even argued that the working class could never be a fully active revolutionary force without the peasantry's participation.[50]

"Workerist" militants strongly disagreed with this analysis. The revolutionary movement, they argued, could come only from the towns, and it was there that the PCF should concentrate its efforts. The regional Communist leadership constantly worried about the lack of members in urban areas and factories, but their recruitment drives regularly ended in dismal failure. In Creuse—a rural department if ever there was one—worried leaders urgently called on small-town workers to join the Party to counter the "large" influx of new peasant members in the wake of the 1928 elections.[51]

This *ouvriérisme*, largely a reflection of the Communist Party's national policy, was not beneficial to its cause. It made little sense to devote the bulk of one's efforts to the towns when previous recruitment attempts there had been unproductive and when the majority of potential members and voters lived in the countryside. Corrèze Communists, more representative and attuned to the countryside than their neighbors, ignored outside directives

---

[49] Docteur [Jules] Fraisseix, *Au long de ma route: Propos anecdotiques d'un militant Limousin* (Limoges, 1946), 122; *TCO*, 22 August 1925.

[50] *TCO*, 26 April 1924 (Dordogne), 15 January 1927 (Corrèze), 6 June 1925.

[51] *PCTC*, 15 October 1922; AN F⁷ 13118, "Parti communiste français: Région limousine: Rapport moral, 1929;" *TCO*, 19 May 1928.

and centered their efforts on the rural world. In Haute-Vienne, the leadership was firmly in control of the working-class militants of Limoges, better known for their sectarianism than for their effectiveness as organizers, and they were replaced in the late 1920s by a series of incompetent full-time cadres parachuted in by PCF headquarters in Paris. These hard-line outsiders, who had no knowledge of the countryside, pursued disastrous *ouvriériste* tactics and spent much time engaging in petty disputes. Their presence in the Haute-Vienne Communist leadership in the 1930s was clearly a factor in the Party's poor showing there.[52] In Haute-Vienne and Dordogne, the constant tensions between the workerists and those who backed action among the peasantry undermined the Communist Party's smooth functioning.

Workerism had other negative consequences. Peasants remained wary of the city, and *ouvriériste* propaganda that criticized their limited political knowledge only reinforced their suspicions of communism. Militants who argued that the peasantry's role in the class struggle was secondary and that peasants should dutifully follow the workers' example also reinforced a culture of inferiority among rural members. The declaration of Buneteau, a peasant delegate from St-Amand-Magnazeix (Haute-Vienne), at the Communist Party's regional congress in March 1937 was revealing: "We are with you [the workers], to support you, but we are counting on you to push for our demands because we peasants are *too stupid*, too divided for that."[53] And Maurice Bans recalled: "City people were there to help us, to emancipate us, to make us understand, because it was often hard for a peasant to put all this in his head at one time."

"Why?" I asked.

He laughed. "I don't know. The people who came made us understand that the working class and the peasant class had the same interests."

"In other words, maybe they had greater ideological knowledge?"

"Maybe."[54]

Some peasant militants internalized an *ouvriériste* discourse that trivialized their own political intelligence and ability. Their lack of self-confidence put a brake on their political initiatives while they waited for the working class (or Party headquarters in Paris) to take the lead. The often suicidal, absurd tactics of *ouvriéristes* who never reconciled themselves to the PCF's rural character hampered communism's growth and blunted the efforts of rural militants. The *ouvriériste* mentality, with its top-down approach to politics, was diametrically opposed to the rural militants' more open and re-

---

[52] The Party's leadership in 1921 and 1922 was composed entirely of Limoges militants; *Prol C*, 6 February 1921, 26 February and 15 October 1922.

[53] *TCHV*, 26 March 1937; emphasis mine.

[54] Interview with Maurice Bans.

ceptive practices. By and large, Communists in the countryside succeeded because they kept workerists of all stripes at arm's length. This was a tribute to their political savoir faire.

Cells

The PCF's members grouped themselves into an impressive network of rural cells. No other political party could rival their presence in the Limousin and Dordogne countryside, and this in itself was a major achievement. The cell was at the heart of the Party's life in small villages, a novelty where little sustained, organized political activity existed.

It was one thing to recruit members but quite another to group them into active cells and turn them into true militants. This problem was magnified in rural areas. The Communists made extensive efforts to sow the seeds of militancy outside areas of Party strength, and they founded cells in almost half of all Corrèze and Haute-Vienne communes during the years between the wars (table 6.4). In the more militant Corrèze, some 60 percent of cells manifested some activity, and these cells provide a reliable indicator of the Communist Party's organizational strength in the countryside. By the 1930s the Communists had an active presence in one-fourth of Corrèze's communes (table 6.4). The map of active Communist cells in Corrèze reveals their strong implantation among the Party's electoral strongholds (compare map 14 with maps 11 and 12). The presence of an active cell had a clear impact on the PCF's score at the polls—the Communist vote rose by an average of 15 percent in villages where the Party had an organized structure.[55]

The vast majority of Corrèze cells took root in small communes. As early as 1921, a PCF Central Committee member noted with satisfaction that "four-fifths of the cells are village sections, which recruit among smallholding peasants, particularly on the Millevaches plateau."[56] In 1930 village cells accounted for fifty-four of Corrèze's fifty-nine cells and all of Creuse's cells. Eighty-seven percent of the Party's 181 cells in Limousin and Périgord were located in the countryside.[57] Most militants also lived in rural areas, and the proportion of urban members rarely surpassed the 20 percent mark. In Tulle (Corrèze) 44 percent of the Party's members in 1921 had joined cells in hamlets within the city's limits, and a large number of these militants worked the land. Of the eighteen active Tulle Communists in 1925, seven,

---

[55] Corrèze, influence of active cell on Communist vote, 1936: regression coefficient b: 15.50; t-test: 9.80[†]; r^2: .50, controlling for percentages of migrants and peasants, population per km², long-term population change, percentage of civil burials, median delay between birth and baptism in 1910, and mean farm size per commune.

[56] *PCTC*, 25 December 1921.

[57] ADHV 1M172, CS Limoges to PHV, 10 July 1930. Dordogne had 45 village cells out of a total of 50, Haute-Vienne 29 out of 42.

Table 6.4. Communes with existing and active Communist cells, Limousin and Dordogne, 1921–1939 (percent)

	Corrèze	Creuse	Haute-Vienne	Dordogne
Existing cell, 1921–1939	48.7%	26.3%	46.9%	19.8%
Active cell, 1920s	21.1			
Active cell, 1930s	26.9			

Source: See table 6.3.
Note: A cell is defined as "existing" when we have some record of its presence. An active cell met at least once.

including Jean Bouysse, were small landholders or sharecroppers and all belonged to the Syndicat des Travailleurs de la Terre, of which Bouysse was one of the leaders. In the Tulle municipal elections of that year, the PCF's list of twenty-three candidates included eight peasants.[58]

With the exception of Limoges and Périgueux and their *ouvriériste* tradition, there were not two communisms, one urban and one rural, in Limousin and Dordogne. In midsized industrial or commercial towns the PCF's strength depended on catering to the peasants who lived within the town's boundaries (and beyond) and winning their approval. The working-class militants of St-Junien (Haute-Vienne) understood this well, and so did those of Bergerac (Dordogne), who played an important role in diffusing the PCF's platform in southwestern Périgord. Urban-based Communist militants who planned to run for office beyond the confines of their town could not avoid appealing to rural voters. To have done otherwise would have been political suicide.

Were urban militants more active than their rural counterparts? In Tulle, Limoges, and Périgueux, severe internal dissensions and power struggles riddled Communist cells; relationships between leaders were strained and acrimonious, and Party functions were occasions for heated exchanges and accusations. The activity of urban cells suffered greatly as a result, and urban groups envied the success of cells in the surrounding countryside.

The work of some rural cells was disappointing too, but for different reasons. Here hard-hitting political debates—common in larger towns—were exceptions; the problem was too little activity. The large number of cells was partially to blame. Joseph Lasvergnas complained that eight cells were too many for the urban and rural sectors of St-Junien; so few members attended meetings that militants' efforts were wasted and they grew discouraged.[59]

[58] Archives de la Fédération du Parti Communiste de la Corrèze (Tulle), Parti Communiste, Comptes, Section de Tulle, 1919–1924. ADC 4M282, commissaire police Tulle to PC, 3 April and 15 July 1925. *TCO*, 2 May 1925.
[59] ADHV 1M170, CS Limoges to PHV, 20 September 1927.

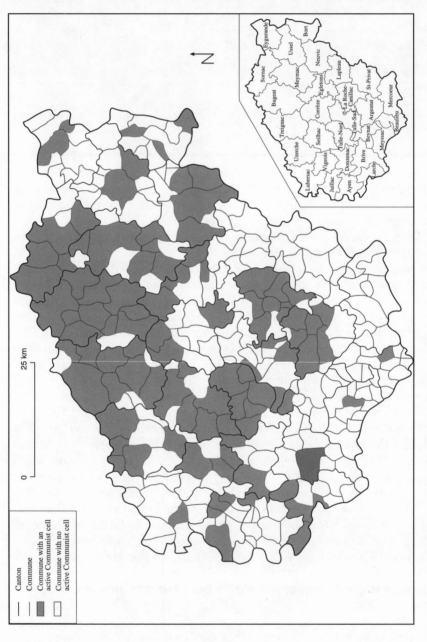

Map 14. Corrèze: active Communist cells, 1920–1939

In the countryside it was difficult to consolidate cells: many villages were widely separated, and it was hard for members who lived in distant hamlets to get to the village center for meetings. As a result, cells were too small to promote militancy. The PCF's continuous attempts to increase the total number of cells led it to create groups that contained only three, four, or five militants at the outset.[60] It was both discouraging and difficult to hold cell meetings with so few members. During the late 1920s and early 1930s, Party leaders incessantly complained of "skeletal" and inactive village cells that emerged from their lethargy only during election periods.[61]

This state of affairs grew out of the circumstances surrounding the establishment of many cells. During propaganda and electoral campaigns, Communist leaders carried their message to small villages and took the opportunity to found cells. After a rally the PCF speaker would gather with a few sympathizers, who designated a cell secretary and a treasurer. The visiting Communist leader would give them a few words of encouragement and perhaps help them hold their first meeting before leaving to speak in another village. The new cell would be left to fend for itself. Half of the cells never met once on their own initiative; after the initial enthusiasm had died down, the forces of inertia proved too difficult to conquer.[62] Numerous cells thus were more active on paper than in reality. One principal reason for the absence of militancy was the lack of dedicated militants to run cells, organize meetings, galvanize members, and twist arms when necessary.

In theory, cells were called upon to meet monthly, and while many announced their intention to do so, few actually did. No matter how dedicated the membership, it was impossible to hold meetings from May to October when peasants were busy in the fields. The cell of Davignac (Corrèze) was one of many that suspended meetings from early July through mid-September because of the harvest. A cell gathered at most eight or nine times a year; most cells met half that often. The cell of La Coquille, one of the most active in northern Dordogne, met on the first Sunday of January, April, July, and October.[63]

Absenteeism was a major problem even in Party strongholds. The secretary of the cell in Gros-Chastang (Corrèze), where the Party obtained impressive backing (45 percent in 1936), complained in 1935 that some comrades rarely came to the twice-yearly meetings. In Pérols-sur-Vézère, one of Corrèze's more active cells, militants wondered in 1921 whether they should

---

[60] *Prol C*, 24 February 1924.

[61] Leaders blamed the lack of cell activity on an enduring concern with elections inherited from the old SFIO. *TCO*, 23 February 1929. On the "skeletal" nature of cells see AN F^7 12750, CS Limoges to SG, 1 December 1925 and 1 April 1929; AN F^7 13130, CS Limoges to PHV, 5 August 1932; ADHV 1M172, CS Limoges to PHV, 10 July 1930; ADHV 4M174 and ADD 4M195.

[62] *TCO*, 27 December 1924; 26 September and 14 November 1925; 18 January 1930.

[63] *TC*, 19 June and 3 July 1921; *Prol C*, 20 March 1921.

expel those who never came, and three years later the cell called on its members to stop neglecting meetings.[64] The absenteeism problem persisted throughout the interwar years, and troubled militants and leaders alike. "It is your absolute duty," Clément Chausson admonished Corrèze militants in 1938, "to attend your cell meetings. Neither hunting nor fishing nor visiting friends is a valid excuse." As mayor and cell secretary of the village of Moustier-Ventadour (Corrèze), Chausson was well acquainted with the problem; in late 1937 he publicly chided fellow militants for their lack of participation in Party activities.[65]

The degree of militancy varied greatly among cells. It was one thing to meet a few times a year and sponsor a "red dance," but it was quite another to gather regularly, plan activities that appealed to the majority of a commune's inhabitants, and bring in outside speakers for public meetings. A sizable number of cells in Corrèze, many of them in Communist-run villages, boasted between fifteen and forty militants. Ten percent of St-Gilles-les-Forêt's (Haute-Vienne) 202 inhabitants in 1937 were Party members, and the figure may well have been higher in other communes.[66] In many villages, long periods of hibernation alternated with shorter periods of activity. Albussac's (Corrèze) cell remained dormant throughout much of the 1920s but sprang to life in the mid-1930s, when the agricultural crisis attracted new members and spurred them to action. In early 1936, Communist militants in surrounding villages joined together and built a small, one-room building to serve as a meeting place. Albussac's *maison du peuple* was proudly inaugurated by some five hundred people, including major Corrèze Communist leaders.[67]

Such examples of cooperation between cells were few and far between; most cells worked in complete isolation. In 1936, militants in Bonnefond (Corrèze) accused the neighboring cell of Bugeat, one of the most active in Corrèze, of falling asleep at critical times and failing to establish relations with other cells in the canton. The cell secretary of St-Cyprien (Dordogne), on the banks of the Dordogne River, was so isolated that he was forced to write to the Communist paper to find out the names of cell secretaries in neighboring villages.[68]

Collecting dues proved difficult in rural areas. Members lived on the margins of the market economy and often had little cash at their disposal. Few ever purchased the monthly dues stamps to paste on their Party cards; on average, Corrèze militants bought between seven and nine stamps a year, and

---

[64] *TCO*, 11 October 1924 and 19 January 1935; interview with Marcel Darnetz, Gros-Chastang, 8 August 1984; *PCTC*, 2 October and 24 December 1921, 8 January 1922.
[65] *TC*, 30 April 1938 and 25 December 1937.
[66] *TCHV*, 29 January 1937.
[67] ADC 1M77, gendarmerie nationale, brigade d'Argentat, 10 April 1936; *TCCHV*, 30 May 1936; interview with Henri Peuch.
[68] *TCCHV*, 22 December 1936; *TCO*, 1 January 1927.

the figure was lower for rural members. Payments from rural cells came to a halt from early April to late October.[69] Léon Champeix, former treasurer of the Communist Party in Corrèze, recalls the difficulty he faced collecting funds in the countryside:

> In the cities people paid their dues fairly well. People are grouped together, they have cell meetings, they're all there, you can keep an eye on them, and the militants are better informed and do better work. In the countryside, though, you know, peasants, they're not very interested in a meeting. Oh, they'll buy a stamp or two or three, and then it's all over. And they'll pay their dues according to how much money they have. So if this month—these were not rich people—they can buy a stamp, they'll buy it, and if they can't, they won't. So it [the collection of dues] was completely, completely irregular.[70]

These financial troubles caused headaches at Party headquarters, but there were ways around them. The departmental Communist federation could pay for stamps and yearly membership cards out of its own funds, and cells picked up the tab for members who were too poor to pay. In any case, finances were less important than recruiting new members and promoting cell activity.[71]

Cell attendance clearly was linked to the quality and interest of the meetings. A successful *réunion de cellule* had to be prepared in advance. In 1984 André Plazanet remembered that at St-Clément (Corrèze) two or three comrades would meet beforehand and discuss the agenda. "There was a solidarity that no longer exists," he said, and he told how the two militants who owned cars would pick up the older militants and bring them to cell meetings. Those meetings, Plazanet noted with a sigh of disappointment, "were better followed then than they are today."[72] St-Clément's cell, composed of peasant smallholders like Plazanet, even published its own handwritten newspaper.

Cell meetings began with a discussion of international and national politics and then turned to local issues. Discussions were often backed up by an article from the Communist press. "We taught our comrades to read an article [from *L'Humanité*]," recalls Henri Peuch, "and how to extract the principal ideas from it."[73] This exercise was of both pedagogical and political

---

[69] *Prol C*, 27 January 1924; Parti Communiste Français, *Conférence régionale*, 28–29. On the collection of stamps at a national level, Annie Kriegel, *Le pain et les roses* (Paris, 1968), 185.

[70] Interview with Léon Champeix. See his appeal in *TC*, 4 December 1937. The financial accounts of Tulle show that the town's rural cells lagged far behind in their payments. Archives de la Fédération du Parti Communiste de la Corrèze (Tulle), Parti Communiste, Comptes, Section de Tulle, 1919–1924.

[71] The treasury of the Corrèze PCF had only 338 francs to its credit when it was seized by the judiciary in 1940. The Tulle section had a bit over twice that amount and so did the Party paper. ADC 58W2145.

[72] Interviews with André Plazanet and Henri Peuch.

[73] Interview with Henri Peuch.

value. The bulk of the meeting was spent discussing an upcoming meeting, collecting funds to support various causes, and organizing the distribution of leaflets, the pasting of posters, the sale of newspapers, and recruitment efforts. "Ideological discussions," wrote Léon Champeix, "were very rare. Convinced, we did not question the dogma."[74] Questioned, he explained: "Well, you understand, we agreed on the Party's political line. We weren't going to discuss dogma, we weren't going to talk about Karl Marx's *Capital*! The last time I talked about Karl Marx's *Capital*, I read a few chapters, and I guarantee you it's difficult reading."[75]

The result was that members had virtually no knowledge of ideological questions and sometimes little more than a cursory familiarity with the Party's political line on issues unrelated to the rural world. Discussions rarely became heated during cell meetings, and few militants were ever expelled for purely political reasons (village feuds played a greater role). "Don't get the idea that the general ideological level was terribly high," Robert Bos warned me. "There are the cadres, there are those who really understand, and then there's the great mass."[76]

Even cell secretaries tended to have little political and ideological baggage. "Their ideological background was formed in two ways," Léon Champeix told me. "First through action, protest movements—defense of people's rights, defense of working-class demands, defense of this and that, campaigns in communes to get water or fix a path. From an ideological perspective their knowledge came from the newspaper, from speeches that carried some ideological weight, and from brochures. Many of them had never read the *Communist Manifesto*, I'm certain of that. They'd heard about Karl Marx, and of course we knew about Lenin."

"More than Marx?"

"Ah, maybe more. Much more. Yes, certainly. Militants knew about Marx, but they had never read *Capital*. I've never read *Capital*, I've only read extracts."[77]

Doctrinal matters assumed secondary importance in the life of a village cell. Members agreed on the outlines of the Party's rural policy; usually they lacked the interest and knowledge necessary to discuss other political problems in any detail. Granted, some cells had small collections of Party brochures and Marxist works for popular consumption, but few people actually read them. The PCF's theoretical organ, *Les Cahiers du Bolchévisme*, had all of eleven subscribers in Corrèze in 1938, and in all likelihood they were Party leaders.[78] The cell library of Egletons, run by Clément Chausson,

[74] Champeix, "Souvenirs," 78.
[75] Interview with Léon Champeix.
[76] Interviews with Robert Bos, Tulle, 24 August 1983 and 30 July 1984.
[77] Interview with Léon Champeix.
[78] Dordogne had ten subscribers, Haute-Vienne eleven, and Creuse three. Parti Communiste Français, *1937–1938: Du Congrès d'Arles à la Conférence de Gennevilliers: Une année de lutte pour le pain, la liberté et la paix* (n.p., n.d.), 256–57.

Table 6.5. Effect of subscriptions to Communist papers on Communist vote, Corrèze and Haute-Vienne, 1928 (coefficients of regression [b] and determination [R^2])[a]

	b	R^2
Corrèze	16.53[†]	.49
Haute-Vienne	17.97[†]	.21

Sources: ADC 4M282, 3M197; AN F[7] 13118.

[a] Controlling for percentages of migrants and peasants, *population per km², long-term population change, percentage of civil burials,* median delay between birth and baptism in 1910, and mean farm size per commune; in Haute-Vienne, for italicized variables and median delay between birth and baptism in 1900. Figures are based on subscriptions as a percentage of population. $N = 279$ (Corrèze) and 210 (Haute-Vienne).

[†] Significant at .01 level.

was one of the best furnished in Corrèze: its seventy-one volumes included a few Marxist classics (Marx's *Communist Manifesto, The Eighteenth Brumaire,* and *The Civil War in France*; Lenin's *State and Revolution*), nineteen pamphlets on the Soviet Union (from *Le mouvement stakhanoviste* to *La démocratie soviétique* and a hagiography of Stalin), and brochures on the Party's program. Few militants besides Chausson, who had patiently collected these volumes, ever read more than a couple of pamphlets.[79]

The regional Communist press was much more effective than brochures or pamphlets in diffusing the Party's policy and discourse. In small villages, newspapers were passed from hand to hand, and often from household to household. Militants studied articles at cell meetings, and newspapers, especially in PCF-run communes, could be found at the café. A newspaper attentive to the concerns of village readers gave added legitimacy to the PCF. By uniting people in isolated villages, the Party press contributed to a growing sense of shared cultural, social, and political identity. Indeed, in both Corrèze and Haute-Vienne, the Party's score improved as the percentage of subscribers to the Communist press rose (table 6.5). Circulation figures were far less sensitive than membership to changes in the political climate and in the PCF's national fortunes. Success depended on publishing a local newspaper that carried news from the small villages along with political commentary: the *Travailleur de la Corrèze* counted 1,750 subscribers in Corrèze in 1921 and over 2,000 on the eve of World War II; between 1922 and 1936, however, it was replaced by a Limoges-based regional paper, *Le Travailleur du Centre Ouest*, which never mustered much more than 1,000 subscribers in the same department. Subscribers, even if they sympathized with the Party's views, showed less enthusiasm for a paper that carried news on neighboring areas but little on their own. *Justice*, a small Communist monthly for the Bergerac region, published in defiance of the Dordogne Communist

[79] ADC 1M71, Gendarmerie Nationale, 27 September 1939. The cell librarian of Chamberet (Corrèze) also complained about the lack of readers. *TCO*, 31 March 1928.

leadership's wishes, boasted more subscribers in one area of Dordogne than did the regional PCF weekly in the entire department.

Subscription lists seized by the police provide a snapshot of the circulation of the Communist press: the 737 Corrèze subscribers to the *Travailleur du Centre Ouest* in 1932 came from almost half of Corrèze's towns and villages.[80] The great majority of subscribers (over 60 percent) lived in the countryside: the twenty-two communes with the highest ratio of subscribers to population were all small villages. In Haute-Vienne, St-Junien led twenty-two rural communes in proportion of subscribers. In the class-against-class period, when the official Communist newspaper focused its efforts on urban areas and downplayed rural matters, the *Travailleur*'s performance in the countryside was impressive.

Militancy and Sociability

There was much more to cell meetings than discussing political and organizational issues. Cell gatherings were also a form of sociability. It was surely no accident that numerous cells met in the key site of village social and cultural life, the café. Marcelle Etienne, of the tiny, isolated village of Toy-Viam (population 166 in 1936) high on the Millevaches plateau, remembers the cell meetings attended by her father, Léon Arvis, a peasant smallholder, occasional carpenter, and Communist municipal councillor: "They'd meet once a month, I can still see them. The treasurer, who was our neighbor then, had a metal sugar box, and that was the treasury. Every month he would stop by on a Sunday evening and pick up my father and they'd go to the bistro in Toy-Viam for their meeting. The *monsieur du bistro* was also a Party member. The meeting would take up an evening. Of course, they'd have a drink, but they still held their meeting, they distributed books and all that."[81]

In Chanteix (Corrèze), militants met at the Café Mayne; in Sornac (Corrèze), they gathered at the café-restaurant Tatet, owned by card-carrying Germain Tatet; and in Beaumont (also in Corrèze), a militant's café in the hamlet of La Méchaussie served as the cell's meeting place. This pattern was repeated throughout Limousin and Dordogne. The cell at Le Châtenet-en-Dognon (Haute-Vienne) met at the *débit de boisson* owned by Party member Léonard Lepetit; in Sarlande (Dordogne), members assembled at the café of Henri Laurent, also a cell member; and in Lalinde, they met at the Pasquet restaurant.[82] Café owners, who often farmed plots of land on the side, played an important role in Communist cells, if only because they provided

[80] ADC 4M282. This figure dropped to 37% in Haute-Vienne, AN F[7] 13118.

[81] Interview with Marcelle and Louis Etienne, Toy-Viam, 2 July 1984.

[82] AN F[7] 13098; AN F[7] 13130; *Prol C*, 20 January 1924; interview with François Monédière.

Figure 2. A meeting of Communist cell delegates in the canton of La Roche–Canillac, Corrèze, October 1928. Front center, holding the hammer, Antoine Parel, peasant and Communist mayor of Gros-Chastang; holding the sickle, Fernand Salles of La Roche–Canillac, correspondent of the local PCF paper. (Photo courtesy of the Fédération du Parti Communiste Français de la Corrèze.)

a convenient and congenial place for members to gather. Georges Lacassagne laughed when he recalled the cell meetings at a bistro in Gros-Chastang. "We had to finish our meeting fast, so we could play cards! The meeting didn't last long." [83]

It is not difficult to imagine that during and after cell meetings a few bottles were brought out. The discussion would move away from politics and turn to crops, agricultural prices, the weather, village and personal issues. In most Limousin and Dordogne villages, where entertainment was virtually nonexistent, cell meetings were occasions for socializing, drinking, and breaking the monotony of rural life. An active cell gave militants a chance to gather with friends and discuss politics, share a few drinks, play cards, and perhaps sing some songs. Camaraderie and shared interests united members at least as much as belief in the Communist Party's ideology. The cell fulfilled an eminently political purpose while simultaneously playing a key role as a vector of village sociability.

When cell delegates from the *canton rouge* of La Roche–Canillac met in October 1928, they posed for a rare photograph (figure 2). Communist militants did their best to incarnate the respectability that was prized in rural

[83] Interview with Georges Lacassagne.

Figure 3. A Communist public meeting in Sornac, Corrèze, ca, 1937. The X
identifies Waldeck Rochet, one of the Party's experts on the peasant question, editor of *La Terre*, and future secretary general of the Communist party. At the center
of the front row, with straw hat and bushy beard, is Marius Vazeilles, Corrèze PCF
deputy and long-time rural Communist leader. (Photo courtesy of the Fédération
du Parti Communiste Français de la Corrèze.)

areas. Gathered in back of a café (witness the bottles in the window), dressed
in their Sunday best, they proudly displayed their Communist sympathies:
sporting red roses, they held the national and local Party newspapers for all
to see, and exhibited their local flag.[84] In a touching gesture, Antoine Parel
(with the hammer), Gros-Chastang's Communist peasant mayor, and the
correspondent of the Communist paper, Fernand Salles (with the sickle),
used their own tools to display the PCF symbol. Three women—wives of
militants or working in the village *bistro*?—peered through the window at a
militant fraternity that had little room for them. A decade later, Sornac (Corrèze) hosted a meeting in honor of Waldeck Rochet, the PCF's peasant expert, and prominent Corrèze leaders (figure 3). In this quiet *bourg* the meeting was a major event, and the symbolism of antifascism dear to the left
(raised fists, Phrygian cap) was clearly apparent. The presence of five women,
this time in the front ranks, was a sign of their slowly emerging presence
within the PCF.

Sociability was not limited to meetings, however. In Communist bastions

[84] At the center of the flag, the emblem of the PCF-aligned Confédération Générale du Travail Unitaire, which did little organizing in rural areas and had no local branch. The flag was
probably brought back from St-Etienne by a militant who worked there on a seasonal basis.

friendship networks interlocked with Party sympathies. Civil marriages between Communist militants and daughters of comrades were not infrequent, and the Party paper announced them with pride. In St-Priest-la-Feuille (Haute-Vienne) a young Communist couple entered the town hall accompanied by the singing of the "International." When the PCF mayor had pronounced them man and wife, in a dual reference to the world of politics and the Catholic Church he congratulated the newlyweds on their "emancipatory sentiments." Wedding feasts were defining events in the life of a society where a man kept his wedding suit till he died. Communism was a family affair.[85]

The PCF's impact on the community went far beyond organized politics and friendships. Active cells and Communist municipalities worked hard to expand their presence, and brought attention to their existence by planning entertainment for local inhabitants. Along with the Jeunesses Communistes, they sponsored, particularly after 1933, a large number of *bals rouges* (red dances) for the young; in some communes the Communists actually held more dances than cell meetings. In small villages the Party dance provided much-needed entertainment. Communists took advantage of these occasions to distribute propaganda leaflets, sell newspapers, and engage in discussions; sometimes a Party militant climbed on a stool and gave a short speech.[86] Cells often emphasized their antimilitaristic convictions by holding dances for army draftees (*bals des conscrits*). At least two Corrèze villages organized red Christmases (*Noël rouge*): in St-Jal some 300 to 400 merrymakers joined the festivities in 1933, and two years later revelers in St-Setiers listened to a speech by a militant and recordings by the Communist leaders Marcel Cachin and Jacques Doriot; they then sang revolutionary songs before hitting the dance floor. Finally, during the Popular Front period, a few rural cells north of Tulle projected Soviet movies, but this never became a widespread practice.[87]

Communist-sponsored fêtes became increasingly common after 1934. The most famous, at Moustier-Ventadour, took place within the imposing ruins of the village's medieval château. This *fête touristique* featured exhibitions of folk dancing (*la bourrée*), poetry readings in langue d'oc, a dance for the young, and food and drink for all. The keynote speeches assumed secondary importance. Chamberet's proletarian fête (which catered to peasants, not workers) offered more traditional activities: participants climbed

---

[85] *TCCHV*, 31 October 1936.

[86] The Jeunesses Communistes of Viam (Corrèze) organized a *bal* at the village train station in December 1935, and three militants took the opportunity to give speeches. The Corrèze Communist leader, Clément Chausson, spoke at the *bal populaire* in St-Yrieix-le-Déjalat that same month. *TCO*, 4 and 12 January 1936.

[87] *TCO*, 30 December 1933 (St-Setiers), *TCCHV*, 4 January 1936 (St-Jal). On movies, *TCCHV*, 3, 10 and 17 October 1936. In Dordogne the Party held thirty-nine movie showings (*Le temps des cerises*; *La vie est à nous*) but how many of them took place in the countryside is not known. See Parti Communiste Français, *1937–1938: Du Congrès d'Arles*, 261.

a greasy pole (*mât de cocagne*), watched a frog race, participated in a sack race and a kilometer run, listened to speeches, sat down to a banquet, and finished the evening with a *bal populaire*.[88]

Fêtes and festive Christmases were family activities, distinguished from the more militant ones largely reserved for men. The fêtes gave the PCF a chance to promote regional culture, whether in the form of folklore or the use of langue d'oc and the Limousin patois used to sing the local "peasant" version of the "International," "L'internationalo daous païsan." Communists also made special efforts to reach out to the young through dances, of course, but also through fêtes to raise money for schools.[89] They were keenly aware that stemming the tide of out-migration and curbing the attraction of city life called for economic, social, and cultural solutions. While the Communists could do little to counter economic stagnation, they could attempt, however modestly, to revitalize a fragile social and cultural life.

Such efforts by rural militants made an essential contribution to the social and cultural environments of small villages while portraying the Communists as defenders of the community. In comparison with neighboring regions and other parts of France, this area had little organized sociability and associational life. Such traditional activities as the *veillées* were declining, and church-related events were not popular, especially in villages where the PCF was strong. Farmer's markets (*foires*), which had been key sites for male sociability, no longer enjoyed the importance of times past. War and out-migration had so devastated the younger generation that some of the responsibility for sociability and entertainment shifted to the older people by default. The postwar years were a watershed in rural popular culture.[90] Communist-sponsored social activities helped fill the gap, and in the process strengthened a sense of local identity. Communism was more than just politics: it was also a way to affirm a set of shared values and to reinforce the bonds within communities hard hit by depopulation and economic crisis.[91] Social and cultural events embedded the PCF in everyday life and added to its legitimacy both in its strongholds and in neighboring areas. By inte-

[88] On Moustier Ventadour, *TC*, 11 September 1937, in ADC 1M77; on Chamberet, uncataloged poster, Bibliothèque Nationale.

[89] PCF leaflet from Janaillat (Creuse), 1935. Bibliothèque Nationale, packet 1722.

[90] For figures on associations, *Limousin et Limousins: Image régionale et identité culturelle*, ed. Maurice Robert (Limoges, 1988), 190–91. On changing sociability in the countryside, Jean-Claude Farcy, "Le temps libre au village, 1830–1960," in *L'avènement des loisirs, 1850–1960*, ed. Alain Corbin (Paris, 1995), 230–74.

[91] On culture, sociability, and communism, Michel Cadé, "Le bonheur pour pratique dans les Pyrénées-Orientales," *Vingtième siècle: Revue d'histoire* 27 (1990): 91–96; Georges Dauger, "Les fêtes de la Creuse," ibid., 77–80; Jean-Noël Retière, "La sociabilité communautaire, sanctuaire de l'identité communiste à Lanester," *Politix* 13 (1991): 87–93; Michel Hastings, *Halluin la Rouge*, and "Communisme et Folklore: Étude d'un carnaval rouge: Halluin 1924," *Ethnologie française* 16 (1986): 137–50; Noëlle Gérôme and Danielle Tartakowsky, *La fête de l'Humanité* (Paris, 1988); Tyler Stovall, *The Rise of the Paris Red Belt* (Berkeley, 1990); Fourcaut, *Bobigny, banlieue rouge*; Gérard Vincent, "Etre communiste? Une manière d'être," in *Histoire de la vie privée*, ed. Philippe Ariès and Georges Duby (Paris, 1987), 5:427–57.

grating Communists within the local community, fêtes and other activities proved an effective counterpoint to an anticommunist discourse based on fear—fear of social change and especially fear of land confiscation.

By establishing an organized, active political structure in small villages, rural Communist militants changed the face of politics in significant parts of the Limousin and Périgord countryside. Traditional political parties relied on a solidly entrenched leadership—often people of social prominence, in the case of Radicals or conservatives—to ensure their continued influence; the Communists depended on a different relationship between leaders and the base. Communist leaders, who could rely neither on patronage nor on pulling strings in Parisian ministries, made up for their lack of connections by an impressive presence in the region's villages. Marius Vazeilles and others played a crucial role in disseminating the PCF's intelligently crafted rural discourse. The role of cells and grass-roots members was equally important, if not more so. Militants in small communities preserved, created, and sustained local networks of sociability and culture while informally popularizing the Party's watchwords. Helped by sympathizers, they provided leaders with valuable feedback and advice. Militancy was not dictated from above; on the contrary, the dedication of members at the village level made the Party's organizational presence possible. The rural Communist message was transmitted successfully thanks to a renewed and original practice of politics that stood in marked contrast to the more traditional approaches of other parties. This was one of the keys to the Party's achievements.

7 Organizing the Peasantry

Philippe Gratton has underlined the key role played by Communist-backed agricultural trade unions in the Party's remarkable success in Corrèze. The successful establishment of a class-based agricultural union was, in Gratton's view, the sine qua non of a solid and durable Communist presence in the countryside. Rural communism was more the product of growing class antagonisms than it was the end point of a *toujours plus à gauche* tradition. The left did well at the polls where it successfully organized those who worked the land.[1]

This explanation of rural communism needs to be questioned. Under the leadership of the tireless Marius Vazeilles, the Communists did establish a network of peasant unions in the Corrèze highlands and the Tulle area. These unions, however, proved more ephemeral than enduring, and their existence was linked to political crisis (in the postwar years) or to economic depression (in the mid-1930s). The Communists would learn much from their attempts to organize smallholding peasants, tenant farmers, and sharecroppers during the 1920s and 1930s, and they did reap political benefits for their efforts. But from their perspective, this ambitious experiment ended in failure. Communists did, however, breathe new life into the staid world of agricultural syndicalism. Seen from a broader perspective, Corrèze provides a good example of the fragmentation and politicization of rural trade unionism during the interwar years, and provides evidence to support the argument that "peasant unity" in the twentieth century is little more than a myth; in the rural world, as in the rest of society, professional organizations have increasingly been organized along political lines.[2]

---

[1] Philippe Gratton, "Le communisme rural en Corrèze," in *Les paysans français contre l'agrarisme* (Paris, 1972), first published in *Le mouvement social* 67 (1969): 123–45.

[2] Ronald Hubscher and Rose-Marie Lagrave, "Unité et pluralisme dans le syndicalisme agricole français: Un faux débat," *Annales ESC* 48 (1993): 109–34; Claude Mesliand, *Paysans du Vaucluse, 1860–1939* (Aix-en-Provence, 1989), 1:432; and for an earlier period, Yves

The Syndicats des Paysans Travailleurs

The Communist Party pursued a dual tactic in the countryside, organizing militants in village cells and establishing a network of agricultural trade unions whose purpose was to bring peasants over to the Party's views by defending their demands and supplying them with tools, seeds, and fertilizers. The Syndicats des Paysans Travailleurs (SPT) were often the PCF's top priority, but they were also the area where the Party was least successful in the long run.[3] Organizing peasants within Communist-leaning agricultural *syndicats* proved to be a far more difficult task than militants had suspected.

The nationwide Communist agricultural trade union movement was born high on Corrèze's Millevaches plateau in August 1920, thanks to the perspicacity, dedication, and political vision of Marius Vazeilles, who, along with Renaud Jean, became the principal leader and theoretician of Communist peasant trade unionism. Vazeilles toured villages urging peasants to form their own *syndicat* and single-handedly published a monthly paper that was mailed to all union members, *Le Travailleur de la Terre*, which became in 1924 *Le Paysan Travailleur*. Vazeilles was the first to understand the need for a union that would defend the interests of struggling peasants while gradually introducing them to Communist politics.[4] He envisaged Syndicats des Paysans Travailleurs reaching out both to the Party faithful and to sectors of the peasantry that remained indifferent to Communist watchwords. Vazeilles and other Corrèze peasant militants grasped the importance of organizing peasants outside the Communist Party's rigid structure.

The existence of an agricultural trade union closely linked to the Party was an original characteristic of Corrèze communism. In no other French department did these *syndicats* establish such firm roots during the interwar years.[5] The Syndicat des Travailleurs de la Terre de la Corrèze, which changed its name in late 1924 to the Syndicat des Paysans Travailleurs, eventually gave birth to the nationwide Communist agricultural trade union movement during the 1920s and 1930s. The Syndicats des Travailleurs de la Terre were grouped together at the departmental level in the Fédération des Travailleurs de la Terre, which joined the nationwide Conseil Paysan Français in the mid-1920s, and it was this organization that gave birth to the Confédération Générale des Paysans Travailleurs (CGPT) in 1929.[6]

Rinaudo, "Syndicalisme agricole de base: L'exemple du Var au début du XXᵉ siècle," *Le mouvement social* 112 (1980): 79–95.

[3] See Parti Communiste Français, Région de la Corrèze, *Conférence régionale des 10 et 11 décembre 1938 à Tulle* (n.p., n.d.), 14.

[4] See his *Syndicats et comités de paysans travailleurs: Constitution, administration, fonctionnement, union* (Paris, 1928).

[5] Communist agricultural unions met with success in Renaud Jean's stronghold, Lot-et-Garonne, and could also be found in other rural Communist zones of strength: the lower Rhône valley, Var, Alpes-Maritimes, the southwest (Landes, Gers), and Allier.

[6] To avoid confusion I will refer to the individual Communist-backed unions by the name of Syndicat des Paysans Travailleurs, and to the umbrella organization as the CGPT.

The Corrèze Fédération des Travailleurs de la Terre grew rapidly in the years after its founding in mid-1920. At the outset, it benefited from the postwar crisis of Corrèze radicalism, the decline of the traditional system of patronage, and the temporary vacuum in the world of agricultural syndicalism. The department's most influential interwar agricultural union, the Radical-leaning Fédération des Associations Agricoles Corréziennes (FAAC), was itself gingerly taking its first steps during the same period. The Communist peasant union, which began with 600 members in three *syndicats*, counted 1,000 members in March 1922 and close to 3,000 in 1925—over 80 percent of whom were grouped in 39 unions. The monthly printing of *Le Travailleur de la Terre* rose from 1,400 in 1922 to 5,000 in 1925. The dramatic decline in the Party's membership during the same period suggests that the union's success was independent of the PCF's broader fortunes. The growth of the Syndicats des Paysans Travailleurs came to an end after 1925. Three factors contributed to the movement's loss of momentum: the increasingly effective competition of its Radical-inspired opponent; the end of the postwar social crisis in the countryside; and the shift of Vazeilles's attention to other matters, under pressure from Renaud Jean and others in the PCF who were wary of his semiautonomous agricultural unions. The monthly *Paysan Travailleur*, published in Meymac (Corrèze), was gently forced into a merger with the Party's nationally distributed agricultural weekly, *La Voix Paysanne*, and the union's local activity slowed noticeably. The *syndicats* gained renewed strength thanks to the mid-1930s agricultural crisis (perhaps some 2,000 to 3,000 members in 1934–35), only to decline again once economic conditions improved.[7]

Communist agricultural trade unions enjoyed far less influence in the rest of Limousin and Périgord. They were nonexistent in Creuse, and in Haute-Vienne they never gathered more than 485 members. In Dordogne the union gained strength in the early 1930s, particularly along the banks of the Dordogne River and in the Bergeracois just north of the Lot-et-Garonne border. By 1934 the CGPT claimed some 1,233 militants in southern Dordogne and published its own short-lived newspaper, *L'Aurore Paysanne*.[8] These unions—unlike their Corrèze counterparts, which did best in areas of polyculture and livestock raising—were active in regions where wine, tobacco, and even fruits and vegetables were the predominant crops; properties in these areas tended to be smaller than in Corrèze, and sharecropping was more important. The success of the SPTs thus was not limited to areas of polycul-

[7] *TC*, 12 September 1920; *Le Paysan Travailleur*, October 1924, June 1925; *TT*, April 1922, March 1924; *Prol C*, 3 June 1923; ADC 4M282 and 1M71.

[8] ADHV 7M26; ADD 4M205, CS Périgueux to PD, 15 June 1934. On Dordogne membership, ADD 1Z34 and 7M8. *L'Aurore Paysanne* had a monthly printing of some 1,000 copies, ADD 1M83. Traditional unions had far more extensive memberships: the Fédération Départementale des Planteurs de Tabac de la Dordogne had 11,258 members in 1935 and the Union des Syndicats Agricoles du Périgord et du Limousin 20,205 members in 1936. ADD 7M10.

ture with an emphasis on cattle raising. Local organizers also benefited from the assistance of Renaud Jean, whose stronghold, Lot-et-Garonne, bordered those areas of Dordogne where the CGPT did best.

Agricultural Crisis

The crippling agricultural depression that swept through the countryside during the interwar period marked the lives of most people in Limousin and Dordogne. The crisis, which hit in 1933 and intensified over the next two years, proved a key opportunity for the Communists to recapture ground they had lost during their sectarian class-against-class period, and to gain a hearing from voters who had not always been sympathetic to their views in the past. Thanks to the Party's organization, its rural militants, and its agricultural trade unions, Corrèze and Dordogne Communists could orchestrate a widespread protest movement against deteriorating economic conditions in the countryside that accelerated the shifting balance of local politics. The Communist Party's successes in rural syndical organization, however, proved to be short-lived.

While a substantial number of Limousin and Dordogne peasants practiced polyculture and thus were largely self-sufficient as far as food was concerned, they had no protection against the fall in agricultural prices that began in the early 1930s and accelerated in 1933.[9] Most peasants always had a head of livestock, some poultry, eggs, dairy products, potatoes, and a few sacks of wheat or rye to sell at the market so that they could buy tools, fertilizers, grain, wine, and clothes and pay the tax collector. Starting in 1933, peasants found it increasingly difficult to sell their products, and the situation worsened considerably over the next two years.[10]

Peasants who sold grain and livestock were hard-hit by the drop in prices. In northern Dordogne, central and northern Corrèze, and parts of Haute-Vienne and Creuse, many farmers had specialized in raising pigs and *veaux de lait*, milk-fed calves, whose meat was considered a delicacy in urban areas.[11] At the fairs of Brive and Tulle (Corrèze) the nominal price of *veaux de lait* declined by 48 percent between 1930 and 1935; adjusted for deflation (*francs constants*), the price of *veaux de lait* fell 29 percent. But for peasants it was largely a question of perception: what mattered was the actual price paid per kilo at the local market; peasants, like most other small producers and con-

---

[9] According to Gordon Wright, *Rural Revolution in France* (Stanford, 1964), 41, agricultural prices dropped by 50% nationwide between 1930 and 1935.

[10] See AN F⁷ 13033 (Dordogne, 1933–34); ADD 3M82, PD to MI, 22 September 1933; AN F⁷ 13024 (Corrèze), ADC 1M76, 3M346; AN F⁷ 13029 and F⁷ 13042 (Haute-Vienne, 1934–35); AN F⁷ 13629, 13024, and 13032 (Creuse, 1933–35).

[11] *Veaux de lait* were sold at three months of age: they were fed only with milk and never saw daylight so as to produce the "white meat" prized by consumers.

Table 7.1. Decline in sale prices of agricultural goods, Corrèze, 1929–1935 (percent)

	Period	Francs	Francs constants
Pigs	(1929–35)	−56.0%	−41.0%
Calves	(1930–35)	−48.0	−29.0
Beef cattle	(1931–34)	−60.4	−53.2
Rye	(1929–35)	−45.6	−27.2
Wheat	(1932–35)	−51.8	−43.0

Source: ADC 6M444 and data provided by the Direction Départementale de l'Agriculture et de la Forêt, Tulle. To adjust for deflation (*francs constants*) I have used the price index table in INSEE, *Annuaire statistique de la France* (Paris, 1961), 509.

Note: Figures are based on the mean yearly price at the fairs of Tulle and Brive. The decline has been calculated between the highest and the lowest average yearly price.

sumers, spent little time adjusting prices to account for inflation or deflation. In the mid-1930s the French had yet to perceive the fall in prices, especially in Limousin and Dordogne, where peasants' contact with the consumer economy was restricted.[12]

The across-the-board collapse of agricultural prices differentiated this crisis from earlier ones. *Veau de lait* and cattle prices at local markets declined consistently from mid-1931 on; peasants could still make ends meet, however, by selling other goods, especially pigs, which not only were one of their principal sources of income but also provided a better return on investment than calves.[13] By late 1933, the fall in prices extended to a wide range of other farm products: the price of pigs tumbled even more than that of *veaux de lait*, and Corrèze led French departments in hog production. Wheat (not a major cash crop in this region) and rye declined in value, and once again Corrèze, the nation's largest rye-producing department (a measure of the poverty of the soil), was particularly struck (table 7.1).[14] In the past, peasants had compensated for declining rye or wheat prices by selling potatoes, and if potatoes proved hard to market, they could recoup part of their investment by fattening pigs with them; by 1934, however, this was no longer a viable option. As the price decline broadened, the butter, eggs, cheese, and vegetables that peasant women sold to generate extra income dwindled in value as well. Granted, some of these products never reached the marketplace: in Nontronnais and parts of Limousin, peasants exchanged wheat for bread at the village bakery; they also might slaughter pigs (for *charcuterie*),

[12] Alfred Sauvy, *Histoire économique de la France entre les deux guerres* (Paris, 1984), 1:195–96 and 3:282.

[13] SP Nontron to PD, 13 September 1933, ADD 1M82; interview with Léger Peyraut, Lamazière-Basse, September 1, 1984.

[14] Statistique Générale de la France, *Annuaire statistique, 1934* (Paris, 1935), 104, 108.

but the bulk of their small-scale production was destined for the market and provided a critical source of income for rural families.[15]

Economic historians have challenged the conventional notion that peasants, of all social groups in France, suffered most from the economic crisis. On the national level, the peasants' purchasing power did not decline dramatically, nor did their indebtedness reach the levels of the late nineteenth century. But these estimates mask substantial regional differences: the Limousin and Dordogne peasants, with their emphasis on livestock production and their low level of productivity, clearly saw their income decline more sharply than that of peasants in other areas. And whatever the measurable severity of the crisis, it had a catastrophic impact on popular opinion in the countryside.[16] In Limousin and Périgord, the significant drop in agricultural prices outpaced the decline in the prices of fertilizers, seeds, plows, and tools. Peasants thus faced a reduction of their revenue, and its impact was all the greater because their *perception* was that the prices of the goods they purchased were constantly rising. In Dordogne, most peasants other than those who grew tobacco—an important crop in the Dordogne valley and in the southern half of the department—saw their incomes fall between 1933 and 1935.[17] The depletion of their savings (if any) in the dark years of 1934–35, prefects noted with growing anxiety, had consequences for their political outlook. In areas where pigs, *veaux de lait*, and other livestock constituted the peasantry's principal source of income, the price collapse resulted in a severe economic crisis that also affected rural artisans, merchants, and small shopkeepers whose economic well-being was linked to the peasants'.[18]

Small farmers, whose living conditions were anything but comfortable, found it increasingly difficult to make ends meet. Having worked hard to raise crops and livestock, they were filled with a profound feeling of injustice when their goods found no buyers. Henri Peuch recalled: "I remember having seen my father buy little pigs at 275 francs each and selling them

[15] AD Creuse 7M33 as quoted in Guy Avizou, "Agriculture et agriculteurs Creusois face à la crise des années 1930," *MSSNAC* 43 (1987), 130. On women, interview with Léger Peyraut. On the exchange of wheat for bread, SP Nontron to PD, 13 September 1933, ADD 1M82.

[16] Gilles Postel-Vinay, "L'agriculture dans l'économie française: crises et réinsertion," in *Entre l'état et le marché: L'économie française des années 1880 à nos jours,* ed. Maurice Lévy-Leboyer and Jean-Claude Casanova (Paris, 1991), 81–82. For a good corrective, Robert O. Paxton, *Le Temps des chemises vertes: Révoltes paysannes et fascisme rural, 1929–1939,* trans. Jean-Pierre Bardos (Paris, 1996), 48. For older estimates that underscore the profound economic crisis in the countryside, Sauvy, *Histoire économique,* 1:194 and 2:314; Serge Berstein, *La France des années 30* (Paris, 1988), 51; Pierre Barral, *Les agrariens français de Méline à Pisani* (Paris, 1968), 220.

[17] Sauvy, *Histoire économique,* 2: 72. ADD 4M205, SP Bergerac to PD, 14 November 1933; ADD 3M90, PD to MI, 13 November 1935.

[18] This was particularly true in Nontronnais (Dordogne), Haute-Corrèze, and the area north of Tulle (cantons of Tulle-Nord, Seilhac, Treignac, Uzerche). See AN F7 13024, PC to MI, 16 April 1934; and ADD 2Z27, SP Nontron to PD, 5 March 1936.

seven or eight months later at 250 francs each—so he lost 25 francs per head. We bought a pair of young oxen for 2,900 francs and we sold them three years later—after having trained them—for 3,200 francs. And they were twice as heavy! I remember helping my father sell little pigs—unsaleable, totally unsaleable. My father finally sold a few at the Beynat fair, and he still had two that he exchanged for a pair of pigeons." [19]

Léonard Leblanc agreed: "It was impossible to sell pigs. I know that my parents sold pigs that weighed a hundred kilograms for less than what they had paid for them as piglets. . . . So that disgusted me." [20]

Declining livestock prices resulted in capital losses for peasants, only aggravating their financial situation. Henri Peuch and many others had little choice but to emigrate. Those who remained struggled along as best they could. A poor peasant family whose budget was analyzed in the PCF paper cut corners on shoes, clothes, and food. A family farm north of Tulle that employed and supported three couples could produce only a meager profit from the sale of eight calves and as many pigs, thirty lambs, and some butter and fruit in the course of a year. [21] The head of the farm noted bitterly that family members drank less than half a liter of wine a day, and meat was on the table twice a week at most. Léon Champeix elaborated: "The sale of a few calves and pigs just allowed [peasants] to buy some fertilizer and barely helped them buy some clothes. They had a suit, and often they still had their wedding suit, which they kept their entire life—in any case, they never got dressed up. They'd go out sometimes on Sundays, but very rarely. They had a very rustic life, a rather rough life." [22]

In view of the precariousness of their living conditions, Corrèze peasants felt deeply wronged when they had to bring their unsold goods home from the market. Their sense of injustice was strengthened by the slaughter and burial of surplus cattle, which the state purchased at rock-bottom prices in order to support the market. Old militants—rural artisans such as Joseph Masdupuy and peasants such as François Monédière—rarely showed as much emotion and indignation as when they recalled those painful times. Masdupuy remembered:

Back then, you know, we struggled so that the poor could gain a bit of power alongside the rich, you see, because we were dominated by a clan of the rich—it goes without saying. You know we were poor in France at the time—it wasn't a rich country. At that time I remember we had a certain Queuille who was a Corrèze Radical [deputy and minister of agriculture from 18 December 1932 to 8 November 1934], and he had the surplus cows bought up [slaughtered] and

[19] Interview with Henri Peuch, Brive, 23 August 1983.
[20] Interview with Léonard Leblanc, Lacelle, 2 September 1983.
[21] *TCCHV*, 28 March 1936; *VP*, 26 January 1935.
[22] Interviews with Léon Champeix, Brive, 30 July and 29 August 1984.

buried at Marcillac-la-Croisille. Thirty or forty cows at each fair. Well, you know, those cows were in good health, not sick, nothing. Well, I was opposed to that. They could have distributed some [meat] to the poor—we had some very poor people here. They could have organized a distribution, this is what I always asked for and what the Communist Party was asking for. Well, it would have brought a lot of well-being to society, a society that was poor, that was really miserable.[23]

"They dug mass graves with bulldozers," François Monédière recalled, "and they buried the cattle with lime—the meat wasn't distributed to those who needed it. And our farmers, poor farmers, from small families, sometimes with only a few hectares of land, had very, very limited means, and they couldn't buy meat. They were very moved to see that meat was being buried."[24]

The state and its local representative, Henri Queuille, were not the only culprits. Scandalized to see market prices for livestock tumbling while the retail price of meat appeared not to change, peasants pinned the blame on the intermediaries, especially the urban merchants, who always seemed to get the better of the deals concluded at local fairs.[25] Prefects agreed. At the height of the crisis, peasants in Nontronnais sold their calves at 3 francs per kilo while veal in the butcher shop sold for four times that amount. In reality the retail (and wholesale) price of meat *declined* in the early 1930s, though not in the same proportion as the price of livestock at the fairgrounds; moreover, whether the price difference was attributable to various taxes and *octrois*, to the rising number of intermediaries, or to a combination of the two is open to debate.[26] François Monédière, an active Communist in the agricultural trade union movement, argued that tolls and taxes accounted for 25 percent of the final price of meat; intermediaries also took a big cut, and rising transportation costs were also to blame.[27]

But here, as elsewhere, it was clearly a matter of perception. And in the popular imagination, as well as in the discourse of the authorities, the intermediaries were a convenient target. The subprefect of Nontron (Dordogne) argued that the number of intermediaries and brokers who took their cut on *veaux de lait* had risen since World War I. This was the explanation for the troubling disparity between wholesale and retail prices. Rare was the broker

[23] Interview with Joseph Masdupuy, Gros-Chastang, 3 September 1984.
[24] Interview with François Monédière, Beaumont, 31 July 1984.
[25] AN F⁷ 13024, PC to MI, 16 April 1934. This was equally the case in Dordogne; see ADD 4M205, SP Bergerac to PD, 14 November 1933. For similar reactions in Vaucluse see Mesliand, *Paysans du Vaucluse*, 1:494.
[26] Sauvy, *Histoire économique*, 1:159–60, places the emphasis on taxes, while Annie Moulin, *Les paysans dans la société française* (Paris, 1988), 185, stresses the role of intermediaries. Postel-Vinay, "L'agriculture dans l'économie," 82, also stresses that market prices of livestock declined more than wholesale ones.
[27] VP, 21 December 1935.

or intermediary who did poorly, even in times of economic crisis. The state, he suggested, should do more to bring the profession under control.[28]

For the peasants, and especially those close to the Communist Party and its affiliated trade unions, the issue of the intermediaries tied in nicely with a broader vision that explained the peasantry's plight in terms of an age-old conflict between *les petits* and *les gros*. One Communist SPT conveniently put the two concepts together and pinned the blame on *les gros intermédiaires*. The intermediaries, speculators, brokers, bigwigs (*gros bonnets*), to whom one could add the big trusts, constituted a small stratum of society— usually urban—that made its living at the peasantry's expense. Doing away with them would be an important step in solving the peasantry's problems and bridging the ever-increasing divide between urban and rural France. And this is precisely what the Communist Party proposed to do.

Of the four Limousin and Dordogne departments, Corrèze, which depended most on livestock raising, was hardest hit by the agricultural crisis, and here demonstrations had the most significant impact. By any standard, all four departments were badly off, but Corrèze was predisposed toward rural protest in a way that the other departments were not. Better organized here than in the rest of Limousin and Périgord, Corrèze Communists and their affiliated agricultural trade union had an unrivaled network of dedicated, competent, seasoned rural militants. Most important, the crisis had made injustice—of which the slaughter of cattle was only one example— more visible here. And it was one such injustice that sparked a widespread protest movement that was to continue for the better part of two years.

Protest in the Countryside

The fair at Tulle, one of the largest in Corrèze, attracted peasants from a wide surrounding area. To enter the fairgrounds, peasants paid an entrance fee (*droit d'octroi*), and while this fee was tolerable in prosperous times, it became increasingly unpopular as the agricultural crisis unfolded.

"People brought their goods to the fair and they didn't sell them," François Monédière explained. "Sometimes you had to return two or three times to sell your goods, your meat, your pigs, and you had to pay, each time you returned to the fair you had to pay. They didn't give you your money back if you didn't sell."[29]

Robert Bos concurred: "To sell their goods the peasants sometimes had to go to the market four or five times, and bring their livestock with them—and each time they had to pay an entrance fee."[30]

[28] SP Nontron to PD, 29 July 1935, ADD 6M449.
[29] Interview with François Monédière.
[30] Interviews with Robert Bos, Tulle, 24 August 1983 and 30 July 1984.

In late March 1934, the Communist-supported CGPT began to organize mass meetings at agricultural fairs throughout Corrèze to protest against the entrance fees and the rural crisis. For the first time, the abolition of the fees, which the Communist Party and its affiliated agricultural union had demanded since the early 1920s, met with widespread approval.[31] The CGPT led a major protest in Ussel on March 24, and six days later 2,000 to 3,000 peasants gathered at Tulle's fair for the department's largest demonstration since the Great War. They listened to Marius Vazeilles, Pierre Verdier, and Jean Bouysse call for an end to the entrance fees and for immediate agricultural reforms, and also heard from a member of the right-wing Parti Agraire. They then marched, 2,000 strong, toward the prefecture, and narrowly avoided incidents with the police.[32] Shortly thereafter the Comité Paysan de la Corrèze, essentially a front for the CGPT, asked Jacques de Chammard, the Radical deputy-mayor of Tulle, to abolish the entrance fees at the town's fair. De Chammard, who underestimated the extent of rural discontent, stalled. When the Communist agricultural trade union called a big meeting at Tulle's largest annual fair, the Foire Saint-Clair (June 1, 1934), and instructed peasants not to pay the entrance fee, de Chammard, in a major political blunder, banned the meeting and let it be known that the fees would be maintained.[33] Despite the presence of the police, a large number of peasants, encouraged by militants singing the "International," managed to break into the fair with their livestock without paying. Faced with a situation that threatened to get out of hand, de Chammard and the police backed down and agreed to let the CGPT hold a meeting that afternoon; after waiting out a rainstorm, Marius Vazeilles and Antoine Bourdarias spoke to over 1,200 peasants, while militants handed out *La Voix Paysanne* and sold CGPT badges. The peasantry's victory was finalized two weeks later when Tulle authorities abandoned their attempts to collect the fees at the June 13 fair.[34]

The CGPT, and through it the Communist Party, capitalized on its success by launching an extensive propaganda campaign in the Corrèze countryside and on a more limited scale in Dordogne. The CGPT's leading peasant militants (all PCF members) held numerous meetings at fairs and denounced the government's lack of action in the face of the Depression. They called on peasants to join their local Syndicat des Paysans Travailleurs to defend their interests and draw up a list of demands. The solutions they proposed, which paralleled the Communist Party's short-term platform, were what struggling

[31] *TT*, May 1922 and March 1923; AC Lagraulière, *DCM* Lagraulière, 1922.

[32] ADC 7M22, PC to MI, 31 March 1934; *TCO*, April 7, 1934; ADC 1M68, 1M76.

[33] ADC 7M22; AN F⁷ 13132. De Chammard was criticized also by the clerical *Croix de la Corrèze*, 3 June 1934.

[34] ADC 7M22, commissaire de police de Tulle to PC, 2 June 1934; AN F⁷ 13024, PC to MI, 18 June 1934. The police estimated the crowd at 350 to 400 peasants, and the *Corrèze Républicaine et socialiste* (5 April 1934) at several hundred; I have used the figures provided by Vazeilles in *TCO* and *VP*, 9 June 1934.

peasants wanted to hear: higher prices for their produce, interest-free loans, a moratorium on the payment of debts, the abolition of property taxes, and indirect taxes on basic necessities. Since peasants could no longer earn a decent living, they asked the state to indemnify them with payments analogous to unemployment benefits.[35] The public, which in the early 1930s had been sparse at both PCF and CGPT meetings, came out in large numbers: 70 people gathered in St-Hilaire-les-Courbes (population 553), 1,500 in Lagraulière to celebrate the first of May in 1934, 150 in Seilhac, 200 in Beynat (in an area refractory to communism) and Vigeois, 400 in St-Clément, 600 in Ussel to listen to Renaud Jean and in early 1935 perhaps 1,000 there and 2,000 to 3,000 in Tulle. Communists did not fail to underline the impressive mobilization of *young* peasants.[36] In late December 1934, the CGPT organized a major peasant congress in Tulle attended by some 600 rural delegates, two-thirds of whom were not members of the CGPT. The congress had been preceded by some thirty "peasant assemblies," where, according to the Party, peasants of all political persuasions gathered to choose delegates.[37] This arrangement was in keeping with the CGPT and PCF policy of reaching out to those who did not share their views in the hope of gaining their support. While the peasant congress and the peasant assemblies gave the appearance of democracy and pluralism, Communist militants firmly controlled them from start to finish and ensured the adoption of the Party's watchwords.

In the course of 1934–35 the department administration wrote countless reports detailing the Communist Party's skillful exploitation of the agricultural crisis and its rapidly increasing popularity in the area north of Tulle and in Haute-Corrèze. Convinced that a show of force—and, if necessary, repression—was the best way to stop communism's progress, the administration issued a pressing call to the government for additional units of riot police.[38] Throughout 1934 and early 1935, the Communists and the CGPT stepped up their demonstrations and called on crisis-stricken peasants either to pay their rents, interest payments, and especially taxes in kind or to stop paying them altogether. They issued similar calls in Dordogne and Lot-et-Garonne.[39] When peasant militants in the village of Soudaine-Lavinadière (Corrèze) decided to stop their payments, the authorities cracked down. They threatened to seize the land, crops, and possessions of those who re-

[35] ADC 7M22 and ADC 1M68; *VP*, 9 June 1934.
[36] *TCO*, 5, 12, 19 May 1934, 5 January and 23 February 1935; ADC 7M22; AN F⁷ 13132; *VP*, 27 April 1934.
[37] ADC 7M22; ADC 1M76, PC to MI, 27 December 1934; *TCO*, 5 January 1935.
[38] ADC 1M76, PC to MI, 27 December 1934 and 29 June 1935; ADC 1M69, PC to MI, 23 January 1935; and ADC 7M22, PC to MI, 26 January 1935.
[39] *L'Aurore Paysanne*, 15 June 1934. On Lot-et-Garonne, Gratton, *Les paysans français contre l'agrarisme*, 137. The CGPT called for a tax strike in southern Dordogne, see AN F⁷ 13269, MI to ministre des finances, 27 October 1933, and petitions in ADD 7M9 and ADD 7M10. The *grève de l'impôt* was a tactic that the right-wing peasant leader Dorgères used with greater success on the national level. See Paxton, *Le temps des chemises vertes*.

fused to pay their taxes, and the prefect suspended the Communist mayor of Soudaine-Lavinadière, who had refused to authorize the seizures. The CGPT countered by holding a large meeting in nearby Chamberet, which attracted 500 peasants and a substantial police contingent. The CGPT speakers denounced the prefect's muscle-flexing and vowed to defend threatened peasants by all possible means.[40]

There was no better publicity for the Communists than defending those who could not pay their debts, rents, and taxes. Party militants rose to support small peasants whose possessions were being auctioned off to satisfy tax collectors and property owners. These sales were known as *ventes-saisies*, and Renaud Jean had been the first to organize protests against them in August 1932. Two weeks after being elected *conseiller général* of the canton of Jumilhac-le-Grand (Dordogne) in October 1934, Gustave Saussot, an automobile and tractor mechanic in La Coquille, led 100 Communists in a successful effort to stop the auction of a sharecropper's harvest that had been seized at the owner's request.[41] A little over a year later, Saussot was sentenced to one month in jail for impeding the "freedom of public auction," but, as the prefect noted, the punishment "won him much popularity among the sharecroppers and small farmers who are numerous in this district."[42] In 1936 Saussot was elected Communist deputy of Dordogne, and it was clear that his role in the *vente-saisie*, which he mentioned twice in his electoral leaflet (though he referred to the sharecropper as a *petit paysan* and a *petit cultivateur*—a clear sign that Saussot was reaching out to this key constituency), had given a major boost to his electoral fortunes.[43]

The *affaire Vinatier* in neighboring Corrèze raised an even greater scandal. When Vinatier, a small tenant farmer in Soudaine-Lavinadière and the father of five, fell behind in his payments, the landowner decided to put Vinatier's possessions on the block. Three hundred Communist militants, including Antoine Bourdarias, forced the bailiff to cancel the auction by making speeches and buying the goods at ridiculously low prices. The authorities responded by indicting Vinatier and ten local Communist leaders for disrupting a public sale.[44] When the auction of Vinatier's goods resumed a month later, 150 riot policemen kept close watch on the large contingent of peasants (600 to 700), many of them Communists, who had come from numerous villages in Corrèze. The cell of nearby Viam trucked in thirty peasants, and close to forty militants drove the 70-odd kilometers from Albussac

---

[40] ADC 1M69, commissaire de police de Tulle to PC, 21 January 1935.

[41] AN F⁷ 13133, PD to MI, 31 October 1934. On the CGPT's involvement in *ventes-saisies* in other departments, see Gratton, *Les paysans français contre l'agrarisme*, 134–37, and for Allier, Sally Sokoloff, "Communism and the French Peasantry, with Special Reference to the Allier 1919–1939" (Ph.D. thesis, University of London, 1975), 236.

[42] ADD 3M90.

[43] ADD 2Z85.

[44] *TCCHV*, 1 and 8 February 1936.

to support Vinatier as well. The leader of Albussac's cell, Henri Peuch, describes the action as "one of the most important our cell participated in."[45]

When the bidding for Vinatier's belongings began, Clément Chausson, a well-to-do Party leader, purchased a light plow, which he promptly gave back to Vinatier, and when the tenant farmer's wheat was sold the peasants cried out, "Wheat for the children! Bread for the kids!" The protesters failed to prevent the sale of Vinatier's possessions, however, although they did collect close to 700 francs on his behalf.[46] Once again the Communists, who had a keen sense of the pulse in rural areas, posed as the defenders of the poor and the downtrodden. But injustice in this case took a particular form: Vinatier had considerable debts because the livestock he had taken on had been worth more at the beginning of his lease than it was worth now, and he had to pay the owner the difference. It mattered little that Vinatier was actually turning over more animals than he had started off with. The Communists proposed that "a tenant farmer should be required to return only the number of animals that he started out with (of the same quality and the same weight). Chaland, the *propriétaire*, gave the tenant farmer [Vinatier] two cows and now he is taking back four, and he claims that the tenant is cheating him. Honest people will be the judges."[47]

In Corrèze, the CGPT and the Communist Party achieved concrete results (the abolition of the market fees) and their constant agitation in the countryside discouraged the authorities from holding a larger number of *ventes-saisies*. But the CGPT's successes were limited to the local sphere. Their attempts to stabilize agricultural prices met with complete failure—and, given the nature of the enterprise, how could it have been otherwise? In Haute-Corrèze some SPT members agreed not to sell their pigs, cattle, and *veaux de lait* below a set price at the local fair in 1933, but militants quickly abandoned these efforts when they realized that their actions had no effect on an oversupplied market and only demoralized the members while showing them the limits of the CGPT's influence.[48] To bring pressure on middlemen and the market, the Communists needed a much larger, more disciplined, more nationally influential agricultural trade union. Some *syndicats* thought the solution was to control rising costs. In Gros-Chastang (Corrèze) the SPT called on peasants to go on a "light strike" if the power company failed to lower rates by 30 percent. But this proposal, too, only underscored the union's powerlessness in the face of the nationwide agricultural crisis.[49]

[45] For Viam, interview with Maurice Bans, Viam, 7 October 1983; and on Albussac, interview with Henri Peuch.

[46] *TCCHV*, 15 February 1936.

[47] *TCCHV*, 8 February 1936.

[48] *TCO*, 2 September 1933.

[49] *La Croix de la Corrèze*, 24 February 1935. Both the FAAC and the CGPT campaigned for lower rural electric rates; see *La Défense Paysanne de la Corrèze*, 28 February and 15 September 1935.

Rural protests and demonstrations against farm foreclosures also erupted in other regions of France. In Allier, Lot-et-Garonne, and Landes, the Communists took the lead in these episodic and not always well coordinated movements, and capitalized on growing discontent among the peasantry. Jean Renoir's *Vie est à nous*, a film produced by the PCF at the time of the Popular Front, brought the peasantry's plight into the national limelight. Renoir's film recounted in heart-wrenching scenes a story similar to the Vinatier affair: the public auction of the furniture, livestock, and wheat of a debt-ridden tenant farmer in St-Aubin-le-Monial (Allier). Here, as in Corrèze, peasants made ridiculously low bids and eventually bought up the tenant farmer's possessions and returned them. *La vie est à nous* exemplified the Communist Party's attempt to place rural injustice and exploitation at the center of its Popular Front campaign—a campaign that resulted in impressive PCF breakthroughs in the countryside. But Communists were not the only ones to mobilize peasants. Henry Dorgères's peasant movement of the extreme right, the Greenshirts, which reached its short-lived apogee in 1935, was in the forefront of protests against *ventes-saisies* (notably in western and northern France). Dorgères himself was sentenced to three months in prison for leading one such protest in 1933, and his call for a tax strike in 1935 earned him a six-month sentence; once again a jail term enhanced a militant's popularity in the countryside.[50]

Peasant movements of the 1930s had little in common with their predecessors of centuries past. The rural revolts that shook the Corrèze during the French Revolution differed in both form and content. The bands of roving villagers directed their wrath against noble and bourgeois privilege and power. They attacked and pillaged châteaus and tried to reclaim forest, hunting, and fishing rights. These rural riots, often fueled by rumors, were part of a larger protest against the social order. In 1848 such protests were accompanied by traditional food riots, and sometimes violent demonstrations against taxation.[51] Twentieth-century rural protests took on a very different form, even if occasionally their motivations were similar. Well-organized, unarmed, and peaceful demonstrators had clearly defined goals and identifiable leaders, and appealed directly to the state and public opinion. Political parties tried to channel rural discontent for their own purposes, and agricultural trade unions increasingly did the same. Finally, protests became part of social and democratic life in the countryside, rather than sporadic outbreaks during periods of nationwide revolution or localized social upheaval. If anything, interwar rural agitation foreshadowed that of the post–World War II period, when peasants increasingly challenged the state head on (blocking

---

[50] Paxton, *Le temps des chemises vertes*, 132–40, 220–23.

[51] Jean Boutier, *Campagnes en émoi: Révoltes et révolution en Bas-Limousin, 1789–1800* (Treignac, 1987); Alain Corbin, *Archaïsme et modernité en Limousin au XIXe siècle* (Paris, 1975) 1:496–97, 511–14.

roads, intercepting trucks of imported food) while playing on the public's sympathy for their cause.

Challenging Radical-Led Peasant Unions

The rural unrest of the mid-1930s accelerated the ongoing decline of Corrèze radicalism. Peasants and Communist agitators constantly placed Radical personalities and organizations on the defensive. Jacques de Chammard forfeited his political future by his intransigence in the face of peasant protests, and Henri Queuille, the leader of Corrèze radicalism and minister of agriculture, adopted a low profile and even avoided fairs in his home district for fear of encountering demonstrations.[52] Queuille was the target of much criticism, and as a member of the government he had little margin for maneuver. In June 1934 he defended his policies before the Conseil Général, but he could do little more than call upon peasants to organize and bring production under control. It was testimony to communism's growing influence that Queuille chose to invoke the Lot-et-Garonne peasant Communist leader Renaud Jean, whom he referred to as "this wise man," to justify his opposition to price supports for livestock; in doing so he managed to point out that Renaud Jean had criticized the Corrèze Communists' position on this issue.[53] The rural crisis and its accompanying political consequences may explain why Queuille chose the safety of a Senate seat instead of standing for reelection as deputy in 1936. The ever-present Communist Marius Vazeilles was elected in his place.

The CGPT managed to steal the limelight from its staid but influential opponent in the field of agricultural syndicalism, the radical-oriented Fédération des Associations Agricoles Corréziennes (FAAC), headed by Joseph Faure, who had represented Corrèze in the Senate ever since 1921. Although the FAAC (better known as the Fédération Faure) outdistanced the CGPT in membership (23,000 members in 1934),[54] it was not an activist organization but a traditional agricultural union that saw its principal task as the provision of tools, seeds, and fertilizers to its members at low cost.

The Communists had infiltrated the FAAC in the 1930s. PCF militants within the Fédération Faure formulated demands that were carbon copies of the CGPT's. They gained control of a few village unions, elected a Party member—François Monédière of Beaumont—to the FAAC's board, and pressured the organization's leaders to work jointly with the CGPT. But Senator Joseph Faure, a staunch believer in measured parliamentary reform, could not bring

[52] ADC 7M22.

[53] *La Montagne Corrèzienne*, 24 June 1934; *La Croix de la Corrèze*, 13 May 1934; *VP*, 21 April 1934.

[54] ADC 7M22, CS to PC, 24 February 1935.

himself to approve any form of protest. Communists in the Fédération Faure thus bypassed the leadership's opposition and implemented "unity at the base" with the CGPT, and they were followed by a significant number of disgruntled FAAC rank-and-file members. In one instance, the Communists, having taken over the FAAC *syndicat* of the village of Veix, defected to the CGPT—but this was an isolated case.[55]

Fédération Faure members accounted for so many of the rural protesters in 1934–35 that Joseph Faure's authority was gravely compromised. Faure, a smallholding peasant in Argentat (Corrèze) before he became the Republican notable par excellence, had founded the FAAC, organized a regional association of unions covering fourteen departments, and been instrumental in the creation of the Chambres d'Agriculture. His talent as a back-room organizer was not matched by his ability to speak in public. Elected president of the Assemblée Permanente des Présidents de Chambres d'Agriculture in 1927, Faure could go only so far in criticizing the agricultural establishment of which he was a linchpin. As a result, paralysis and disillusionment overtook the agricultural union that he had painstakingly built from scratch since World War I.[56] The CGPT, and through it the Communist Party, had thus successfully—if temporarily—destabilized their principal opponent in the countryside. To the Communists' disappointment, however, they were never able to sign the joint-action pacts they sought with the FAAC or, more surprisingly, with the right-wing Parti Agraire et Paysan Français.[57] But their plans to do so show that they were ready to form an alliance with anyone, even the extreme right, if it promised benefits.

More than any other group, the Communists profited from the agricultural crisis. It gave them an opportunity to train and recruit militants and broaden their network of sympathizers. Their efforts paid off handsomely at the polls in municipal (1935), cantonal (1934, 1937) and legislative elections (1936) when Limousin and Dordogne Communist candidates advanced in areas where protests had been strongest (the districts of Tulle-Nord and Ussel in Corrèze; Nontron and Bergerac in Dordogne). Unlike the Party, however, the CGPT was unable to profit from its extensive activity in 1934–35. As prices rose and the situation in rural areas improved under the Popular Front, the CGPT found it increasingly difficult to mobilize its members. Peasants who had joined the union and attended its meetings during hard

[55] ADC 7M22, CS Tulle to PC, 2 April 1934; *TCO*, 30 March 1935.

[56] On Faure's loss of authority, ADC 7M22; biographical information in "Mémoire de Joseph Faure, 1875–1944," *Chambre d'agriculture*, March 1975; AN F[7] 13628, police report of 2 April 1936; ADC br. 20.

[57] The CGPT reached a tentative accord for unity of action with the FAAC and the Parti Agraire in the fall of 1935 after negotiating for close to nine months, but the agreement was denounced two weeks later after Joseph Faure backed down. See *TCO*, 28 September and 5 October 1935; ADC 7M22, PC to MI, 19 September 1935. See also *La Croix de la Corrèze*, 13 and 27 January 1935. On national CGPT efforts to collaborate with the Parti Agraire and Dorgères's Front Paysan see Gratton, *Les paysans français contre l'agrarisme*, 146–56.

times saw little need to continue their political activity now. The secretary of St-Mexant's (Corrèze) Syndicat des Paysans Travailleurs complained in 1938 that dues-paying members were interested primarily in purchasing grain and fertilizers; they didn't understand, he complained, that the union's job was also to discuss peasant demands.[58] When the CGPT was dissolved along with the Communist Party in the fall of 1939, the activities of the fifteen remaining SPTs were purely professional.[59]

Politics and Peasant Unions

The Syndicats des Paysans Travailleurs fulfilled a dual purpose: first to supply peasants with fertilizers, tools, and grain at reduced prices, and then to defend the peasants' interests and contribute to their politicization. Plans to sell produce directly to consumers, set up cooperatives, and undertake agricultural research rarely moved beyond the discussion stage.[60] A large SPT might own a threshing machine or a crusher to lend to its members, and the departmental union purchased a truck to facilitate deliveries. It was clear, however, that the SPTs could not compete with the FAAC in material benefits, nor did its members exhibit the kind of cooperative spirit that would have promoted the union's smooth functioning. Meymac's *syndicat* complained that it had difficulty making bulk purchases because members failed to sign up in advance to order fertilizers and grains. In 1935, when the union's influence reached its peak, Marius Vazeilles called upon peasants, as he had done on numerous occasions ever since 1920, to help the SPTs survive by patronizing the union's stores. Peasants joined in times of crisis to defend their interests, but cooperation and mutual aid did not figure high on their list. Moreover, some unions were poorly managed, and internal dissension and personal rivalries discouraged both current and prospective members.[61]

The union was open to all "toiling" and "authentic" peasants: sharecroppers, tenant farmers, and peasants who worked their land with the help of their family or even with a few agricultural workers. Pending the creation of specific trade unions to serve their needs, agricultural wage laborers and servants also could join. Only those property owners who did not cultivate the soil themselves were unwelcome. The PCF-backed agricultural union opened its ranks to peasants of all political persuasions, and indeed, the

[58] *TC*, 12 February 1938.

[59] *TC*, 20 November 1937; ADC 1M71, CS Tulle to PC, 21 October 1939.

[60] See the statutes of Meymac's union in *TC*, 17 October 1920, and those of Gros-Chastang in ADC 7M16–21. See also ADD 7M8.

[61] *VP*, 29 September 1929, 13 January 1934, 27 April and 5 November 1935; interview with Marcel Darnetz, Gros-Chastang, 8 August 1984. For personal disputes see *TCO*, 10 February 1934.

union's aim was to recruit far beyond the Communist Party. A rough estimate indicates that at least half the union's members did not belong to the
PCF. On the other hand, the leadership remained firmly in the hands of
Communist militants throughout the interwar years: of the fourteen leaders
of the Corrèze Fédération des Travailleurs de la Terre in 1922, at least nine—
including the federal secretary and his assistant—were card-carrying members of the PCF.[62]

The Syndicats des Paysans Travailleurs built their propaganda on com-
monsense watchwords—"Land to the one who works it," "He who does
not work should not eat," "Let us gather together with other peasants"
(*groupons-nous entre paysans*). There was little here for a peasant to dis-
agree with. The *syndicats'* simple, straightforward message mixed vulgarized Marxism with appeals to social justice and the struggle against *les gros*.
Leaders relentlessly argued that the *paysan travailleur* faced two main enemies: those who derived income from the land without working it themselves, and the army of intermediaries who built "enormous fortunes" on the
peasants' backs.[63] Themes that provided peasants with identifiable, familiar
enemies were bound to be popular in rural areas.

The geography of the SPTs was concentrated in two distinct areas of PCF
strength: in northern Corrèze and among villages northeast of Tulle (the
cantons of Tulle-Nord and Seilhac) (map 15). In contrast to the PCF, the
union displayed little strength outside these two areas, largely because a few
Communist militants played key roles in setting up and running the local
unions. A union required more structure than a Party cell: it needed a small
barn to store supplies and someone in charge to order and distribute goods.
Men such as Marius Vazeilles encouraged and advised those who took on
such duties. Vazeilles was responsible for founding numerous Syndicats des
Paysans Travailleurs in northern Corrèze, and his policy of establishing one
union to serve two or three communes explains why the union seems underrepresented in this traditionally Communist bastion. On the whole, the SPTs
could rarely compete with the more powerful FAAC, which offered its members a wider range of products and services at lower cost. In the 1920s, SPTs
were established in only 23 of the 111 communes where the FAAC had local
unions, and 8 of those villages were PCF strongholds. Like the PCF, the peasant union had great difficulty expanding outside of areas where it had done
well from the beginning, and it failed to establish itself in 155 villages where
no agricultural trade unions existed.

The strong links between the SPTs and Communist votes demonstrate the
close connections between politics and agricultural trade unionism that developed between the two wars. The presence of an SPT was an excellent
predictor of solid Party support at the polls, a reflection of the fact that *syn-*

[62] *PCTC*, 19 March 1922.
[63] *TT*, July–August 1922; *Le Paysan Travailleur*, March 1925.

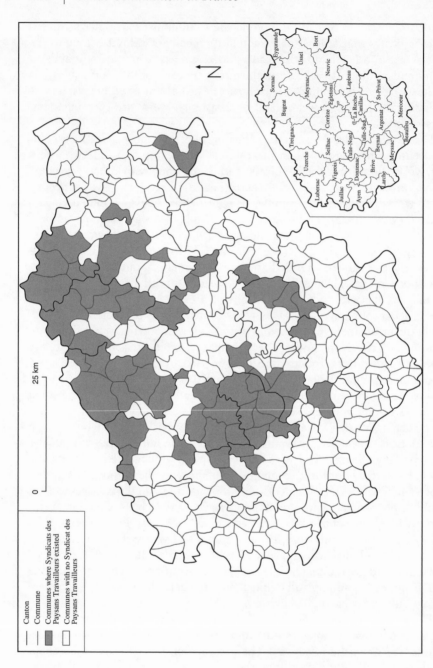

Map 15. Corrèze: communes where Syndicats des Paysans Travailleurs existed, 1920–1939

Table 7.2. Effect of Syndicats des Paysans Travailleurs (SPT) on Communist vote, Corrèze, 1924–1936 (coefficients of regression [*b*] and determination [R^2])[a]

	Existence of SPT		SPT meetings	
	b	R^2	*b*	R^2
1924	12.70[†]	.36	3.23[†]	.31
1928	9.98[†]	.36	2.41[†]	.33
1932	16.38[†]	.42	6.34[†]	.36
1936	21.31[†]	.49	8.72[†]	.44

Sources: Regional Communist press; *Le Travailleur de la Terre*; *Le Paysan Travailleur*; *La Voix Paysanne*; *La Terre*; ADC 3M196–97, 3M200, 7M16–22, AN C10045, and numerous other files in ADC 1M and 4M series and AN F[7] series.

[a]Controlling for percentages of migrants and peasants, population per km[2], long-term population change, percentage of civil burials, median delay between birth and baptism in 1910, and mean farm size per commune. N = 279.

[†]Significant at .01 level.

dicats had been initially established in Communist bastions. The mere existence of an SPT, however, was more significantly associated with Communist voting than was the number of SPT meetings per village. In other words, increased syndical militancy did not necessarily increase support for the Party (table 7.2). On the opposite side of the political spectrum, the right-wing Entente Paysanne, a precursor of Dorgères's movement, was associated with conservative voting in 1924 and 1928. But these relationships did not apply to the Radical party and the Fédération Faure. The Radical vote actually declined in villages where the FAAC was established, and the Radicals did not do best in communes with high percentages of Fédération Faure members. It was conservatives and Socialists who found themselves occasionally profiting from the FAAC presence (table 7.3). The Fédération Faure was a union in flux; with no clear connection to the world of electoral politics, it did little to help the Radical Party stave off its long-term decline. At the ballot box the Radicals did not benefit from the influential, notable-run agricultural union with which they enjoyed close ties. This was a fundamental difference between Radicals and Communists, and in this arena, as in many others, the Communists were a step ahead of their centrist rivals.

The Communist Party's objective had been to create an agricultural union that was—to use the term often applied to the Party itself—*pas comme les autres*, and they intended to do so by emphasizing politics. But to the Syndicat des Paysans Travailleurs' regret, politics rarely advanced beyond the editorial columns of the monthly newspaper. The large majority of members displayed little enthusiasm for the few scheduled meetings, whether the order of the day was fertilizer or politics. A recurrent complaint was that the leadership worked hard while members remained largely apathetic. In Bonnefond (Corrèze), "insouciant and unconscious" members skipped the

Table 7.3. Influence of agricultural syndicalism on voting, Corrèze, 1924–1936 (coefficients of regression [*b*] and determination [R^2])[a]

	b	R^2
Entente Paysanne		
Right		
1924	6.89*	.19
1928	8.75*	.28
FAAC		
Right		
1928	5.26[†]	.28
1936	5.69[†]	.29
Radical		
1928	−7.00[†]	.08
1932	−8.06[†]	.08
Parti Socialiste		
1928	−4.78[†]	.41
1932	4.79[†]	.12
FAAC membership, 1931		
Radical		
1928	−.02	.05
1932	.04	.23

Sources: ADC 7M16–21, 3M196–7, 3M200, AN C10045.

[a] Controlling for percentages of migrants and peasants, population per km², long-term population change, percentage of civil burials, median delay between birth and baptism in 1910, and mean farm size per commune. N = 279; for right in 1936, 210; for Radical in 1936, 227; for Parti Socialiste in 1928, 148.

* Significant at .05 level.

[†] Significant at .01 level.

scheduled general assembly in the midst of the agricultural crisis. The leaders of Meymac's *syndicat* put their finger on the problem when they noted that members were interested solely in getting supplies at the union's store. Time and again Marius Vazeilles urged members to remember that the purpose of their union was to defend the peasantry's interests.[64] The unions themselves were to blame for this state of affairs, for they often recruited on purely economic grounds: "Hurry up, comrades [and join]," wrote a member of Peyrelevade's (Corrèze) peasant union, "for the secretary has just ordered more lime, fertilizers, and clover seeds."[65] Of politics there was no mention.

Attempts to stir up support for the leadership's national and international political agenda met with meager success. The Corrèze's Communist peas-

[64] *L'Aurore Paysanne*, 15 May 1934; *TCO*, 3 February 1934; *TT*, April 1923, October 1924; *VP*, 5 November 1932 and 3 March 1934.

[65] *TCO*, 21 February 1925.

ant unions were by far the largest French contingent in the Moscow-based Peasants' International (Krestintern), founded in October 1923. Marius Vazeilles, along with two other Corrèze peasant leaders, Pierre Verdier and Jean Bouysse, traveled to Moscow to attend the Peasants' International's first congress, and Vazeilles, one the Krestintern's most enthusiastic backers, was elected to the International's board. Upon the delegates' return, they attempted to develop "internationalist" sentiments among the union's membership. Vazeilles soon conceded, however, that despite his persistent efforts, members remained indifferent to the Peasants' International.[66]

The Communist Party's attempt to gain a foothold in the world of agricultural trade unionism met with both success and failure. For the first time, the Party demonstrated that smallholders, sharecroppers, and tenant farmers could organize themselves in a politicized agricultural organization. The sustained activity of the Syndicats des Paysans Travailleurs in the early 1920s and the mid-1930s contributed to PCF successes in the countryside, if only because they popularized the Party's catchwords, focused attention on militants who would run under the Communist banner at election time, and provided new recruitment sources for Party members. When the time came to supply members with seeds, fertilizers, or tools, however, the Syndicats des Paysans Travailleurs were poorly equipped to compete with the richer Fédération Faure. Communist militants capitalized only temporarily on the growing dissatisfaction with traditional agricultural organizations whose response to rural problems was passive and parliamentary. The Communists, who first understood the importance of protest and direct action in the countryside, proved incapable of translating their successes into an enduring peasant mobilization. In times of economic trials the CGPT's militancy attracted a broad range of supporters, but during more prosperous periods this was precisely what frightened off potential members, and thus put a brake on the *syndicats'* expansion. The combative and political character that was the Syndicat des Paysans Travailleurs' principal asset was also something of a liability.

Peasants who organized during times of crisis rarely sustained their commitment to a union over the long run. Union work required time and energy, and as soon as results were forthcoming (or if they could not be seen on the horizon), membership declined. Peasants and the Communist Party thus operated at cross-purposes: the peasants had a largely short-term and utilitarian vision of trade unionism, whereas for the Party the trade union was the critical arena for rural politicization. In the end, most of the SPT's most com-

[66] *TT*, November–December 1923, February and July 1924. See also Conseil paysan international, *1ère conférence internationale paysanne tenue à Moscou, dans la riche salle du trône du palais du Kremlin les 10, 11, 12, 13, 14, et 15 Octobre 1923* (Paris, n.d.); *Conférence paysanne internationale: 2ème Congrès, Moscou, novembre 1927* (Berlin, 1928); Franco Rizzi, *Contadini e comunismo: La questione agraria nella Terza Internazionale, 1919–1928* (Milan, 1980), 143–62; George D. Jackson, Jr., *Comintern and Peasant in East Europe, 1919–1930* (New York, 1966); AN F[7] 13627.

mitted members belonged to the PCF, and it was within the local cell that they engaged in politics and participated in social and cultural activities. For the peasantry neither politics nor sociability was the union's fundamental raison d'être.

Despite the crippling agricultural downturn of the 1930s, and despite the Fédération Faure's close association with the Radical elites often blamed for the crisis, the SPTs did not overturn the hegemony of the Radical union. This was the SPTs' greatest failure, and it was a lesson that the Communist Party would ponder over the years to come. At the outset, the Communists had been faced with a choice: either infiltrate existing agricultural trade unions or set up their own; and in Corrèze they clearly opted for the second alternative while dabbling with the first. After World War II, however, the PCF distanced itself from this solution and capitalized on its leading role in the Corrèze Resistance to enhance its presence in the Fédération Départementale des Syndicats d'Exploitants Agricoles (FDSEA), Corrèze's leading agricultural union. François Monédière, who had led Communist efforts to infiltrate the FAAC during the interwar years, played a leading role in the world of agricultural syndicalism in the 1940s and 1950s. And even when the technique of *noyautage* and infiltration reached its limits in the early years of the Cold War, the Communists consciously backed away from the agricultural union (MODEF) that was sympathetic to its views. Here, as elsewhere, the lessons of the interwar years had not been lost.[67]

The whole issue of agricultural trade unionism forced the Communists to think hard about the exact nature of their achievements. Marius Vazeilles and others remained convinced that rural syndical organization was a precondition for large-scale Party successes, in much the same way that the PCF thought unions (or at least organizing on the factory floor) were the key to a solid working-class base. Historians have made similar arguments.[68] But there is little evidence to support this interpretation. The peasant unions were not a precondition of the Party's implantation, merely its by-product. Without a strong Communist organizational presence to begin with, the Syndicats des Paysans Travailleurs would have faced insurmountable odds. Communism in Limousin and Dordogne owed its enduring success to rural supporters, and not, by and large, to the work of the Communist agricultural trade union movement. Setting up peasant unions was difficult enough; using them to ground larger social and political movements proved to be an even more elusive goal.

---

[67] On agricultural syndicalism in postwar Corrèze see Alain Bastardie, "Le syndicalisme paysan en Corrèze depuis 1945" (mémoire de l'Institut d'Etudes Politiques, 1970–71); and John T. S. Keeler, *The Politics of Neocorporatism in France: Farmers, the State, and Agricultural Policy-Making in the Fifth Republic* (New York, 1987), 154–77.

[68] Gratton, "Le communisme rural en Corrèze"; Sokoloff, "Communism and the French Peasantry," 271.

8   Governing at the Grass Roots

The exercise of municipal power in and around large cities has been a key component of French communism's strength. The Party's municipal power base gave it access to resources, financial and otherwise, much needed for its expansion. Municipalities served as a training ground for Party cadres and elected officials, and were a recruiting base for new generations of militants.[1] Beginning in the 1920s the Party carefully forged a discourse that underscored the exemplary administration of its municipalities. Generations of militants prided themselves on the Party's administration of local government, which demonstrated that Communists, too, could exercise power, and at the same time demonstrated convincingly that they alone did so in the interests of the working class. Communist municipalities presented themselves as beacons of hope and models for the future in an otherwise hostile environment. In the 1980s and 1990s, PCF leaders, in charge of a ship that was taking on water on all sides, made the preservation of municipal power their top priority.

Communist municipal power, however, was not confined solely to urban working-class areas. In the mid-1930s, the Communists ran thirty-three villages in rural Corrèze, or close to 10 percent of all the PCF-directed communes in the country.[2] Only in industrial Nord did the Communists control

[1] On Communist municipalities see Raymond Pronier, *Les municipalités communistes* (Paris, 1983); Fernand Dupuy, *Etre maire communiste* (Paris, 1975); Jean-Paul Brunet, *Saint-Denis la ville rouge: socialisme et communisme en banlieue ouvrière, 1890–1939* (Paris, 1980) and his *Un demi-siècle d'action municipale à Saint-Denis la Rouge, 1890–1939* (Paris, 1981); *Sur l'implantation du Parti communiste francais dans l'entre-deux-guerres*, ed. Jacques Girault (Paris, 1977); Annie Fourcaut, *Bobigny, banlieue rouge* (Paris, 1986); Tyler Stovall, *The Rise of the Paris Red Belt* (Berkeley, 1990).

[2] The figure reaches 14% when one adds Communist municipalities in Creuse, Haute-Vienne, and Dordogne. Parti Communiste Francais, *Deux ans d'activité au service du peuple: Rapports du Comité Central pour le IXe Congrès national du Parti communiste français, Arles, 25–29 décembre 1937* (n.p., n.d.), 82–84.

a larger number of municipalities. While small municipalities may have contributed less to the Party than large urban ones, they are no less interesting. Benefiting from a degree of independence from PCF headquarters unparalleled in larger towns, rural Communist mayors improvised, at least until the late 1930s. Those in charge of municipalities in the countryside fashioned a perception of the Party's ideology and a practice of municipal power that corresponded neither to the official PCF line nor to urban undertakings. PCF mayors and their municipal councils were less likely to reproduce the models of Communist administration prevalent in cities. Their legacy suggests how difficult it was to put new ideologies into practice and inaugurate new forms of village politics, and displays the limits of the Party's challenges to the established order. Moving from a hard-hitting critique of capitalism to local governance proved far more difficult for the Communists than they expected.

The PCF's municipal strength was not in keeping with its electoral influence. In Corrèze, where five villages have consistently reelected Party candidates to office since 1920[3]—a distinction shared by only a dwindling number of urban municipalities—the Communists invested over a decade of militancy before establishing themselves solidly on the municipal level: the number of villages under their control fluctuated from eleven in early 1921 to nine in 1925 and fourteen in 1929 before jumping to thirty-three in 1935, by which time the Party could boast over 350 municipal councillors spread over one-quarter of the department's towns and villages.[4] At their apogee, Communists headed eleven percent of Corrèze's municipalities, far less than the Radicals (55 percent in 1935), who, despite their losses, still dominated local politics, but more than the Socialists, who proved even less capable of breaking the Radicals' lock on municipal power.[5] In the other three departments Communist municipal strength was more limited. Not until after World War II did the Communists move into town halls on a large scale. As late as the 1977 municipal elections they gained control of 141 communes in Limousin and Périgord, but 113 of them had fewer than 1,000 inhabitants.[6] The Party's power base has remained largely rural.

Rurality was the central unifying characteristic of Communist municipalities in Limousin and Dordogne. With the exception of a brief reign in the railroad center of Périgueux (Dordogne) in the early 1920s, St-Junien (Haute-Vienne) was the only important industrial town under Communist

---

[3] Except during the Vichy regime, when prefects named administrators to replace PCF mayors. The five villages are Chanteix, Lagraulière, Lacelle, Tarnac, and Toy-Viam.

[4] ADC 3M344–345.

[5] The Socialists controlled 5% of all Corrèze communes in 1939. In Haute-Vienne, where the powerful SFIO had destroyed Radicalism as a political force by the end of World War I, the Socialists still had to contend with the Radicals on the municipal level. In this department, the Socialists controlled 35% of all communes in 1935 and the Radicals 18%. ADHV 3M559.

[6] In the mid 1930s the PCF ran fourteen communes in Haute-Vienne, and only six in both Dordogne and Creuse. For 1977 figures, Pronier, *Les municipalités communistes*, 437–47.

control. The spreading influence of Communist municipal power moved not from urban areas to the countryside, but rather from the smallest villages toward larger centers of population. From their rural bastions, Communists fanned out and conquered larger *bourgs* and towns. This was anything but an urban political movement.

The first Communist municipal administrations had been elected on the Socialist ticket in 1919, and had joined the new party at the time of the Tours Congress. These villages—eleven in Corrèze, three to four in Haute-Vienne—remained faithful to the PCF over the next decades and beyond. The Socialists in these communes had originally reached power on an anticapitalist, antimilitaristic platform, and owed their success to the people's disaffection with Radical notables of all stripes who enjoyed a lock on the running of municipal administrations. In Lagraulière (Corrèze), the Socialists, virtually nonexistent before World War I, brought an end to the reign of the conservative Radical mayor by assembling a last-minute list of candidates (they even lacked the time to print and distribute a program) composed largely of peasant war veterans. But socialism and, as of 1920, communism represented not radicalization of Radicalism but a break with the past: the majority of the future Communist municipal councillors elected in 1919 had not held office before, and only a few had been involved in Radical village politics.

The conquest of local power was a difficult, long-range enterprise that depended more on the charisma, connections, and popularity of personalities than on structured political organizations. It was difficult for new contenders to establish their credibility. The Communists denounced the pervasive emphasis on personalities rather than issues in small communes, and did their utmost to place politics first. Many of the PCF's most charismatic leaders had never headed rural municipalities, and their lack of credentials cost the Party dearly.[7] Lacking administrative experience and the legitimacy of better-known PCF leaders, those Communists elected to office in the countryside worked in relative isolation. The promise of social change soon took a back seat to more familiar village disputes and rivalries.

Running for Local Political Office

Unlike their opponents, rural Communist candidates for municipal office did not hesitate to emphasize politics. The PCF's well-rehearsed slogans occupied a prominent position in village campaign literature: the fight against militarism and the war, the struggle against fascism, the denunciation of capi-

---

[7] Two notable exceptions: Jules Fraisseix, Communist deputy of Haute-Vienne (1928–32) was mayor of the small town of Eymoutiers from 1919 to 1939, and the Corrèze Communist leader Clément Chausson headed the village of Moustier-Ventadour between 1929 and 1939.

talist exploitation, and protests against the agricultural crisis of the 1930s. Communist Party candidates called upon voters to cast their ballots more against the reigning order than for a given conception of a new society. By backing the PCF, electors disavowed the rapacious bourgeoisie and capitalism, and aligned themselves with the old struggle—of which the Communists claimed to be the heirs—of *les petits* versus *les gros*.[8] Municipal Communist discourse perpetuated a Manichean vision of the world that pitted the poor and exploited against the rich and greedy; in a word, *le peuple* against capitalism. This long-standing dualism, which lay at the root of society's ills, was but a continuation of the struggle against feudalism. Indeed, PCF candidates often accused outgoing mayors of behaving like kings who believed they had a hereditary right to remain in office.[9]

PCF candidates, however, preferred to steer away from such sensitive matters as the dictatorship of the proletariat and the problem of socialization and collectivism: these themes were hot potatoes even in the reddest of rural communes, and the candidates themselves, especially after the early 1920s, did not consider them to be communism's goal.[10] The land issue was conspicuous by its absence from municipal electoral discourse. Candidates, armed with little or no ideological ammunition, hesitated to meddle in such a sticky matter, best left to their more experienced leaders.

Communist municipal platforms were a judicious mixture of political, administrative, national, and local concerns. Broadly speaking, the degree of politicization was inversely related to the likelihood of a Party candidate's election. When the popular Communist mayor of Lagraulière, Guillaume Brousse, stood for reelection in 1925, he distributed an electoral leaflet stressing his accomplishments over the past six years and his plans for the future; he addressed his *administrés* as "Brousse, mayor of Lagraulière," and mentioned only in passing that he had run as a Communist for the Conseil Général in 1922. Nowhere did he claim to be a Communist or mention that the other sixteen candidates on his ticket, whose names he failed to list, were for the most part also PCF members. Worried that the Radicals might stage a comeback, Brousse focused attention on his personality and administrative achievements and avoided any mention of politics, save for a few barbs directed against *messieurs les aristos* and *les bourgeois*. In future years, however, as Brousse consolidated his power, and under strong pressure from his

[8] For more on this theme see Pierre Birnbaum, *Le peuple et les gros: Histoire d'un mythe* (Paris, 1979); Patrick Le Guirriec, "Communisme local, résistance et PCF: Les trois éléments du pouvoir dans une commune bretonne," *Etudes rurales* 101–2 (1986): 226–27; Pierre Vallin, *Paysans rouges du Limousin* (Paris, 1985).

[9] See the campaign literature for PCF candidates in the Corrèze villages of Sornac, 1929, ADC 3M453; Lamazière-Basse, 1935, ADC 3M392; Chanteix, 1935, ADC 3M368; and Lagraulière, 1925, ADC 3M391.

[10] For exceptions see Sornac (Corrèze), 1923, ADC 3M336. I have seen only one *profession de foi* that mentions the dictatorship of the proletariat—see Viam (Corrèze) 1935, ADC 3M465.

comrades on the municipal council, his electoral programs became increasingly political.[11]

The promise of a different kind of municipal administration was as important as political and ideological considerations in attracting voters. Just as they did in larger cities, PCF candidates stressed that their mayors "had everywhere been magnificent achievers," despite the active opposition of prefects.[12] The Communists emphasized the classic issues: electrification and running water for the village center and the outlying hamlets, upgrading of roads and paths, improved maintenance for schools, communal buildings, and the cemetery. To distinguish themselves from their adversaries they placed particular emphasis on the social aspects of their platform: hot soup for schoolchildren, free schoolbooks and supplies, increased relief for the destitute and the elderly, municipal libraries, and support for secular schooling. Communists claimed they would govern impartially and do away with the favoritism characteristic of the Radicals and the right: in Pérols-sur-Vézère (Corrèze) they pledged that only the truly needy, not the friends and families of municipal councillors, would be placed on welfare rolls.[13] But this emphasis on administrative matters depoliticized the Party's message. Save for the heading "Liste communiste," some platforms made no mention of politics, and others omitted even that reference, leaving both voters and prefects puzzled when the time came to pin a political label on them. Village politics were a highly contentious affair, governed by enduring family feuds and social cleavages; Communist candidates who downplayed their Party affiliation reflected, by and large, the pulse of their communities.

Well aware that rural voters were keenly sensitive to the personalities, professions, social status, and family ties of candidates, village militants selected candidates who reflected the geographic, demographic, and occupational diversity of the commune, and who represented each hamlet as well as a diverse network of family relations. The most dedicated, politically engaged Communist militants rarely made it to municipal office. Prominent militants did not always possess those qualities necessary for a good candidate: tact and diplomacy, a solid network of friendships and influence, and a respected image within the community. Better a hardworking peasant than an exemplary Communist to head a rural commune. In Communist Gros-Chastang (Corrèze), the mayor, Antoine Parel, was chided for caring more about *la politique* than about the upkeep of his plot of land. Marcel Darnetz explained, "At the time this was not a mark in his favor, because people are demanding—they have respect for good peasants, for those who raise good crops, for those who do a good job of working the soil." [14]

---

[11] ADC 3M391.

[12] Châteauneuf-la-Forêt (Haute-Vienne), 1929, ADHV 3M555.

[13] Pérols-sur-Vézère (Corrèze), 1929, ADC 3M414; St-Martin-Château (Creuse), 1929, Bibliothèque Nationale, uncatalogued.

[14] Interview with Marcel Darnetz, Gros-Chastang, 8 August 1984.

Smallholding peasants formed the great majority of those who ran for office under the Communist banner. Even in larger *bourgs*, peasants dominated municipal councils: in the market center of Lagraulière (Corrèze), peasants accounted for thirteen of sixteen Communist municipal councillors in 1935, and the Party found its staunchest, most faithful electoral backers among cultivators in the outlying hamlets, while shopkeepers and merchants in the village center were its most dedicated opponents.[15] The thirty-three Corrèze Communist mayors in 1935 included nineteen *cultivateurs*, five merchants, four artisans, and one shopkeeper. Because artisans often assumed key positions in the village cell, they often played second fiddle on the municipal stage.

Communists interested in preserving municipal power had to bend to the unwritten rules of village politics. A mayor, especially a Communist one, needed to make up in respectability and esteem what he lacked in influence. While his political views may well have been known by all, if he chose to place politics front and center, he risked alienating part of the constituency that had contributed to his initial success.

Village Communism?

The true problems began once the Communists accepted the keys to town hall. The mayor and his council soon realized that their political and administrative margin for maneuver was limited. Communist municipal councils could transmit as many resolutions to the prefect as they pleased, but these had only a symbolic importance. One could protest vigorously against the agricultural crisis, support imprisoned Party leaders, ask for the dissolution of the fascist leagues, condemn militarism on paper, but as soon as municipal councils tried to back a cause with financial support, the prefect could, and usually did, impose his veto. In Lagraulière, the municipal council voted funds in support of a small tenant farmer whose possessions had been auctioned off when he failed to pay his rent, only to meet with the prefect's disapproval.[16] The prefect not only exerted his powers in the political domain, he kept a sharp eye on administrative and financial matters as well. If he judged that a given project was too expensive, poorly prepared, contrary to the general interest, or simply unnecessary, he vetoed it. But the prefects appear to have been impartial in this particular role: there are no indications that they overtly discriminated against Communist municipalities when the time came to approve new school buildings, new roads, water projects, and the like.

There are, of course, subtler ways of helping your political allies, and in

[15] Interview with Armand Soleilhavoup, Lagraulière, 5 July 1984.
[16] AC Lagraulière, *DCM* Lagraulière, February 1936

Limousin strategically placed friends and political figures could often get a village's dossier advanced and approved. In this sense the Communists' political isolation was a liability. The PCF's opponents—the Radicals in particular—did not fail to underline how well positioned they were to ask their senators, deputies, and *conseillers généraux* for as many favors and subsidies as possible.[17] In an area where politics often rhymed with patronage, connections with important political figures served as a key electoral argument. The Communists understood this so well that in the most sectarian period in the Party's history, they selected the outgoing *conservative* mayor of Bugeat (Corrèze) to head the newly elected municipal council (their lack of administrative experience and self-confidence also surely contributed to this decision). In a nearby village the Communists likewise chose a political opponent—a retired rentier, no less—as their mayor.[18] In other villages, however, the PCF claimed that it was not necessary to be in the "prefecture's favor" or to bow before the authorities to obtain what one was entitled to.

Once in power, the Communists cultivated their ties with elected officials at all levels. They often boasted that a *conseiller général* who did not share their political leanings supported their endeavors and had proved to be a model of impartiality.[19] Electors were not being short-changed at a higher level because they had elected a Communist municipal government. Soon enough, however, Communist mayors became indebted to their political opponents, and this became a major source of conflict within the Party. In 1925 the newly elected Communist municipal government of Gros-Chastang (Corrèze), led by its mayor, Antoine Parel, sent a message expressing its "confidence and entire devotion" to the Radical *conseiller général*, Dr. Aussoleil, and thanked him for a job well done. (The municipal councillors, obviously impressed by their new posts, also addressed their congratulations to the *président du conseil*, Paul Painlevé—not a gesture one would expect from a PCF municipality). This was the beginning of a long and, for the village of Gros-Chastang, profitable friendship between the Communist mayor and the Radical *conseiller général*. But friendship had its price: when Parel supported Aussoleil's bid for reelection in 1931, he was scolded by the Party and forced to recant and repent in the columns of the Communist newspaper.[20] Another Communist mayor made a costly political mistake when he addressed a letter of profuse thanks to his *conseiller général*, only to find this letter used against him when he ran for office a few months later.[21]

---

[17] Lagraulière (Corrèze), 1935, ADC 3M391.

[18] In both communes the Communists later ousted the mayors they had installed in office. For Bugeat see ADC 3M347, 3M309, and *TCO*, 28 November 1931. For Pérols-sur-Vézère, *VP*, 12 November 1929.

[19] St-Georges-la-Pouge (Creuse), 1929, Bibliothèque Nationale, uncatalogued.

[20] ADC 1E dépôt 89/3, *DCM* Gros-Chastang, 1 June 1925; interview with Charles Martignac, Gros-Chastang, 3 July 1984; *TCO*, 1 August 1931.

[21] Electoral poster of Gustave Vidalin, canton de Seilhac (Corrèze), 1922, Bibliothèque Nationale, packet 1497.

Few conflicts erupted between Communist mayors and the omnipresent prefects. Only in Ambazac (Haute-Vienne) did the fiery mayor, Gabriel Texier, make a profession of irritating and provoking the prefect, and as a result, he was suspended from his duties more than once. In other villages, clashes with the central authorities were the exception rather than the rule: the mayor of Lacelle (Corrèze), suspended from his post in 1931 after raising the red flag over the unfinished post office building, enjoyed a cordial relationship with the prefect at other times.[22] Communist mayors, little versed in municipal administration, relied heavily on the prefecture for guidance: it was not in their interest to defy the departmental bureaucracy and the representatives of the state. To exercise power effectively, Communist villages cultivated their local networks of influence. Isolation was not a realistic possibility.

Communist mayors found themselves sandwiched between the necessity of developing political ties with their opponents and the need to hold the Party line. The meager benefits of municipal power disappointed PCF militants. Mayors could do little to help the Communist Party: the prefect's supervision of communal finances (not to mention the poverty of communal budgets) made it impossible to funnel out funds to support PCF activities. Neither was it possible to hand out jobs to Party militants. At best, a municipality could offer the cell a meeting room in town hall and the Communist-sponsored agricultural trade union a place to store fertilizers and tools.

To counter their limited range of influence, Communist mayors took the political initiative and proposed to democratize village life. The Party's democratic discourse was a breath of fresh air in an otherwise stagnant political environment. PCF candidates promised that municipal councils would consult their constituents regularly and would not make important decisions behind closed doors. In Lacelle (Corrèze) the outgoing Party list pledged to organize "popular general assemblies. Nothing that concerns the peasants will be decided without consulting them." The tune was similar in other communes.[23] These promises, however, remained dead letters once the Party was installed in office; at best, the mayor held meetings to inform the public of his accomplishments. PCF candidates also promoted themselves as champions of direct democracy in the countryside: electors (and in some communes the Party) would be free to recall municipal councillors. Again, however, such methods—publicized by some militants as "Soviet"—never saw the light of day.[24] But not all promises went unfulfilled: Communist mayors and municipal councillors did resign in large numbers in 1933, after four

---

[22] *TCO*, 15 November 1930.

[23] Lacelle (Corrèze), 1929, Bibliothèque Nationale, uncatalogued. In some villages Communists promised to call upon the people to approve all expenditures over a given sum. See Pérols-sur-Vézère (Corrèze), 1929, ADC 3M414.

[24] *TCO*, 18 February 1928; Peyrelevade (Corrèze), 1929, ADC 3M416.

years in office, in protest against the law that lengthened their term in office from four to six years.

There was nothing remarkable about the Party's municipal achievements. Communist municipalities—and they were not alone—lacked funding, and proved cautious in spending the taxpayers' money. Mayors and their municipal councils merely did what they could to upgrade roads, build new paths, maintain school buildings, electrify the village center and outlying hamlets, and provide running water and sewers—projects common to most municipalities. Few PCF mayors and councillors had the administrative experience, imagination, and entrepreneurship necessary to promote innovation in communes with limited means. Bugeat (Corrèze) was a rare exception. There Communists engaged in a modest program of public works and tried, at the same time, to make up for their lack of finances by encouraging citizens to contribute money to support the schools and donate their labor to the commune.[25] In most villages, Communist mayors could only voice their powerlessness in the face of continued rural out-migration and economic crisis. The mayor of Singleyrac (Dordogne) remarked bitterly in 1937 that "artisans have disappeared from the commune and so have the good peasants; misery will stay." Communists could do little to prevent this rural exodus. In Toy-Viam (Corrèze), the Communist municipality turned down the prefect's suggestion to subsidize apprenticeships for artisans, arguing that the salvation of rural artisanship walked hand in hand with a critical issue over which it had no control: an improved standard of living for the village's peasants.[26]

From a financial perspective the Communists distinguished themselves by their prudence: Party-controlled communes rarely engaged in deficit spending (the prefect would not have allowed it), and their yearly budgets were models of fiscal conservatism. In Toy-Viam (Corrèze), expenses outpaced receipts in only six of seventeen budgets, and these deficits were easily covered by the budgetary surplus from years past; the situation was similar in other PCF villages. But these surpluses merely provided a safety cushion in small communes where the people were so poor that an increase in taxes was unthinkable.[27] A balanced budget was a convincing electoral argument: rural households, living on the margins of the market economy, rarely engaged in deficit spending, and there was no reason why municipalities should do so either. Guillaume Brousse claimed he governed Lagraulière with the same relentless attention to savings that he applied to his household finances. Gros-Chastang's Communist candidates for reelection in 1935 boasted that they had never raised taxes or borrowed money in their ten years in office. In an-

[25] *L'information municipale* 16 (July–August 1938): 124–26. The municipality of Communist Gros-Chastang asked inhabitants to donate labor to repair a village path. AC Gros-Chastang, *DCM* Gros-Chastang, August 1927.

[26] ADD 7M20; AC Toy-Viam, *DCM* Toy-Viam, 9 March 1933 and 2 September 1934.

[27] AC Toy-Viam, *DCM* Toy-Viam, 1920–39; ADC 2 O Toy-Viam 2, July 1936.

other village, Communist candidates criticized the outgoing municipal government for having put the commune in debt and for planning to undertake public works projects beyond the village's modest means; taxes, they implied, were high enough as they were.[28] Even in the 1980s, small Communist villages remained financially strapped: in Viam (Corrèze), which has been administered by the PCF ever since 1935, the church (admittedly not the municipal council's number one priority) was dangerously near collapse, much as it had been over thirty years before, when the historian Gordon Wright passed through the village.[29]

Of the three distinctive trademarks of urban Communist municipal management—the suspiciously large sums spent for supplies, general administration, and maintenance; a significant budget for health and welfare; and a sustained effort undertaken on educational matters—only the last also characterized rural PCF communes. Despite campaign promises to the contrary, municipalities spent only modest amounts on social welfare: Lacelle and Bugeat (both in Corrèze) spent nothing on medical and social assistance beyond required expenditures. In contrast, St-Denis, the PCF's suburban stronghold north of Paris, devoted between 17 and 22 percent of its regular budget to such expenditures.[30] Rural Communists did make a greater effort in the educational realm, however, allotting between 4 and 5 percent of their budgets for optional items such as school supplies for poor children.

Schools and other communal buildings suffered from the municipality's neglect. In Chanteix (Corrèze), the school roof leaked badly, classrooms had no ceilings, the floors were in pieces, the windows were broken and impossible to open, the lighting was poor, and the building was only marginally heated in winter. When the prefect intervened after an outbreak of meningitis to get the school disinfected and the most elementary repairs done, he found the mayor distinctly uncooperative. Part of the problem was that the mayor was on bad terms (*brouillé*) with the schoolteacher. Moreover, Chanteix and its Communist-run neighbor Lagraulière, where one school was described as a shack, never agreed to build the joint school that the Ministry of Education thought was necessary; parish-pump politics made cooperation between neighboring Communist villages impossible.[31] Lagraulière had no school lunch program; children, locked out of the school at noontime, soaked their old bread crusts in the soup they obtained at local restaurants,

[28] René Vergne, "Rétrospectives de Lagraulière et d'ailleurs, 1926–1930," manuscript, 1975, in ADC; Gros-Chastang (Corrèze), 1935, ADC 3M387; ADC 3M340.

[29] Gordon Wright, *Rural Revolution in France: The Peasantry in the Twentieth Century* (Stanford, 1964), 201.

[30] See the *comptes administratifs* for Lacelle in ADC 2 O 95/2, and for Bugeat (1935) in ADC 28W1322a. The budgets differentiate between *dépenses obligatoires* and *dépenses facultatives*; Brunet, *Un demi-siècle d'action municipale*, 151. These figures are calculated as percentages of the *dépenses ordinaires*.

[31] ADC 2 O Chanteix 2; ADC 28W1279.

and ate outside in the wind and cold.[32] PCF municipalities, however, were only partly responsible for the often sorry state of village buildings: Tarnac (Corrèze) waited over six years for subsidies to renovate a school. The same commune's project to build tennis courts and a small sports facility never received financial support from the state, nor did nearby Toy-Viam's (Corrèze) original proposal to build a community center (*foyer familial*) as a way of combating rural out-migration.[33] Unless Communist communities found alternative financing, their projects would remain forever on the drawing boards. For rural Communists, the state's fiscal conservatism and its neglect of poor, isolated rural areas was a double-edged sword: on the one hand, the pervasive sense of isolation and abandonment contributed heavily to PCF successes; on the other hand, the state's control of the purse strings made it impossible for Communist-run villages to undertake original programs of social reform.

Ambitions and Rivalries

Communist mayors presided over villages beset by rivalries, tensions, and conflicting ambitions. There was no agreement within the Party, or within the municipality, or within the community at large. This was a highly contentious society, even if, on the surface, communes where the Communists reached power without opposition or with decisive majorities appeared to be havens of political consensus. It was never an easy matter to reach agreement on building paths, levying taxes, and regrouping plots of land (*remembrement*).

Mayors' authority was often resented and challenged by fellow municipal councillors and the Communist cell. Mayors ran villages with little input from the Party cell; indeed, they vigorously resisted the cell's intrusion in village politics. Some mayors had more to fear from their cell comrades than from their political opponents. The cell in Tarnac led such a vicious campaign against the outgoing Communist mayor and village baker, Léon Banette, that he chose not to run again in 1935. The ensuing elections nonetheless saw two Communist lists—one sympathetic to the outgoing mayor—oppose each other, and the campaign was an exercise in mudslinging such as Tarnac had never seen before. Banette, first elected as a Socialist in 1919, was accused of careerism, of being too "refined" in his manners, of having "reigned" over the commune; worse yet, he had favored a

---

[32] Vergne, "Rétrospectives," 6. Other PCF municipalities, however, did set up lunch programs for children who lived outside the village center.

[33] Tarnac's subsidies were eventually paid out under Vichy. ADC 28W1319. On the state of the schools and sports facilities, ADC 2 O Tarnac 4 and *TC*, 7 August 1937; AC Toy-Viam, *DCM* Toy-Viam, 15 September 1929.

large property owner at the expense of *les petits*. "This was your *politique*, your communism. It was not ours," wrote the cell secretary.[34] The opposing lists—not to mention Banette, who defended his honor from the sidelines—accused each other of not being Communist, not knowing why they were Communist, and being too timid in their communism. Beneath this bitter political struggle lay a complex family feud.[35] Here, as in many other villages, family quarrels and village politics went hand in hand. The conflict reached a comical level after the elections, when Banette and the new PCF mayor, who owned two of the few automobiles in the village, collided on a nearby country road.[36]

Other Communist mayors were similarly criticized for their lukewarm communism, but quite often their popularity was a corollary of their refusal to be simple Party transmission belts. Guillaume Brousse survived as mayor of Lagraulière for twenty years precisely because he was able to mediate between opposing factions on his council; when consensus proved impossible, Brousse would threaten to resign.[37] Armand Soleilhavoup, Communist mayor of Lagraulière, recalled the difficult relations between Brousse and the PCF: "[Brousse] was not an exemplary Communist militant, and quite often he didn't even take out his card. This doesn't mean that he wasn't Communist, that he didn't follow the Party, but he was an independent sort and he would never—because he was a character, he was stubborn—have let the Party tell him what to do."[38]

Jean Dupuy, one of Brousse's most virulent opponents in Lagraulière's cell, explained what the hard-liners had against him: "At one time Brousse had taken out his [Party] card but he didn't want us to say so. 'If I declared myself Communist,' he said, 'we'd have been beaten.' He liked his *mairie*. He saw it his way. He didn't even want the Party to look over our administration. We, we wanted the Party's help and participation. Brousse was a Communist, if you will, but a Communist who . . . He didn't want to increase taxes, he didn't want to move that way, he didn't want to put the commune into debt, he didn't want to move forward, you had to push him."[39]

This was the basis of Brousse's success. He went neither too far nor too fast. Change, in Communist communities as well, was slow in coming.

Petty disputes, personal ambitions and hatred forged lasting divisions within Communist municipal councils. Chanteix went through five Com-

---

[34] *TCO*, 31 March, 6 and 13 April, 4 May 1935; ADC 3M340. This was not the only occasion when two Communist lists opposed each other at election time—see Lagraulière, 1933, ADC 3M391.

[35] ADC 3M340. The outgoing mayor's principal critic was his cousin, who criticized the mayor for having addressed him rudely when he was a child. *TCO*, 18 May 1935.

[36] *TCO*, 14 September 1935.

[37] Brousse did resign in 1939, but changed his mind after reaching an agreement with his municipal council. ADC 3M391.

[38] Interview with Armand Soleilhavoup.

[39] Interview with Jean Dupuy, Lagraulière, 1 August 1984.

munist mayors during the interwar years; four of them quit in disgust.[40] Communist municipal councillors resigned for a variety of reasons, ranging from the alleged poor treatment of their children in school to, more commonly, the fact that they had not been selected as senatorial delegates. In Lacelle, never more than half the outgoing Party municipal councillors stood for reelection, and while they attributed their decision to weariness and lack of time, it was not unrelated to the high degree of contentiousness in village politics. Lagraulière's Communists squabbled for over twenty years over what inscription to engrave on the village's *monument aux morts*, and as a result they never built one; their dispute over a cross—was it or was it not too close to the public school?—led to bitter clashes with the curé and the prefect and eventually made it all the way to the Conseil d'État.

What did Communist municipalities have to show for five, ten, or twenty years of rule? In terms of concrete, tangible results, the answer is relatively little. Communists proved no more enterprising than many of their neighbors, and displayed much conservatism in their municipal management. Unlike their urban counterparts, they had neither the budgetary means nor the administrative know-how to undertake major programs of social reform. They met with more success promoting rural sociability, but more often than not the municipality left the initiative to the Party cell and limited its role to organizing an annual fête. Asked if his father's Communist municipality differed from those headed by other parties, Louis Freyssinet, who followed in his father's footsteps, replied, "You really can't say so. There wasn't much difference with other municipalities, because we had so few means." Another militant I interviewed was more faithful to the myth of Communist management: he claimed that rural Communist municipalities had demonstrated that it was possible to do something with limited resources.[41] Rural Communist mayors could only watch helplessly as the tide of rural depopulation gradually undermined the social fabric of their villages. To put it bluntly, ever since the 1920s the Communists have presided over social and economic decline in the countryside.

Rural voters subscribed more to an image of communism than to a proven record of municipal management. Villagers repeatedly reelected PCF municipal leaders no matter how dismal their record or how virulent their internal disputes. Nor did constituents seem concerned about the wide gap between promises and reality—they hoped that Communists would do a better job of managing scarcity, but they believed that solutions to the social crisis could not be found at the village level. Mayors and their constituents saw social and political reform as a top-down affair; in this sense they played into

---

[40] ADC 3M368.
[41] Interviews with Louis Freyssinet, Ste-Fortunade, 1 September 1983 and 30 June 1984. Freyssinet's father, Alfred Freyssinet, was the Communist mayor of St-Germain-Lavolps from 1932 to 1939; interview with Jean-Baptiste Vars, Meymac, 3 October 1983.

the hands of the state, which had a vested interest in making sure that its authority remained unchallenged.

The Communists proved unable to reinvent politics at the municipal level. The weight of petty rivalries, the personalization of issues, the legacy of patronage politics, and the meager financial resources proved to be barriers too difficult to overcome. Less understandable was the lack of imagination and innovation shown by PCF municipalities. Communist mayors had difficulty breaking out of the cultural constraints of village politics. By persuading their electors that change was inevitable in the future, they absolved themselves of their failings in the present.

Conclusion

Communism has arguably been the object of greater scholarly concern than any other political or social movement in modern France. The reasons are complex: the polarization of political life; the enduring divisions of the left; the nagging question of the French Communist Party's relation to Moscow and the International; the perception that the PCF differed greatly in form and content from other political parties; communism's influence among intellectuals in the 1940s, 1950s, and 1960s; the presence in the academic community of present and former PCF members who feel compelled to write about the Party's past; and the availability of sources. Today the historiography of French communism finds itself at a crossroads. The collapse of communism in Eastern Europe in 1989 and the former Soviet Union in 1991, coupled with the declining strength and growing marginalization of the PCF in the 1980s and 1990s, has led to new questions and approaches even as interest in the history of communism has declined.[1] Just as the collapse of fascism led to a long-term historiographical reassessment of that movement, so, as communism recedes in time, will some of the central problems that frame its study change. Some scholars have pinned their hopes on newly accessible archives in Moscow, and doubtless these files will reveal much about the relationship between French Communists and the International, the "relative autonomy" (or more likely the lack of it) of PCF policy, the nitty-gritty disputes within the Party apparatus, and the depressing subservience of Communist leaders in France to their Russian comrades.[2] Much of this new evidence will contribute to refining the dominant model

---

[1] Marc Lazar, "Après 1989, cet étrange communisme . . ." in *Passés recomposés: Champs et chantiers de l'histoire*, ed. Jean Boutier and Dominique Julia (Paris, 1995), 243–53.

[2] On this last issue see Arkadii Vaksberg, *Hôtel Lux: Les partis frères au service de l'Internationale communiste*, trans. Olivier Simon (Paris, 1993); and, for preliminary findings from Russian archives, *Communisme* 32–33–34 (1993).

of PCF historiography: a top-down political history concerned with institutions, policies, and personalities. While these developments will fill in crucial blanks of *l'histoire événementielle* and shed considerable light on the complex inner workings of the Party bureaucracy, they will not be sufficient to help us reconceptualize the history of French communism, and explain the PCF's prominence on the political and social scene for the better part of the twentieth century. Neither "Moscow's hand" nor the ruthlessness and sectarianism of the apparatus can help elucidate the PCF's enduring grass-roots support.

The PCF's "anthropological diversity" was critical to its success.[3] It became a national party precisely because it established bases of support among a varied spectrum of occupational groups in a range of geographical settings, urban and rural. The Party's voters elected mayors, departmental representatives, and deputies in cities, in rural departments with industrial traditions, and in agricultural departments. Communism was not just a working-class or suburban phenomenon, and its supporters were not just people who were discontented with industrial and urban development. Nor did rural Communists share the perception of communism held by skilled metalworkers, for example, or the *mal-lotis* (poorly housed) of the grim Paris suburbs. Communism struck another chord in the countryside; it served a different purpose, appealed to other perceptions and sensibilities, and it did so within a particular historical, social, and economic context.

Rural communism's enduring success was related to the considerable independence local leaders enjoyed from PCF headquarters in Paris, not to mention from the Third International.[4] However centralized and pyramidal the PCF's leadership and bureaucracy were, they did not always have the capacity to micro-manage everything at the local level. Even when they attempted to do so, the forces of passive resistance were stronger than has been commonly thought. On the surface, the relationship between center and periphery was one of authority and submission, but in practice it was complex and contradictory. Isolated rural areas, devoid of any recognizable working class, were not high on the Party's list of priorities, and often the PCF was content to give a free hand to peasant leaders such as Marius Vazeilles in Corrèze and Renaud Jean in Lot-et-Garonne. To some extent, it was a case of benign neglect, and the PCF's rural achievements must have come as a pleasant surprise to the better part of the Communist apparatus (although for some *ouvriéristes* it was a bitter pill to swallow). When the Party did decide to intervene, it found it difficult to do so within a milieu about which it

---

[3] For an overview, Marc Lazar, "L'invention et la désagrégation de la culture communiste," *Vingtième siècle: Revue d'histoire* 44 (1994): 9–18; Michel Hastings, "Le communisme saisi par l'anthropologie," *Communisme* 45–46 (1996): 99–114.

[4] On the theme of autonomy, Michel Hastings, *Halluin la Rouge, 1919–1939: Aspects d'un communisme identitaire* (Lille, 1991).

knew too little; the few attempts at "parachuting" working-class militants into Limousin and Dordogne leadership invariably met with failure. As a result, rural militants enjoyed more independence than their urban counterparts, and they continued to do so as long as they kept a low profile. Grassroots propagandists, well aware of the fears and interests of their constituents, carefully tailored their discourse to local circumstances. This was nothing but smart politics, but it was a difficult balancing act nonetheless. Militants needed to exercise care not to antagonize the PCF hierarchy while at the same time demonstrating considerable political savvy in recruiting new supporters.

The example of rural communism highlights the hybrid nature of the PCF and of political parties generally. Political formations are more varied sociologically than is commonly assumed, serve purposes sometimes at odds with their ideology, and do not function as hierarchically as is often thought. They are both constructed from the top down and fashioned from the bottom up by the actions of voters, sympathizers, and militants. Parties in rural areas thrive on autonomy, and succeed when they are not the instruments of urban militants and cadres.

Perceptions of Communism in the Countryside

Rural communism was not the end point of a long-standing leftist tradition in the countryside that began with the Démocrates Socialistes and continued down the line with Radicals of various stripes, Socialists, and Communists. Neither the PCF nor any other party profited from a deeply entrenched voting tradition. True enough, the Communists were the party whose electoral roots reached farthest back in time—but those roots went no deeper than earlier twentieth-century socialism. Socialists (before 1920) and later Communists did not continue an electoral tradition; rather, they founded a new, radically different one that endured through the 1930s, and even beyond.

The Communist vote during the interwar years distinguished itself from its rivals in important ways. No other political party in Limousin and Dordogne was characterized by such an exemplary stable geographical implantation on the village level. The PCF proved unable to lure voters away from other political parties in significant numbers, and it also failed in its attempt to find new electors in areas where it had done poorly in the past. Once established, the Party became a prisoner in its own bastions. This was a source simultaneously of strength and of weakness.

The PCF's inability to expand beyond fixed boundaries was linked to the nature and structure of its electorate. The Communists forged an original base of support composed of smallholding peasants, tenant farmers, agricultural workers, rural artisans, village shopkeepers, and the last remaining temporary migrants; their backing did not originate, as some have argued, among the most proletarianized (rural workers) or poorest (sharecroppers) elements of rural society. Support for the Party was not related to massive depopulation, temporary migration, patterns of settlement, or family structure. By any measure, lack of religiosity was by far the best predictor of Party support. The PCF established itself in areas characterized by a strong detachment from Catholic practice, hostility to religion, and the absence of political parties (the Radicals) that had made anticlericalism their bread-and-butter issue. The PCF's program of future social change and present economic defensiveness, coupled with its effectiveness in recreating networks of sociability in the countryside, had success in areas where the Church's presence had been reduced to a bare minimum and where, by extension, the Radicals and other local elites had lost their raison d'être. These were also areas of medium and large property holdings, where peasants practiced polyculture and raised cattle and sheep on the poor soils. More dependent on the vicissitudes of the market than their counterparts in areas of smaller holdings, peasants were particularly hard hit by the fall in livestock prices in the early 1930s, and the ensuing social and economic crisis made them that much more receptive to the Party's watchwords.

During the 1920s and 1930s, sectors of rural society found that the Communists best represented both their fundamentally defensive economic outlook and their political progressivism. Attached to a mythical image of the Russian Revolution, profoundly marked by the experience of the Great War, rural inhabitants of Limousin and Dordogne voted for a party that in their eyes would defend and even expand their small property holdings while ushering in a reign of economic and social justice. Peasants, rural artisans, and shopkeepers backed those who promised to protect them from the destabilizing effect of economic change by establishing a highly protected rural economy. High prices, the Communists pledged, would be guaranteed for small producers, while the profits that the "big trusts" and other predators made at the peasantry's expense would be drastically reduced. Of collectivism and even cooperation there was little talk. This was an egalitarianism with limits.

The Communists intelligently adapted their propaganda to the often binary worldview of rural inhabitants.[5] There were those who profited (*les bourgeois, les gros*) and those who "slaved hard" (*les travailleurs, les cultivateurs*) "to ensure that some would have *la belle vie*," and it was time to do away with this state of affairs.[6] This kind of argument, based on the duality

---

[5] For an earlier period consult Pierre Vallin, *Paysans rouges du Limousin* (Paris, 1985), 356–57, and more generally Pierre Birnbaum, *Le peuple et les gros: Histoire d'un mythe* (Paris, 1979).

[6] There are numerous examples of this rhetoric. See *TCO*, 16 August 1930.

of good and bad, poor and rich, workers and exploiters, was transposed into historical terms to make it even more vivid: capitalism was but a new feudalism, capital itself was but the king in disguise, and the peasants were nothing but serfs.[7] The day would come, wrote a Dordogne peasant, when "we will carry out our Revolution, the true revolution, the revolution of the poor, the revolution of justice."[8] For many rural supporters, communism was synonymous with *la fin des gros* (the overthrow of the rich). A voter in the village of St-Front-la-Rivière (Dordogne) expressed this sentiment well when he wrote, "Long live Saussot! Down with *les gros*!" on the ballot he cast for the Communist candidate in 1936.[9]

There was little paradox in the support of peasants, artisans, shopkeepers, and other rural inhabitants for the Communist Party. But the communism they subscribed to was not the political animal of the cities. Rural supporters perceived the Party both as the representative of revolution—which eventually would bring about a socially egalitarian democracy of property holders—and as the one political organization that would shield them from economic change and the pernicious effects of the free market. By setting up village cells, sponsoring dances and festive occasions, reviving sociability networks, organizing agricultural trade unions, establishing an active political organization in the countryside, and giving voice to demands emanating from rural society, village militants and sympathizers also affirmed an identity and a set of shared values that differentiated them from their opponents. Communism provided a minimal amount of social cement to communities that desperately needed it.

During the interwar years the exercise of local power was not what brought the Communists support in the countryside. Once elected, Communist officials at all levels could do little for their constituents. The Party's deputies had little impact in Paris, and were in no position to render the services that were the trademark of Henri Queuille and other Radicals and the source of their popularity. Communist departmental representatives were too few and until 1934 too isolated politically to accomplish much, and in any case the prefect, not the Conseil Général, wielded authority. The PCF did not fare better on the municipal level. Today old militants candidly admit that virtually nothing distinguished Communist rural municipalities from those run by Socialists, Radicals, or even Conservatives.[10] There was (and still is) little that Communists could do to stem the tide of rural depopulation, help small peasants stay on the land, and resist changes in agriculture that, in the long term, threatened the existence of their electorate.

[7] For references to feudalism and serfs, see handbills in ADD 4M192 and *Le Paysan Travailleur*, May 1925.

[8] *Le Travailleur de la Dordogne*, 7 July 1934.

[9] AN F[7] 12582.

[10] Interviews with André Plazanet, St-Clément, 1 September 1984; Jean-Baptiste Vars, Meymac, 3 October 1983; Louis Freyssinet, Ste-Fortunade, 1 September 1983 and 30 June 1984.

The Apogee of Rural Communism

The dizzying succession of events in 1939–40—the Nazi-Soviet pact, the dismantling of the PCF's organization, the staggering defeat of May–June 1940—brought the fruitful decades of rural Communist organizers' hard work to a bitter end. Throughout Limousin and Périgord the police interrogated Party militants, searched offices and cell meeting places, seized the local PCF newspapers and the meager funds in the Party bank accounts, suspended Communist mayors and municipal councillors, and dissolved the Communist Party and its affiliated organizations.[11] The region's three rural deputies—in company with other PCF representatives from the countryside—broke with the Party in the fall of 1939 and the winter of 1940.[12] The Communist Party's suicidal twists and turns were difficult to explain to an electorate that had never made a practice of slavishly following the Party's every change in policy, an electorate more interested in the nuts and bolts of politics than in questions of form and tactics. By early 1940 Communist leaders, overly concerned with the working class, had lost touch with the countryside and could only note that the "Party's rural implantation seems to have disappeared."[13]

Within a few years, however, Limousin and Dordogne emerged as strongholds of the Communist resistance and of the Resistance *tout court*. Relying on networks of former militants, the Communists organized small groups of resisters. In the forests of southeastern Haute-Vienne and northern Corrèze, Georges Guingouin, a schoolteacher and Party militant in St-Gilles-les-Forêts (Haute-Vienne), patiently forged an effective, powerful maquis that enjoyed considerable independence from the Communist resistance in other parts of the country. When the Party, showing more ideological dogma than tactical intelligence, accused Guingouin of "indiscipline" because he was organizing peasants and not the urban proletariat, he ignored the critique.[14] After the Liberation, the PCF, riding on the crest of its Resistance popularity, doubled its score at the polls and established itself as the leading political force in Limousin and Dordogne. Even in Haute-Vienne, which had been the main interwar bastion of the SFIO, the Communists managed to overtake their Socialist rivals by June 1946. By that November, when the Communist Party achieved its highest electoral score in history (28.8 percent of the vote),

---

[11] ADC 1M71, 1M73; ADD 2Z114; ADHV 1M175.

[12] Bernard Pudal, *Prendre parti: Pour une sociologie historique du PCF* (Paris, 1989), 85.

[13] Philippe Buton, "Le Parti, la guerre et la révolution 1939–1940," *Communisme* 32–33–34 (1993): 48.

[14] See Jean Chaintron, *Le vent soufflait devant ma porte* (Paris, 1993), 245–46, 332–34; Georges Guingouin, *Quatre ans de luttes sur le sol limousin* (Paris, 1974); Georges Guingouin and Gérard Monédiaire, *Georges Guingouin, premier maquisard de France* (Limoges, 1983); Sarah Farmer, "The Communist Resistance in the Haute-Vienne," *French Historical Studies* 14 (1985): 89–116; Michel Taubmann, *L'affaire Guingouin* (Limoges, 1994), 76–77.

Corrèze (39.9 percent) ranked second in Party support, behind Pyrénées-Orientales; Creuse (39.2 percent) and Haute-Vienne (38.6 percent) followed close behind. By 1951, the PCF did better in Corrèze (40.4 percent), Creuse (39.9 percent), and Haute-Vienne (39.1 percent) than in any other departments in the country—and this pattern was repeated, with a few variations, through the better part of the 1950s. In 1962, Corrèze trailed only Seine in its backing for Communist candidates. Thus the PCF's strongest electoral bastions during the Cold War were far from the country's industrial heartland. The post-Liberation years witnessed the growing ruralization and deproletarianization of the PCF's membership and electorate.[15] The Party's rural presence, which had been restricted to Limousin, Dordogne, and a few other departments during the interwar years, now extended to large parts of the countryside. French communism was increasingly a rural phenomenon.

What accounts for these achievements? The patient groundwork and successful interwar rooting of the PCF in the Limousin and Dordogne countryside made the later successes of the Resistance and Liberation possible. To reverse a common proposition: it was not the Resistance that gave birth to rural communism, but rural communism that created favorable conditions for the PCF's success in the Resistance and beyond. Most observers have argued the opposite, emphasizing that Communist strength in the countryside was a post–World War II phenomenon that could largely be explained by the Party's newfound Resistance legitimacy. Sophisticated analysts of postwar communism, recognizing that the PCF's rural strength had more complex origins, have pointed out that it also benefited from "socialist and communitarian" traditions in regions characterized by sharecropping and complex family structures.[16] Yet the PCF's rural strength was long in the making and needs to be situated historically; explanations based on political or social traditions (which are, interestingly, rarely used to explain urban working-class political behavior) are not entirely satisfactory.

Did rural communism have an impact on the PCF as a whole? Or did the Party merely reap the fruits of its rural strength? To the degree that the Party was concerned with its electoral and militant support, it had to pay attention to the countryside, especially during times when the weight of the working class in its ranks was declining. But peasants never found themselves near the center of the Party's interests and strategy. Nor did the PCF ever give hard thought to the significance of its appeal among declining (the peasantry, workers in deindustrializing areas) or marginal (the unemployed) social

[15] Election results from ADC 118W3471a, 58W2210; Ministère de l'Intérieur, *Les élections législatives du 17 juin 1951* (Paris, 1953); Claude Leleu, *Géographie des élections françaises depuis 1936* (Paris, 1971); on ruralization, Philippe Buton, *Les lendemains qui déchantent: Le Parti communiste français à la Libération* (Paris, 1993).

[16] Marc Lazar, *Maisons rouges: Les Partis communistes français et italien de la Libération à nos jours* (Paris, 1992), 193. One recognizes here the arguments of Hervé Le Bras and Emmanuel Todd, *L'invention de la France: Atlas anthropologique et politique* (Paris, 1981).

groups. In the 1950s and 1960s, the structure of PCF peasant policy remained unchanged. During times of prosperity it was difficult to cry famine, but one could still identify an enemy on the outside: the trusts, the rich, and now the Germans, who, the PCF argued, bought up precious French farmland and reaped the benefits of the Common Market. Having successfully resisted the German occupation, the peasantry was now losing the war against the "revanchist" enemy to the east.[17]

Some Broader Implications

The story of the encounter between rural society and the Communist Party also carries larger lessons concerning the role of the French state, the changing face of politics in the French countryside, and the place of rural communism within European societies.

The endemic rural vote for the Communist Party, to which one could couple the strong support for peasant movements of the extreme right (Dorgères's Greenshirts) in the 1930s, demonstrates the state's long-term inability to uproot opposition in the countryside. Persistent economic crisis and decline, a singular resistance to political change, the backwardness of local elites, the lack of investment in infrastructure—all testify to the state's immobility and lack of interest in rural areas. Successive governments were content with the status quo at a time when massive social change had destabilized rural communities. They thought that winning the Great War was enough, when in fact the conflict left psychological and physical wounds that ripped the fabric of social life, even in the most isolated rural areas. During the interwar years and beyond, elites and governments were more often turned toward a mythical peasant past than occupied in finding innovative solutions to social and economic change in the countryside. Rural communism was a grass-roots response to the state's immobility in the face of the massive upheaval brought about by the slow disappearance of peasant society. It represented new forms of politics in the countryside, as political relationships based on patronage and fueled by rumors gave way to increasingly structured forms of social action. In the years after World War II, the solution finally came from the outside: it was the Common Market and its Common Agricultural Policy (coupled, it is true, with the economic growth of the Thirty Glorious Years) that provided the necessary cushion to accompany social and economic change in rural regions.

In the mid 1930s, the growing strength of rural communism and of Henry Dorgères's "rural fascist" peasant movement underscored the crisis of rural society—an economic crisis that was also one of social and political legiti-

---

[17] Waldeck Rochet, *Ceux de la terre* (Paris, 1963).

macy. And parallels did exist between the two movements: both of them organized protests against the state (tax strikes, actions against tax collectors) and property owners (demonstrations against crop seizures) to build popular support. Both appealed to a peasantry resentful of urban society and disgruntled with urban politicians. But the similarities stop there. *Dorgérisme* was a short-lived movement that reached its apogee between 1933 and early 1936. When conservative notables, increasingly confident that they could defend their interests on their own and uncomfortable with Dorgères's unbending radicalism, withdrew their support, the movement slipped into low gear. Communist strength, on the other hand, did not depend on an alliance (however informal) with notables—quite the contrary. Dorgères, furthermore, was at his best rousing large crowds, and the Greenshirts depended heavily on his oratorical skills and charisma. The PCF had no rural leader of Dorgères's magnetism and effectiveness (only Renaud Jean came close), and its meetings in the countryside could not match Dorgères's in intensity. But the PCF had a grass-roots electoral presence that Dorgères did not. While Dorgères's movement may have been a product of the peasantry's ever more problematic relation to the nation (and thus may be representative of a more wide-ranging crisis), it was episodic, and could not compete with the PCF's half-century-long presence in parts of *la France profonde*.[18]

Those familiar with French rural history may find parallels here with the extensive debate concerning the politicization of the peasantry in the mid- and late nineteenth century. By the fin de siècle, and certainly by the Great War, the question was no longer when peasants came to politics, how they "modernized" (always a dubious proposition), or how they became integrated in the larger nation-state, but rather how they used the political arena to forward their own agenda. The rural communist movement of the 1920s bore greater resemblance to its post–World War II successor than to radical social movements of the past. The development of communism in the countryside was not linked to the diffusion of urban values or to the marketing networks dear to modernization theorists; on the contrary, it demonstrates the autonomy and inventiveness of politics in the countryside, the uncanny ability of rural inhabitants to shape the behavior and actions of political parties. Like many political movements, the Communists incorporated features of past traditions (tax revolts, for example) in their forms of action and gave them contemporary resonance. Unlike the nineteenth-century inhabitants of Limousin who voted for the left out of attachment to traditional values and hostility to innovation, their twentieth-century counterparts turned to the political arena to defend their identity and economic interests, demand social change, and give root to a culture of democracy. The last of the *fureurs*

---

[18] The definitive study of *dorgérisme* is Robert O. Paxton, *Le temps des chemises vertes: Révoltes paysannes et fascisme rural, 1929–1939*, trans. Jean-Pierre Bardos (Paris, 1996).

paysannes, sparked by the rumors and fears ever present in rural society, ended in 1870.[19] Society was still riddled by conflict after that time, but violence was no longer a credible alternative.

Communist successes among the peasantry went well beyond France or even Europe. In parts of Asia, to take but one example, Communists successfully organized sectors of rural society, although the form and historical context of this mobilization makes comparisons with Europe difficult. In Vietnam this development was intimately linked to a war of decolonization and nascent nationalism, and in China to social revolution and civil war. In all cases, communism's appeal to the peasantry took root within societies virtually devoid of industry, where the precapitalist peasantry had more in common with its European counterpart of the eighteenth or nineteenth century than with the rapidly changing agricultural sector of the mid–twentieth century. Marxism appealed to peasants on substantially different grounds in Europe, where peasants (rightly or wrongly) were not seen as the standard bearers of social change, and in the Third World, where those who worked the land constituted a vast reservoir for social and political action—not to mention a potential threat to the stability of the state.[20]

A comparison within Europe, however, suggests interesting parallels while placing the French example within a larger perspective. This was far from the first time that the left had developed a significant base in the countryside. One need only recall rural anarchism and socialism in southern Spain (Andalusia), as well as rural socialism in both France and Italy, to recognize that there were no insurmountable barriers to prevent left parties from appealing (albeit on different terms) to rural inhabitants.[21] It was no accident that the most powerful Communist parties in European democracies (with the exception of the German Communists under Weimar)—the French, Italian, and Finnish—were those that had the strongest rural roots. Even in the post–World War II years, when the weight of the peasantry declined, the importance of the rural sector could not be circumvented. In the Liberation years, the support of the countryside was critical if one wanted to assume and preserve power, whether through a coup of sorts or through the ballot box. During that period, Communists had difficulty increasing or even preserving their share of the working-class vote. The declining numbers of the working class and, in the French case, the PCF's growing deproletarianization made support from the agricultural world all the more critical.

---

[19] Alain Corbin, *Archaïsme et modernité en Limousin au XIXᵉ siècle, 1845–1880* (Paris, 1974) 2:1002–3, and *Le village des cannibales* (Paris, 1990).

[20] On the Asian example, *Peasant Rebellion and Communist Revolution in Asia*, ed. John Wilson Lewis (Stanford, 1974).

[21] Temma Kaplan, *Anarchists of Andalusia, 1868–1903* (Princeton, 1977); George A. Collier, *Socialists of Rural Andalusia: Unacknowledged Revolutionaries of the Second Republic* (Stanford, 1987).

There are, of course, key differences among the French, Italian, and Finnish cases. The French example demonstrates that communism's influence in rural areas largely predated the Resistance movements of World War II. It also shows that Communists could succeed in a country where most peasants owned their own land, so that "land hunger" was not a key issue. Finally, the French Communists made breakthroughs in a rural environment characterized by a solidly entrenched representative democracy and structured political parties of the left and right.

In Italy, in contrast, the PCI established itself in rural areas on the heels of the aura it acquired in the antifascist struggle; this was particularly the case in the south, where the Communists, who barely existed before 1943, reaped the benefits of rural agitation in the wake of the agrarian decrees drawn up by the Communist minister of agriculture. In the northern half of Italy (Emilia-Romagna, Tuscany, Umbria, Marches), the left's strength in the countryside was nothing new; witness socialism's strength in the socially explosive post–World War I years.[22] After World War II the Communists in this region quickly drew lessons from the disastrous mistakes of the early 1920s and worked hard to reconcile the diverging interests of landless laborers, sharecroppers, and small owners. They also successfully guided and capitalized on the major—if unsuccessful—sharecroppers' struggles in central Italy in 1945–47. In the post-Liberation years the Italian Communists faced a substantially different task than their French counterparts: Italy's political landscape and social fabric needed to be built anew; the nation had only the briefest experience with universal manhood suffrage. After twenty years of fascist dictatorship, the PCI's role was in part to consolidate "progressive democracy"—a less pressing concern on the other side of the Alps, where the Vichy regime was seen more as a distasteful interlude than as a sign of profound troubles in French political culture. Finally, the Italians understood that a successful strategy could not avoid addressing the eternal "southern problem." The stagnation of the impoverished south, dominated by landed proprietors and clientelist politics, while the industrial north prospered forced the Italians to pay more attention to rural issues than the French ever did.[23] Because the Italian rural sector was far more important than the French one, the peasant issue was all the more critical in the eyes of the PCI.

In both Italy and France, communism established itself in a variety of geo-

[22] Adrian Lyttelton, *The Seizure of Power: Fascism in Italy, 1919–1929* (Princeton, 1973); Paul Corner, *Fascism in Ferrara, 1915–1925* (London, 1975).

[23] On Italy, Sidney Tarrow, *Peasant Communism in Southern Italy* (New Haven, 1967); Paul Ginsborg, "The Communist Party and the Agrarian Question in Southern Italy, 1943–48," *History Workshop Journal* 17 (1984): 81–101, and *A History of Contemporary Italy: Society and Politics, 1943–1988* (London, 1990); Jean Besson et al., *Sociologie du communisme en Italie* (Paris, 1974); Lazar, *Maisons rouges;* Giuseppe Maione, "Mezzogiorno, 1946–1950: Partito comunista e movimento contadino," *Italia contemporanea* 163 (1986): 31–64; Paolo Cinanni, *Lotte per la terra e comunisti in Calabria, 1943–1953* (Milan, 1977).

graphical settings and chronological periods. The French recruited small-holders in Côtes-du-Nord and Limousin, sharecroppers in Lot-et-Garonne, and agricultural workers along the Mediterranean littoral. The Italians found support among sharecroppers in their central Italian strongholds (Emilia-Romagna), but also (on different terms) among the socially fragmented agricultural populations of the Mezzogiorno. In France and central Italy, communism often developed in areas of declining religious practice; the Italians, however, proved more sensitive to the Catholic electorate, and more deft at reappropriating some of the symbolic aspects of Catholicism to their own advantage.[24]

The Finnish case is of equal interest. Finnish "backwoods communism" developed largely after World War II (the Communist Party was banned between 1930 and 1944) in the northern and eastern parts of the country. In these woodland areas, 45 percent of the rural electorate (versus 26 percent of the urban) supported the Communists. Here communism received backing from economically marginal small farmers, many of whom supplemented their income during the winter months by working as lumberjacks. Forest work was strenuous and seasonal, economic conditions (outside the 1945–48 timber and reconstruction boom years) were difficult, and rural unemployment was high. Standard explanations of Finnish backwoods communism have linked it to declining religious practice, high unemployment, the absence of social and cultural networks in the countryside, a poor standard of living, and rural out-migration. In the 1960s, sociologists argued that it was a by-product of modernization—more a protest vote, devoid of ideological content, by people uprooted and isolated by social change, than an outgrowth of divisions within the left dating back to the period of independence and Civil War (1917–18). Others have suggested that in eastern Finland communism established itself not in economically homogeneous regions of small farmers but precisely in those areas where struggling small-holders and better-off farmers coexisted. Whatever the case may be, communism in Finland, like its counterparts in France and Italy, found a durable home in some of the country's rural areas. And if the French and Italian examples are any indication, Finnish backwoods communism was not a mere protest vote but a rich phenomenon that demonstrates the social complexity of both the Communist movement and rural political life.[25]

Pockets of rural Communist strength could be found in other European

---

[24] David I. Kertzer, *Comrades and Christians: Religion and Political Struggle in Communist Italy* (Cambridge, 1980); Liliano Faenza, *Comunismo e cattolicesimo in una parrocchia di campagne* (Milan, 1959).

[25] The classic analysis of backwoods communism is Erik Allardt, "Social Sources of Finnish Communism: Traditional and Emerging Radicalism," *International Journal of Contemporary Sociology* 5 (1964): 49–72. See also Allardt, "Community Activity, Leisure Use and Social Structure," *Acta Sociologica* 6 (1962): 67–82; Jaakko Nousiainen, "Research on the [sic] Finnish Communism," *Scandinavian Political Studies* 3 (1968): 243–52; Onni Rantala, "The Political Regions of Finland," *Scandinavian Political Studies* 2 (1967): 117–40.

countries as well, but nowhere did they prove as enduring as in Limousin and Dordogne. Peasants and Communists met as partisans in the mountains of northern Greece, and their encounter was successful because the Party was attentive to older communal values and interests. The same was no doubt true in parts of Yugoslavia. In Norway, where communism found some support among rural foresters and outside industrial areas, one finds echoes of Finland's situation. After 1974 the Communist party built a bastion among agricultural workers in the south of Portugal (Alentejo and to a lesser extent Algarve). Elsewhere it did less well. During the Weimar years, the German Communist party (KPD) recruited few agricultural workers (2.2 percent of its members in 1927) and virtually no peasants; nationally it gathered no electoral support among the "self-employed." In a few areas, however, the KPD did manage to appeal to those who lived on the land, and the Party was not necessarily the purely urban phenomenon observers have thought it to be. After World War II, the KPD recruited peasants and agricultural workers in Saxony (14.7 percent of all members in Halle-Merseburg). Thus, even for one of Europe's most heavily proletarian parties, the countryside was not a terra incognita.[26]

The plasticity of communism's appeal—sociologically, geographically, culturally—had everything to do with its rural success. The Party's well-adapted grass-roots program, its effective rural leaders, and its ability to rekindle sociability networks all played a part. But the crucial issue was the promise of land. Communism simultaneously appealed to people who had no land (sharecroppers, agricultural workers, tenant farmers); to property-owning peasants who felt their holdings were too small or were threatened by economic circumstances; to small owners who also worked seasonally in the forests, in rural industry, or as agricultural laborers; and to shopkeepers and artisans whose well-being depended on the peasants' prosperity. It was not always easy to reconcile these competing interests. The French were successful at this exercise because the declining importance of sharecroppers and agricultural workers encouraged the PCF to focus on the property-holding peasantry. In Italy, the weight of the landless made it more difficult to appeal to property-owning peasants, who by and large remained faithful to Christian Democracy. In the Mezzogiorno, small owners felt threatened by more militant agricultural workers who had an eye on large properties. The Party could reconcile the two only by putting a brake on the militancy of the poor-

---

[26] Riki Van Boeschoten, "The Peasant and the Party: Peasant Options and 'Folk' Communism in a Greek Village," *Journal of Peasant Studies* 20 (1993): 612–39; Per Selle, "The Norwegian Communist Party in the Immediate Postwar Period," in *Modern Political Ecological Analysis*, ed. Sten Berglund and Søren Risbjerg Thomsen (Åbo, 1990): 265–96; Eric Weitz, *Creating German Communism, 1890–1990: From Popular Protest to Socialist State* (Princeton, 1996), 245, 329; Jürgen W. Falter and Reinhard Zintl, "The Economic Crisis of the 1930s and the Nazi Vote," *JIH* 19 (1988), 74; Klaus-Michael Mallmann, *Kommunisten in der Weimarer Republik: Sozialgeschichte einer revolutionären Bewegung* (Darmstadt, 1996), 96–97, 329.

est sectors of rural society and identifying a common enemy on the outside (the northern capitalists and their agents).

What broader role did rural communism play in French and Italian societies? One line of argument has been that communism's rural efforts ultimately contributed to a rapprochement between the peasantry and an urban working class that was often viewed with suspicion in the countryside. By showing that workers and peasants had similar interests, by valorizing industrial work in a society marked by a rural ethos, the Communists contributed to a pacified social system, facilitated the gradual integration of the declining peasantry into urban areas, and ensured themselves a replenished stock of voters. The case of Limousin and Dordogne, however, brings this formulation into question. Reductionist workerist discourse, propagated by the Communists as a way of reaffirming the superiority of the working class, impoverished rural political culture. Workerism did not bridge the gap between peasants and workers; on the contrary, links between the two groups remained largely superficial. Rural Communists defended themselves with consummate skill against the tactless intrusions of urban militants poorly versed in agricultural issues. Communism in the countryside was a defensive reaction against outside enemies (capitalists, urban society) and not the result of a deeply felt solidarity with urban workers. It served more to preserve and nurture a threatened rural identity than to promote integration with urban social groups.

A second line of argument, which has received renewed life with communism's collapse, suggests that one way to account for communism's influence in the twentieth century (and its present decline) is to see in it a form of secular religion.[27] To simplify a complex argument, during the better part of the twentieth century communism fulfilled people's need for core values and beliefs; now, however, the growing atomization and individualization of society has rendered such needs less compelling and reduced the attraction of communism. The PCF's strength in some rural areas has been explained as a transfer of faith.[28] The case of Limousin and Périgord, where Catholicism was never fully established and hostility to religion was endemic, shows that such an explanation is problematic. Here communism had deeply entrenched social and political roots. The enduring belief in the revolution to come (*le grand soir*) had more to do with utopian visions of social change than with a deeply felt need for a surrogate faith.

While rural communism did not achieve its ends—reaching power at the center, achieving a "social revolution" of sorts in the countryside—it did

---

[27] Marc Lazar, "Communisme et religion," and Stéphane Courtois, "De la contre-société à la contre église: La dimension religieuse du phénomène communiste français," in *Rigueur et passion: Mélanges offerts en hommage à Annie Kriegel* (Paris, 1994); Stéphane Courtois and Marc Lazar, *Histoire du Parti communiste français* (Paris, 1995), 24–25.

[28] Ronan Le Coadic, *Campagnes rouges de Bretagne* (Morlaix, 1991), 56–60, and "Comment peut-on être Breton, paysan et communiste?" *Communisme* 45–46 (1996): 187–94.

have a major, though unintended, impact. The Communists were often the first to introduce more contemporary and organized forms of politics into rural areas dominated by patronage (Corrèze) or clientelism (southern Italy). This enterprise, to be sure, was not always successful: Jacques Chirac's election in a Corrèze PCF stronghold in 1967 eventually reintroduced, through the back door, a variant of the patronage politics that the PCF had worked so hard to eliminate. But on the whole, Communists did transform the political landscape in those rural areas where they enjoyed a firm presence. In France, communism was solidly anchored in the ballot box. The PCF worked consistently in the electoral arena, and through its persistent campaigning did more to cement universal suffrage and the practice of democracy than many rival parties did—admittedly something of an irony for a party whose functioning was profoundly undemocratic. The Communists worked hard to defend rural areas condemned to decline, succeeded in preserving rural identities, and provided a renewed practice of democracy.

The Limousin and Dordogne are among those few regions where the Communist Party escaped complete marginalization in the 1980s and 1990s. In the 1988 presidential elections the PCF candidate, André Lajoinie, himself of Corrèze and of peasant origin, did better in Limousin (12.1 percent—nearly double his catastrophically low national score) than in any other French region. In the March 1993 elections, Dordogne (16.2 percent) and Corrèze (15.7 percent) occupied, respectively, the seventh and eighth positions nationally in terms of PCF support; in these departments, and in Creuse and Haute-Vienne as well, communism is in the midst of a long-term decline, and it is only a matter of time before here, too, the Party's influence on the political scene becomes negligible.[29] The transformation of the French countryside and the continuing depopulation of the region have sapped the PCF's strength. The Party's aging rural electorate and its supporters in deindustrializing towns such as Tulle (Corrèze) and St-Junien (Haute-Vienne) hold out little promise for the future. Unless the Communist Party can adapt to changing social and economic structures—and precious little evidence indicates that it can—it will be condemned to the sidelines of history, and rural communism will soon be a memory of times past. The days (in 1935) when the authorities, acting on a misinformed tip, searched for Leon Trotsky in, of all places, rural Corrèze (where one village militant, who bore some resemblance to the Russian leader, was affectionately known as "Trotsky") are now long forgotten.[30] Today, dissatisfied rural voters are increasingly likely to cast their ballots for other political parties, and in other regions of the country, even for the right-wing Front National. They no longer see in the PCF a party that

[29] The PCF obtained 9.2% of the vote in 1993: *Le Monde*, 23 March 1993.

[30] ADC 4M282; interview with Louis Freyssinet. When the rural militant Antonin Bonnet-large of Sornac died, his brother placed his portrait on his dresser next to those of Lenin and Trotsky.

can protect their interests, defend local communities, provide a reassuring sense of identity and values, and propose a compelling model of social change.

The rural communist movement forged in the 1920s on the bleak Mille-vaches plateau, in the undulating hills around Tulle, and in northern Dordogne was not the end product of a tradition, but a new and profoundly original movement that filled a crucial social and political void in the aftermath of the Great War. Over time, however, communism founded a unique social and electoral tradition. Contemporary observers thus are not entirely off the mark when they explain the remaining pockets of Communist strength in the countryside as the residue of a leftist tradition and sensibility. The key difference is that this is a Communist tradition dating back to the early twentieth century, not a leftist one reaching back to the Démocrates-Socialistes and Radicals of the nineteenth. Today the movement the Communists built is largely a hollow shell. The small property owners, rural artisans, and shop-keepers who formed the Party's backbone are relics of another age. Just as the decline of the working class and the disappearance of the *mal-lotis* have hurt the PCF in urban areas, the Party has been ravaged in the countryside by the social and economic revolution of the decades since 1950. In the future, forests will continue to take the place of marginally profitable agricultural land, and nearer to the cities and tourist areas city dwellers in search of rurality will restore old farms and build tasteless villas. The physical and political landscape will hardly be recognizable to those who knew it earlier in the century. When the older generations of Party faithful have disappeared, few historical markers will remain, save for a few gravestones and monuments to the PCF resistance, attesting that here, in the heart of rural France, the Communist Party established one of its most loyal and durable bastions.

Appendix

This appendix provides a brief overview of the data base used in the quantitative analysis. The significance and interpretation of the statistical procedures used in this book are explained in chapters 2 and 3, and more technical remarks can be found below. Readers interested in further details may refer to the specialized literature listed in the chapter notes.

The Data Base

The quantitative analysis is based on first-round voting results for all communes of Corrèze (289), Creuse (266), and Haute-Vienne (205), and for Dordogne's 47 cantons.[1] Data on religious behavior (civil burials, median delay between birth and baptism) and demography also were gathered for Limousin's 760 towns and villages. More detailed figures on the social composition of the electorate, the percentage of migrants, farm size, patterns of settlement, the number of war dead, agricultural trade unions, and PCF militancy are available only for Corrèze. Although it entails a considerable amount of work, it is highly profitable to work with electoral results and social, religious, and demographic data at the village level. The commune is

---

[1] Electoral results are from AN C7208 (1906); C7228 (1910); C7243, C7251 (1914); C10002, C10006 (1919); C10011, C10016 (1924); C10021, C10027 (1928); C10031–10032, 10039 (1932); C10045–10046, C10055 (1936); ADC 3M65 (1849), 3M189–3M202 (1906–36); ADCR 3M304 (1928); ADD 3M90 (1936); ADHV 3M162 (1910), 3M164 (1919); *Le Journal de Bergerac* 17 and 24 May 1924; *L'Union Sarladaise*, 18 May 1924. The Socialist candidate in the district of Bellac (Haute-Vienne) in 1910, Château, was disqualified for not filing his candidacy on time, and his votes were declared void. I have reconstituted his support with the *bulletins nuls* in AN C6781. Creuse and Haute-Vienne 1849 results are based on Jacques Bouillon, "Les élections législatives du 13 mai 1849 en Limousin," *Bulletin de la société archéologique et historique du Limousin* 84 (1954): 467–96.

the fundamental political entity in rural France, and it is here that men and women vote and participate in the political process. While inhabitants may have a strong affinity to their village or town, they display little attachment to a canton, whose function is often purely administrative. The communal approach provides a more accurate representation of the relationship between political behavior and economic, cultural, and social factors. It has rarely been adopted because the cartographical method is poorly suited to the study of large numbers of units over time. Faced with such problems— and faced, until recently, with a lukewarm response from the historical establishment—few historians have undertaken communal investigations on a large scale.[2]

For the voting study I have classified over six hundred candidates who ran for deputy between 1898 and 1936 in Limousin and Dordogne. Some candidates are easy to locate politically, but not all: in Haute-Vienne the Républicains Socialistes were neither Republican nor Socialist (and thus not on the left); in neighboring Corrèze and Creuse they were usually to the left of the Radicals. Political labels during the period under study were the source of much confusion, and candidates did not hesitate to describe their political affiliations in ways that would win them votes—even if the characterization they chose was at odds with their political views.[3] In Limousin, where open identification with the right was usually tantamount to political suicide, a proliferation of right-wing candidates presented themselves before the electorate with left-sounding political labels. Before World War I, rightist candidates often adopted the Republican or Radical rhetoric and used it for their own purposes. At the same time, some Radical and Radical-Socialist candidates moved progressively toward the right—while carefully preserving the better part of their Radical language—and many of them ended up there after (if not before) the Great War.

I have identified the political leanings of candidates by looking at their self-attributed political labels, analyzing their campaign literature, examining patterns of withdrawal between the first and second rounds of voting, consulting newspapers to determine the public perception of candidates, and checking secondary works as well as police reports. By confronting accounts assembled from a broad range of sources it is possible to see through the murky political rhetoric and locate candidates on the political spectrum.

Since many of these candidates ran for marginal and sometimes ephemeral political parties, it has been necessary to combine their results with those of other candidates who voiced similar opinions. The votes of all radicals—in

[2] For the standard argument against communal data see Pierre Barral, "La sociologie électorale et l'histoire," *Revue historique* 238 (1967): 128.

[3] On the fallacious nature of political labels, André Siegfried, *Tableau politique de la France de l'Ouest sous la Troisième République* (Paris, 1913), xv; Michel Offerlé, "Le nombre de voix: Electeurs, partis et électorat socialiste à la fin du 19e siècle en France," *Actes de la recherche en sciences sociales* 71–72 (1988): 11.

the broad sense of the term—have been consolidated, as radical-leaning candidates often adopted differing political labels, ranging from Républicain Socialiste (in some departments) to Radical Socialiste, Radical Indépendant, and just plain Radical. The statistical analysis of the Radical vote thus covers a larger range of political groups (the center left) than other parties, even if the Radicals are by far the dominant party in this category.

Any classification scheme such as this one contains a measure of arbitrariness, and categorizing candidates is rarely a clear-cut task. Local observers have occasionally classified Radical candidates on the right for the simple reason that they seem to have received important support from the right-wing electorate—a plausible occurrence in a region where the right was not regularly represented by a candidate. In some of these elections, one or more candidates on the left were clearly receiving conservative votes on the first ballot, for reasons ranging from *la politique du pire* (voting for a Communist in order to defeat a Socialist) to choosing a candidate ideologically closest to the right. For my part, I have not categorized candidates in accordance with the imputed political preferences of some of their supporters.[4]

Finally, a word about the electoral system. In all elections save those of 1919 and 1924, candidates ran for office in specific electoral districts, and needed an absolute majority of votes on the first round or a plurality on the second to be elected. In 1919 and 1924, candidates ran on a department-wide list affiliated with a major political party, and a single-round proportional system decided the outcome. In Corrèze, Socialists and Radicals presented a joint Cartel des Gauches ticket in 1924, and in Dordogne the Socialists presented no candidates and supported an entirely Radical Cartel list. This is the reason the Socialist vote in that year is absent from the statistical analysis for those two departments.

Data on the social composition of the electorate have been gathered from voter registration lists for Corrèze's 289 communes. Electoral lists have rarely been used by students of French elections. I prefer them to census lists because they provide a more accurate picture of the registered electorate. In general, I have not found census lists to name a person's occupation more accurately than voter registration rolls. Some investigators have cautioned that voter registration lists provide only with an elector's declared occupation at the time of his initial registration, and that officials were not required to note changes in later years. I have compared electoral lists for 1920, 1930, and

---

[4] For the 1936 elections I included Jacques de Chammard, the Radical-Socialist deputy of Corrèze, who was opposed to the Popular Front, within the left. De Chammard, first elected on a Radical-Socialist ticket in 1924, remained the local representative of radicalism, and his opposition to the Popular Front did not move him from the center-left to the right of the political spectrum; see ADC 3M198, 3M302. I have also classified Chambonnet, the Radical candidate in the district of Aubusson (Creuse), within the Radical category. He was not nominated by the Radical-Socialist Party and opposed the Popular Front.

1939 and have found a number of voters whose names appear in all three years with two or three occupations listed—a clear indication that the occupation of some voters was updated. This finding is not surprising in small villages where the people in charge of voter registration lists knew their electors well. In Lyon, Jean-Luc Pinol found the same or similar occupations listed on voter registrations and the census; he argues that those differences that exist are of little consequence on the aggregate level.[5]

Correlation Analysis

The correlational analysis has been conducted for each department separately because a detailed regression analysis for all of Limousin and Dordogne reveals considerable regional differentiation in the base of support of political parties. The correlational study was undertaken for each of Limousin's fourteen electoral districts also, but the results are ambiguous and not always easy to interpret. The intensity and strength of the Communist Party's geographical stability varied from district to district. In some electoral districts the Communist Party was a model of territorial permanence, while in others it had difficulty assuming the geographical heritage of socialism. In short, what may be true of a department's communes taken together is not necessarily true of the communes in any particular district.

Transition Tables

The transition tables (ecological regression) were obtained by running least squares regressions where the dependent variable was the percentage of registered voters casting their ballots for party a in election a, and the independent variables the percentages of the registered electorate voting for parties a, b, c, d, etc., along with nonvoters and ineligibles in election b. The data I have used are based on the registered electorate in each of Corrèze's 289 communes, a figure that, to take two examples, accounts for over 95.5 percent of all eligible men over the age of twenty-one in both 1932 and 1936. I have included nonvoters and ineligible voters (those eligible to vote in one election but not the other) in the regression equations; this last category is of particular importance in Corrèze. Poverty and difficult living conditions had driven large numbers of Corrèze's inhabitants to migrate either temporarily or permanently ever since the nineteenth century, and this trend continued, albeit at a slower pace, well into the twentieth century. As a result, the num-

[5] Jean-Luc Pinol, *Les mobilités de la grande ville: Lyon, fin XIX*[e]*–début XX*[e] (Paris, 1991), 348–84, and *Espace social et espace politique: Lyon à l'époque du Front populaire* (Lyon, 1980), 8, 9, 46, 168.

ber of registered voters often declined substantially between successive elections: Corrèze lost 10 percent of its registered voters between 1919 and 1924. In order to estimate the behavior of voters who participated in the first election but were no longer registered to vote in the second, in most cases I inverted the way transition tables are usually calculated and used the first— not the second—election as the common denominator. In other words, instead of asking how those who voted in 1919 cast their ballots in 1924, I have asked how those who voted in 1924 voted in the previous election.

Some analysts argue that regressions should be weighted by the square root of the number of electors to control for important variations in population between villages. I compared the results of both the unweighted and weighted regressions and found few notable differences. I opted for the transition table that produced the fewest "illogical results" (outside the 0 to 100 percent bounds) or that corresponded best to the historical evidence. The percentages in the unweighted transition tables are mean percentages; those in the weighted tables are the actual percentages. The transition tables are based on 290 cases because the town of Tulle was divided into two electoral precincts belonging to separate cantons.

Multiple Regression Analysis

The interpretation of the multiple regression study is based on coefficients that conform to the broadly agreed-upon .05 level of significance (starred * in the tables). Coefficients for which the *t*-test is greater than or equal to 1.96 are significant at the .05 level—that is, there is only a 5 percent chance that the null hypothesis (i.e., that the relationship between the two variables is equal to 0) is actually true. Coefficients with a *t*-test greater than or equal to 2.58 are significant at the .01 level (indicated by a dagger † in the tables).

All the regression equations have been submitted to standard regression diagnostics. I have studied the residuals closely in order to identify potential outliers, check for heteroscedasticity, and verify that the basic assumptions of regression analysis have not been violated. I have also regressed all the independent variables against one another to check for potential multicollinearity problems. Weighting the regressions by the square root of the registered electorate—to control for potential heteroscedasticity caused by important population differences between communes—produced little change in the coefficients, and I have thus preferred the results of the unweighted regressions.

Archives

This book is based on detailed research in national and provincial archives. Space considerations prevent me from providing a complete listing of the documents consulted; detailed references can be found in the chapter footnotes.

Archives Nationales de France (CARAN)

Série C	Assemblée Nationale (official election results)
Série F¹ CIII	Public opinion
Série F⁷	Police Générale (Communist Party; socialism; social, political, and economic problems; elections; agriculture; strikes; unemployment)

Archives Départementales de la Corrèze (Tulle)

Série 1M	Administration Générale du Département. Rapports de Préfets (War of 1914–18; public opinion; Communist Party; banning of PCF; Socialist Party; reports on social and economic life; monuments to the war dead; press surveillance)
Série 3M	Elections (legislative, cantonal, and municipal elections: reports on campaigns; electoral propaganda; election results)
Série 4M	Police (Communist Party; suspicious individuals)
Série 6M	Population, Economie, Statistiques (census; agricultural statistics)
Série 7M	Agriculture (agricultural trade unions; demonstrations; agricultural statistics; reports on agriculture)
Série 10M	Travail et Main d'Oeuvre (strikes)
Série O	Administration Communale (village administration and statistics)
Série W	Administration Générale du Département après 1940 (Communist Party under Vichy)
Série Z	Sous-Préfecture de Brive (surveillance of Communist Party; public order)

Série 1 E
    dépôt   (municipal councils)

Archives Départementales de la Creuse (Guéret)

Série 3M   Elections

Archives Départementales de la Dordogne (Périgueux)

(See Archives Départementales de la Corrèze for a broad description of the kinds of documents contained in these series)

Série 1M   Administration Générale du Département. Rapports de Préfets
Série 3M   Elections
Série 4M   Police
Série 6M   Population, Economie, Statistiques
Série 7M   Agriculture
Série W   Administration Générale du Département après 1940
Série Z   Fonds des Sous-Préfectures, 1800–1940
1Z   Sous-Préfecture de Bergerac
2Z   Sous-Préfecture de Nontron
4Z   Sous-Préfecture de Ribérac
5Z   Sous-Préfecture de Sarlat

Archives Départementales de la Haute-Vienne (Limoges)

Série 1M   Administration Générale du Département. Rapports de Préfets
Série 3M   Elections
Série 4M   Police
Série 6M   Population, Economie, Statistiques
Série 7M   Agriculture
Série 10M   Travail

Archives Communales

Archives Communales de Gros-Chastang (Corrèze)
Archives Communales de Lagraulière (Corrèze)
Archives Communales de Toy-Viam (Corrèze)

Archives de la Fédération du Parti Communiste Français de la Corrèze

Index